Caribbean Reasonings

Caribbean Political Activism:
Essays in Honour of Richard Hart

Other Titles in the Caribbean Reasonings Series

After Man, Towards the Human: Critical Essays on Sylvia Wynter

Culture, Politics, Race and Diaspora: The Thought of Stuart Hall

George Padmore: Pan-African Revolutionary

The Thought of New World: The Quest for Decolonisation

The George Lamming Reader: The Aesthetics of Decolonisation

M. G. Smith: Social Theory and Anthropology in the Caribbean and Beyond

Caribbean Reasonings
Series Editors
**Anthony Bogues
Rupert Lewis
Brian Meeks**

Caribbean Reasonings

Caribbean Political Activism:
Essays in Honour of Richard Hart

edited by
Rupert Lewis

IAN RANDLE PUBLISHERS
Kingston • Miami

First published in Jamaica, 2012 by
Ian Randle Publishers
11 Cunningham Avenue
Box 686
Kingston 6
www.ianrandlepublishers.com

Introduction and editorial material
© Centre for Caribbean Thought, University of the West Indies, 2012

NATIONAL LIBRARY OF JAMAICA CATALOGUING-IN-PUBLICATION DATA
Caribbean Political Activism : Essays in Honour of Richard Hart / edited
    by Rupert Lewis

    p. : ill. ; cm. – (Caribbean Reasonings)
Includes index.
ISBN 978-976-637-614-7 (pbk)

1. Hart, Richard, 1917-   2. Political activists – Jamaica
3. Political activists – Caribbean Area 3. Jamaica – Politics and
Government 4. Labour movements – Jamaica   5. Labour
Movement – Caribbean Area 6. Jamaica – Economic conditions –
20th century
I. Lewis, Rupert   II. Series

322.4   dc 22
ISBN 978-976-637-614-7

All rights reserved. While copyright in the selection and editorial material is vested in the Centre for Caribbean Thought, University of the West Indies, copyright in individual chapters belongs to their respective authors and no part of this publication may be reproduced, stored in a retrieval system or transmitted in any form or by any means electronic, photocopying, recording or otherwise, without the prior express permission of the author and publisher.

Cover Image: Richard Hart
Cover and book design by Ian Randle Publishers
Printed and bound in the United States of America

Table of Contents

Preface / **vii**

Acknowledgements / **ix**

Introduction: Richard Hart's Evaluation of
Early Modern Jamaican Politics / **xi**
Rupert Lewis

1. Preserving the Record:
   The Role of the Political Activist/Historian / **1**
   John A. Aarons

2. The Logic of Richard Hart's *Slaves Who Abolished Slavery*:
   Black Abolitionism and the Agency of
   Emancipated Nationhood / **8**
   Clinton Hutton

3. Richard Hart and the 'Resurrection' of Marcus Garvey / **24**
   Robert A. Hill

4. Insights from the 1938 (All Jamaica) Economic
   and Industrial Conference / **41**
   Mark Figueroa

5. The Present in the Past: Caribbean Economic
   Development since Independence: The 1960s–2000s / **59**
   Derick Boyd

6. Alexander Bustamante and Constitutional
   Government in Jamaica, 1944–47 / **76**
   Robert Buddan

7. Seaforth in the Eye of the Storm: The Role of Rastafari
   in Major 1938 Events / **91**
   Louis E. A. Moyston

8. The 1930s Labour Rebellions in Barbados and Jamaica:
   Considering Violence and Leadership in Decolonization / **102**
   Maziki Thame

9. The Early Political History of Wilfred A. Domingo,
   1919–39 / **118**
   Margaret Stevens

10. Black Marxist: Champion of the Negro Toilers / **144**
    Rodney Worrell

11. Self-Liberation: The Cases of Occupied Haiti and the
    Anglophone Caribbean's Labour Rebellions / **159**
    Myrtha Désulmé

12. Imagining Freedom: Afro-Jamaican Yearnings and
    the Politics of the Workers' Party of Jamaica / **171**
    Obika Gray

13. Grenada, Once Again: Re-visiting the 1983 Crisis and Collapse
    of the Grenada Revolution / **199**
    Brian Meeks

14. Grenada, Education, and Revolution, 1979–83 / **227**
    Anne Hickling-Hudson

15. Foreign Policy and Economic Development in Small States:
    A Case Study of Grenada / **254**
    Patsy Lewis

Contributors / **291**

Index / **293**

Preface

Caribbean Political Activism: Essays in Honour of Richard Hart is a long overdue tribute to one of the foremost activists to have emerged out of the labour upheavals of the 1930s in the Caribbean.

Richard Hart was born in Jamaica on 13 August 1917, and years after having sat the English Law Society examinations in Jamaica he became a solicitor in 1941. 'He practised for many years in Jamaica and its then dependencies, the Turks and Cayman Islands, and represented the trade unions in Antigua and St Kitts at Commissions of Inquiry in 1951, 1960 and 1962.' In 1962 also, he enrolled as a solicitor in Britain and in 1965 migrated to England where he was employed as a solicitor in local government, holding the post of Head of the Legal Department of the Waverly District Council, a local government authority in Surrey, from 1968–82. In 1982 he was appointed Legal Adviser to the People's Revolutionary Government in Grenada, and in May 1983 became Attorney General, a post he held for only a few months until the American invasion of Grenada in October 1983. From 1985 until his retirement from legal practice in 1989, he was in private practice with a firm of solicitors in Surrey.

In addition to his legal work, he has made an exceptional and selfless contribution to the English-speaking Caribbean in its struggles for decolonization over some 70 years, and has connected this activism to the reinterpretation of Caribbean history. Furthermore, he understands that the domestic realm of party politics is inextricably bound up with British and American interests in the region. It was therefore no coincidence that in 1952 when he was expelled from the People's National Party of Jamaica along with Ken Hill, Frank and Arthur Henry, a year later the British army overturned the democratically elected government of Cheddi Jagan of British Guiana. Thus the Cold War policies of the United States and the United Kingdom removed those from the political scene whom they saw as inimical to their interests, and they did so with the support of the nationalist political elites who had learnt how the game of political independence was to be played.

Hart's activism has been accompanied by the effort to reconstruct and analyse the political experience of the region from enslavement to political independence. His major historical publications have been *Slaves who Abolished Slavery – Blacks in Bondage* (Volume 1) and *Blacks in Rebellion* (Volume 2). Ever mindful of the need to write popularly accessible histories, he produced *From Occupation to Independence – A Short History of the Peoples of the English-Speaking Caribbean*. Hart is also the author of a three-volume study on Jamaican politics from the 1938 riots until independence. The first volume is entitled *Towards Decolonisation – Political, Labour and Economic Development in Jamaica, 1938–1945*, the second *Time for a Change – Constitutional, Political and Labour Developments in Jamaica and Other Colonies in the Caribbean Region, 1944–1955* and the third volume surveys *End of Empire – Transition to Independence in Jamaica and Other Caribbean Region Colonies*.

His writings and command of historical and political subject matter have led to his being invited as visiting lecturer to several Canadian and American Universities: the University of Havana, the University of Guyana, the University of the West Indies in Jamaica and Trinidad, and the University of Paris. He has also been conferred with honorary doctorates by the University of the West of England in 2004, the University of the West Indies in 2005, and the University of Hull in 2011.

Caribbean Political Activism: Essays in Honour of Richard Hart offers a critical reflection not only of aspects of Hart's work as politician, historian, and archivist, but also delves into the achievements as well as the fateful experience of the left in Jamaica and Grenada in the post-independence years of the 1970s and 1980s. It is to the credit of the Centre for Caribbean Thought that these issues were discussed at the conference in his honour during a period of self-imposed silence in the face of what appeared to be triumphal global neo-liberalism from the 1980s. Hart's enduring example, whatever its shortcomings, enabled the opening of the mouth and the process of learning to speak once more the language of transformation.

Acknowledgements

The essays in this collection were originally presented as papers at the Fifth Annual 'Caribbean Reasonings' Conference entitled 'Politics, Activism and History: The Life and Times of Richard Hart' 8–10 June 2006 and held at the University of the West Indies, Mona, Jamaica. The conference was sponsored by the Centre for Caribbean Thought, Department of Government, University of the West Indies in collaboration with the Africana Studies Department, Brown University in Providence, Rhode Island.

I am grateful to my colleagues, Professor Brian Meeks, Director of the Sir Arthur Lewis Institute of Social and Economic Research and the Centre for Caribbean Thought as well as Professor Anthony Bogues, past Chair of the Africana Studies Department of Brown University and Associate Director of the Centre for Caribbean Thought, for their contribution to the series of conferences staged by the Centre for Caribbean Thought. These conferences started in 2001 and have been dedicated to examining the contribution of outstanding Caribbean thinkers. They also spawned the book series 'Caribbean Reasonings', now part of the Ian Randle Publishers' catalogue.

Christine Randle of Ian Randle Publishers has provided support and encouragement in the publication of these conference papers. I am also indebted to Professor Emerita Maureen Warner-Lewis, an honorary Fellow of the Centre for Caribbean Thought, who has not only copy-edited this volume but has been in communication with each contributor thereby ensuring that the book would not be further delayed. Ms Eleanor Williams, staff member of the Centre for Caribbean Thought, also helped in the early stages.

Introduction

Richard Hart's Evaluation of Early Modern Jamaican Politics

Rupert Lewis

Richard Hart is a symbol of the nationalist awakening and the twentieth century struggle for decolonization in Jamaica and the Caribbean. He has contributed to Jamaica's political awakening by his selfless commitment to social, political and economic transformations and to regional unity since the 1930s. His year of birth was 1917 and that year was significant for two reasons. Hart was born towards the end of the First World War, 1914–18, and the West Indian veterans of this war were triggers of the early twentieth century movement against colonialism.[1] Secondly, 1917 was the year of the Russian Revolution the influence of which had a major ideological and political impact on the world in the twentieth century and on Hart's political thinking. Richard Hart's life spans key moments in the twentieth century and the relationship of these moments to the process of twentieth century political decolonization.

He was one of Jamaica's best known political subversives of the colonial order from the 1930s until the 1960s. Through independent reading he was a Marxist who thought about issues of decolonization from a class standpoint. His radicalism resulted in him being imprisoned by the British colonial government in the 1940s, expelled by the People's National Party (PNP) in 1952 in the early years of the Cold War and kept under surveillance by the Special Branch in Kingston under Jamaica Labour Party (JLP) and PNP administrations of Alexander Bustamante and Norman Manley. Hart was a consistent advocate for mass-based democratic political parties, for trade unions, for political sovereignty, for a greater role of the state in the economy but his radical advocacy of these ideas posed a threat to British imperialism and their local political successors as well as the Jamaican upper classes who financed political parties.

Hart's background made him an unlikely radical. He was from the upper middle class and most of his associates in his youth had been light complexioned (Bogues 1978, 5). In his diary entry dated 24 May 1938, Hart, then approaching 21, wrote: 'Bustamante and Grant had walked through the police untouched and along South Parade to King Street. My companion and I walked down to the fountain and out into South Parade. A few scattered policemen were still advancing in a sort of semi-circle, but we wore neckties and jackets and are both of fairly light complexion so we passed through unmolested' (Hart 1938a). Hart's colour was protective armour from the batons and bullets of the special constables in the midst of a riot in which one of his brothers was a special constable (Bogues 1978, 6). His father Ansell Hart was a lawyer and a historian who wrote an authoritative book on George William Gordon who had been executed by the British in the 1865 revolt. Ansell had a well-stocked library which included Marxist literature which his son read.

To be a communist in the 1930s and 1940s meant 'progressive' as many working-class and middle-class intellectuals joined mass movements (Bogues 1978, 7). These two decades were marked by an acute economic crisis in the Western capitalist countries, the rise of right-wing and left-wing political movements, and the beginning of the Second World War. Hart's radicalism has to be understood in the context of the leftward swing in Europe and of the liberal American federal government agenda of President F.D. Roosevelt in the United States in response to the depression in the 1930s, the Spanish Civil War and the Italian invasion of Ethiopia, which drew many in Europe and the colonies to the class politics of Marxism and the growing tide of nationalist anti-colonialism. Later on the alliance between the Soviet Union, the United States and Western Europe in the fight against Hitler also saw widespread support for socialism until the end of the war and the start of the Cold War.[2] It is in this global political climate that Hart's Marxism developed. Radicals in Kingston were reading Stalin's pamphlet on the *National and Colonial Question* and Lenin's *State and Revolution* as well as John Strachey's *The Theory and Practice of Socialism* (Bogues 1978, 10). The 1930s were therefore a decade of political significance marked by the rise of German, Spanish and Italian fascist movements on the one hand and anti-fascist and socialist movements, on the other. The international climate provided fertile ground for the political left. Italy's invasion of Ethiopia in 1935 sparked off a wave of protests in the West Indies and the United States and added a Black Diasporic dimension to the emergence of popular fronts bringing together communists and democrats in a political struggle that defeated Hitler in the Second World War. Political protests took place throughout the Caribbean in response to local conditions as well as the European crisis caused by the war. There were disturbances in British Honduras in 1934, St Kitts and St Vincent in 1935; in St Lucia in 1936; in 1937 in Barbados and Trinidad and Tobago and 1938–39 in British Guiana and Jamaica.[3]

The 1930s labour rebellions in Jamaica and the Caribbean were defining moments in Hart's life and he has drawn on the energy and vision of that historical moment throughout his long political career. Hart set an example of selfless political activism since 1936/1937 when at age 19 he started writing for *Public Opinion*. Indeed his support of progressive class-based politics in the Caribbean started before the PNP was created. He became a founder member of the People's National Party in 1938; in 1939 he acted as secretary of the Trade Union Advisory Committee, forerunner of the Trades Union Congress (TUC). He was President of the Railway Employees Union from 1942–48 and Vice President of the TUC until 1953. In 1942–43 he and others were imprisoned without trial by the colonial government (Hart 1989, 10). He represented the PNP and the TUC at the founding conference of the Caribbean Labour Congress in Barbados in 1945 and was its Secretary from 1946–53. From 1953 until 1957 he was legal adviser to the Sugar and Agricultural Workers Union in Jamaica; from 1954–63 he was a member of the People's Freedom Movement and its successor, the Socialist Party of Jamaica. He edited the *Mirror* newspaper in Guyana, 1964–65, and relocated to England in 1965 where he continued his political work in the West Indian community. In 1974 he founded the Caribbean Labour Solidarity in London. His work among the Caribbean Diaspora in London has also seen him take up all the significant issues of trade relations with the Caribbean, British racism, human rights, defense of the Grenada Revolution as well as the broader issue of Caribbean sovereignty in the *Cutlass* newsletter which he edited.

Hart is therefore a regional political activist. At the founding meeting of the Caribbean Labour Congress in 1945 in Barbados, Norman Manley sent a message in which he endorsed Richard Hart: 'Comrade Richard Hart who represents us at the Conference is a foundation member of the People's National Party and a trusted and invaluable worker both in the Trade Union and Political field...I ought to add that we do not have in our ranks anyone who has more closely studied West Indian history or kept himself better informed as to the course of events in recent years in other West Indian Countries'(Caribbean Labour Congress, 36–37). This endorsement testifies to Hart's regionalism and few Caribbean political activists have this enduring record. Years later, on the invitation of Maurice Bishop he served as legal adviser to the People's Revolutionary Government of Grenada and became its Attorney General in May 1983. His record of political activism has therefore lasted throughout most of the twentieth century and into the twenty-first century.

In addition to Hart's formative years of political activism in Jamaica, his work in Guyana in the 1960s and Grenada in the early 1980s has made him a significant influence on twentieth century Caribbean political radicalism. His political experience has been linked to the emergence of the Caribbean working class and this connection has been decisive in his development as a human being: it has shaped his political choices and has brought him some political success as well as defeats. But these defeats have not daunted his commitment to the political struggles of working people. He represents the Marxist tendency in Jamaican radicalism; the other tendency that has had widespread mass support from Garveyism through to Rastafarianism and Black Power is Black Nationalism. Neither of these tendencies – Marxism and Black Nationalism – has commanded significant electoral support although both of them have had an influence on the dominant two political parties, with Black Nationalists supporting both parties at one time or the other and Marxists having an influence in the People's National Party from 1938–52 and during the first Michael Manley government of 1972–80. In addition, his extensive political writing on twentieth century English-speaking Caribbean politics and history has put him in the ranks of important Caribbean historians.

Hart's Political Histories

Four books by Richard Hart on the history of Jamaican politics from 1938 to 1962 are *Rise and Organise – The Birth of the Workers and National Movements in Jamaica (1936–1939)*; *Towards Decolonisation: Political, Labour and Economic Development in Jamaica, 1938–1945*; *Time for a Change: Constitutional, Political and Labour Developments in Jamaica and other Colonies in the Caribbean Region, 1944–1955;* and *The End of Empire – Transition to Independence – In Jamaica and other Caribbean Region Colonies* (Hart 1989, 1999, 2004, 2006). These books cover a formative period in the economic, cultural and political development from colony to nation, and demonstrate the transition to independence that in many ways continued British authoritarian political values together with class and racial prejudices drawn from the plantation system. At the same time, this transition introduced universal adult suffrage and brought the masses into electoral politics.

Rise and Organise – The Birth of the Workers and National Movements in Jamaica (1936–1939) has a different and unusual quality. It draws on his diaries of 1938 which are like political field notes on the islandwide protests and captures the actions of the masses and the response of the colonial state; the imprisonment of Bustamante which further endeared him to the workers, the tactical responses of the left in issuing leaflets, for example, to indicate clearly to the governor that the strikes would continue unless Bustamante was released. There was also the issuing of a leaflet critical of Norman Manley's mediating role in which he had called on the workers to go back to work prior to Bustamante's release. Later on there was Buchanan's open letter to Bustamante when he left the union with a critique of the labour leader's autocratic style. Hart helped to edit the *Jamaica Labour Weekly* during the imprisonment of its editors Hugh Buchanan and Stennet Kerr-Coombs. There was Manley's request that Hart and the left not participate in a Kingston and St Andrew Corporation (KSAC) by-election in 1938 because of his fear that the communist label would prejudice Noel Nethersole's chances at the polls. Hart agreed but Nethersole lost just the same. Hart's adherence to Marxist ideas helped to shape his democratic organizing among the working class in particular, but anti-communism in the colonies was virulent and was a powerful tool in isolating these Marxists who were depicted as anti-religious in a society where every political meeting started and closed with prayer. Furthermore, these communists were portrayed as wanting to expropriate property on an island where small peasant holders were deeply attached to their plots of ancestral hillside land.

The other volumes: *Towards Decolonisation: Political, Labour and Economic Development in Jamaica 1938–1945; Time for a Change:*

Constitutional, Political and Labour Developments in Jamaica and other Colonies in the Caribbean Region, 1944–1955 also include a considerable body of field notes, letters and confidential comments from Colonial Office officials that enable us to understand the motion of political life.

Hart represents for me that fascinating encounter between political involvement and the writing of history based on serious reflection at a moment of political foundation. Richard Hart's methodology reflects a strong interest in documentation as he is a systematic writer of notes, diaries, letters and now emails, which constitute a database for his political analyses. He has preserved the records of popular organizations and tells the following anecdote: 'I recall an occasion, in the 1950s, when I temporarily rescued a minute book of one of the trade unions affiliated to the former Trades Union Council. This had been placed in the toilet at the offices of the Trade Congress on Hanover Street where it was being used, page by page, for an uninspiring purpose' (Hart 1999, xvi). He is meticulous in his use of sources, strongly committed to evidence (this reflects his legal training), forensic in his insights and is an authority on British Colonial Office documentation. The right to organized political life, which we take for granted today, whether this be in the form of trade union organization, political parties, the right to freedom of association, of expression, were all hard-won rights secured in the struggle against British colonialism and the local political class, supported by the sugar oligarchy and merchants.

Behind the Legends

The generation born after the Second World War benefitted directly from independence in the 1960s with access to higher education, greater political representation, vastly improved prospects for employment in the government bureaucracy and in the private sector. In addition, there were the struggles that eroded racial barriers which continued for decades after the 1930s. The legendary Alexander Bustamante and Norman Manley are credited with many of these achievements. However, Hart's historical writings remind us that they themselves were political beneficiaries of a movement of hundreds of thousands of estate workers, dockworkers, small farmers and the progressive middle classes and business people who were the collective makers of the radical shift that took place in 1938, which opened new space for political action and forced the authorities into new compromises. Hart offers us a sober look behind the legends of party politics and introduces us to other personalities who are today virtually unknown but on whom the political legends depended.

Among these characters were A.G.S. Coombs who formed the Jamaica Workers and Tradesmen Union in 1937 along with Hugh Buchanan. Hart describes A.G.S. Coombs who lived from 1901–69 as 'a tall, powerfully built man, he had been a policeman from 1919 until 1922. His departure from the Police Force was said to have been a consequence of his defiance of a white officer whom he had bested when they came to blows. Thereafter he became a soldier in the West India Regiment, leaving the army in 1926 or 1927 with the rank of Corporal or Lance Corporal.' In a letter to a local newspaper he described himself as a 'peasant of low birth, very limited education and a very poor man' (Hart 1999, xi). There was the fiery St William Grant, the Garveyite who was Bustamante's right hand man, Aggie Bernard who raised money and cooked and fed the workers during the labour strikes, and Robert Rumble, a small farmer and the leader of the Poor Man's Improvement Land Settlement and Labour Association in Clarendon. Overseas there were Wilfred Domingo, W. Adolphe Roberts, Rev. Ethelred Brown, and the Garveyite Jaime O'Meally of the Jamaica Progressive League in New York who called for self-government before the PNP was conceived. And there is Edgar Daley of Islington in St Mary, one of the protesting banana workers who, armed with a stick, was bayoneted and his back broken by blows but who shouted defiantly 'No, not a rass!' (Hart 1989, 91).

It is in response to this level of commitment that Hart's socialism grew in counterpoint to the British Labour Party inherited socialism of Norman Manley and others in the leadership. The important point about Hart's political thinking at this time was that Jamaica was a plantation society and was in no position to build socialism as it had no industrial base. Hence the priorities for the foreseeable future were on self-government, independence, regionalism and the building of democratic institutions. The smokescreen of anti-communism meant that Hart and the left were portrayed as Stalinists who wanted to impose a dictatorship and take over what little personal property ordinary people had. British policy in the colonies ensured that people like Hart would be targeted for political marginalization and pressure was brought to bear on the organizations in which they functioned. Hart's four volumes on Jamaica's pre-independence political history document the actions against the left from Colonial Office files (Munroe 1992; Horne 2005; 2007).

The Politics of the British Empire

Winston Churchill, the British Prime Minister, had declared 'I have not become the King's first Minister in order to preside over the liquidation of the British Empire' (Hart 1999, 138). How did the empire maintain itself? It did so ideologically through validating institutions such as family, school and church as Brian Moore and Michele Johnson have shown in their book *Neither Led nor Driven – Contesting British Cultural Imperialism in Jamaica, 1865–1920* and they did so militarily as Caroline Elkins documented in *Imperial Reckoning: The Untold Story of Britain's Gulag in Kenya*, a well documented exposé of British atrocities in Kenya in the 1950s. This ideological and military power ensured the growth of Britain's global colonial investments. In 1938 when the rural and urban masses demonstrated against poor economic conditions, the browns and whites volunteered in large numbers to put down the protests and there was considerable support for the British Empire not only among white people but among blacks as well.

Hart's volumes on Jamaican politics 1938–62 include extensive citations by him from Colonial Office papers. These officials who wrote from the standpoint of the British Empire which they had served in postings in Africa, the Caribbean, the Middle East, India and elsewhere had a good grasp of the emergent political class in the colonies and their class analysis is as good in many respects as any first-rate Marxist analysis. They were accustomed to ruling and understood the bigger stakes behind any challenge. They understood the class trends in the nationalist movement, knew who could be bought off, who could be pressured, whose vanity could be appeased by making him a Member of the British Empire or granting him a coveted knighthood. The political class at that time was male. They understood the social, economic and political relations of the plantation system they had created in the Caribbean and felt they understood Norman Manley but found Bustamante unpredictable, but knew his weaknesses.

The 1938 protests marked the death knell of the political order implemented in the era after the Morant Bay Rebellion of 1865 which saw the execution of George William Gordon and Paul Bogle and the killing of several hundred people. The introduction of the Crown Colony system gave the governor full control and eliminated the representative element until the constitutional changes of 1884 and 1895 which reintroduced the elected element, numbering nine and then 14 for those years. J.A.G. Smith, a veteran member of the old Legislative Council from the 1920s felt that Jamaica was not ready for adult suffrage in 1939. Hart quotes an amusing but very instructive note by Governor Richards who wrote 'I frightened the life out of J.A.G. Smith the other day... by referring to the approaching days of universal suffrage, in private conversation. He looked at me and said "But you could never allow that. It would not work & the people are not ready for it"' (Hart 1999, 40). But after the 1938 rebellion the people had moved beyond J.A.G. Smith. As Hart points out, in '1938, when the population of Jamaica was 1,173,645, there were 61,621 registered voters. This works out at about 10 percent of the adult population. In the previous election, held in 1935, only 25,668 of these registered voters voted' (Hart 1999, 3). Hart was foremost among those who not only called for the end to British rule but challenged the country to envision an entirely new political order that was democratically rooted not only in universal suffrage but in political parties, unions, and citizens associations where everyone had equal rights.

Secondly, in 1938 there was a national movement with two components – the political movement was the People's National Party, the intellectual author of which was O.T. Fairclough, who among others encouraged Norman Manley into political life. The other component was the labour movement around the charismatic Bustamante who had the support of the largely agricultural working class. Bustamante was the decisive figure in Jamaican political leadership from 1938 until the early years of independence (Eaton 1975, Jones 2009). He had a strong trade union base, the union belonged to him, he controlled the union's finances and there was no audit of its accounts. In fact the constitution affirmed that the union was under Bustamante's personal control. Rule 17 read 'Mr Alexander Bustamante shall be the permanent President of the Union, and shall hold office during his lifetime…The President shall preside as Chairman at all meetings of the Union and the Managing Executive Committee….' Rule 19 stated 'The General Secretary, the Assistant General Secretary, the Treasurer, and the Field Organizers shall be appointed by the President...They and each of them shall act according to the instructions of the President and be appointed and dismissed at his discretion...' Bustamante had control of the funds of the Bustamante Industrial Trade Union (BITU). Under Rule 30 (m) it stated: 'There shall be a standing subcommittee of the President, the Vice-President, General Secretary, Assistant General Secretary and Treasurer, which shall control all the finances of the Union and the employment and terms of employment of all paid officers and paid employees of the Union.' Three of these persons were appointed by Bustamante (Hart 1999, 19–21). It was not a democratic organization and the Jamaica Labour Party which was formed in 1943 to contest the first elections based on universal adult suffrage was also developed in that mould. No one challenged the leader. The sociology behind this kind of autocratic leadership was the authoritarian structure of agrarian plantation systems with its rigid hierarchical top-down structure.

The workers and farmers, who became staunch supporters of Bustamante and who benefitted from his direct engagement with the colonial authorities in 1938 and subsequently from his negotiating skills, were able to improve their wages, advocate policies which allowed them to send their children to school in shoes, and have better working and living conditions. They discounted their own militancy and saw Bustamante, the light-skinned Jamaican, as their charismatic saviour. Hart's evaluation of Bustamante is of importance as he noted 'in the upheaval of 1938, tens of thousands of manual workers, who had hitherto shown every sign of subservience to their employers and "social superiors" had, so to speak, got up off their knees. After years of apparent docility they were now prepared to fight for better wages and conditions. Bustamante was the leader around whom they had rallied' (Hart 1999, 21). As Hart pointed out, Bustamante's political elevation was a miracle as the crowds transformed him from a moneylender into someone sent from God to deliver them from oppression (Hart 1938b). There was an uneasy relationship between the political movement for self-determination and the labour movement led by Bustamante which focused on bread and butter issues. Activists like Hart were more democratically oriented and influenced by British Labour Party ideas about trade union and party organization. Nevertheless, Bustamante was on the platform at the launch of the PNP and Norman Manley appeared as legal counsel for Bustamante on numerous occasions. Moreover, in 1940 at a public meeting marking the second anniversary of the labour uprising Bustamante stated categorically, 'For some months I have made up my mind not to allow anything whatever to separate me and the Bustamante Industrial Trade Union from the People's National Party…I now join hand and heart with Mr Norman Manley on my left here and with the other officers of the PNP on my right to work in friendship so that we will achieve something if not today, tomorrow, worthwhile for the masses' (Hart 1999, 52). Moreover, Richard Hart, Ken Hill and Frank Hill among others worked to build and increase the membership of the Bustamante Unions when Bustamante was imprisoned by Governor Richards from September 1940 until February 1942. Richards had intended to keep Bustamante in detention for the duration of the war. Hart provides figures to show the growth of the BITU. 'In February 1942 the membership of the BITU had risen to 20,612 of whom 13,741 were described as paying – a dramatic increase from the corresponding figures in May 1940 when the total membership had been 10,707 and the paying membership only 3,271' (Hart 1999, 104). So Bustamante's absence from the streets saw increased trade union political activities that were strengthening his union and there were misgivings that the left would emerge stronger as a result of their work. It was therefore in the interest of the Governor to release Bustamante to split the national movement. Hart brings some evidence to show that Bustamante cut a deal with the Governor and part of that deal was the denunciation of the PNP and the struggle for self-government. Bustamante's speeches on his release were hostile to self-government. Whether or not a deal was cut, Bustamante's alliance with the PNP was fraught with mutual suspicion and contradictions. One of these contradictions was his stout resistance to any form of democracy within the trade union. He developed a form of proprietary unionism which meant that employees of the Unions were entirely dependent on him and were expected to be loyal to the chief.

For a brief time therefore, there was a single nationalist movement; however the British played on existing tensions and it seems inevitable that these tensions would have led to splits between the charismatic style of Bustamante and those in the nationalist movement influenced by the British Labour Party and trade union constitutional approach to party and union management. Bustamante recognized that he had an independent working-class base and in 1943 organized the Jamaica Labour Party with a very pragmatic, bread and butter programme. In the first general election 'held under full adult suffrage on 14 December 1944' the JLP won 29 seats, the People's National Party 19, the Jamaica Democratic Party and five other organizations won nine. There were 68 independent candidates (Hart 2004, 7).

Hart explains the PNP response to the 1944 defeat: 'The election result was a bitter pill for Norman Manley and the PNP to swallow.' The PNP had initiated and successfully led the campaign for the extension to every man and woman of the right to vote and had pioneered the demand for self-government. But given the class structure of Jamaica, the messianic image that Bustamante had acquired as a result of the events of 1938 and his role as leader of by far the largest trade union, the result of the election was not surprising.

Bustamante's messianism is best analysed in the hero and the crowd metaphor used by Archie Singham in his analysis of the rise of the trade union and political leader Eric Gairy in Grenada as a result of the upheavals in 1951, the equivalent of Jamaica's 1938 (Singham 1968, 309–23). The sense of the crowd is a much looser aggregation than working class and John Hearne in the novel *Voices Under the Window* captures the unpredictable actions of the mob in Kingston and the way it drove fear into the privileged sectors resulting in a changed political environment of representational politics. The protests of 1938 and later years, however, did not deliver the kind of political change hoped for as far as the class consciousness and organization of the masses were concerned. Hart argued that 'this appreciation by the workers of their strength had not however been accompanied to a similar degree by a growth in working class self-confidence. Instead of accepting as their leaders persons of their own class and complexion, such as A.G.S. Coombs and H.C. Buchanan, they had entrusted leadership to Bustamante, a brown middle class, albeit sympathetic, careerist who appeared to have demonstrated his identification with their cause' (Hart 2004, 10).There is much in this assessment to agree with but it does pose a number of questions. Hadn't Bustamante satisfactorily demonstrated his capacity for bold leadership at the moment in 1938 when it mattered? To what extent has Hart overstated the capacity of the working class at the time, given its agrarian base, its small farming activities which made it a small owning class as well as a wage-earning class? Moreover, given the deep biases in the society towards a light-skin wouldn't workers too feel that a Bustamante was preferable to a Coombs? As Hart himself demonstrates in his political narrative, the way Jamaican politics evolved witnessed a not surprisingly strong preference for Bustamante as a counter to the nationalism and radicalism of the PNP and while the planters and business class felt for a time that they could enter the political fray on their own, they concluded after their defeat in 1944 that Bustamante was the best political leader with whom to strike a deal. To what extent did working class self-confidence and embrace of Bustamante demonstrate the kind of mix that reflected frustration and unwillingness to put up with low wages and poor working conditions as well as the persistence of the view that light-skinned persons had a better capacity to intervene on behalf of the poor? Drawing more on the actual historical circumstances of an island still marked by its legacies of slavery and colonialism, it is quite unlikely that the agrarian working class would act according to the theoretical ideas found in the texts of Lenin or Marx. Leaders like Bustamante who had an instinctive grasp of the paradox of rebelliousness and subservience were better able to emerge as political leaders. The democratic struggle would prove much more difficult and complex and while 1938 provided an opening, it was also a kind of closure as those leaders who emerged out of that ferment through their organizational efforts and the support of the British gained legitimacy for themselves and their political organizations. Legitimacy in Jamaican and Caribbean politics remains a function of domestic and imperial support. Domestic support was built up through political work and the implementation of policies that were of benefit to the people in education, health, and infrastructure. Imperial support from Britain or the United States in the era of the Cold War was determined by the ability to steer clear of policies and alignments that challenged Western hegemony and the extent to which left wing politicians were marginalized or excluded from the political process (Horne 2005).

The third proposition is that the nationalist movement had different social and racial forces, with the mass of the black population concentrated in the labour movement while the middle classes solidified within the PNP. There was an influential brown and black Anglophile middle class that was colonial-minded, who respected and loved Britain but who were outraged at practices of racism on which basis they were excluded from promotion in the police force, the judiciary, the civil service and the educational system. These institutions were manned by significant numbers of British males and, in a few cases such as in all-girl high schools, by British females as well as brown and black teachers steeped in that educational tradition and the prejudices associated with it. The racism of the time had led to the growth of Black Nationalism that expressed itself in the Garvey movement and the Rastafarian movement. Some of the adherents of these movements were active in the trade unions and in politics. Garveyites were spread throughout the national movement, in the BITU, the PNP and in their own formations. The Garveyite newspaper the *New Negro Voice* gave strong support to Bustamante. One of the most active Garveyite divisions was the Harmony Division which celebrated their fourth anniversary in 1942. There is a report of 'Mr Richard Hart, one of our youngest in the legal circle' who spoke at the anniversary of the Harmony Division and said: 'Impressions made him feel that it was a shame to acknowledge himself a Jamaican. He lost the foolish idea when he went to study in England… one afternoon in Hyde Park he saw many speakers. A black man had an audience before him that was larger than all the other audiences put together. He understood it was Marcus Garvey and after his oration, he had to go and introduce himself as a Jamaican and he felt justly proud. Since his return he has interested himself in Negro writings and became race-conscious. He said Mr Garvey had done his duty and wiped out the "Yes massa and yes missis" idea out of at least 50 percent of the people. It was therefore our duty to wipe it out of other 50' (*New Negro Voice*, 11 April 1942, 2, 8). In a 1975 interview Hart pointed out 'the key people in the PNP structure (at group level) had all been in the Garvey movement, many of them had lived in Latin American countries abroad – Cuba in particular, Costa Rica and Panama' (Bogues 1978, 3).

Race consciousness was a central issue in the emergence of twentieth century Jamaican nationalism. The Rastafarian movement whose central figure at the time was Leonard Howell was seen by Cecil Nelson of the PNP leftist organization, the Negro Workers Educational League, in the following way in 1940: 'We do not know Mr Leonard Howell and we hold no brief for the Ras Tafari Society, but…they represent a united Negro Movement with a membership drawn exclusively from the working class; so naturally we sympathise with them and regard them as comrades. Their methods are different from ours but we feel that ultimately they will join us in the class struggle to achieve emancipation of the...working class' (Hart 1999, 51).

The Role of the Early Jamaican Left

The young Hart at age 21 represented a different ideological viewpoint from Norman Manley in 1938 and especially Bustamante. Manley, at the time, was a prominent lawyer approaching 45 and he was drawn into mediation between labour on the one hand and on the opposing side the owners of sugar estates and wharves as well as the Governor who protected British interests.[4] Bustamante, who was 54 years old, had definite ideas that the he would be the sole proprietor of the trade union movement that evolved out of the nationwide disturbances of 1938 but one must not underestimate the uncertainty about his political future at the time. The huge advantage he had was that he stood tallest in the eyes of the people. Hart in his book on 1938 draws our attention to the early Jamaican Marxists of the 1930s. Among them was Hugh Buchanan who Hart describes as Jamaica's first active Marxist who had been introduced to Marxism by Cleveland Antonio King. King had been a member of the illegal Cuban Communist Party. Buchanan enjoyed a strange connection with one Audley Thomas, 'a senior civil servant in to the Colonial Secretary's Office', who had a good collection of Marxist works to which Buchanan had access. (Hart 1989, 18). Hart says that it was from Buchanan that he first obtained a copy of Lenin's *State and Revolution*. Buchanan who was a tile maker and small businessman became the first General Secretary of the Bustamante Unions at the outset and then resigned because of Bustamante's autocratic behaviour. Buchanan was the figure around whom Jamaica's first Marxist group started to meet. Among the original members of the group were Wellesley McBean, Frank Hill, Albreath Morris, Cecil Nelson, Lionel Lynch and Richard Hart (Hart 1989, 19).

Hart became active in the Negro Workers Educational League which was formally affiliated to the People's National Party. This was the Marxist group within the PNP. Hart's assessment of their role reads: 'Members of the Marxist left played a leading part in organizing PNP groups all over the country but we nevertheless maintained our own organizations within the party. The main organization of the left was the Negro Workers Educational League which was formally affiliated to the party. In addition to this there was the somewhat ill-defined "Inner-Circle" of leading comrades, designed to co-ordinate and guide the work of the left within the party and the trade union movement' (Hart 1989, 120).

The idea for the PNP to adopt socialism did not come from the left. It came from O.T. Fairclough, a right-winger who was introduced by Norman Manley in 1940 and it took the left by surprise. In his speech Norman Manley appeared to be very much on the defensive saying much more about what socialism was not than what it was. It was not revolutionary socialism, it was not anti-religion, 'it involved a fundamental change...it does involve a demand for the complete change in the basic organization of the social and economic conditions...' (Hart 2004, 74). Hart wrote, 'The recommendation in the draft Statement of Policy that the party declare itself socialist forced Jamaican Marxists to re-examine the situation. They came to the conclusion that there was no alternative but to support the proposal. It was nevertheless regarded as important that socialism should be clearly defined and that it should be emphasized that socialism was the party's ultimate, not its immediate, objective' (Hart 2004, 70). From Manley's speech his version of socialism was one entirely in keeping with the stance of the British Labour Party with a focus on state ownership, welfare policies and competitive party politics. In the context of a plantation society with a colonial state the reform prognosis for a developed capitalist economy could hardly be appropriate for Jamaican conditions. Manley's socialism seemed very dependent on the lead of the British Labour Party. In the context of the 1939–45 war when the Soviet Union was in alliance with the Western Alliance the international climate was one that facilitated easy adherence to socialism as it was identified with freedom. However this socialist spirit was to give way as global conditions were to shift with the dawn of the Cold War after the Second World War which led the leadership of the People's National Party to eventually jettison the left.

A socialist spirit infused the first meeting of the Caribbean Labour Congress (CLC) where Hart represented Jamaica in 1945. Other territories represented were Jamaica, St Kitts, Antigua, St Lucia, Barbados, St Vincent, Grenada, Trinidad and Tobago, British Guiana,

Bermuda, and Suriname. Hart functioned as the secretary of the CLC. Among the delegates were Vere Bird, leader of the Antigua Trades and Labour Union, who went on to become Prime Minister; Grantley Adams later Barbadian Prime Minister; prominent trade union leaders Hubert Critchlow, General Secretary of the British Guiana Labour Union; prominent Caribbean and Grenadian leader, T. A. Marryshow; Albert Gomes of Trinidad and Tobago who became that island's first Chief Minister.[5] Bustamante ignored this development and this became a characteristic posture in that the PNP has historically been more drawn to a regional agenda than the isolationist JLP. But an indication of the eventual anti-communist trend within the regional movement was evident in the posture of Grantley Adams of Barbados who in 1948 at the time that he was President of the Caribbean Labour Congress 'was selected by the British Government to be one of its representatives at a meeting of the Trusteeship Committee of the United Nations Organisation's General Assembly...An item on the Committee's agenda on 13 October 1948 was a proposal by the representative of the Soviet Government that the governments of countries controlling non-self-governing territories should be required to submit reports on the political, constitutional, economic, social and educational development of the territories they controlled. Speaking on behalf of the British Government Adams not only opposed this proposal but also launched a completely irrelevant attack on the Soviet Government' (Hart 2004, 96–97).

The British Government was astute in selecting a person of African descent to declare an offensive against a motion that was clearly geared towards laying the political basis for freedom and decolonization. A majority of Caribbean nationalist leaders were willing to play this anti-communist role but others like Cheddi Jagan were not (Palmer 2010).

Hart's assessment of the role of the left in the early development of the PNP emphasizes two points:

> The first was the achievement of bringing the nationalistic message of the party to the working class. Indeed, there were areas in western Kingston and western St Andrew...which 'respectable' middle-class members of the party did not dare or care to visit, where the only public meetings at which the call for self-government could be heard were those organized under the red flag of our Negro Workers Educational League....The left also influenced the entire thinking

of the party during the first decade of its existence in determining the content of the nationalism. The Marxist thesis was that the Crown Colony system was being maintained because it was the most effective political superstructure for exploitation of the resources and peoples of the colonies by the British capitalists. By explaining the connection between economic exploitation by foreign capital and the role of the colonial state, we were able to convince all strata of the party that the demand for self-determination was based on something more substantial than an emotional quest for national prestige. Self-government, we argued, could provide the opportunity for the economic development of our resources for the benefit of the people. And because our Marxist strata, including nationalistic elements among the bourgeoisie and petty bourgeoisie, we were able to ensure that the nationalism of the PNP was not narrowly anti-colonialist but also, in the broader economic and political sense, anti-imperialist (Hart 1989, 120–21).

Economic development for the benefit of the people meant dealing with agrarian reform, however, the left tended to neglect this question. Hart argues that the PNP's approach to agriculture was modest and as a result of farmers conferences in 1947, it resolved to advocate taxation of land on its unimproved value and 'admission duty free of general farm supplies including grain and feed concentrates and materials necessary for the establishment and operation of plants for processing and other agricultural industries'(Hart 2004, 48). Hart claims that the left was not involved with these meetings and had they been involved 'a proposal that large properties, not engaged in the production of the island's principal export crops, should be acquired and broken up for distribution to farmers with inadequate or no land would at least have been considered.' The left seemed not to have been as active around the land issue which was critical to socio-economic change since this was where the bulk of the population derived its livelihood.

Richard Hart's theoretical perspective was premised on the struggle for self-government, the development of democratic trade unions and mass parties and a voice for the working class in the nationalist struggle but it underestimated land reform. The politics of the left was that of building class alliances and Hart saw the national movement as being socially heterogeneous but focused on what it had in common which was its opposition to British imperialism. He saw politics not simply in terms of personalities but personalities embodying social and racial interests. Post-colonial political development therefore would be a complex terrain of competing interests within the nation.

What were the foundations of Jamaican politics evident in the Hart narratives? The years 1938–44 were critical in laying the foundations for Jamaican politics. Firstly, it established an organized working-class base through the trade union movement that played a critical role in electoral mobilization after the granting of universal adult franchise in 1944. The BITU was the mass base for the JLP and the TUC in the 1940s was the mass base for the PNP. This gave rise to political unionism as the parties had at their core mass base the organized working class and sharp rivalries between the two parties were expressed in the sphere of working-class representation. The BITU spread was much larger and its influence greater than the TUC particularly in rural Jamaica. The union divide became the foundation for the political divide and the union clashes in the 1940s became the base for political tribalism. The use of violence in trade union rivalries engendered political violence in subsequent decades (Sives 2010). The most famous case was the 1946 Mental Hospital strike led by F.A. Glasspole of the TUC where Bustamante who was then Chief Minister sent 3,000 BITU members to break the strike and this resulted in the deaths of two people.

Secondly, the political parties developed a system whereby the masses would be appeased by political rhetoric and strong personalities but at the level of policy formation the interests of business and the middle classes prevailed. Richard Hart can count himself among those in the national movement who consistently assessed the class basis and interests behind national policies and engaged in political education and discussions at party conferences to advance the interests of the mass base of the national movement. Political education is a requirement for organizations seeking social, economic and political transformation. This is not the case for organizations that basically seek to make adjustments to the status quo.

Thirdly, Bustamante had mastered the art of political demagogy. At times he was for self-government at other times he was said it was a means to install 'brown man rule.' This was particularly effective in the 1944 election when the PNP leadership had significant numbers of recruits from the brown middle class. There were times when Bustamante was pro-Federation and times when he was anti-federation and it all depended on what was politically advantageous. His relationship with the British blew hot and cold: there were times when he cursed the British and times when he appeared to genuflect. It all depended on political advantage. There is the classic example when the governor proposed a new constitution which included the retention of special powers, which Norman Manley opposed. Bustamante told the Governor he agreed with the retention of powers but had to speak against it at public meetings. Bustamante was mostly anti-communist and he used it effectively to his advantage long before the Cold War. Manley was more politically predictable but the worry of the British was the left wing of the PNP and their influence. He therefore found himself on the defensive when it came to explaining that the party was socialist and not communist and he became anti-communist when he saw the extent to which the British and Americans and the local business class were hostile to a PNP that included a left wing. In the 1940s the big debate concerned the affiliation of the TUC to the World Federation of Trades Unions (WFTU), with Manley insisting that the TUC break with the WFTU. The PNP right wing sought to disentangle the TUC from the WFTU which had connections to the Soviet Union and the international communist movement while at the same time justifying contacts with the International Confederation of Free Trade Unions that had the support of capitalist countries. The left insisted on its right to determine its international affiliates in the trade union movement. It was obvious that the PNP accommodated different class and ideological trends and had a more rational internal decision-making process, while the JLP functioned on the basis of loyalty to Bustamante.

Hart was expelled by Norman Manley and the party leadership in 1952 along with Arthur Henry, Ken Hill and Frank Hill. Arthur Henry was organizer of the railway workers; Ken Hill, organizer of the postal and telegraph workers; Frank Hill had been a journalist as well as a union organizer (Horne 2005, 237). Ken Hill served as President of the Tramway Transport and General Workers Union and 'joined the Marxist left wing in 1939.' He was the most effective politician, becoming Mayor of the Kingston and St Andrew Corporation in 1951 (Hart 2005, 154). In addition, he was elected to the executive of the PNP, was Vice President of the Trades Union Council, secretary of the Tramway, Transport and General Workers Union (Hart 2004, 64,

66), and became President of the TUC in 1948 (Hart 2004, 75). He also served as Vice President of the PNP when he was re-elected to the position at the annual party conference in 1949. Ken Hill won the seat for West Kingston when Bustamante retreated and ran instead in a rural constituency in Clarendon. After the expulsion in 1952 his political career went downhill. Frank Hill was a journalist who wrote for *Public Opinion* and in the 1940s was President of the Public Works Employees Union, served as officer of the TUC and became a member of the Executive Committee of the PNP (Hart 2005, 18, 106). Arthur Henry was treasurer of the TUC. Richard Hart had this to say about Henry's contribution: 'the creation of the Negro Workers Educational League (NWEL) was not…the creation of Arthur Henry, though he may have been the member who suggested its formation to the Marxist group, which became known as the "Inner Circle."' The NWEL was the openly functioning organization of the left in 1939 to which converts were recruited. It was affiliated with the PNP. I was its Secretary until I was succeeded by Frank Hill. Arthur Henry was the editor of its organ *The Worker and the Peasant* (Hart 2005, 52). Although the 4-Hs (Richard Hart, Arthur Henry, Frank Hill and Ken Hill) were not members of a communist party, their ideological histories, their reading, their political ideas in the context of the Cold War and pressures from Washington, London and local elites were sufficient for the PNP to jettison the left. Moreover, the feeling was that the PNP's electoral chances would improve as there were capable leaders in the centre and on the right who could give strong support to Norman Manley.

Clearly, it was the electoral prospects that were uppermost in the minds of the party leadership. The narrow electoral loss of the PNP to the JLP in the 1949 elections was partly laid at the feet of the left. According to Hart: 'The PNP's 32 candidates had received 203,048 votes or 43.5 percent of the valid votes cast, thus exceeding the total of the JLP's 31 candidates (199,638) or 42.7 percent. But the JLP's independent ally Sir Harold Allan had received 8,714 votes. The JLP had won 17 seats, the PNP 13 seats and independent candidates 2' (Hart 2004, 139). Considerable pressure was brought particularly by the *Gleaner* for Manley to expel the left and certainly traditional business interests were of the same mind. The expulsion of the left closed an important chapter in Jamaica's politics in relation to the considerable effort made to bring workers into democratic union structures, the struggle for party democratic procedures to ensure that ordinary people had a voice, and that the agenda for self-government and regionalism would be carried forward. The left had little impact outside of the PNP though considerable efforts were made by Richard Hart and others in organizing the Sugar and Agricultural Workers Union and the politically-engaged People's Freedom Movement. But these activities remained on the margins of national political life. The left stood very little chance of political survival outside of the mass-based parties and trade unions they had helped to build from the late 1930s. The 1950s and '60s were therefore very difficult times for Hart and his colleagues.

The PNP in the 1950s developed the National Workers Union to push the Trades Union Council out of the sugar industry and to become the second strongest union after the Bustamante Industrial Trade Union. Thus was political unionism consolidated with the two major political parties having strong union affiliates. The reasons for the expulsion of the left had been in the making since the end of the Second World War when Winston Churchill declared the Cold War against the Soviet Union in 1946 (Hart 2004, 88). This political line of anti-communism was pursued through economic, political, cultural and military policies backed by billions of American dollars. When Grantley Adams adopted a position of anti-communism it signalled that the leading figures in Caribbean nationalism would adopt that course and those who departed from it would pay a heavy political price. Vere Johns, an influential Jamaican journalist, wrote:

> I think it is high time for Government to keep out of this country certain Communist literature…I think the PEO Library at 64 Barry Street with its Communist literature and hung pictures of Lenin and Butcher Stalin should be immediately closed by the police and all that inflammatory stuff burned – including the two pictures… [There] should be a law making it punishable by imprisonment for anyone here to be in possession of any banned literature. Special attention should be paid to Chinese Communists in Jamaica… Ferdinand Smith has gone to Vienna to soak up more Red poison and he should be notified by Government that he will not be allowed to re-enter Jamaica, birth or no birth. Let Moscow welcome him – he has forfeited the right to be a citizen…And deport Hart while you are at it (Gerald Horne 2005, 242).

Bustamante was effective with his brand of anti-communism, arguing with more wit than logic, 'I cannot divide completely. If I have one pair of shoes, I cannot give you one and keep one' (Horne 2005, 243). It is this assault, particularly in the powerful publications of the *Gleaner*, that supported the PNP right wing and forced Manley to purge the leadership of its left wing.

By the 1950s the Cold War and the growth of American influence took centrestage as the British ended their political rule. American influence was felt throughout the Caribbean but was strongest in British Guiana where the British Guianese were informed in no uncertain terms that independence should not be granted to Cheddi Jagan. With the exception of Cuba after 1959, the Caribbean continued to be the backyard of the United States and some leaders were very pleased with the American presence as it enabled them to step up their anti-communist crusade in the expectation of politically driven bi-lateral aid. Norman Manley and Alexander Bustamante made it very clear that Jamaica was aligned with the West: Bustamante even declared that the US could have a base in Jamaica any time they wanted and this did not have to be tied to aid.

Hart makes us aware of the way anti-communism functioned as a powerful force to defang the anti-colonial movement and to bring the PNP into line with the Jamaica Labour Party. The PNP went on to win the 1955 election after being in the political wilderness as an opposition party since 1944. But the PNP made life difficult for Richard Hart and Ferdinand Smith by limiting their freedom of movement, banning left-wing publications from socialist countries and from Britain, and supporting employers who denied representational rights to unions that had left-wing trade union activists in their leadership. In the years before independence in 1962 there was little to choose between both political parties.

Notes
1. For an excellent discussion of the West Indian Diaspora in the United States, especially New York, and its involvement in African American struggles for civil rights and West Indian agitation for self-government, see James 1998 and Hill 2011.
2. For a good discussion of the Jamaica left and the Cold War, see Munroe 1992.
3. Hart 1989 provides coverage of this period. See also Bolland 2001 for an excellent discussion.

4. Vic Reid (1985), Jamaican novelist, has written on Manley and captures very much the spirit of the nationalist movement of the 1930s to the 1960s, the persona of Bustamante as well as the left wing inside the PNP.
5. See Caribbean Labour Congress 1945.

References

Bogues, Anthony. 1978. Interview with Richard Hart. London, 8 August 1978. Richard Hart Papers, Centre for Caribbean Thought files, University of the West Indies, Mona.

Bolland, O. Nigel. 2001. *The Politics of Labour in the British Caribbean – The Social Origins of Authoritarianism and Democracy in the Labour Movement.* Kingston: Ian Randle Publishers.

Caribbean Labour Congress. 1945. Official Report of Conference held at Barbados – From 17 to 27 September 1945, 37, Richard Hart Papers, Centre for Caribbean Thought files, University of the West Indies, Mona.

Eaton, George. 1975. *Alexander Bustamante and Modern Jamaica.* Kingston: Kingston Publishers.

Elkins, Caroline. 2005. *Imperial Reckoning: the Untold Story of Britain's Gulag in Kenya.* New York: Henry Holt & Co.

Hart, Ansell. c1972. *The Life of George William Gordon.* Kingston: Institute of Jamaica.

Hart, Richard. 1938a. Diary fragment. Richard Hart Papers, Centre for Caribbean Thought files, University of the West Indies, Mona.

———. 1938b. Letter to Walter O'Meally, June 1. Richard Hart Papers, Centre for Caribbean Thought files, University of the West Indies, Mona.

———. 1989. *Rise and Organise – The Birth of the Workers and National Movements in Jamaica (1936–1939).* London: Karia Press.

———. 1999. *Towards Decolonisation – Political, labour and economic development in Jamaica 1938–1945.* Kingston: Canoe Press.

———. 2004. *Time for a Change - Constitutional, Political and Labour Developments in Jamaica and other Colonies in the Caribbean Region, 1944–1955.* Kingston: Arawak Publications.

———. 2005. A Brief Commentary on Louis Lindsay's Myth of Independence. In Louis Lindsay, *The Myth of Independence: Middle Class Politics and Non-Mobilization in Jamaica.* Working Paper 6. Kingston: Sir Arthur Lewis Institute of Social and Economic Studies (SALISES).

———. 2006. *The End of Empire- Transition to Independence in Jamaica and Other Caribbean Region Colonies.* Kingston: Arawak Publications.

Hearne, John. 1955. *Voices Under the Window.* London: Faber and Faber.

Hill, Robert (ed.). 2011. *The Marcus Garvey and the Universal Negro Improvement Association Papers – The Caribbean Diaspora, 1910–1920.* Volume XI. Durham and London: Duke University Press.

Horne, Gerald. 2005. *Red Seas – Ferdinand Smith and Radical Black Sailors in the United States and Jamaica.* New York: New York University Press.

———. 2007. *Cold War in a Hot Zone – The United States Confronts Labor and Independence Struggles in the British West Indies.* Philadelphia: Temple University Press.

James, Winston. 1998. *Holding Aloft the Banner of Ethiopia – Caribbean Radicalism in Early Twentieth-Century America*. New York: Verso.

Jones, Ken. 2009. *Bustamante – Notes, Quotes and Anecdotes*. Kingston: Ken Jones Publisher.

Moore, Brian and Michele Johnson. 2004. *Neither Led Nor Driven: Contesting British Cultural Imperialism in Jamaica, 1865–1920*. Kingston: University of the West Indies Press.

Munroe, Trevor. 1990. *Jamaican Politics: A Marxist Perspective in Transition*. Kingston: Heinemann Publishers.

———. 1992. *The Cold War & the Jamaican Left 1950–55 – Re-opening the Files*. Kingston: Kingston Publishers Ltd.

New Negro Voice, 11 April 1942.

Palmer, Colin. 2010. *Cheddi Jagan and the Politics of Power – British Guiana's Struggle for Independence*. Chapel Hill: The University of North Carolina Press.

Reid, Victor. 1985. *The Horses of the Morning: About the Rt. Excellent N.W. Manley, Q.C., M.M. National Hero of Jamaica. An Understanding*. Kingston: Caribbean Authors Publishing Co. Ltd.

Singham, A.W. 1968. *The Hero and the Crowd in a Colonial Polity*. New Haven and London: Yale University Press.

Sives, Amanda. 2010. *Elections, Violence and the Democratic Process in Jamaica 1944–2007*. Kingston: Ian Randle Publishers.

1 | *Preserving the Record: The Role of the Political Activist/Historian*

John A. Aarons

There is an aspect of the life and work of Richard Hart which is perhaps not as well known as the other aspects of his life such as his career as a political activist and his work as a historian and writer. It is nevertheless an activity of great value and one which has earned him the grateful thanks of scholars, librarians and archivists. This is his work in not only collecting documentary materials on the social and political events in which he was involved, but in depositing them in research institutions (particularly in Jamaica) for scholars and other interested persons to use. His collections are of great value as they represent unique sources of primary information on significant events in modern Jamaican and West Indian history.

As he himself noted, 'much of the contemporary material on trade unions and political organizations in the late 1930s, the '40s and '50s that have been preserved was collected by me.'[1] In one of his works he lamented the fact that 'during the period with which this book is primarily concerned, very few contemporaries shared my enthusiasm for preserving written records of events. Copies of minutes, memoranda, correspondence and even publications were often discarded when they had served the immediate purpose for which they had been prepared.'[2] He records that even after he had rescued an early volume of minutes belonging to a trade union, which he found in a bathroom, and placed it with other records, it later disappeared!

Some of the collections which he assembled covered specific subjects such as the Caribbean Labour Congress which he served as Assistant Secretary and then Secretary. He deposited the papers for the period 1945–54 in the then Institute of Social and Economic Research (ISER), now the Sir Arthur Lewis Institute of Social and Economic Studies (SALISES). The collection consists of original letters, copies of Hart's replies, newspaper clippings, articles and pamphlets.[3] One wonders what would have happened to the collection had he not safeguarded it and ensured its preservation for posterity.

One of Hart's greatest gifts to political scientists is his collection of pamphlets, reports, circular letters etc., of the People's National Party (PNP) covering the period 1938–56 which he presented to the then West India Reference Library – now the National Library of Jamaica – in 1957. These were his materials and he compiled them into three volumes. In his introduction, contained in the first volume, he said: 'I regret to say that it appears to be the only collection of this material in existence. But it is an important collection because it contains the best source material on the birth and growth of the national movement in Jamaica.'[4]

The great value of the collection can be seen from his assertion that the pamphlet containing the speeches, *This Jamaica* by Norman Manley and *Don't Shoot the Pianist* by Sir Stanford Cripps at the launching of the Party on 18 September 1938 was 'the only available copy belonging to the PNP and was in Mr Manley's possession who readily agreed to surrender it, accepting a typed copy instead.'[5]

In 1994 he deposited another large collection of materials at the National Library of Jamaica covering a variety of subjects. These include the Caribbean Labour Congress and copies of documents from the Colonial Office as well as copies of newspapers such as *Jamaica Labour Weekly*, *The Worker* and *The Masses*. These newspapers are of particular value as they were often produced by political parties or political activists and are excellent sources of information on current events. It is difficult to track down copies of them as they were often published infrequently, in small numbers and without any organized distribution system.[6]

For several years his collection on political and trade union activities in Jamaica and the Caribbean covering the period 1937–64 was deposited at the Institute of Commonwealth Studies in London. The collection was microfilmed by an academic publishing company and is available for purchase on eight microfilm reels.[7] Although Richard Hart returned to live in England in the 1990s, he remained a Jamaican at heart and he always intended that the collection should be in Jamaica. Finally, in 2004 the collection was repatriated home and it is now at the National Library of Jamaica.

The index to the collection at the National Library states that the 'Richard Hart Papers consist mainly of handwritten documents, newsletters and newspaper clippings. These documents range from personal and business letters to resolutions and propaganda leaflets. The documents trace the contribution of Richard Hart to Jamaica's political and social development during 1937 through to 1963. Interestingly, also in the collection is a copy of the Detention Order for Richard Hart from the Governor under the Emergency Powers (Defence) Acts of 1939 and 1940 which landed him with three other comrades in detention camp.'[8]

Although the bulk of the collection relates to Hart's involvement with the People's National Party it also includes material on the [Jamaican] People's Educational Organization (PEO) and the [Jamaican] People's Freedom Movement (PFM), 1952–62, including PEO managing committee minutes, 1952–55 and PFM committee minutes, 1954–55, 1960–62; papers on the Jamaica Youth Movement, 1941–44. Where else today could one find this type of information but in the Hart Collection?

Richard Hart's most recent donation of materials to an institution in Jamaica was to the Centre for Caribbean Thought at the University of the West Indies, Mona. The collection consists chiefly of materials on Grenada in the 1980s and '90s. Hart had been a supporter of the Grenada Revolution which had brought Maurice Bishop's New Jewel Movement to political power in the country. He was appointed Attorney General in May 1983 and served in that position until the Government was overthrown in October of that year. The collection contains valuable materials on developments in Grenada after the United States invasion and, in particular, the trials of members of the New Jewel Movement who had been arrested and tried for the murder of Maurice Bishop. Among the papers are copies of affidavits from the accused persons, transcripts of the court cases, accounts of the treatment of the prisoners, petitions for their release, newspaper articles and other items concerning the trials and the international reactions.

The great value of the collections which Richard Hart donated to the institutions mentioned lies not only in the extraordinary breath and width of their contents, but also in their formats. This is because a large number of the items consist of political pamphlets, leaflets, speeches, newspapers, programmes and other ephemeral materials (often cyclostyled) produced for particular events and often on poor quality paper. They fall outside the normal publication distribution channels and are not covered by legal deposit legislation. To acquire these types of materials, libraries have to establish links with political activists or party offices. Frequently, when contact is made with the particular party headquarters, the office itself does not even have copies for its own records, much less for deposit in libraries.

The question which should be asked today is: who is collecting these types of materials? The National Library has copies of political manifestos and party programmes but the collection is far from comprehensive, as it has to rely on the goodwill of persons or groups involved to respond to requests for materials. Early in 2006, Jamaica went through a long election campaign for the presidency of the governing People National Party (PNP). Thousands of copies of manifestos, promotional material and programmes must have been produced by the contenders. How many of them have been preserved for posterity in order to record an important event in our political history?

Today, we need persons in our political life like Richard Hart who have a sense of history, are conscious of the role they are playing and see the importance of collecting and preserving a comprehensive collection of the documentary materials relating to the activities in which they are participating. They also need that generosity of spirit, and sense of stewardship, to make them available to other persons by depositing them in libraries and archives.

Several institutions today, including the Jamaica Archives and Records Department, are responsible for collecting and preserving for posterity the records being produced today. However, as custodians they can only collect or acquire materials which are produced by organizations or institutions and then maintained for their own purposes. At times these institutions, which include government entities, do not recognize that one day these records may have historical and archival value and therefore should be properly organized and stored.

In Jamaica, as a result of the Access to Information Act, government bodies are now taking the management of records more seriously. Subject to certain exemptions, records for the past 30 years are accessible to members of the public who now have a 'right to information'. The Act, however, will only be effective if it is used by members of the public, including the academic community. Although some key records such as Cabinet Minutes fall into the 'exempt' category, records are only exempt for 20 years, although the Minister has the authority to shorten or lengthen the period. Cabinet Minutes for the period since Independence are still at the Cabinet Office and it is understood that very few scholars have made requests for access to them.

It will be recalled that in England, when the '30 Year Closed Period' for records at their national archives was in force, every January, historians would eagerly await the release of cabinet and other records which fell outside the closed period. In fact, the 'closed period' used to be 50 years but due to agitation from researchers among others, it was reduced to 30 years. Now with their Freedom of Information Act in force, the '30 year closed period' has gone, although some records fall into the 'exempt categories' and are not available for inspection.

Historians and other researchers, both here and in the region, can assist their national archives to acquire from government institutions records of historical value, by making requests to see these records. This demonstration of interest might help the government entities to realize the value of their records. For example, in the early 1970s, a request from a young researcher named Robert Hill to have access to the confidential records pertaining to Marcus Garvey, then stored in the basement of Headquarters House, led to those records being transferred to the Jamaica Archives and opened to researchers.

Of course, there is no guarantee that the requests will be successful. In the Hart papers at the National Library there is an interesting exchange of letters between Hart and the Colonial Office in 1991 regarding the availability of certain files on politics and trade union activities in Jamaica between 1942 and 1961 housed at the British National Archives. Hart was asking for access to some files which were closed for public inspection. He was particularly frustrated by the fact that a file on the Caribbean Labour Congress was closed in 1947 for 75 years and would not be available until 2012. 'One wonders,' he said, 'what the Foreign and Commonwealth Office thinks there is about the British Government's activities at that time that needs to be hidden for a further period of time.'[9]

Frustrating as this might be, at least researchers are aware that the file existed and would be available at some time, however long the wait. Unfortunately, the situation is not the same here as government entities do not normally have the same level of concern over their non-current records. The Access to Information Act in Jamaica only refers to records within the past 30 years. It is assumed that records of long-term value before that date are in the Jamaica Archives and Records Department, but this is not necessarily so. At the moment the Archives is working on acquiring these records, especially those dating back to the 1950s and '60s as many of them are still stored in their original locations.

Unless historians and archivists are vigilant, important records will not find their way into archival custody. This is very important as historians and social scientists researching Jamaican history after 1962 have not got the 'safety net' the historians of the previous eras had in knowing that comprehensive collections of official records were safely housed in London.

There is also the need to encourage non-government bodies such as companies, political parties and trade unions to preserve their records, not only for their current administrative, legal or financial purposes, but also for their long-term historical value. One of Richard Hart's concerns, which should be shared by all historians and political scientists, was that there was a danger of presenting a lopsided version of our history if certain primary source material was not available. As an example, Hart notes that very little documentary materials exists on the early days of Jamaica's other major political party, the Jamaica Labour Party and its affiliated union, the Bustamante Industrial Trade Union (BITU). Even the PNP, he said, did not take care of its own records. He bemoans the fact that the early minutes of meetings of the party had been kept for some time but could not now be found. 'Have they been lost,' he asks or 'only misfiled and will they resurface?' [10]

The political activists of today should realize that the work they are doing will be critiqued and analysed by generations to come. To understand the issues, social scientists and historians will need to consult the records and if they are not available, an inaccurate account of events might result. The activists themselves might need to consult the records of current events for their own writings. The extent to which generations to come will be able to read and understand events taking place today will depend on what records have been preserved and thus are available for research purposes. Libraries, archives and other research institutions require the help of scholars to ensure that the records of today are available for tomorrow as many of the materials of value would not normally find their way into the institutions.

One of the best ways of honouring Richard Hart is to follow his example of collecting materials and depositing them in libraries and archives. As a true nationalist, he deposited them in institutions in his home country and did not offer them for sale on the international market. He has set a fine example and scholars will always be in his debt.

Notes

1. Richard Hart, *Towards Decolonization: Political, Labour and Economic Development in Jamaica, 1938–1945* (Kingston: Canoe Press, University of the West Indies, 1999), xvi.
2. Ibid.
3. Richard Hart Collection: papers relating to the Caribbean Labour Congress during the period in which Hart was Assistant Secretary and then Secretary of the organization, 1945–54. See Item 1282 by K.E. Ingram, *Manuscript Sources for the History of the West Indies* (Kingston: UWI Press, 2000).
4. Richard Hart, Introduction, PNP Collection, MS 126a, National Library of Jamaica.
5. Ibid.
6. Caribbean Labour Congress. Papers collected and introduced by Richard Hart, 1945–52. See Item 1113, in Ingram, op. cit.
7. Microform Academic Publishers, *Richard Hart Collected Papers on Microfilm, 1937–1966*, www.microform.co.uk. The company also produced a set of 'political newspapers and ephemera relating to the independence of Jamaica' on microfiche (22 items).
8. Index to the Richard Hart Papers, MSS. 2115A, National Library of Jamaica.
9. Richard Hart, 'A Documentary Treasure Hunt: Assessing Colonial Office Files in the Public Record Office,' *Social and Economic Studies* 45, 1, (1996): 195.
10. Hart, *Towards Decolonization*, xvii.

2 | The Logic of Richard Hart's *Slaves Who Abolished Slavery*: *Black Abolitionism and the Agency of Emancipated Nationhood*

Clinton Hutton

In the nationalist movement which emerged in the British West Indian colonies in the 1930s, and which assumed organized political expression in the founding of the People's National Party in Jamaica in 1938, Richard Hart, one of its founders, posited that one of its guiding principles ought to be rooted in the legacy of the agency of Black emancipation as a philosophical, cultural and psychological compass upon which to locate national emancipation.[1] The implication here is that the agency of the Jamaican nation state, of Jamaican sovereignty and vision, is best served if it were consciously and subconsciously rooted in the epistemic, ontological and psychological legacy of Black abolitionism.

Since that time, Hart has articulated in political campaigns and published a number of studies on the historical significance of Black agency in abolishing slavery and making freedom in Jamaica/the Caribbean and in constituting the superstructural basis for national sovereignty. The best known and most important of these studies are the two volumes of *Slaves Who Abolished Slavery*. Volume 1 (1980), is subtitled *Blacks in Bondage*, while Volume 2 (1985) is subtitled *Blacks in Rebellion*.

Inspired by the nationalist upsurge and labour movement of the 1930s, Hart took interest in 'Slave Rebellions and Maroon Wars of Jamaica [ ] in or about the year 1940' (1985, i) and commenced research on slavery and anti-slavery resistance '[s]oon afterwards' (i). Hart's coinage of the banner title, *Slaves Who Abolished Slavery*, is a profound statement on the epistemological source of emancipation – its motive forces/agency and meaning which came from a tradition authored by the enslaved themselves and signalled a philosophical departure from a historicism emanating from the intellectual roots of enslavement and white supremacy.

It seemed obvious to Hart that an important aspect of the political mobilization discourse for the making of an independent state must necessarily be rooted in black abolitionist political culture. In this respect, Richard Hart tells us in the preface of *Slaves Who Abolished Slavery* (Volume Two) that as early as the 1940s, he 'began to speak from political platforms about the resistance of the slaves to their enslavement, about Sam Sharpe, Tacky and other participants in the many slave rebellions and about Cudjoe and other leaders in the Maroon wars' (i). Hart further notes that, after 'an initial period of surprise, [his] colleagues in the trade union and political movements began to understand [his] purpose' (i).

But how far did Hart's colleagues understand or want to understand his purpose and to let it shape their own agency in light of what Hart calls 'the formidable historical legacy of a widespread lack of racial self respect'? (Hart 1985, i). 'This historical legacy of self denigration,' Hart notes, 'was only partly attributable to the objective circumstances of generations of enslavement and cruel exploitation' (i). For, as he further notes:

> It was also the contrived effect of a system of education and indoctrination deliberately designed to promote a loyalty to the prevailing imperialism and an acceptance of the domination of whites over blacks (i).

Moreover, Hart argues that the British model of this system of education and indoctrination, cast in a mode of gripping subterfuge, was particularly effective in shaping the epistemological compass of most historians. Masked in the image of British liberalism, this system of education and indoctrination, as far as Hart is concerned, engendered in most historians an epistemological compass aimed at perpetuating the superstructural system of white domination and silencing and erasing black agency from the authorship of freedom and justice, and thereby depriving the nationalist project of its essential ontological building blocks. It is in the following statement, more than any other, that Hart's explanation for the epistemological, ontological and agential ethos of most historians emanating from the British model of education and indoctrination, is best articulated.

> Revelling in Britain's liberal image earned by the abolition of the slave trade and slavery, most historians have paid little or no attention to the frequent and formidable rebellions and conspiracies of the slaves, or the extent to which these events influenced the British decision. The suspicion is unavoidable that this is only partly to be explained by ignorance of the facts. The reluctance to investigate and assess the role of the blacks suggests a desire, perhaps sub-conscious, to erase the record of their decisive participation in the anti-slavery struggle (iii).

What we have here in Hart's assertion, is the description of the undeniable truth of a historical process and a historicism/historicity which denied Africans historical agency. Eric Williams[2], whose study of *British Historians and the West Indies* (1964), began to germinate around the same time when Richard Hart began to speak from political platforms about the resistance of Africans to their enslavement as part of the mobilization discourse for national sovereignty, makes a similar point. According to Williams: 'The British historians wrote almost as if Britain had introduced Negro slavery solely for the satisfaction of abolishing it' (182). Slavery in the epistemic and ontological culture of white supremacy thus became a state/school for civilizing Africans rescued by Europeans from the state of nature, from their zoological state of existence into a state of freedom, freedom from themselves.

One can understand why Hart and Williams focused on the British model of education and indoctrination in the shaping of the epistemic culture and agency of most historians. After all, they were British colonial subjects in the vanguard of the struggle for national liberation and the articulation of an epistemology of national sovereignty in their respective countries, Jamaica and Trinidad and Tobago. But what they have said for the British model could easily have been said for the French, or indeed, the German with its Kantian and Hegelian voices of history. With respect to the French model of historiography, historicism and historicity, Pompée Valentin Vastey (Baron de Vastey) a soldier of the Haitian Revolution cum statesman and author, notes that:

> Hayti has no general history written by a native of the country. The few detached fragments which we possess are chiefly from the pens of European writers, who have principally confined themselves to those parts more immediately connected with themselves, and who, when led by the subject to speak of the native inhabitants, have done

so with the spirit of prejudice and partiality which never fails to appear whenever there arises a question involving the competition of Blacks with Whites (Vastey 1969, 15).

Vastey further notes that:

> It should be borne in mind that those historians had nothing to guide them except statements furnished by Whites, in which facts and events were most strangely garbled, truth was exhibited in a false light, and the scale made to preponderate to one side, without at any time inclining to the other (15).

What can be said here is that ideas of Haitian statehood and the meaning of sovereignty in the early nineteenth century began a tradition of questioning, excavating, articulating and centering history rooted in a cognitive agency and epistemology unthinkable in the discursive culture of empire. And, whether this anti-slavery/anti-colonial history arose to confront British, French, Iberian or any other version of European imperialsm, one of its centre-pole assertions is articulated in 1907 by Theophilus E. Samuel Scholes, the Jamaican medical doctor and author, thus:

> (a) THE white, or colourless race, has asserted that it is the superior race, and that the coloured are inferior races. (b) This superiority which it claims for itself, and the inferiority which it attributes to the coloured races, it bases upon certain physical, mental, and moral distinctions that it alleges to exist between itself and the coloured races. (c) And in virtue of this superiority which the colourless race claims for itself, and of the inferiority which it attributes to the coloured races, it announces the right to possess the inheritances of those coloured races and the duty to shape their destiny (Scholes 1908, 1).

Discursively, Vastey, Scholes, Hart and Williams reflect, to an important degree, an episteme antithetical to empireism and acquired empireism. Writing over 160 years before Richard Hart, Pompée Valentin Vastey points to the dire consequence of this phenomenon (acquired empireism/acquired racism) for freedom, justice and sovereignty, when some blacks and browns in Haiti joined with Napoleon's forces to reimpose slavery on that land. Vastey refers to these counter-revolutionaries as 'these…indigènes, Blacks and

Mulattoes in their outward complexion alone, but Ex-colonialists in heart and principle [who] were and yet are, the most inveterate enemies of their brethren and their country [who] deserve to be slaves' (Vastey 1823, 30).

The radical post-slavery political movement led by Paul Bogle[3] against the plantocracy in Jamaica in 1865, came face to face with this phenomenon, which it termed 'black skin, white heart.' One person who would have been placed into this category was a man who tells the *New York Daily Tribune* that black people, like those following Bogle, were more than fools for wanting to come out of the safety of White people's law:

> Massa Black people too fool! – Yes wosser dan fool, dem no free man already. Buckra no make one law fe we all, teef go a me ground law no da fe me? Him nock me down, law de fe me? Neber see de day when me will trus black negro fe make law to govern me, or protect me little and much *(New York Daily Tribune* 17 November 1865).

Another Black man tells the same issue of the *New York Daily Tribune* that:

> I is owner of five acres of land, me hab me house, and me coffee walk – me hab me cart and horse, what going hat me fe take myself out a white people law so go trus [ ] black negro? Dem no walk in tomorrow, knok me down, and take way my place, who me going to fe ax protection? Tan safely me breda! Go plant we coffee and coco, make dem in St Thomas in de East keep dem fool to demself.

About a month later, a man addressing himself as 'A Negro' vigorously protested in a letter, penned by him to the *Colonial Standard*, 'the doings' of Bogle's men in the 'bloody slaughter of their superiors... as a type of negro character.' According to this 'Negro' of the pen:

> No one regrets the late rebellion of St Thomas in the East more than I, neither do I believe that Her Majesty [Queen Victoria] has amongst all her subjects any that is more loyal than I; I would stake my loyalty against that of the proudest son of English blood, or of English aristocracy. [T]he late rebellion of the East was the work of a few of the basest sort of negroes, men of no education and of any position in the country...The *English Times* says "[George William] Gordon was a black man." Doubtless, if he had been black he would

have been less aspiring and thereby saved the country from the disgrace brought upon it...The intelligent black man regards the white man as his friend – political factionists cry colour! Colour!! (*Colonial Standard* 21 December 1865).

The political action and ideas of blacks supporting white domination were evidently rooted in an ontological complex and agency in which some blacks deemed themselves racially inferior to whites in much the same way in which whites deemed them. And it is this ontological complex, this expression of the nature of being, which engendered a type of blackness with an agency to perpetuate white domination, that Theophilus Scholes (1905) described as 'the unenviable and despicable position of the average Europeanised Ethiopian' (60). According to Scholes:

> In the colleges he may have absorbed as much Latin, Greek, and Hebrew as, could they take on concrete form, would suffice, as cargo, the largest transatlantic liner. Yet before a human being with pale face, in abject servility, he will crouch and cower. Having, from the dawn of consciousness upwards, been taught to associate with the white skin everything possessing superior merit, he ends with the conviction that he himself is but a mass of demerit and inferiority; and so, upbraiding his Maker for the "curse of a black skin," instead of the "blessing of a white skin," for the "curse of curly hair" instead of the "blessing of straight hair," for the "curse of black eyes" instead of the "blessing of blue eyes," he journeys through life, ashamed of himself and of every other member of his race (60).

Here we can see that the problem with the production of Caribbean history does not lie just in the epistemological and ontological ethos of metropolitan historians who Vastey and Williams wrote about with respect to the French and British models respectively, but also with the same ethos regarding agency in the production of historical narratives emanating from the Caribbean itself. An additional problem tied to this ethos is what Wilfred A. Domingo refers to as the reticence displayed by 'most' Jamaicans in discussing racial prejudice. W.A. Domingo, a leading figure in the emerging nationalist movement in Jamaica in the late 1930s, states that:

> Most Jamaicans are reticent about discussing racial prejudice. Many of them say it is not a major problem. I maintain it is one of our major problems. It has vast economic and social implications...The tendency of most Jamaicans, especially those who are not black, is to deny its importance (Brown 1947, 81).

Some 80 years before Domingo's statement, the *Morning Journal* newspaper in Jamaica made a similar statement:

> There are many connected with the injured class, who from the highest motives of charity...would desire that the prejudices of colour be forgotten, and deceive themselves that those prejudices have already been buried in oblivion (qtd. in *Falmouth Post* 31 August 1858).

In Hart's logic, the dismissal, nay denial, of the existence of an invidious and insidious race/colour complex, the expression of a self-denigratory cultural ethos and amnesia about black imagination and agency in the framing/weaving of an anti-slavery/anti-colonial culture of freedom, reflect the cultural bases of a way of knowing, thinking and constructing meaning antithetical to the framing of a history narrative of national sovereignty. The inverse of this state of affairs is to be found in the ontological, epistemic and creative culture of the 'slaves who abolished slavery.'

It is in this inverse complex in Hart's logic and, indeed, in Vastey's and Williams's, that the aquifer of authenticity in discourses in Caribbean history is located. Hence, as obscured as it was, encrusted in the intellectual, epistemological, ontological and political complex of White supremacy, Jamaica (the Caribbean) did have a history of its own, Hart opines, '[a]nd there were aspects of that history which, if brought to the people's attention, could provide abundant inspiration for future struggles against oppression' (Hart 1980, ii). Meanwhile, Vastey (1969) tells us that 'to give a correct history of any country,' historians should be mindful that 'a thorough acquaintance with its inhabitants and transactions is an indispensable requisite' (15–16). He rules out authenticity from 'the pens of European writers' (15) because they were 'so blinded...by the prejudices which they entertained against blacks, prejudices of which they are even at this moment [some two decades after Haytian independence] unable to divest themselves'(19). As for Eric Williams, 'the West Indian historian of the future has a crucial role to play in the education of the West Indian people in their own history and in the merciless exposure of the shams, the inconsistencies, the prejudices of metropolitan historians' (Williams 1994, 183).

This West Indian history of which Williams, Hart and Vastey spoke, must of necessity be a central plank in the post-colonial socialization complex and in informing Caribbean political thought and policy. The post-colonial Caribbean nation state requires sovereignty of self and the imagination and the centering of an epistemological and ontological corpus rooted in the rich legacy of the evolving culture of generations of Africans who resisted slavery and post-slavery colonial oppression.

The logic of Hart's conception and production of history is in a profound way congruent with the logic of black resistance to slavery and post-slavery colonial oppression. This resistance to modern European history making, that is, to the discursive ritualization/articulation of occidental mythologies about the inherent intellectual, aesthetic, linguistic, cosmological, spiritual, epistemological, ontological and cultural superiority of Europeans over non-Europeans, forms the basis of what Eric Williams denotes as the West Indian's 'own history.'

In this West Indian history, black agency was and remains central to the making of Caribbean civilization and nation statehood. Moreover, the African diasporic aesthetic complex and the values of freedom, equality, justice and sovereignty, which blackness engendered in resisting colonialism, became key epistemic and ontological instruments in the shaping and reshaping of the modern world.[4] Yet, despite the significant progress Caribbeanist history scholars[5] have made in the production of Caribbean history, it has not, in the context of socialization and time, fundamentally shaped the imaginative and subterraneous ontological culture of Caribbean consciousness.

Power in praxis is still, to a great extent, consciously and subconsciously defined in the epistemic and ontological culture of empire. So, even while Robert Osborn, the prominent Coloured member of the House of Assembly in Jamaica, tells that body on 31 December 1858 that 'God has destined that the wrongs of Africa should be vindicated in these [Caribbean] lands,' in the same breath he asserts that '[t]here is a vein in the hearts of coloured and black men which none can touch but coloured men' (qtd. in the *Colonial Standard*, 13 January 1866).

While Osborn's conception and assertion of leadership and definition of the agency of power seek to obviate the hegemony of whiteness, he argues these on the basis of values rooted in an acquired racist epistemological and ontological complex. His opposition to Edward Vickars' bid to become a member of the House of Assembly because he was black-skinned (Wilmot 1977, 306), denotes that epistemological and ontological complex, which James Lynch[6] ascribes to persons of African descent 'who pride themselves on the color of their skins, feeling that a light complexion imparts superiority.' Lynch opines that '[i]t is questionable whether there is in existence a more contemptible feeling than this, for while it assumes superiority over the darker skin, it confesses inferiority to the lighter, or white, person' (Foner 1972, 317).

Osborn, like other coloured or brown persons in his social position who shared his worldview, wants to end white domination, like most people of African descent. He assesses that in a relatively short period of time, given the existence of a permissive demographic context,[7] persons of his class would assume the positions of power held by the white minority. The basis of this right to power rested in the assumed occidental genetic and cultural endowment of the Coloured, which endogenously equipped them to assume positions of whiteness, which black-skinned black people were bound to respect. In this model, elite or aspiring elite blacks were particularized and assumed to be junior partners.

This Brown Complex, modified under the banner, 'Out of many one people,' in the Jamaican case, won out in the nationalist movement which assumed power in the 1960s.[8] It marginalizes the traditions of Emancipation Day rituals and the legacies of black anti-slavery struggles. It engages in the symbolic manipulation of Garvey(ism) and the black aesthetic, and of spiritual and folk/popular cultural traditions in order to co-opt/pacify/obscure the socio-political, economic, cultural and ontological interests of the black majority, and ultimately of all Jamaicans. It declares the articulation of the sovereign interests and aspirations of blackness to be racist, divisive, nay subversive and antithetical to social harmony, national stability and the integrity of the nascent nation state and hence, needing proscription.

In this post-colonial model of governance, the race and colour problem no longer exists. Hence, those who are raising it as an issue are not acting in concert with the requirements of extant historical realities, but are bent on living in the past and opening up old wounds. There is thus a need for the encystation of that model of history, inspired by the tradition of black resistance, a need to repudiate, to silence, to obscure the meaning of history seemingly at odds with social harmony and national stability.

Richard Hart's conception, articulation and use of black emancipatory history to engender national consciousness and identity, was not the Garveyite model, although he was obviously sympathetic to it and inspired by it. The conceptual and methodological framework he employs to weave a post-colonial history narrative is located in the Marxist philosophical tradition. Hart's assertion that national emancipation ought to be informed by the cultural and ideational legacies of the enslaved who abolished slavery is in keeping with his interpretation of the Marxist ontological-epistemic principle: social being determines social consciousness. It is in this context that Hart indicates that the consciousness of the colonialists and the acquired colonial consciousness of the colonized must be combated, obviated and replaced by an anti-colonial nationalist philosophy rooted in the epistemological and ontological legacy of the most uncompromising anti-colonial ethos, black abolitionism.

In Volume 1 of *Slaves Who Abolished Slavery: Blacks in Bondage*, Hart documents the genesis, condition, scope and justification for the European enslavement of Africans. This narrative is chillingly explicit and intimate in its exploration of the depth, breadth and inventiveness of the brutality and inhumanity of slavery which Hart, citing the planter historian, Bryan Edwards, agrees was 'the leading principle' of modern large-scale enslavement. Bryan Edwards notes:

> In countries where slavery is established, the leading principle on which the government is supported is fear: or a sense of that absolute coercive necessity which, leaving no choice of action, supersedes all questions of right. It is vain to deny that such actually is, and necessarily must be, the case in all countries where slavery is allowed (Hart 1980, 89).

Hart's approach in detailing with amazing intimacy instances of European ritualistic violence against Africans to invoke a culture of fear, and to maintain slavery, as well as his brief but useful attempt at theorizing this breed of violence, was an inspiration to conduct an exclusive study of violence against enslaved Africans. This study, entitled 'Dem Days was Hell': Manufacturing Violence, Shaping Social Psychology: Aspects of the Lived Dystopia Europeans Imposed on Africans in the Americas,' (Hutton, forthcoming) gives intimate details of the execution of a plethora of violence as performance rituals and offers explanations for the inventiveness and use of violence in the process of slave-making.

And this study, which reading Hart inspired, led me to do another study on how Africans cope with such sustained brutality, spanning four centuries. The name of this study is 'The Creative Ethos of the African Diaspora: Performance Aesthetics and the Fight for Freedom and Identity.' It was to a great extent, in the process of coping with the brutality of slavery, that the cosmological roots of African diasporic art and aesthetics emerged in the Caribbean. The emergence of African diasporic spirituality and religious expressions and the weaving of royalty as a metaphor of being, as well as the ontology of double personality (playing fool to catch the wise) and of fortitude, what is called *talawa* in Jamaica and *neg genm* in Haiti, were also fashioned in this way.

It is when the stark brutality of enslavement is considered alongside the culture that the 'Blacks in bondage' spawned to cope with it, indeed to resist it and to overcome it, that the true measure of African heroism can be appreciated and the contribution to the making of modern freedom and the values of civilized relationship among peoples is best understood. Hence the logic of Hart's assertion of the centrality of the legacy of black abolitionism in the articulation of a history narrative germane to national sovereignty.

Despite the fact that Volume 1 of *Slaves Who Abolished Slavery* is about *Blacks in Bondage*, Hart's inclusion of chapter 8, '*The Revolution in Saint Domingue*,' invokes the theme of Volume 2, *Blacks in Rebellion*. Apart from delineating the Haitian Revolution as a historical phenomenon in the pantheon of the making of global freedom, Hart uses the Revolution – that iconic and epic expression of the agency of black abolitionism in the global struggle to free humanity from the ontological construction of the European as free and the Other as unfree – to expose the importance and historic limitations of white abolitionism in ending the trafficking of Africans and in abolishing slavery. Hart had begun to deconstruct the European epistemic and ontological complex which Eric Williams (1994) summarizes thus: 'The British historians wrote almost as if Britain had introduced Negro slavery solely for the satisfaction of abolishing it' (182).

Volume 2 of *Slaves Who Abolished Slavery: Blacks in Rebellion*, focuses solely on blacks' struggles against slavery in Jamaica, from the Maroon wars to the insurrection led by Sam Sharpe. Hart sees a limitation in this volume and tells us that he does not 'deny that the scope of the work would have been improved by accounts of parallel events in other territories' (1980, iii). As in Volume 1, Hart's careful, extensive use of a wide range of primary as well as secondary data has helped him to recreate the major, minor and aborted insurrectionary moments in Jamaica and delineate their individual and cumulative impact on Jamaica, the Caribbean, Britain and, by extension, the world.

In Hart's analysis, it was the primacy of the struggles of enslaved Africans in Jamaica, the Caribbean and the wider Americas, that made possible the end to the trafficking in Africans and the abolition of slavery and set the stage for the making of sovereign spaces and peoples. In *Slaves Who Abolished Slavery*, the explicit arguments denoting black agency in ending slavery and in culturing an epistemic and ontological complex that ought to be, in Hart's estimation, the basis on which to locate national emancipation, are not nearly as obvious in Richard Hart's publications on the rise of the nationalist movement and the development of the process of decolonization.

Although it was the rise of the nationalist movement which inspired Hart's location of the epistemological and ontological ideation of national sovereignty in the legacy of black abolitionism, his publications such as *Rise and Organise: The Birth of the Workers and National Movement in Jamaica (1929–36)*, *Towards Decolonisation: Political, Labour and Economic Development in Jamaica (1838–1945)* and *The End of Empire: Transition to Independence in Jamaica and other Caribbean Region Colonies*, do not explicitly bear witness to Hart's assertion.[9] In a sense, therefore, the *Slaves Who Abolished Slavery* discourses appear to be autonomous from the discourses in Hart's nationalist/decolonization narratives.

However, there is a more implicit and more cautious way in which the connection with the nationalist agenda is linked to the legacy of black abolitionism. This is located in Richard Hart's Marxist conception of national sovereignty and the motive forces and method of organization required to realize it. For Hart, 'the history of the working-class is the history of the people of Jamaica'[10] and consequently, the basis for national sovereignty. This working class in the nationalist struggle came from the old working class, the enslaved Africans who, by their preponderance of numbers and position in the slavery state, constituted 'the embryo of the Jamaican nation' (1974, 2). Moreover, enslaved Africans not only produced the modern working class, but also the middle classes. According to Hart:

> The working class not only reproduced itself, it also gave birth, albeit at the pleasure of the masters and their minions, to the future middle classes. The original intermediate stratum, consisting of the white indentured servants and a few free poor whites who served as tradesmen and book-keepers, disappeared. Brown children born to black mothers replaced them. As this new middle stratum subdivided into upper and lower middle classes, some of the former no doubt wished to forget their proletarian ancestry (2).

Since it is assumed that social being determines social consciousness, there is an implicit assumption of the necessity for the articulation of a working class consciousness (including the legacy of the consciousness of the old working class which gave birth to the new working class) in the struggle for national emancipation.

As stated earlier, the view that the legacy of black abolitionism ought to inform the construction of the epistemological and ontological complex of national sovereignty was defeated as divisive and opening up old wounds. However, this position cannot be sustained. In this respect, Richard Hart's views in *Slaves Who Abolished Slavery* remain very relevant. Neither can the old modes of socialization in Caribbean history be sustained.

We have to be more effective in socializing our people in the ways and meaning of Caribbean history/Caribbean civilization. More creative ways must be imagined and made flesh, along with those already proven to work well, to transform the growing body of historical research into popular documentaries (for television/cable etc.) and themes in the production of the visual and performing arts. We have to find creative ways in making better use of historical sites, in rethinking/recreating/creating historical sites and museums to make them more exciting/sombre places for learning, contemplation, reflection and communion. We have to find imaginative ways to commemorate historical events and make historical experience relevant to national development materially, spiritually, culturally and intellectually. Finally, we have to centre Caribbean history more in the education system as well as design more innovative ways of training history teachers.

Notes

1. Having read Hart's *Slaves Who Abolished Slavery* in two volumes and ascertained from the preface the reasons leading him to research and to write these two volumes, I interviewed Richard Hart in 1990 to get him to elaborate on the link he sees between black emancipation and national emancipation. He was manifestly clear that the legacy of black emancipationism ought to become the basis for the articulation of national sovereignty.
2. The late Eric Williams, historian, lecturer, became the first Prime Minister of an independent Trinidad and Tobago in 1962. He is author of the classical Caribbean history text: *Capitalism and Slavery* (1944). Hart notes that '[t]he first, immature, draft of [his] manuscript,' *Slaves Who Abolished Slavery*, 'was read and criticized by Eric Williams, who had then recently published his classic *Capitalism and Slavery*.' Moreover, Williams subsequently published, as an article in his *Caribbean Historical Review* in 1950 from Hart's manuscript, the chapter, 'as it then stood' on 'Cudjoe and the First Maroon War' (Hart 1980, v). Two years after (1952), the Education Department of the Trade Union Congress in Jamaica published Richard Hart's booklet, *The Origin and Development of the People of Jamaica*, a political education history text asserting that it was the enslaved population which constituted the embryo of the Jamaican nation.
3. Bogle and his movement clashed with the paramilitary forces of the plantocracy and merchant class on 11 October 1865 in Morant Bay, Jamaica. This event is known as the Morant Bay Rebellion in Jamaica's political historiography. See Hutton 1992.
4. See Hutton 2007a and 2007b.
5. This class of scholars include, among many others, Kamau Brathwaite, Elsa Goveia, Walter Rodney, Michel-Rolph Trouillot, Barry Higman, Roy Augier, Bridget Brereton, Verene Shepherd, Carl Campbell, Franklin Knight, Hilary Beckles, Patrick Bryan, Aline Helg and Richard Hart. Other scholars whose works are not necessarily in the discipline of history, but whose contributions are important to the visioning of Caribbean history include, among others, Rex Nettleford, Maureen Warner-Lewis, Wilson Harris, Earl Lovelace, Carlos Moore, Paget Henry, Rupert Lewis, Joan Dayan, Donald Cosentino, Erna Brodber, Aimé Césaire, Brian Meeks, Frederick Hickling, Frantz Fanon, George Beckford, Anthony Bogues, LeRoy Clarke, Philip Moore, C.L.R. James and Robert Farris Thompson.
6. Lynch, an African American abolitionist, made a speech at the May 1865 meeting of the Young Men's Literary and Debating Society of Philadelphia, denoting four ways in which 'Coloured men' (black and brown) in

consequence of their internalization of white prejudice, were 'standing in the way of their own race.'
7. Osborn tells the House of Assembly that '[t]he Government of this country [Jamaica] will within twenty years, be left to the Brown and Black men. The Hon. Member for Metcalfe will by that time be gone. The honourable gentleman, Mr Speaker, is only fighting a shadow; for it is in the course of God's Providence that the change to which I allude should occur, and there is no altering it. God has destined that the wrongs of Africa should be vindicated in these lands,' however, '[t]here is a vein in the hearts of coloured and black men which none can touch but coloured men' (qtd. in the *Colonial Standard*, January 1866).
8. See Thame 2009.
9. Perhaps the best example of how this was done is to be found in the tradition of Marcus Garvey.
10. The logic here is that the application of Hart, say, to Guyana, would locate the motive forces of national sovereignty in the African and East Indian working class.

References

Brown, Wenzell. 1947. *Angry Men – Laughing Men: The Caribbean Caldron*. New York: Greenberg Publishers.
Colonial Standard. 1865. *The Colonial Standard and Jamaica Despatch*. December 21.
Colonial Standard. 1866. *The Colonial Standard and Jamaica Despatch*. January 13.
Falmouth Post. 1858. *The Falmouth Post and Jamaica General Advertiser*. August 31.
Foner, Philip S. 1972. *The Voice of Black America: Major Speeches by Negroes in the United States, 1797–1971*. New York: Simon and Schuster.
Hart, Richard. 1974. *The Origin and Development of the People of Jamaica*. Montreal: International Caribbean Service Bureau.
———. 1980. *Slaves Who Abolished Slavery: Volume 1 Blacks in Bondage*. Jamaica: Institute of Social and Economic Research, University of the West Indies.
———. 1985. *Slaves Who Abolished slavery: Volume 2 Blacks in Rebellion*. Kingston: Institute of Social and Economic Research, University of the West Indies.
———. 1989. *Rise and Organise: The Birth of the Workers and National Movement in Jamaica (1936–1939)*. London: Karia Press.
———. 1999. *Towards Decolonisation: Political, Labour and Economic Development in Jamaica 1938–1945*. Barbados. Jamaica. Trinidad and Tobago: Canoe Press.
———. 2006. *The End of Empire: Transition to Independence in Jamaica and other Caribbean Region Colonies*. Kingston: Arawak Publications.
Hutton, Clinton. 1992. Colour for Colour; Skin for Skin: The Ideological Foundations of Post-Slavery Society, 1838–1865 – The Jamaican Case. PhD. Thesis. University of the West Indies, Mona.
———. 2007a. The Creative Ethos of the African Diaspora: Performance Aesthetics and the Fight for Freedom and Identity. *Caribbean Quarterly*, Volume 53, Nos. 1&2.
———. 2007b. The Historic Values of the Haitian Revolution in the Making of the Modern World. In *The Jamaican Historical Review*. Vol. XXIII.
———. Forthcoming. The Drums Were Never Silenced: Essays on Enslavement Freedom and Identity.

New York Daily Tribune. 17 November 1865.

Scholes, Theophilus E. Samuel. 1905. *Glimpses of the Ages or The 'Superior' and 'Inferior' Races, So-called, Discussed in the Light of Science and History.* Vol. 1. London: John Long.

———. 1908. *Glimpses of the Ages or The 'Superior' and 'Inferior' Races, So-called, Discussed in the Light of Science and History.* Vol. II. London: John Long.

Thame, Maziki. 2009. Caribbean Racial Contract?: Race, Power and Identity in Jamaica and Barbados. PhD. Thesis. University of the West Indies, Mona.

Vastey, Baron de. 1969. *An Essay on the Causes of the Revolution and Civil Wars of Hayti, Being a Sequel to the Political Remarks upon French Publications and Journals Concerning Hayti.* Tr. From French W.H. M.B. 1823. New York: Negro Universities Press.

Wilmot, Swithin. 1977. Political Development in Jamaica in the Post-Emancipation Period. PhD. Dissertation, Oxford University.

Williams, Eric. 1964 [1994]. *British Historians and the West Indies.* New York: A&B Books Publishers.

3 | Richard Hart and the 'Resurrection' of Marcus Garvey

Robert A. Hill

> Considering the fact that at the time of his death
> he had sunk almost into oblivion,
> what has taken place has been a veritable resurrection!
>
> Richard Hart, *The Life and Resurrection of Marcus Garvey*
> (London: Karia Press, 2002)

> The Black Moses, we were told, would take the chosen across the Atlantic,
> the Red Sea of slavery, to Africa or Abyssinia, because
> 'the black man cannot sing his song in the white man's land'. . .
> Much of it is pure Garveyism, and the visitor manages to glimpse
> some of the massive spell that Garvey still yields, a generation after his
> death in an obscure London suburban house.
>
> Prof. Gordon K. Lewis on speaking of the Jamaican 'Apocalypse'
> of Prince Emmanuel Edwards (*Sunday Gleaner*, 2 March 1958)

Of all of Richard Hart's many achievements as a scholar, political thinker and militant, the aspect of his work that has been most significant for me personally has been his contribution to the study of the Garvey movement. Since the 1960s, he has served as a role model of what a Garvey scholar should be. In making the ideology of Garveyism the subject of serious scholarly discussion, his intellectual contribution has been seminal. Equally important, is his role in helping to preserve the records of the Garvey movement in Jamaica, without which it would have been nearly impossible to document the history of the movement. It would not be an exaggeration to say that Richard Hart blazed the trail that we who have come after him have followed and are still pursuing fifty-odd years after he pointed the direction that we should travel.

I am very grateful to have this opportunity to acknowledge a deep and abiding debt to the individual whose multifaceted life and work we are here to recognize and celebrate. Additionally, it is a moment for us to pause and take stock of where we have been and whence we have come since those early days in the 1960s when the 'remarkable cult of revival' that marked the rebirth of interest in Garvey got underway. In this assessment of Richard Hart's remarkable contribution to the evolving interpretation of Garvey, one discerns a process of analytical disambiguation in Hart's attempt to fix the function of the Garvey phenomenon within a broader emancipatory framework of working class struggle.

For the purpose of this chapter, the remarks made will concentrate on Hart's landmark 1967 essay, 'The Life and Resurrection of Marcus Garvey,' published in the London-based journal, *Race: The Journal of the Institute of Race Relations* (Vol. IX, No. 2 [October 1967], 217–38). Although almost 40 years have passed since the essay appeared, I still remember the impact that its publication had upon me as if it was yesterday. It was published just as I had commenced an MSc degree in Government at the University of the West Indies. Not only was the essay carefully researched and documented, and the treatment of the subject illuminating – the author represented also a sort of legend, someone with whom both my uncles, Ken and Frank Hill, shared a particular political history and filiation as part of the famous (or infamous) 'Four Hs.' The decision was made early on to write my MSc thesis on the Garvey movement and the Crown Colony state in Jamaica. As a result, both the essay and author held an unusual significance for me, personally and intellectually.

Over the years I have gone back and re-read this essay many times to check certain things and it has never ceased, after repeated readings, to exert its influence and to be a fresh source of inspiration and insight. The dexterity with which the author handles what is an incredibly complex history, the felicity of his prose, and the unflinching assurance with which he confronts the ambiguous political legacy of Garvey are only some of the essay's intellectual purchase on the phenomenon of Garvey. Fundamentally, by setting the standard that one would come to aim at, Hart's essay was an inspiration and instrumental in helping to make me what I aspired to become.

Hart's 'The Life and Resurrection of Marcus Garvey' marked the literary apotheosis of 'Garvey's posthumous rehabilitation in Jamaica,' marking an extraordinary reversal of fortune for a man whose final years were marked by so steep a decline – 'almost to the point of oblivion, of a man who had once inspired millions' is how Hart describes it.[1] The author himself played no small part in helping to foster the rehabilitation of Garvey in Jamaica, as he himself obliquely alludes in the essay, when he states: 'The small left wing party, generally regarded as Communist, unveiled his [Garvey's] torso, sculptured by a leading member at their party hall,'[2] a reference to the People's Freedom Movement and its role in the Garvey revival.

'By the mid-1950s,' Hart informs us, 'no aspiring Jamaican politician dared conclude a major speech without a complimentary reference to the black messiah.'[3] It would be truer to say that the spirit of Garvey has always been the special province of the Jamaican left. The erection in of a special memorial to Garvey November 1956 by the municipality of Kingston and St Andrew in what was then the King George VI Park (now National Heroes Park) had its origin in the resolution introduced in the Kingston and St Andrew Corporation [KSAC] by Ken Hill in September 1948. The report in the *Daily Gleaner* of 10 September 1948, states:

> At yesterday's meeting of the Council of the Kingston and St Andrew Corporation, Councillor Ken Hill gave notice of the following resolution:
>
> WHEREAS THE LATE MARCUS GARVEY, through his teachings and his work, first fired the souls of the Negroes of the British Caribbean with racial pride and national consciousness and thereby assisted greatly in laying the foundations of the national movements now striving for self-determination for the people of this area;
>
> AND WHEREAS the said Marcus Garvey was not only a member of the Kingston & St Andrew Corporation but a son of the soil of Jamaica who acquired international fame which will go down in history;
>
> BE IT HEREBY RESOLVED that this Council erect a suitable statue in his memory at a prominent place in the city and parish of Kingston;
>
> AND BE IT FURTHER RESOLVED that a special committee of this Council be appointed to make the necessary recommendations to give effect to this resolution.[4]

Ken Hill, the leader of the left wing of the People's National Party (PNP), in the Fall of 1945, had been deputed to represent the Universal Negro Improvement Association (UNIA) at the Fifth Pan-African Congress in Manchester, England, in place of the UNIA selected delegate, L.A. Thoywell-Henry, when the latter did not arrive in England in time. Upon his return to Jamaica, Hill gave a special report to a welcome meeting of the UNIA's Harmony Division on 23 December 1945.[5] Following passage of the resolution in the KSAC approving the erection of a statue of Marcus Garvey, Hill was appointed chairman of the special sub-committee to make recommendations on the proposal.[6] In 1952, as the Mayor of Kingston and St Andrew, Hill wrote the following letter to the *Daily Gleaner:*

> THE EDITOR, Sir:–To perpetuate the memory of the late Marcus Garvey, I have got the Council of the Kingston and St Andrew Corporation to agree to erect a statue in the City of Kingston. The success of my proposal will, however, depend upon the financial assistance which is received from the Government and patriotic citizens of our country.
>
> The Government, I believe, will be prepared to pay one-half of the cost on the understanding that the other half is subscribed by citizens. I have therefore had a special fund opened in the Bank of Nova Scotia under the auspices of the KSAC Council. Public subscriptions are invited and will be lodged to this Special Account of the Corporation…The work and worth of Mr Garvey do not require me to eulogise in words. I take this opportunity of requesting readers formally to be good enough to subscribe to the Fund and to get as many of their friends and other loyal, patriotic Jamaicans to join in doing the same thing.
>
> It will be appreciated that the earlier the money is subscribed the earlier the statue will be erected.[7]

A bronze bust of Marcus Garvey was completed by the Jamaican sculptor Alvin Marriott in July 1954 and the following year plans were approved for the erection of the memorial. According to the *Daily Gleaner,* 'It was decided that Mr Ken Hill, on whose initiative it was decided to erect the statue, should be co-opted a member of the committee. Mr Hill lost his seat as an ex-officio member of the Corporation Council, and as a member of the committee, during the last general elections.'[8] On 4 November 1956, thousands of people gathered to attend the official ceremony unveiling of the bust of Marcus Garvey.[9]

This event, which marks the first official acknowledgment of Garvey in Jamaica, was the result of the initiative of the Jamaican Left introduced by Ken Hill. 'Then in 1964, to the rising chorus of a remarkable cult of revival,' in Richard Hart's words, 'his [Garvey's] remains were exhumed and reburied with honour in Kingston, Jamaica.'[10] The official reburial of Garvey in Jamaica, which took place on 22 November 1964, is physically linked to the 1956 memorial in the form of the bronze bust sculpted by Alvin Marriott that today adorns the mausoleum of the official Marcus Garvey shrine in National Heroes Park. It should be noted that the individual who was mainly responsible for the repatriation to Jamaica of Garvey's remains in 1964 was Leslie Alexander, a Kingston real estate agent, who before then was a militant figure in the Trade Union Congress and the left wing of the PNP prior to its expulsion in 1952.[11]

The programme of civic and political education that was such a feature of the left within the PNP, and that formed the basis of its ideology of patriotism and nationalism, had Garvey at its centre from its inception. It formed the backdrop to Hart's comment cited above, namely, 'By the mid-1950s no aspiring Jamaican politician dared conclude a major speech without a complimentary reference to the black messiah,' embodying as it did a key part of the cultural work of the left. The only other group in the society that could rival the Left was the Rastafarian community, who, according to Hart, 'outdid everyone with their announcement that he [Garvey] was the reincarnated Moses . . . apparently unaware of Garvey's scathing denunciation of Haile Selassie during his London exile in the thirties.'[12]

At the time that Hart's essay was published in 1967, the 'resurrection' of Marcus Garvey was nearing its crescendo after having been steadily climbing from the previous decade. Equally as important, Hart's essay appeared just as a new generation of students was embarking on a whole new exploration of Garvey's legacy as part of their qualification for advanced degrees. Given the changed ideological and cultural climate of the late '60s, marked by the rise of Black Power consciousness all across the Caribbean, the unfolding of the worldwide anti-imperialist movement spawned by the Vietnam War, the movement toward the decolonization of knowledge systems throughout the Caribbean and the Third World, and, finally, the eruption of student radicalism at the various campuses of the University of the West Indies – what it meant to be a Garvey scholar in these altered social and political circumstances took on a new and expanded meaning. The antecedent Garvey 'revival' fed into this rejuvenated field of Garvey scholarship and Hart's essay arrived just as it was getting underway and helped to guide its early steps along the path that was opening up. Three things mark the contours of this new phase of investigation: first, recognition and recovery of Garvey's leading role in the Caribbean anti-imperialist movement; second, the UNIA not only as an organization but also as a social movement with links to the period of post-emancipation; and, third, the role of racial ideology in the formation of the colonial state and the corresponding ideology of 'Africa' in movements of intellectual resistance in the colonial Caribbean.

What is clear from the terms of the new Garvey scholarship outlined is that students of Garvey were coming of age as an inextricable part of the broader process of intellectual maturation in the Caribbean. While it had ties to the Garvey 'revival' and bore a certain allegiance to the wider aims of the movement, it nevertheless marked a new departure and thus should not be collapsed into or conflated with the earlier 'revival' movement of public recognition. Once again, it was the Caribbean left, in a climate of a reawakened Pan-African nationalist consciousness and a rediscovery of Marxism that now attempted to rescue and redeem Garvey from the trammels of condescension bestowed on him by the postcolonial state. In this connection, Hart's unflinching Marxist analysis was both formative as well as bracing.

Hart's interest in Garvey stretched back 30 years. The trajectory of his interest in Garvey is traceable to his student days, as described in the introduction to the much enlarged version of his 1967 essay which was published in 2002. Here he recalls his chance encounter with Garvey in England and rehearses his subsequent political contacts with the Garvey movement in Jamaica:

> I had a brief meeting with Garvey when I was a student in London in 1936. He had just finished addressing a large crowd that had assembled as usual on a Sunday afternoon at Speakers Corner, Hyde Park, and was standing on the pavement at Marble Arch when I introduced myself to him. I had arrived too late to hear his speech.

Apart from my recollection of his impressive personality and of his telling me that a partner in my father's law firm in Kingston had done some legal work for him, I cannot recall anything else of our brief conversation....

In the 1940s I went on several occasions to Liberty Hall on Upper King Street in Kingston, where one of the two Jamaican Divisions of the UNIA had continued to hold its meetings. On one of these occasions I was the guest speaker. I recall that many of the leaders of Groups of the People's National Party at that time had had their introduction to politics as members of the UNIA when Garvey was its leader. Some of them had been members of UNIA branches in Costa Rica, Cuba or Panama.

Although Garvey's fortunes had declined and his contemporary influence had subsided to a very low point by the time of his emigration to Britain in 1935, a remarkable revival of interest in him occurred in Jamaica in and after the 1940s. In the 1950s, I organised a three session study course on Garvey, his ideas and activities for the People Educational Organisation in Kingston. Amy Jacques Garvey, his widow, assisted in this project, attending some of the sessions.[13]

Although Hart's stated purpose in 'The Life and Resurrection of Marcus Garvey' was a modest one – it was, he stated, 'little more than an introduction' to what he hoped would be 'a far more detailed and extensive study' of Garvey's 'teachings and their effect' – there is an unmistakable note of caution expressed at the outset that can easily be overlooked in the rush to rehabilitate Garvey's memory. 'It is, however, interesting to note,' Hart writes, 'that Garvey's posthumous rehabilitation in Jamaica has been instinctive, almost spontaneous.' And then he warns:

> It has not been based, as such reappraisals should be if they are to be of more than passing interest, upon an analysis of his writings and speeches. Such an analysis is undoubtedly necessary.[14]

The essay itself is broken down into five sections, viz., Garvey's 'early life and formative influences'; his 'activities in the USA'; Garvey's 'Jamaican period' after his deportation; an examination of Garvey's 'philosophy and teachings' that returns the focus to Garvey's American period; and, finally, a broad assessment of Garvey's 'impact and effect' in the USA and Jamaica. Included with the essay are also two appendices, the first being a description of the various published collections of Garvey's writings and speeches and the holdings of his various newspapers, the second being to supply the text of Garvey's 1930 election manifesto in Jamaica.

It will be seen from this summary that the author's focus falls mainly on the American and Jamaican periods of Garvey's activities. What is clearly missing from the essay is any discussion of Garvey's wider impact on Africa or the activities of the Garvey movement in Africa generally, information about which was still then, in the '60s, almost completely absent from most accounts, including that of his widow Amy Jacques Garvey's *Garvey and Garveyism* (1963). The omission was subsequently made explicit, when the author observed: 'That very few Africans were ever involved in his plans is neither here nor there in assessing the effectiveness of his message.'[15]

Despite this limitation, however, the essay marks a new point of departure in a number of significant areas that are worth recalling and making explicit today. Among the essay's important innovations in terms of documentation were:

- Recovery and use of oral history as a primary source of fundamental importance in the reconstruction of Jamaican social history. The essay draws upon several oral sources – W.A. Domingo, socialist, editor of Garvey's *Negro World* newspaper, and subsequent opponent of Garvey, whom Hart interviewed while both men were interned in Internment Camp in Jamaica, 1942–43;[16] Marcus Garvey's widow, Amy Jacques Garvey, who 'told the writer that it had not been worth the expense to probate the Will';[17] Adrian J. McGlashan, whom Hart interviewed in 1958, 'one of the pioneer unionists who some years ago gave the writer an account of the founding of the [Printers] Union, its leading personnel and the strike it conducted in the same year [1907, the year it was founded as a chapter of the American Federation of Labour as the first Jamaican trade union to be organised]';[18] Cecil B. Facey, retired head of P.A. Benjamin and Company, the firm of manufacturing chemists for whom Garvey worked as a young man in Kingston, and whom Hart interviewed at about the same time that he interviewed McGlashan;[19] Vivian Durham, the Jamaican civic activist, who recalled the nascent

Universal Negro Improvement Association in 1914; and Dr E. E. Penso, who helped to arrange Garvey's departure for England in 1935, and who, for example, recalled 'that when he bid Garvey farewell on the ship which was to take him to England in 1935, he tore up before him a number of personal IOUs, irrecoverable in any event, as a parting gesture of good will.'[20] The employment of oral history imparts a tone of authenticity to the text, providing bits of information that would not otherwise be available as well as humanizing the subject. Until Hart's essay, such extensive use of oral sources had been notably absent from writing about Garvey. Perhaps the same might also be said about the state of West Indian historiography in general, thus Hart's innovation applies not only to Garvey but also to the writing of West Indian history at the time.

- Research of institutional records for traces of Garvey's presence, as, for example, when Hart notes in the essay: 'In July 1966, at the writer's request, the Registrar of Birkbeck College checked much of the College records for attendance during 1912–14 as could be found. He drew a blank.'[21]

- Use of Garvey's available Jamaican newspapers, *The Blackman* (1929–31) and *The New Jamaican* (1932–33), as a primary source in documenting the Jamaican period of Garvey's career following his deportation from America in 1927.

- Attention to the vicissitudes that Garvey's political fortunes underwent during his 'Jamaica Period,' 1927–35, in order to balance his American impact and more accurately arrive at a balance-sheet of his activities in Jamaica and his political legacy.

- Reproduction of original documentation (*Appendix II: 'Garvey's Election Manifesto for the General Elections in Jamaica in 1930 published in 'The Blackman,'* 2 January 1930), in order to authenticate the text of the original document and to counteract the deliberate distortions that subsequent commentators had attempted to introduce into the text, including Amy Jacques Garvey herself.

Now, each of these was a notable contribution at the time of writing in broadening the parameters and content of Garvey scholarship. There are two additional features in this 1967 analysis of Garvey that are deserving of comment. Hart's standpoint in the essay is that of Jamaica. It is not the standpoint of race, certainly not in the way that a good deal of the writing on Garvey in the post-1968 period was to become.

In this sense, Hart's priority is the national question. Thus, his evaluation of Garvey's racial ideology is from the perspective of Jamaica as an integrated social totality. 'Garvey's activities, once he had decided to become a Jamaican politician, took an interesting turn,' Hart observes. 'He spoke and wrote in the same racial terms he had used in America, appealing to the black man to unite and respect himself. But Jamaican society was entirely different to the coloured communities of the USA.' Here the priority of the Jamaican question, in contradistinction to the racial question, is asserted. Hart confronts Garvey's racial analysis of Jamaican society, published in the *Blackman* of 6 April 1919, where Garvey spoke of acquiring 'the Negro outlook,' with the following comment:

> What is missing from this analysis is the fact that though in appearance these are divisions of colour, they are also, more basically and with only minor exceptions, of economic and social classes. The fact that the lines of colour follow so closely the divisions into economic classes is of course due to historical factors which need not concern us here.
>
> From this it follows that although Garvey made his appeal in exclusively racial terms, the overwhelming majority of his audiences heard it in terms of class. To them the upliftment of the black man meant improvement in the conditions of the working class.[22]

As an example of how Garvey was forced to change under the quite different circumstances of Jamaica, Hart brings forward as evidence the interesting case of S.M. DeLeon. Referring to Garvey's launch of the Jamaica Workers and Labourers Association in April 1930, Hart merely notes how 'in the USA Garvey had counselled the Negro worker against trade unionism and advised him to accept lower wages in order to survive.' Then he notes:

> The change in content of Garvey's agitation was symbolised in his choice of officers [of the Jamaica Workers and Labourers Association]. Garvey, so bitterly opposed to the efforts of the Communists and Socialists in the USA to enroll Negro workers into the trade unions, selected as Secretary of his committee S. M. DeLeon, one of the first West Indians to go to Moscow for training in the '20s.[23]

The second feature of the essay that I wish to call attention to is Hart's careful analysis of the content of 'the philosophy and teachings of Marcus Garvey,' which Hart was not only in a position to provide, but which he also obviously undertook to supply as a scholarly counterweight to 'the public acclaim' that had, by 1966–67, reached a crescendo.[24] The public clamour surrounding Garvey's rehabilitation was what he had warned against at the outset of the 1967 essay, in so far as it blocked out a substantive evaluation of Garvey's thought. This is still a problem today, for the problem has not gone away. Amidst all the public commemoration of Garvey that continues, there is still far too little enlightening discussion of his actual thought. There are many doubtless reasons that might account for this lack, though it is hoped that what remains may be able to offer one such reason by way of explanation.

The conclusion reached by Hart in his 1967 analysis was two-fold, as applied to Garvey's Jamaican and American periods. Both are remarkably similar. In the case of the former, Hart ends by telling the story of the rumour that circulated 'when the Jamaican masses rose in spontaneous rioting in 1938' to the effect that Garvey would be returning to Jamaica. 'It was only a rumour,' Hart notes. 'Some said the rumour was started deliberately to cause confusion and undermine the influence of the new leaders who had emerged among the people.' Then he offers this assessment:

> It was as well that Garvey did not return. He had fulfilled his function. History had passed him by, and there was nothing more that he had to offer.[25]

In the concluding section of the essay, 'Garvey's Impact and Effect,' Hart writes with the same wistful tone. 'It is well that Garvey passed from the scene at the time he did,' the author once more declares.

What Garvey had to offer to his followers, once he had stirred them into awareness and self respect, would have been of negligible value. But he it was who first stirred the masses up and they will never be the same again.[26]

The nature of Hart's historical judgment tells us as much about Hart as it does about Garvey, as we shall see when we come to examine the larger trajectory of Hart's historical analysis of Garvey.

The publication of Hart's essay resulted in a flurry of correspondence. A summary of the various communications was published in a subsequent issue of the journal.[27] Included were excerpts from letters from Amy Jacques Garvey, Professor E.D. Cronon, author of the classic *Black Moses: The Story of Marcus Garvey and the Universal Negro Improvement Association* (1955), N.W. Manley, Peter Evans, and A.J. McGlashan, each of them adding some qualifying piece of information or correcting some item in the original essay, but all of them, taken together, advancing the scope of knowledge. The level of scholarly attainment achieved by the essay could be said to be reflected in the quality of the correspondence that it generated. It was an intimation of how scholarship functions to move a field forward.

This chapter will now be concluded by examining the trajectory of Hart's evolving views. Let it be said immediately that Hart's analysis shows a remarkable consistency over the years. As far as can be determined, Hart's earliest allusion to the political significance of Garvey was in his essay, 'From Garvey to Roberts,' published in *Public Opinion* in December 1937. In his pamphlet, *The Origin and Development of the People of Jamaica* (1952), published the same year as the occurrence of the split in the PNP, there is a comment on the relevance of the Garvey movement tucked away in the section entitled 'Factors Which Retarded Organisation,' wherein are enumerated the 'hopes of self-improvement [among the workers] other than through organised trade union action.' Hart cites three impediments. The first impediment retarding the growth of labour consciousness was access to individual landholdings after the abolition of slavery, followed by emigration to Central America and the USA. The third inhibiting factor is described thus:

> In the 1920s the terrific development of the 'Back to Africa' agitation led by Marcus Garvey and organised in the Universal

Negro Improvement Association which reached its peak in Jamaica in 1929, also for a time diverted the workers attention from local economic problems (though on the other hand it did so much to develop racial self respect among the people without which no popular movement could succeed).[28]

What stands out in the statement is the parenthetical comment that qualifies the larger judgment, which was fully in keeping with the political orthodoxy of the communist left of the period. Here we have what is a curious ambiguation, as if the psychological variable was being accorded a special autonomous existence where blacks were concerned. That was 1952, the height of communist orthodoxy as well as the low point of Garvey's apparent obscurity. One has to assume that Hart's closeness to and involvement with the Jamaican working class afforded him special appreciation of the continuing influence and thus significance of Garvey's thought among black people in Jamaica. The question for the left was how to recognize and account for the important tradition of black struggle, while at the same time organizing on the basis of the primacy of class solidarity. The result was, by the very structure of social reality, the sort of ideological ambiguity expressed in Hart's qualification, fostered, on the one hand, by the undeniable impact of Garvey's movement on black workers, and the ongoing struggle of classes structured as they were under conditions of domination determined by the Jamaican plantation economy. The outcome has been a complex if unstable ideological perspective, to say the least.

Hart's analysis in his 1967 essay carries forward and applies this split perspective. 'Garvey was unable to recognise the basic change of role that it was necessary for him to make if he was to hold the support of the masses in Jamaica,' Hart observes. 'He did not vigorously pursue the idea of organising trade unions and indeed he was mentally unsuited to it. Nor did he resolutely set about building up a grass roots political party. To him the People's Political Party had meant no more than a convenient political label for a group of candidates. Once the elections were over he forgot about it.'[29] This leaves open the need for an explanation of what exactly it was that Garvey accomplished and the nature of that accomplishment. In Hart's view, 'The really progressive element in Garvey's teaching in the USA was that he successfully challenged the imperialist doctrine of Negro inferiority which millions of Negroes in the Western world had themselves come to accept. In making this challenge he used techniques which fired the imagination of simple people.' He adds: 'Garvey stirred millions of the apathetic into action who but for him might have slumbered on.'[30]

Hart would remain consistent in the stress that he continued to place on this theme of psychological cure. Thus he speaks of Garvey having 'devoted his life, with considerable success, to the task of inspiring self-respect in the Negroes of the New World,' such that even the failure of his goal of African redemption mattered little.

> Though the projected return to Africa never did take place, his efforts were not wasted. Those who had been inspired by Garvey's message now had the self-respect and self-confidence to struggle for their rights and improve their conditions right where they were in the USA and the West Indies.[31]

In a subsequent review of Theodore Vincent's *Black Power and the Garvey Movement*, Hart rebuked the author for his apparent sleight of hand in modifying the first plank in the text of Garvey's 1930 election manifesto. This was changed from 'Representation *in* the Imperial Parliament *or* a larger modicum of self-government' to read 'Representation *to* the Imperial Parliament *for* a larger modicum of self-government.' The net effect of his change was the embellishment of Garvey's nationalist credentials, causing Hart adamantly to insist: 'Garvey needs no apologies.' As justification for this injunction, Hart explains:

> His [Garvey's] contribution to history, at a time when millions of Negroes in the Americas had been reduced to a state of psychological depression in which they had come to believe in their own inferiority, was that he did more than any other man to restore their racial self-respect. Thereby he helped to create a foundation on which all the great protest movements of the 1930s and '40s could be securely built and move irresistibly forward.[32]

This psychological breakthrough was achievement enough, Hart seems to say, and is historically significant enough to bear the weight of Garvey's political failings. 'To gloss over his [Garvey's] mistakes, to credit him with initiating ideas and pioneering developments with which he was not directly associated,' says Hart, by way of criticizing the author's revisionism, 'is a disservice rather than a compliment to his memory.'[33]

Hart's final contribution to the historical discourse on Garvey came in 2002 with the publication of his much enlarged edition of *The Life and Resurrection of Marcus Garvey*, incorporating material that had appeared in print in the intervening years, but to which Hart did not have access when he was writing in 1967. In enlarging the scope of his essay, however, something of its critical edge seems, in my reading, to have been lost. Compared to the quality of the 1967 essay, the conclusion of the 2002 enlarged edition ends on a note of consensus. 'Today his [Garvey's] positive contribution is recognised,' the author declares, 'even among those Americans who could not support him because of his repudiation of the struggle for racial equality in USA, his advice to black workers to stay out of trade unions and accept lower wages than unionised white workers and his repudiation of communism.'[34] The contradictions inherent in Garvey's political record in Jamaica, however, seem to be given a subordinate importance in the following gloss:

> Fortunately there were never any contradictions of this nature to complicate the situation in Jamaica and the rest of the Caribbean area.[35]

What distinguishes Richard Hart's contribution to the analysis of Garvey are, first, the clear distinction that he draws between the trade union struggle of the working class and Garvey's siding with the capitalist class in the economic struggle; and, second, the theorization of the pertinence of the ideology of Garveyism as belonging to the psychological sphere. These preoccupations also enable us to distinguish between Hart's take on Garvey and that of the patriotic-nationalist left of the 1930s, '40s, and '50s, for whom Garvey was made identical with the struggle for national independence. It is in this context that we can discern the shifting currents of the left and its divergent strategic outlook during these three critical decades. By differentiating the perspectives of the left, moreover, we avoid the mistake of assuming any sort of ideological disambiguation that would cloud our understanding of the important ideological cleavages that composed the left. In this sense, analysis of the 'resurrection' of Marcus

Garvey as a collective social product keeps alive the tension inherent in the apprehension of Caribbean thought.

Notes

1. Richard Hart, 'The Life and Resurrection of Marcus Garvey,' *Race* 9:2 (October 1967): 217–18.
2. Ibid., 218.
3. Ibid., 217.
4. 'Statue of Marcus Garvey Proposed,' *Daily Gleaner*, 10 September 1948.
5. 'Welcome Function,' *Daily Gleaner*, 23 December 1945.
6. 'KSAC Names Garvey Statue Committee,' *Daily Gleaner*, 15 October 1948.
7. 'Marcus Garvey Statue,' *Daily Gleaner*, 24 May 1952.
8. 'Garvey's Bust for George VI Park,' *Daily Gleaner*, 11 March 1955.
9. 'C[hief] M[inister]: Garvey Liberated Spirit of Freedom,' *Daily Gleaner*, 8 November 1956.
10. Richard Hart, review of Adolph Edwards, *Marcus Garvey 1887–1940* (London and Port of Spain: New Beacon Publications, 1967), *Race* 9:1 (July 1967): 124.
11. Richard Hart, 'The Life and Resurrection of Marcus Garvey,' 218; cf. 'Despite misgivings about the originator of the proposal, who was regarded as somewhat eccentric, the idea won immediate official approval and Alexander was entrusted with the task' (Richard Hart, *The Life and Resurrection on Marcus Garvey* [London: Karia Press, 2002]), 69.
12. 'The Life and Resurrection of Marcus Garvey,' 218.
13. Richard Hart, *The Life and Resurrection of Marcus Garvey* (London: Karia Press, 2002), 5.
14. 'The Life and Resurrection of Marcus Garvey,' 218.
15. Richard Hart, review of Amy Jacques Garvey, *The Philosophy and Opinions of Marcus Garvey or Africa for the Africans* (London: Frank Cass, 1967), *Race* 9:4 (April 1968): 548. See, however, evidence countering Hart's claim in Robert Hill, *The Marcus Garvey and Universal Negro Improvement Association Papers: Africa for the Africans, June 1921–December 1922*, vol. IX (Berkeley and Los Angeles: University of California Press, 1995); and vol. X: *Africa for the Africans, 1923–1945* (Berkeley and Los Angeles and London: University of California Press, 2006).
16. Richard Hart, *The Life and Resurrection of Marcus Garvey* (London: Karia Press, 2002), 8.
17. Ibid.
18. Ibid., 219; *The Life and Resurrection of Marcus Garvey*, 7–8.
19. Ibid., 7, fn. 1.
20. Ibid., 228.
21. Ibid., 220.
22. Ibid., 225–26.
23. Ibid., 226.

24. Richard Hart, review of Adolph Edwards, *Marcus Garvey 1887–1940* (London and Port of Spain: New Beacon Publications, 1967), *Race* 9:1 (July 1967): 124.
25. Op. cit., 228–29.
26. Ibid., 235.
27. Richard Hart, 'Correspondence,' *Race* 9:4 (April 1968): 527–28.
28. Richard Hart, *The Origin and Development of the People of Jamaica* (Kingston: The Education Department of the Trade Union Congress, 1952), 27.
29. Richard Hart, 'The Life and Resurrection of Marcus Garvey,' 227.
30. Ibid., 234–35.
31. Richard Hart, review of *The Philosophy and Opinions of Marcus Garvey or Africa for the Africans*, 548.
32. Richard Hart, review of T. G. Vincent, *Black Power and the Garvey Movement* (New York: Ramparts Press, 1971), *Race* 13:2 (October 1971): 244.
33. Ibid.
34. Hart, *The Life and Resurrection of Marcus Garvey*, 70. The statement hews closely to the almost identical historical judgment enunciated in Hart's 1967 conclusion, viz., 'Today, even among those who could not bring themselves to support him during his years of maximum influence in the USA, his contribution is generally recognised. Few indeed are the voices of coloured Americans today who do not now acknowledge the American Negro's debt of gratitude to him' ('The Life and Resurrection of Marcus Garvey,' 235)
35. 'Death and Resurrection,' *The Life and Resurrection of Marcus Garvey*, 70.

4 | Insights from the 1938 (All Jamaica) Economic and Industrial Conference[1]

Mark Figueroa

Introduction

In January 1938 the mayor of Kingston, Oswald E. Anderson, convened an All-Jamaica Economic and Industrial Conference at the Ward Theatre in the heart of the city. It was attended by approximately 200 delegates representing a wide range of organizations. Participants included political representatives at the national and local level as well as state functionaries, but in the main they were drawn from what is currently referred to as 'civil society'. It was not Kingston's first major conference during the twentieth century but it was significant for many reasons. These include the specific focus of the conference, the range of participants, the moment in history when it was called and the types of ideas that were expressed. In what follows, an evaluation of the conference is presented making reference to these criteria. Richard Hart is recorded as attending the conference although, when asked, he did not recall attending.[2] In contrast, Howard Cooke provided a vivid recollection of the conference and recalls sitting next to Richard Hart.[3]

From the written record corroborated by Howard Cooke's recollections, the conference captured the excitement of the moment. It embodied the expectation of the early nationalist movement at a point when a section of the Jamaican elite was seized with the idea that they would be able to take control of the leadership of their country and transform it for the benefit of the broad mass of the people. The conference gives a clear insight into elite concerns but it is more difficult to say whether it provides an idea of the issues that were on the minds of the ordinary citizens. The conference can be seen as a window to the cultural life of the country and an understanding of the degree to which intellectual debate surrounding its problems had developed among its citizens on the eve of the 1938 labour rebellion that helped to transform the country and which brought Richard Hart to national prominence. An analysis of the conference also provides insights into trends in Jamaican society that have persisted over long periods of time.

The conference took place at a point when the working people were beginning to make initial stirrings that were transformed into open rebellion between May and June 1938. On January 3 the *Daily Gleaner* published the draft programme for the conference.[4] On the same day, workers at the Serge Island Estate in St Thomas were engaged in a fierce strike which Ken Post suggests, 'marked the fact that the emergence of consciousness of trade union politics among the workers was now irreversible.'[5] The conference can therefore be seen as a significant initiative by Anderson and his associates to come to terms with a growing crisis. All members of the team supported by the Federation of Citizens Associations which included Anderson had been successful in the Kingston and St Andrew Corporation elections of November 1937. Anderson, who had previously served as deputy mayor and acted as mayor, was unanimously elected Mayor and he immediately set about promoting the conference. It appears that there were some objections from those who felt that the scope of the conference went beyond municipal concerns. Anderson defended the all-island approach on the grounds that the state of the national economy impacted on Kingston. For example, persons who flocked to the city in search of employment became a direct call on the Kingston and St Andrew Corporation's (KSAC's) budget when they fell into poverty.

The events of 1938 in Jamaica have been dealt with in a wide range of works both as a direct object of analysis or indirectly in considering associated events and personalities. The most comprehensive of these is Ken Post's *Arise Ye Starvelings*. Nevertheless the conference has received very little attention in the literature on 1938 and is ignored completely by Post. This omission is all the more notable as Post dedicates a chapter to 'The Revolt of the Respectable' in which he notes the success of the Federation of Citizens' Associations in the 1937 elections.[6] In *Rise and Organise*, Hart does not mention the conference.[7] He discusses a number of organizations in which the middle class leaders featured prominently but he does not discuss significant conferences or conventions in his analysis. At a minimum, the conference would have to be seen as part of the growing confidence of the section of the middle class that increasingly comes to support anti-colonial positions in the post-1938 period. The self-assurance with which Anderson proceeded to summon an all-island conference and the willingness of persons representing a wide range of interests to respond were significant. In this regard, Anderson himself represents an important personality whose role in the development of the Jamaican political system has not been fully explored.

Mayor Anderson

I am not aware of any substantial biographical work that has been done on Anderson but his funeral provides one indicator of how he was seen by his peers among the post-war national elite. He died on 8 September 1948. Among his pall bearers were representatives drawn from both sides of Jamaica's post-adult-suffrage political divide, including W. Alexander Bustamante, N.N. Nethersole, and Wills O. Isaacs. Anderson was born in 1881 in Guys Hill, St Catherine and attended school at Ginger Ridge where he served as a pupil teacher. He completed medical studies at Howard University and was admitted to practise medicine in Jamaica in 1908. He was co-opted as an alderman of the KSAC in 1931 and went on to serve as deputy mayor in 1936 and Mayor in 1937. He resigned as Mayor in 1938 when an advertisement appeared in the British press for a post in the Jamaican medical service requiring that the candidate be European. In 1940 he was elected as a member of the Legislative Council for St Andrew and again served as Mayor from 1943–44. He was one of the persons who along with Norman Manley, J.A.G. Smith and Ross Livingstone accompanied Alexander Bustamante when he went to address the workers at Railway Pier No. 1 after his release on 28 May 1938. He also served as vice-chairman of the Trade Union Advisory Committee which Norman Manley brokered following the February 1939 conflict between Jamaica's leading labour leaders Alexander Bustamante and A.G.S. Coombs. He was described as a leading (East Queen Street) Baptist layman and a past master of the Phoenix Lodge of which he was a member for almost three decades.[8] I was unable to locate a good picture of Anderson but the best newspaper picture available, as well as two caricatures from the Jamaican *Daily Gleaner* leave little doubt that he was predominantly of African heritage.[9]

Conference Participants

The organizers of the conference claimed that it was attended by 200 representatives. In its reports, the *Daily Gleaner* listed the names of over 150 persons as participants in the conference.[10] As such the claim by the organizers does not appear to be farfetched. All of the participants are yet to be identified but from those identified it is clear that many of the participants were drawn from the ranks of the most prominent Jamaicans. These included custodes notably F.M. Kerr-Jarrett of St James; members of the Legislative Council including George Seymour; representatives of the various parochial boards and the KSAC including Rudolph Burke, Chairman of St Thomas; and representatives of incipient organizations that would go into the formation of Jamaica's political parties including Ken Hill and N.N. Nethersole of the National Reform Association and O.T. Fairclough of *Public Opinion*.[11] There were about 15 women including some of Jamaica's most outstanding social activists of the time: Edith Clarke, May Farquharson, Una Marson and Mary Morris-Knibb. A range of professionals was present: at least 10 ministers of religion including the head of the Roman Catholic Church in Jamaica, Bishop Emmet, and the Jewish Rabbi H.P. Silverman; five doctors;[12] a number of very prominent educators including the president of the Jamaica Union of Teachers along with past presidents and other prominent members (including the 22-year-old Howard Cooke), the Vice-Principal, J.J. Mills, of Jamaica's premier teachers' college, Mico; various school principals and the secretary to the Institute of Jamaica, Philip Sherlock who eventually became the Vice-Chancellor of the University of the West Indies (UWI) having served on the Irvine Commission whose report led to the establishment of UWI). State functionaries with offices relating to matters such as city engineering and forestry; prominent journalists such as H.P. Jacobs and Nathaniel Parker; and businessmen, the most prominent of whom was James Gore, all attended. Over 20 persons sent excuses for their absence including the Anglican Bishop of Jamaica, the manager of Barclays Bank, and R. Ehrenstein, the member of the Legislative Council for St Thomas whose workers started the year on strike as noted above.

The range of organizations associated with the delegates mentioned included the Jamaica Agricultural Society, Jamaica Imperial

Association, Jamaica Chamber of Commerce, Sugar Manufacturers' Association of Jamaica, Native Industries Protection Committee, Jamaica Welfare Ltd, the Universal Negro Improvement Association, Women's Liberal Club, Young Womens' Christian Association (YWCA), Save the Children Fund, Jamaica Citrus Producers Association, Jamaica Branch of the British Medical Association, Jamaica Birth Control League, League of Coloured People (local representative), citizens associations (Johnson Pen, St Elizabeth, Ocho Rios, and Smith Village were specifically mentioned), various past students associations, artistic societies, sports clubs and associations. It is difficult given the sources used to know whether the organizations with which participants were at one time affiliated were active at the time of the conference. Some organizations were by that time defunct; in other cases the person's affiliation may have related to a later period.

Notable Absences

There were many notable absences for this period. The main persons who had been associated with the organization of labour up to that time were missing from the conference. Neither Alexander Bustamante nor A.G.S. Coombs were recorded as attending the conference but the Jamaica Workers and Tradesmen Union appears to have been represented by P.A. Aiken and C.S. Maxwell. Post records the former as acting as president of the Union following the crisis between Bustamante and Coombs which developed at the end of 1937. C.S. Maxwell became General Secretary after the resignation of H.C. Buchanan.[13] I have only been able to identify two participants: Richard Hart and Ken Hill, as persons who later became prominent trade unionists. I have not been able to identify as participants any of the persons who appear in the accounts of the labour uprising of 1938 in the works of Ken Post or Richard Hart or the 'Eyewitness Perspectives' appearing in Patrick Bryan and Karl Watson's edited collection.[14] It is possible that there were more representatives of the ordinary working people at the conference (including representatives of peasant organizations) and that they were overlooked by the *Gleaner* reporters, but whether they were present or not, it does appear that the conference was dominated by the professional middle classes as significant participation came from elements within the propertied classes.[15] At the same time it is important to note that many significant middle class leaders and businesspersons were also absent from the conference.

The task of assessing how important each absence was is a very difficult one. In addition, it should be noted that the conference started on a Tuesday and finished on a Thursday. For the vast majority of persons, attending the conference would have meant missing work or setting aside professional or business commitments. Many of those who were so inclined may have found it very difficult to attend. An analysis of the conference may therefore be best done in terms of the presence of representatives of the various circles, trends and tendencies that marked the economic, social and political landscape of the period. From the above we can see that there was a very wide range of representation in terms of the contemporary society and persons who would later play a leadership role in Jamaica.

Reactions to the Conference

Judging from the press it does not appear that the more conservative sectors of the propertied classes warmed to the conference despite the presence of persons like Custos Kerr-Jarrett. This was reflected in the *Daily Gleaner's* somewhat negative editorial stand. In summing up the conference, the paper described the affair as 'desultory' in its editorial of 29 January 1938. At the same time it gave the conference considerable coverage and printed the secretary's reply to the editorial. The attitude of the *Daily Gleaner* stood in contrast to the somewhat positive stand of the *Times* (weekly) and the friendly summary that *Public Opinion* (weekly) provided for the conference.

The most nationalist wing of the professional middle class appears to have been firmly behind the conference. The absence of persons like N.W. Manley and Florizel Glasspole may have been accidental but it may also have indicated that up to that time they had a somewhat limited vision of the politics of the country.[16] Ken Post quotes Manley in early 1937 as declining O.T. Fairclough's efforts to get him involved in politics under the rubric that Jamaica's problems were 'social and economic, not political.'[17] The absence of some of the more prominent elected members of the Legislative Council may have had more to do with the dynamics of Jamaica's fractious politics. Here I would echo the call made by Post for 'much more research...on the development of Jamaican parish politics.'[18] In some ways Jamaica's parish politics were more significant than its national politics prior to the development of universal adult suffrage. In parish politics Jamaicans were facing each other whereas in the Legislative Council relations were mediated by the presence of the governor and other officials. Many people blame the extremes of Jamaican politics on the two-party system that developed in the post-war period but there were divisive aspects of Jamaican politics that predate adult suffrage. Perhaps the absence from the conference of certain persons could be attributed to this. The success of Anderson in topping the polls and leading the Federation of Citizens' Associations candidates in a clean sweep of the municipal elections may have made other politicians, aspirants to national leadership and their natural allies, wary of providing him with additional approbation. His boldness, manifest in the calling of the conference, may have also led others to see him as over-reaching his office.

Both Hart and Post identify *Plain Talk* as seeking to speak for the 'little man.'[19] Post also suggests that *Plain Talk* supported the Federation of Citizens' Associations candidates in the 1937 elections.[20] This support was not reflected in the attitude taken to the conference, which was portrayed as a publicity stunt on the part of Anderson. The participants were portrayed as being unsympathetic to the ordinary people. Stennett Kerr Coombs took this perspective in a letter to the *Daily Gleaner*. His complaint, which was echoed elsewhere, was that there was insufficient time to discuss the wide range of topics and the focus of the conference was on the presentations from the platform dominated by 'plutocrats.' 'Men who truly know the conditions… among the poorer classes had little or no real say at all.' 'In glaring letters on…the programme were printed the words: 'MAYOR'S… CONFERENCE,' and by my word, it was indeed!'[21]

From Anderson's point of view, the conference went well. There was a broad participation; the speakers lavished him with praise for his initiative; for the most part the resolutions prepared by the organizers were passed and a Continuation Committee was established. Yet there were a few negatives beyond the adverse press reactions. Within the conference there were times when the floor went into uproar with respect to the way in which the conference was being run. This occurred when the chair intervened in the discussion on labour issues to suggest that only certain persons who were knowledgeable on the issue should speak.[22] There was a similar reaction when the platform suggested that the delegates should only elect a small minority of the members of the Continuation Committee. The attempt to impose time limits on persons was not always well received, especially as it appears to have been unevenly applied. In general, there seemed to be dissatisfaction over the extent to which those who already had a voice (especially the elected members of the Legislative Council) were allowed to dominate the discussions and more generally the tendency of the platform to dominate the conference. These negatives lend weight to criticisms that the conference could have been more democratic in terms of the strata from which delegates and speakers were drawn and the opportunities that were given for the participation of the ordinary citizen. On matters of substance, Anderson also suffered one major defeat when his position on married women in the public sector was voted down by a narrow margin.

Conference Discussions

The conference covered a wide range of subjects. From the economic point of view the programme gave agriculture broad coverage. It also included trade issues and the need for new industries where the word 'industries' was generally used to mean areas of endeavour rather than manufacturing industries. In the course of the conference, presentations were also made which related to housing, transportation and communication. Labour was a specific area as were health and education, and a range of topics was discussed under the heading of social issues. These included poor relief, pensions, gender in relation to economic problems, village life and the cost of living. There are two main sources on which I rely to get an idea of the sentiments of the persons attending the conference. The first consists of a series of resolutions which were presented to the conference (mainly from the platform) and the second comes from the newspaper reports of the presentations of the main speakers and the comments from the floor. The *Daily Gleaner* gave extensive coverage to some but not all of the speeches and recorded many of the resolutions that were considered. A third source would be the records of the Continuation Committee but I have not been able to locate many documents relating to the work of this committee.

In assessing the ideas that emerged from the conference there are a number of measures that we can use. The first relates to the kind of platforms that emerged from similar meetings that took place in the years before and after the conference, as well as those adopted by organizations which took positions that deviated from the status quo during this period of Jamaica's history. Notably among these was the Jamaican section that was convened at the end of the Seventh International Convention of the Negro Peoples of the World held in Kingston between August and September 1934. The resolutions of the conference can also be compared to the positions taken in the programmes of organizations such as Marcus Garvey's 1929 People's Political Party and the early People's National Party, which was established in September 1938. It is not possible to do a complete comparison here. Elsewhere, I have considered this comparison especially as it relates to industrialization.[23] Such comparisons reveal similar perspectives relating to land reform; promotion, protection and marketing of local products abroad as well as social development including matters such as education and health. The views put forward at the conference were not uniformly more forward-looking. This is especially true if one restricts considerations to the resolutions themselves. A second measure relates to the extent to which the ideas expressed at the conference were limited to the narrow vision of possibilities for Jamaica's development that were prevalent at the time. We must consider whether the ideas expressed represented significant departures from the status quo or at least signalled the presence of the embryo of a perspective that came into vogue in the post-war period. My motivation here is to try to understand whether there were persons who had begun to think in terms of a new Jamaica prior to the rebellion of 1938 which in many ways made it difficult to continue the old. In this way it would be possible to identify the continuities before and after 1938 and not simply focus on the discontinuities.

Spectrum of Ideas

Although the ideas of the conference were bound in large measure by the status quo, there were many ways in which they showed important departures. Before speaking to the specific points raised in the conference it is important to note that the very idea of addressing the economic and industrial problems as a whole was forward-looking. Associated with this, was the notion that Jamaica needed to develop a plan for its economy covering a number of years. The conference promoted the idea of developing alternatives to the mainstays of production on which the island was dependent but the notion of Jamaica as a country with a predominantly agricultural future was built into the structure of the programme. A number of sessions were dedicated to the different facets of agriculture while only one was dedicated to alternatives. Even then, many of the alternatives did not focus on possibilities outside of agriculture. They often related to the idea that there were other crops, the promotion of which required greater attention. In the area of trade, the idea of trade promotion and the employment of trade commissioners in target markets represented one of the more forward-looking ideas. Many of the ideas expressed on social issues were quite forward-looking but there was only a partial link made between the social and the economic. Critics of the conference suggested there was a failure to speak to the issue of how social measures would be funded. There was also a limited grasp of the extent to which the social measures could have a positive feedback on production.[24] Arguably the conference was caught in the contradictions of the moment, which were only cleared away by the subsequent labour uprising. There were those who clearly did not see that significant change would have to come, while there were those who presented ideas that would take a long time to come into their own.

A striking manifestation of the degree to which some persons did not grasp that change had to come was a long presentation relating to a method for the construction of cheap housing. This method used compressed earth and thatch. At its foundation this approach is classist and completely missed the mood of the moment. None of the middle class persons who attended the conference were going to live in a house made of compressed earth or covered by a thatched roof no matter how much the speaker claimed it was a method 'adopted…in England, Spain, France…and parts of Australia.'[25] This was precisely the problem of pre-1938 Jamaica. The working people did not expect to have houses as large as those of the rich. They did not expect wages as high as the managers. What they were calling for, from all accounts, was adequate land and/or regular employment and wages that could provide them with a respectable standard of living.[26] By mid-1938, the working people were no longer willing to accept that they were qualitatively inferior. The proposal to give them 'mud huts' to live in was just not going to be accepted no matter how cheap, comfortable and cool they were as compared to houses built with materials that would be considered by the middle classes as appropriate for their homes.

At the other end of the spectrum, ideas were presented on the need for pension schemes, acceptance of the Jamaican language and culture, and the conservation of Jamaica's renewable resources, which probably are yet to be implemented fully. This forward-looking thinking was also manifested in the presentations by James Gore and Quintin Williams on alternatives to the dominant productive structures. Williams seems to have presented the clearest statement on the importance of industrial development. The details of his presentation are not available but the *Gleaner* reporter noted that he started out with a definition of industries and how they related to agriculture.[27] This suggests that unlike many of his peers, including Gore, he used the term 'industry' not in the sense of 'enterprise' but in the sense of 'manufacturing industry.' He made the incisive comment that the absence of raw materials was not a constraint on industrialization and drew on Japan as the prime example. In the elaboration of his discussion on the topic he does not seem to have carried the point forward to demonstrate the kinds of industries that Jamaica could develop based on imported raw materials save for a few such as grain milling, which presumably he would have targeted to the local market. Rather he stuck mainly to those that could be linked to local raw material sources to supply local needs and create new export products. In addition he was concerned with the development of industries to utilize wastes and other by-products and preserve perishable agricultural products. Gore is reported as focusing somewhat less on industry. He spent a lot of time on alternative agricultural crops although he did go into some detail on the question of cement production, which was for many years one of his major concerns. (He also mentioned plaster of Paris and cement products).

In addition to taking into account the unevenness of the ideas presented at the conference it is interesting to note the persistence of ideas on Jamaica's development. There was a call at the time for the launching of a campaign to encourage Jamaicans to buy more local food.[28] Similarly, trade agreements and the negotiation of trade agreements and their likely impact on Jamaica also came up for discussion. The inclusion (in the social discussion) of the topic 'sex as it relates to economic conditions' shows that concerns with respect to mating, family structure and household development have been with us for a long time. There was a call for sterilization, which was once more raised in 2002 this time by a Jamaican parliamentarian, Sharon Hay-Webster.[29] The issue of race was also raised but more obliquely by those who were concerned with racial oppression and more directly by those who were concerned that the black majority might one day assert itself in racial terms.

Insights from the Conference

The conference provides us with a number of insights into Jamaican society on the eve of the 1938 labour uprising. In terms of cultural concerns we can note two contradictory tendencies. There was clearly a growing sense in which sections of the society wished to see themselves as Jamaican. Philip Sherlock's presentation dealt with this in terms of self-expression and art but it was also manifest in the whole range of efforts to come to terms with the country's problems. At the same time the continued deference to Britain and British forms was striking. One manifestation of this was how British visitors were treated during this period.

It appears that British visitors to the island could be immediately accepted as a part of the community. Included on the very crowded programme of the conference was a specially featured talk by 'Mr Wilfred Hill, 70-year-old English industrialist; who has been on his second visit to Jamaica...and who has taken an interest in the city's slum clearance scheme.'[30] The Imperial Trade Commissioner was also afforded a large section on the programme. Above I have spoken of fractiousness in Jamaican politics. Perhaps we could contrast the willingness to listen to others with the difficulty that Jamaicans have had in having dialogue with each other. It appears that many of the features that we see in Jamaica's contemporary political and intellectual culture have roots that go far back into its history.

The dynamic interactions within the conference were also of interest. There were stormy moments between the platform and the floor. There were times when many people were on their feet to speak. *Sotto voce* remarks and humorous interventions were also the order of the day. When Howard Cooke was asked about these aspects of the conference he quickly acknowledged them. In particular he noted the attacks on leaders that came from some quarters as well as the humour of the people that he suggests 'keeps us alive; when it comes to repartee those simple people out there are ready for you.' It is difficult to judge racial and class interactions from the available reports.

Women were only named as approximately 10 per cent of those identified by the *Gleaner* reports, yet a number of them were singled out for the contribution they made to the conference. Edith Clarke and Amy Bailey won praise for providing such interesting presentations on poor relief and old age pensions, subjects that were not expected to gain rapt attention from the audience. Amy Bailey was also outstanding along with Mr V.A. Bailey (relationship not established) in the struggle against the resolution calling for the exclusion of married women from government employment. This issue along with the resolution on the stabilization of the real wages of the working class seemed to have brought out some of the strongest passions.

Reading the contemporary press is suggestive, but being able to conduct an interview with a participant allowed for the confirmation of impressions formed by reading the press. It is not surprising therefore that Howard Cooke speaks of the intensity of the debate and more broadly of the intensity of the period. One of his indices regarding the quality of the debate was that he did not recall 'one man falling asleep,' a curious but apparently significant measure. He identifies the conference as 'a moment of history.' 'Many people are not aware that out of that conference some of the changes that…came in were changes that were talked about and reflected decisions made [there].' The other quality that he emphasises is that 'there was no partisan thing about this conference, every strata of society' was included. 'All these people seemed to be endowed with a desire to remove poverty.' 'I was member of the JUT [Jamaica Union of Teachers]…Anderson was getting all the various organizations from all over the country… people who were interested in social and economic change' 'It was not a political, it was a social gathering…the ferment of change was in the air coming over from the early '30s when Marcus Garvey was dominant.'[31]

What we see is that under the leadership of Mayor Anderson it was possible to bring together a broad cross section of the Jamaican community. At the same time, there were many prominent absences. We do not know why these persons did not attend but we can note that Anderson and his leadership style attracted some negative commentary inside and outside the conference. This underlies the significance of leadership but it may also speak to the fractious nature of Jamaican society that was, at times, evident in the conference. Yet this was mediated through cultural forms that remain present today, for example, the use of humour to defuse tensions. The moment in history was significant. It was clear that there were leaders in the society who recognized that there was a brewing crisis and who were trying to come to terms with the situation. A study of this episode in its context brings to the fore the question as to how a society like Jamaica can resolve its problems and the kinds of leadership that have the best chances of succeeding. It also points to the difficulties of gaining a sufficiently broad based consensus. The distance between the elite and the ordinary citizens also emerged in the context of the conference. This was manifest in the interaction between the platform and the floor as well as the failure to involve a broader representation of the people. This is striking as at the very moment the conference was taking place the workers and peasants were beginning to take action.

The years leading up to the conference and those that followed were filled with social ferment. The hope for change inspired many persons of relative privilege to make considerable sacrifice. Richard Hart turned to trade unionism and political organization leading to his subsequent detention without trial (1942–43). In the year that followed the conference, Howard and Ivy (née Tai) Cooke were motivated to leave their comfortable jobs in Kingston to go and teach in the Portland 'bush' at Belle Castle. The moment of history that produced these developments allowed Mayor Anderson to bring together what was a most significant conference. At the same time, the participants were neither leading nor directing the social processes that emerged later in 1938 and the majority would have wished to have avoided much of what took place between May and June that year. Mayor Anderson's leadership must also be singled out given his ability to bring together the diverse social forces that were represented in the conference. But this leadership proved inadequate to the tasks of the moment and others emerged to lead the people. A reflection on the conference and its context may provide us with insights into the limitations of the different social forces as well as the difficulties of forming and leading broad coalitions for change in the Jamaican context.

Conclusion

Mayor Anderson's conference was significant in terms of its timing, the range of participants that it brought together and the reactions that it produced inside and outside the conference. It is also significant in terms of those who did not attend although we do not now know why they were missing. It gives us an insight into the extent to which many of our cultural forms have long histories.

It raises interesting questions about leadership, social forces and the possibilities for change. The nature of the discussions gives us some insight into the thinking of Jamaica's prominent citizens on the eve of the 1938 uprising but it only provides a limited window to the ideas current in the country as a whole. Given the dominant role played in the conference by the upper echelons of the society, we cannot say whether the views expressed were widely held. Despite this limitation, it demonstrates that people were aware that the country was facing a growing crisis and sought to find solutions to the problems of their country. More research needs to be done to get a greater insight into the nature of the people who participated in the conference and the socio-economic and political dynamics surrounding its occurrence as well as how the ideas espoused during the conference related to other significant occurrences such as the Moyne Commission. Yet even with our limited knowledge of the details of the conference we can get a glimpse into the degree to which ideas that became important in the post-war period were already beginning to germinate in the late 1930s prior to the uprising. At the same time, it is equally clear that certain ideas persisted that would have to be cleared away by the uprising. In this way, 1938 represents both a point of continuity, as well as a discontinuity in Jamaica's development.

Notes

1. In writing this paper I benefitted from the research and or editorial assistance of Dalea Bean, Debbie Dwyer, Kamara Gibson, Stacey Plummer and the research done for a paper by a former student, Louleita Evans, which she completed for the final-year course, 'Selected Topics in the History of Economic Thought.' Howard Cooke, Richard Hart, Sylvia McNeil, G.E.M. Mills and Sybil Wood (née Mills) also assisted by providing details concerning persons named in the *Gleaner* reports of the conference. An earlier version of this paper 'A City Confronts Its Problems: Kingston's Mayor Anderson's 1938 Economic and Industrial Conference' was presented

to the conference: *Citylife in Caribbean History: Celebrating Bridgetown*, 11–13 December 2003, UWI, Cave Hill. Financial assistance was received from the Social Sciences Faculty Office and Research and Publications Fund of the UWI, Mona Campus.
2. Personal communication between Richard Hart and Mark Figueroa.
3. All references to Cooke's perspectives are taken from an interview conducted on 18 February 2006. Additional material can be obtained from Jackie Ranston, *They Call Me Teacher: The Life and Times of Sir Howard Cooke Governor-General of Jamaica* (Kingston: Ian Randle Publishers, 2003). Cooke was born in 1915, two years before Hart. He graduated from Mico Teachers College in 1935, was a founding member of the People's National Party (PNP) in 1938, served in different ministerial capacities and as Governor General from 1 August 1991–15 February 2006.
4. The details of the programme, resolutions of the conference and a list of prominent participants are available in the original conference paper from which this chapter is derived. Space did not allow for their inclusion here.
5. Ken Post, *Arise Ye Starvelings: The Jamaican Labour Rebellion of 1938 and Its Aftermath* (London: Nijhoff, 1978), 266.
6. Ibid., 214.
7. Richard Hart, *Rise and Organise: the Birth of the Workers and National Movements in Jamaica, 1936–1939* (London: Karia, 1989).
8. Sources on Anderson: *Daily Gleaner*, 17 January 1938, 18; 10 September 1948; James Carnegie, *Some Aspects of Jamaica's Politics, 1918–1938* (Kingston: Institute of Jamaica, 1973), 58–59. Hart, *Rise and Organise*, 84, 130–31; Donna Hope, 'Annotations for Marcus Garvey Papers Jamaican Volume' (Dept of Government, UWI, Mona, nd), 3–4; and Post, *Arise Ye Starvelings*, 401.
9. *Daily Gleaner* clippings file, Institute of Jamaica.
10. Reports naming participants appeared in the *Daily Gleaner* on five days: 26–29 January and 31 January 1938, 14, 14, 14, 16 and 13 respectively.
11. Those mentioned here all went into the PNP but there were participants who also went into the JLP, for example, E.R.D. Evans.
12. There were also a number of lawyers but the doctors were easier to identify given their title.
13. Post, *Arise Ye Starvelings*, 259, 327; Coombs who led the JWTU brought Bustamante into the Union in 1937 but they were soon involved in an irreconcilable conflict. Following this crisis Buchanan also left the Union.
14. Post, *Arise Ye Starvelings*; Hart, *Rise and Organise;* Patrick Bryan and Karl Watson, eds., *Not for Wages Alone: Eyewitness Summaries of the 1938 Labour Rebellion in Jamaica* (Kingston: The Social History Project, Department of History, University of the West Indies, Mona, 2003).
15. Based on his letter to the *Daily Gleaner*, 7 February 1938. Stennett Kerr Coombs attended the conference but his name does not appear in the *Gleaner* reports that list those who participated. Along with Buchanan he launched the *Jamaica Labour Weekly* on 14 May 1938 and supported the action of the striking workers. Both were jailed for sedition later in the year.
16. Richard Hart, *Rise and Organise*, 114–16 gives some indication of Manley's development.

17. Post, *Arise Ye Starvelings*, 220.
18. Ibid., 256.
19. Richard Hart, *Rise and Organise*, 21. Post, *Arise Ye Starvelings*, 118.
20. Ibid., 214.
21. *Daily Gleaner*, 7 February 1938, 21.
22. *Daily Gleaner*, 28 January 1938, 14.
23. See Mark Figueroa, 'Pre-War Industrialization in Jamaica: Policy Ideas and Initiatives' (Department of Economics, UWI, Mona, 1992); Mark Figueroa, 'W. Arthur Lewis's Socioeconomic Analysis and the Development of Industrialization Policy in Jamaica, 1945–1960' (PhD diss., University of Manchester, 1993), for a discussion specific to the issue of manufacturing industry.
24. *Daily Gleaner*, 31 January 1938, 13; of all the reported speakers Sherlock appears to have come closest to dealing with these issues.
25. Ibid., 26 January 1938, 14.
26. Claus F. Stolberg, ed., *Jamaica 1938: The Living Conditions of the Urban and Rural Poor: Two Social Surveys, 1938* (Kingston: Social History Project, Department of History, University of the West Indies, Mona, 1990).
27. *Daily Gleaner*, 27 January 1938, 14.
28. When I was drafting the earlier version of this paper in 2003 such a campaign had once more been launched in Jamaica.
29. *Daily Gleaner*, 30 July 2003, A3.
30. *Daily Gleaner*, 26 January 1938, 15.
31. All quotes are taken from an interview on 18 February 2006. The quotes do not necessarily follow the order in the interview.

Bibliography

Bakan, Abigail B. *Ideology and Class Conflict in Jamaica the Politics of Rebellion*. London: McGill-Queen's University, 1990.

Bryan, Patrick and Karl Watson, eds. *Not for Wages Alone: Eyewitness Summaries of the1938 Labour Rebellion in Jamaica*. Kingston: The Social History Project, Department of History Mona, 2003.

Carnegie, James. *Some Aspects of Jamaica's Politics 1918–1938*. Kingston: Institute of Jamaica, 1973.

Figueroa, Mark. 'Pre-War Industrialization in Jamaica: Policy Ideas and Initiatives.' Department of Economics, UWI, Mona, 1992.

———. 'W. Arthur Lewis's Socioeconomic Analysis and the Development of Industrialization Policy in Jamaica 1945–1960.' PhD diss., University of Manchester, 1993.

Hart, Richard. *Rise and Organise the Birth of the Workers and National Movements in Jamaica 1936–1939*. London: Karia, 1989.

Hearne, Leeta, ed. *The Memoirs of Lady Bustamante*. Kingston: Kingston Publishers, 1997.

Hill, Frank. *Bustamante and His Letters*. Kingston: Kingston Publishers, 1976.

Hope, Donna, P. 'Annotations for Marcus Garvey Papers Jamaican Volume.' Department of Government, UWI, Mona, nd.

Johnson, Anthony. *J.A.G. Smith*. Kingston: Kingston Publishers, 1991.

McFarlane, W.G. *The Birth of Self-government for Jamaica and the Jamaican Progressive League 1937–1944*. Kingston: Masterall Printers, 1957.

Post, Ken. *Arise Ye Starvelings: The Jamaican Labour Rebellion of 1938 and Its Aftermath*. London: Nijhoff, 1978.

Ranston, Jackie. *They Call Me Teacher: The Life and Times of Sir Howard Cooke Governor-General of Jamaica*. Kingston: Ian Randle Publishers, 2003.

St Pierre, Maurice. 'The 1938 Jamaica Disturbances: A portrait of Mass Reaction against Colonialism.' *Social and Economic Studies* 27 (1978): 171–96.

Stolberg, Claus F., ed. *Jamaica 1938: The Living Conditions of the Urban and Rural Poor: Two Social Surveys, 1938*. Kingston: Social History Project, Department of History Mona, 1990.

Thoywell-Henry, L.A., ed. *Who's Who and Why in Jamaica 1939–40*. Kingston: by the author.

Workers Week Education Committee. *1938: An Account of the Struggles of the Jamaican Workers' in 1938*. Kingston: Agency for Public Information, 1977.

5 | *The Present in the Past: Caribbean Economic Development since Independence: The 1960s–2000s*

Derick Boyd

Introduction

> There is a chance for Jamaica to transcend its present limitations and to achieve more fully the moral ambitions of Western Civilization – perhaps especially to achieve the values of Enlightenment... Generally, the new national leaders of Jamaica seem to have avoided corruption and opportunism, the twin evils of unworthy leaders in most societies.
>
> Wendell Bell in *Jamaican Leaders* (1964, 172)

The transition of a country from a colony to an independent state is a rare and interesting event.[1] Many of us have been fortunate to observe this phenomenon, directly in some cases, for the Caribbean. The struggle for self-determination is a struggle between the strong and the weak and information is usually sparse, unreliable and subject to considerable manipulation. Indeed, the very process of colonialism is defined by its fundamental inequalities in almost every aspect; not surprisingly, therefore, a characteristic feature of this is poor data on which to base empirical analyses and an understanding of what has taken place.

It is said that academic progress is made by standing on the shoulders of giants and it is very much in this regard that this chapter seeks to extend an analysis that is rooted in two papers of Richard Hart: (i) 'An Historical Approach to Industrialisation in the English-Speaking Caribbean Area (seventeenth century to 1970)' and (ii) 'Changing Perspectives on Development in the 1940s and '50s.'

The first of these papers presents an historical analysis of the industrial features of the Caribbean. The period covered was vast, from the seventeenth century to the 1930s, but the tracing of, primarily, the rise and decline of sugar showed the static nature of industrial development in Jamaica and many other Caribbean countries until well into the twentieth century. From the point of view of *economic development* the central lesson is that as far as the Caribbean was concerned, as colonies of Great Britain, the concept was almost entirely irrelevant. Certain important analytical implications may be derived from Hart's 1990 paper that discusses the transition to independence and self-determination. The paper suggests firm linkages between pre-independence structures and relations that inform analyses of the contemporary political, social and economic performance. It is some of these implications that we seek to develop.

The second paper, 'Changing Perspectives on Development in the 1940s and 1950s', examines the changing views on industrialization and economic development in the Caribbean over those two critical decades. An analysis of the evolution of policy, to which this chapter contributes, allows insights into the explicit and implicit views on the role and functioning of the state in economic development.

If we are to assess the economic performance in the Caribbean since the 1960s it seems desirable to appreciate the chronological context of that process since economic development is not likely to simply appear as if by accident. What these two papers indicate is that a comprehensive assessment of the economic development process in the Caribbean requires that analysis to take place against its historical background (to contextualize the analysis) and requires an evaluation of plans for the transition. In his book *The Practice of Economic Management*, Courtney Blackman wrote:

> In an address to students of the University of the West Indies at the Mona campus in March 1980, I described the 1970s as the 'Decade of Disaster' in the context of Caribbean economic history. I added, 'If you think the '70s were rough, wait until you see the '80s.' We have navigated the '80s even less adroitly than we did the '70s. ... The period 1970–90 may well go down in West Indian economic history books as 'Two Lost Decades.' The question now is, 'How do we get back on track?' (2006, 3)

In this chapter I do not address how to get back on track but rather, I am interested in an anterior question, 'what factors may have determined the track'? Indeed, the issues that I seek to address may give rise to questions concerning the identification of the track or indeed a track. This is not to deny the poor macroeconomic statistics, *in some regards*, for the 1970s and '80s, or the '90s into 2000 come to that. I seek to analyse, however, the extent to which the independent Caribbean was shaped by the dynamics (cultural, institutional, social and economic) forged in its colonial experience, or as C.L.R. James may have termed it 'the future in the present', and the impact it should have on our assessment of the Caribbean economic performance over the years of independence.

The Future in the Present: The Colonial Context

Colonial government of the Caribbean from the seventeenth century had clearly stated objectives. The role of colonial government was to protect the interests of British industrialists and companies whose financial well-being was affected by operations in the Caribbean. The role of economic processes in the Caribbean colonies was fairly traditional. It was to provide raw materials to the industries of Britain and markets for their outputs – as simple as that, although the implications may be far-reaching and complex. Throughout the centuries the social and economic conditions in the Caribbean were a *residual* of the quest to enrich the British colonial interests who influenced and controlled production and trade in and out of the countries. Transition from a slave labour to a wage labour economy over the mid-nineteenth century through to the early twentieth century did not change the historical role of the colonial Caribbean. Colonial government continued up until the 1940s to block any investment that would make Caribbean products which competed with products manufactured in the UK and imported into the Caribbean or competed with the interests of UK firms. The evidence for this is clear (Hart 1998, Bell 1964, Bernal 1988). The Caribbean was not a democracy and Government in the Caribbean did not *explicitly* or *implicitly* pursue the interest of the majority of the inhabitants of the islands. Economic development was not an issue. It was vigorously discouraged with all the consequences that entailed for the vast majority of the population.

Hart's contributions allow us to appreciate the degree to which hands-on colonial government actions effectively stifled economic activity throughout the Caribbean and the colonial territories. Indeed, Hart writes:

> Jamaica in the 1940s was still a predominantly agricultural country. Apart from the processing of the juice of the sugar cane into sugar and rum, the generation of electricity, a few bakeries, biscuit and aerated water factories, a match factory and a couple of foundries, there was very little in the way of industrial development...One of the most convincing arguments for self-government was that if Jamaicans were able to elect their own government such a government would give priority to local interests and encourage industrialisation (1998, 107).

The way of doing business in the Caribbean was founded on the protective/facilitating relationship between government and business. The larger and more powerful the business, the closer and stronger that relationship between government and business would necessarily be. The culture of business was embedded in and functioned on this partnership between government and business. The lesson of business in Caribbean economies is thus founded, not on theoretical and ideological notions of free markets and laissez-faire, but on the harsh realities of the duality between government and business in the pursuit of production, exchange and profits.

The 'sordid story,' as Hart calls it, of the setting up of a cement factory in Jamaica provides an example of not only the extent to which government frustrated industrial development initiatives as late as the 1940s, but beached the colonial relationship into the independence era. In 1941, James Gore, a local businessman, requested permission to establish such a factory. Hart explains that the then Governor of Jamaica,

> Richards informed the Colonial Office by telegram that, in view of the war time interruptions of supplies, it was important that a cement factory should be erected in Jamaica...but he added, 'I do not favour Gore's proposal.' Instead he would 'prefer a local company to be formed in which Cement Marketing Company would have interest'[2] (1998, 110).

The decision to manufacture cement in Jamaica would be allowed but what is a harbinger of things to come was that, it was not Gore who established the cement factory, but indeed, the British cement company in concert with local interests. Hart explains:

> The cement saga ended in 1948, with the enactment of legislation granting a monopoly to manufacture cement in Jamaica to Caribbean Cement Company Ltd. This was a locally incorporated company in which British cement manufacturers had a substantial financial stake. Gore, the entrepreneur who had originally proposed the establishment of a local cement factory, had been forgotten. The group of local investors involved in the project was headed by the Ashenheims who, as solicitors, had done the legal work (end of part II of Hart 1990).

The business culture of official protection and dominant interest preservation provided the basis for this landmark industrial project and arguably could be seen as providing an important marker for what was to follow. This was an inauspicious start for the new and emerging business culture for the post colonial Jamaica and especially so for what was to be an iconic Jamaican industrial development. This was confirmation, if any was necessary, that Government could award economic and financial largesse to the favoured. This was the basis of doing business in the past and the culture for business in the future – *the future in the present*.

Planning for the Future: Structural Transformation and Economic Development

The 1940s and '50s saw the drive for political independence and pronounced changes in the perspectives on Caribbean economic development. Among other factors, the Second World War was important in weakening the grip that the British government had on her many colonial territories. This in turn revealed new possibilities for social and economic development that were largely thought to be unattainable in previous decades. This was true not just for the Caribbean but for many countries subject to colonial domination. There were, of course, competing and overlapping arguments about the way to most effectively pursue economic development but what emerged over the 1940s and '50s was the clear notion that the Caribbean territories could develop as nation states, interdependently or independently, but certainly, independent of their then colonial masters. This is not to say that there was a consensus on this view but it was certainly the majority opinion as evidenced in the 1958 survey carried out by Bell (1964, 132–42).

This period marked a watershed in the government and policy in the region.

> It was a turning to self-government and for the first time to policy responsibility. In 1944, Jamaica had adopted Universal Adult Suffrage, followed by Trinidad in 1946. In the Caribbean things seldom jump and they scarcely jump now. But this was still a new time...Nation builders emerged in the wake of a leader to run institutions and to shoulder responsibilities straddling sundry disciplines and domains (Best 1999, 10–11).

The discipline of Economic Development emerged largely due to the work of W. Arthur Lewis with the publication of several seminal works addressing issues of direct importance to economic development in the Caribbean (Downes 2004). Confidence in critiquing, theorising and developing new perspectives on policy problems was considerably enhanced with the establishment in 1948 of the University of the West Indies (UWI) as a college of the University of London, the establishment of the Faculty of Social Sciences in 1960 and especially so when UWI achieved full university status in 1962. Hart writes:

> In the 1930s and 1940s ideas of industrialization and how it was to be achieved were very different to the ideas on this subject which emerged in the following decade. The approach agreed upon by the progressive political and labour organisations of these colonies at the time was set out in the **STATEMENT on ECONOMIC DEVELOPMENT and FEDERATION** approved at the founding conference of the Caribbean Labour Congress in Barbados in 1945.[3]

> As a perusal of this statement will show, the basic premise of our thinking at that time was that, apart from the existing sugar, petroleum and bauxite industries, local industrial development would be mainly to satisfy the needs of the local regional market. We did not pay much, if any, attention to the possibility of industrial production for a market in the USA. Federation of these colonies was considered desirable to ensure that the market for the products of the proposed industries would be regional rather than insular

in order to ensure that these industries would be of a viable size (Hart 1998, 7).

Government was at the centre of decision-making and in large part acted as the engine of growth. This to some extent was understandable: this was the historical colonial experience; at that time immediately after the Second World War the Marshall Plan, developed and executed by governments, was rapidly re-establishing Europe's industrial base (though for some, this may have been misinterpreted as *establishing* that base); and the emerging dominant Keynesian Demand Management had won the argument of the day that government could effectively control economic movements – Professor Phillips (1958) showed how employment rate could be traded off. In this milieu, government through planning and its expenditures was seen as being able to lead and drive that process of economic development. The Caribbean Labour Congress document mentioned in Hart (1998) above is an illustrative example. That document notes:

> It is clear that private enterprise is not at the present time providing capital investment for the development of our territories at a sufficiently rapid pace. Measures are therefore necessary to encourage greater capital investment...Unrestricted encouragement of capital from outside the area is not a wise policy for several reasons...Provision of capital for economic development by the local government may take several different forms. The mere provision of the necessary capital is not however a guarantee that it will be profitably employed. To ensure the necessary protection it is necessary that the local Government should be more interested in local development than in maintaining a market for manufactured goods from the Mother Country (Hart 1998, 51).

Resources, material and capital were identified as the main obstacles to growth. Poor resource endowments in the form of unlimited supplies of unskilled labour were identified. However, if we have learnt anything about economic development in the last 50 years it is that economic development is less about resource endowment or even the transformation of material resources in outputs and more about the transformation of people. It is the transformation of people that is simultaneously the pre-condition and the outcome of the economic development process.

The Caribbean provides an interesting variety of economic outcomes arising from similar historical background (Boyd and Smith 2006). What is clear from that study is that countries that are as similar as say the countries of the Eastern Caribbean are not the same for a one-size-fits-all policy approach – not even in this case. At the same time, there are institutional frameworks that can obtain across the countries that allow for worthwhile and appropriate checks and balances, such as the currency board arrangements underlying the single OECS currency. This has worked remarkably well in the development of monetary policies underlying a relatively successful economic performance. What is remarkable in the examination of the OECS economies is the degree to which they conform to what Quah (1996) would term a convergence club (Atkins and Boyd 1998), whilst at the same time revealing heterogeneous characteristics. In a study of the inflation characteristic of 12 Caribbean economies, for instance, it was shown that whilst some OECS countries exhibited low inflation outcomes over long periods the persistence profile of the inflation varied considerably across countries, with Antigua-Barbuda and Dominica bracketing the sample with high and low persistence, respectively (Boyd 2006).

If we learnt anything from Hart (2004; 1999; 1998; 1990; among others) it is that Caribbean societies from the seventeenth century to the 1940s were not being prepared for industrialization and economic development under independent government. So that the activities in the 1940s and '50s planning for the future and making the transition into post-independence economic performance was not breaking through a Chinese wall – a paper screen. It was entering the ring into the free-for-all that is every nation's quest for economic advantage and improvement where businesses are the storm troopers.

It is with a degree of level-headedness and insight that Bell notes that the big decisions that the new nation would have to make are not peculiar to emerging nations:

> ...neither the alternative choices regarding a particular policy area nor the total configuration of "big decisions" should be regarded as peculiar to the new nations. In fact, similar processes are constantly going on in the older nations, which are themselves reformulating goals and devising different and more effective means of achieving them; for the older nations too are in a state of flux, of development, of constant change from past to future. Nonetheless, the transfer

of power from a colonial to an indigenous regime forcefully raises a large number of societal policies that become highly problematic, subject to change, and, most of all, potentially amenable to manipulation in accordance with the collective will of the citizens and the leaders of the new nation (Bell 1964, 87–88).

Transition and Post-Independence Macroeconomic Performance

Tempered by the reality of these small open vulnerable economies, the transition to post independence economic activity was, nevertheless, accompanied by considerable optimism. In the first regional study of its kind, the World Bank (1978), for policy analysis purposes, divided the area into the More Developed Countries (MDCs) and the Less Developed Countries (LDCs). The MDCs consisted of Barbados, Guyana, Jamaica, and Trinidad and Tobago. The LDCs consisted of Antigua and Barbuda, Dominica, Grenada, Montserrat, St Kitts, St Lucia, St Vincent and the Grenadines and Belize.

I will focus on only three interesting aspects of Caribbean economic performance since the 1960s:
1. the intra-regional dynamics of per capita income;
2. the comparative growth in per capita income; and,
3. the trend in average out per employed worker as an indicator of welfare and economic performance.

These are illustrated in Table 1 and Figures 1 and 2. I focus on these in order to provide evidence of certain aspects of the internal dynamics of the region that have significant implications for living standards and long-term economic development.

Table 1
GDP PER CAPITA INDICES: CARIBBEAN 1974 AND 2003

Country	GDP Per Capita [1]	GDP per Capita [2]
	1974	2003
Antigua & Barbuda	71	275
Dominica	32	102
Grenada	30	115
St Kitts & Nevis	50	210
St Lucia	44	123
St Vincent & Grenadines	33	94
Belize	49	106
Barbados	68	270
Guyana	45	28
Jamaica	100	89
Trinidad & Tobago	80	220

1. The data in this column was interpolated from World Bank 1978, 6–7.
2. The data in this column was calculated from GDP (constant 2000 US$) divided by Population data.

Sources: World Bank 1978, 6–7; and World Bank, *World Development Indicators*, www.esds.ac.uk download, November 2005.

Table 1 allows a time and cross country comparison to take place for 1974 and 2003. It is constructed relative to the income of Jamaica which is set at 100 so that for comparisons the other incomes can be read as a percentage of the 1974 Jamaica income. For 1974 it shows that GDP per capita in Jamaica was considerably greater than all the other countries. Trinidad and Tobago's was 80 per cent of the Jamaican income, and Grenada and Barbados were 30 per cent and 68 per cent, respectively, of the 1974 Jamaican per capita GDP level. Twenty-nine years later in 2003, the distribution of regional per capita income had significantly changed and the only country with a lower income than Jamaica was Guyana. Jamaica's 2003 per capita income was 89 per cent of its 1974 level and Grenada that had only 30 per cent of the 1974 Jamaican income, in 2003 had an income larger than that of Jamaica. Jamaica and Guyana represent the two cases in which there was an absolute decline in per capita income and a dramatic fall in relative income in the case of Jamaica.

Figure 1

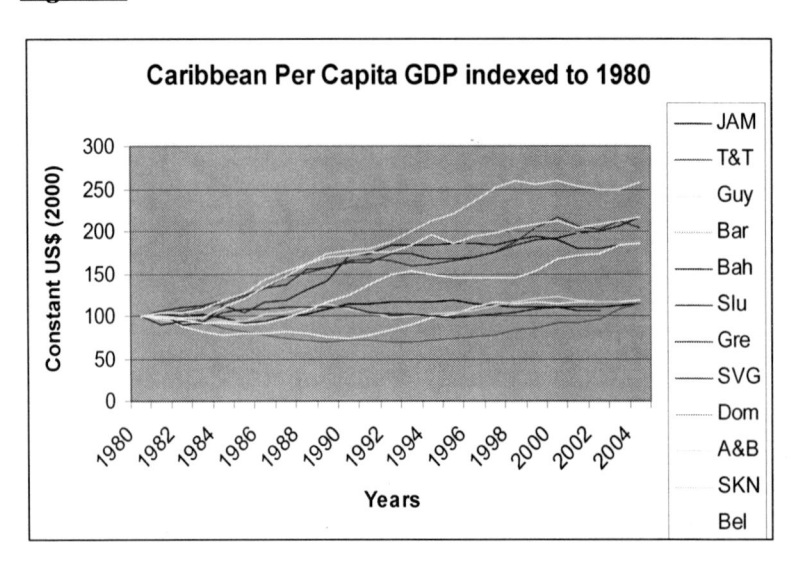

Caribbean Per Capita GDP indexed to 1980

Figure 2

Average Product per Employed Worker: USA, UK, Singapore and the Caribbean

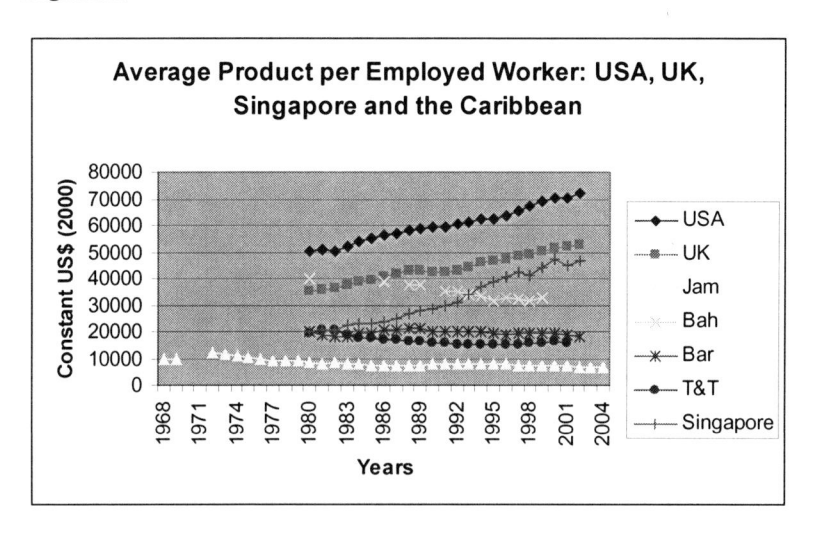

[Chart showing Constant US$ (2000) on y-axis from 0 to 80000, Years on x-axis from 1968 to 2004, with series: USA, UK, Jam, Bah, Bar, T&T, Singapore]

Figure 1 shows that the promise of the MDCs failed to materialize and as they failed to grow they were overtaken by LDCs. The growth profiles of the countries are indexed to their 1980 levels so that the profiles reflect their growth since 1980. The figure shows a dichotomous growth experience with the top group consisting of St Kitts and Nevis, Antigua and Barbuda, St Vincent and the Grenadines, Grenada, Dominica, St Lucia, and Belize. The lower group is made up of Barbados, Guyana, Trinidad and Tobago, Jamaica and The Bahamas.

Figure 2 sheds some light on the productive performance of the countries and their ability to produce goods and services in the independence period. It presents the average value of the output produced by employed workers – this data is not available for all Caribbean countries. The implications of this figure are many and deep seated but three features are briefly noted here:

(i) All the Caribbean economies show a falling trend in average product. Even Caribbean countries with relatively well performing economies such as The Bahamas and Barbados show a declining trend. They do so, however, from significantly higher levels of average output value. In 1999 for the Bahamas the average product of the employed worker was US$32,864 and that for Jamaica US$7,097. This means that on average in Jamaica the employed worker produced 22 per cent of the annual value produced in the Bahamas.

(ii) There is not only a downward trend in value of what is produced on per employed worker over 1976–2003, but what is more, the value of Jamaica's average output is the lowest among the reported Caribbean countries.

(iii) The on-trend decline of the Caribbean countries stands in contrast to the on-trend growth shown for the USA, UK and Singapore reported in Figure 2. Singapore is known to have made considerable progress in economic development and this is evidenced by the performance of its average product per employed worker observable from Figure 2. In 1980, the average product was around US$20,000, the same as for Barbados and Trinidad and Tobago, but while the Caribbean countries' product trended downward, Singapore's product showed a strong upward trend. So that, by 2002, the Singapore value of US$46,880 was nearly the same as that of the UK, and 2.5 times that of Barbados.

The on-trend decline in the average value of what is produced must function as a growing binding constraint on social and economic development, especially in the light of a growing population. This must be so since less goods and services being produced per worker must mean that less is available for consumption, investment, and taxation, all of which need to grow in order to facilitate social and economic development. If each employed worker produces less value year on year then the value of the goods and services available to each household, on the whole, must also fall.[4] A falling Caribbean trend is, therefore, indicative of binding economic constraints with downward pressures on household living standards.

This analysis could further be extended to issues of government revenues and the ability of governments to provide public services and the servicing of public debt.

Historical Dynamics and Economic Performance

In this section I draw out conclusions of performance outcomes in the light of historical factors and dynamics analysed above rather than give an assessment based simply on stated ambitions or plans.

From the historical analyses of the role of the state; the dynamics of production and consumption; poverty and an iniquitous social and economic structure, we are able to discern that the colonial dynamics were aimed at reproducing colonial Caribbean and it did so remarkably successfully over the seventeenth century to the 1930s. The rudimentary industrial structure was the deliberate outcome meant to subvert development in order to support the financial advantages of British companies. The associated social structure was defined by the privileges of the few, largely defined by race, and the long-term impoverishment of the masses. The Great Depression of the 1930s and the Second World War, and the moral bankruptcy, inter alia, of such a system contributed to its vulnerability. The second half of the twentieth century saw the movement for self-determination around the world.

Modern notions of economic development emerged in the 1940s and the 1950s saw the rapid development of plans. The attainment of economic development, however, required the dismantling of the historical social dynamics and its replacement with a new role for the state, the development of a social infrastructure, a business culture, and financial and political conditions consistent with this new vision. There is weak evidence of this dismantling of the old *and its replacement* with a new institutional framework implicit in which are the cultural dynamics able to deliver the new outcome.

If the sordid cement factory story symbolizes anything, it is that the future would be grounded in the past, founded on the existent dominant business relationships and culture. What was there to overturn this in its fundamentals and establish a new order? The vast majority of the people suffered from significant deprivations, and although access to education, health and income improved, the road to social and economic well-being was symbolized by race and ethnic relationships. This largely excluded the majority from meaningful participation in economic development. C.L.R. James wrote, 'the leaders of a revolution are usually those who have been able to profit by the cultural advantages of the system they are attacking,' and this is no less true of epochal changes as seen in a transition from colony to independent nation. The emerging elite could indeed be expected to profit from the cultural advantages of a fairly static system grounded on the manipulation of the ignorant and future outcomes, especially in the area of politics, provided ample evidence of this.

For all its moral bankruptcy and considered brutality, an undeniable feature of the colonial period was reasonably well-functioning institutions. Government, the police, the judiciary, the monetary and financial systems all functioned largely predictably. Indeed, the exploitation and grinding poverty of the majority over a long period of time is evidence of their institutional efficacy. We have already noted the objective of their design and in this they appeared 'fit for purpose.' The extrication of the Caribbean economies from their role as colonies in the 1940s and '50s was not because the basis for economic development was established and they could break through into a process of industrialization in the 1960s; far from it. The quest for self-determination was driven more by the poverty and deprivation of the masses and a slackening of the constraints, more so than by industrialization and economic development being an obvious next step. This drive for self-determination, moreover, was a part of an international drive for independence with long-standing armed revolt in India notable in this respect.

In eschewing the old and bringing in the new, there are many opportunities to make mistakes. In his seminal *Theory of Economic Growth*, W. Arthur Lewis writes:

> Only the best governments can use foreign monies and skills to best advantage. At present most of the less developed countries are in a state of reaction against nineteenth century imperialism. They have acquired a distaste for foreign capital and foreign administration, and they are more anxious to protect themselves from further exploitation than to take advantage of current opportunities (1955, 412).

Nowhere is this truer than in the sphere of monetary arrangements. A comparative analysis of central banking, monetary policy and economic performance indicates that the historical currency board arrangements have served the OECS countries remarkably well (Boyd and Smith 2006). Although this is not a sufficient condition for economic success, the financial constraints implicit in the 'backing' of a currency present in a currency board framework can serve to protect the nation's currency – recent analyses of Ireland and Estonia are instructive in this regard[5] (Honohan 1994; Gulde 1999; Ghosh 1998; Schuler 1992). And, protection of the currency and the financial infrastructure can and does play a crucial role in the functioning of institutional infrastructure, notably so in the ability of the government to finance essential public services such as education, health, and security. The inability of the government to adequately finance the security services leads to a gradual breakdown in the police and in extreme cases the military services.

The process of development requires the structural transformation of the society. The conditions under which this has to be undertaken are ever changing and there is scant evidence that the social, economic or institutional preconditions for economic development processes were in place prior to independence. A capacity-building approach that seeks to improve the ability of the state across what Grindle (1996) refers to as technical, institutional, administrative and political capacities had to be established. Whilst there have been notable successes, there have been failures and there is the issue of whether governments have been good enough (Grindle 2005).

For some Caribbean states the 1990s saw issues concerning governance and corruption eclipsing the earlier themes of public debate concerning balance of payments problems, exchange rate viability, the operations of multinationals or employing IMF monetary and fiscal programmes. The central debate has moved on from technical economic policy relevancies to embrace far more comprehensive and deep seated governance concerns.[5] In his 1958 survey of political attitudes Bell (1964) reported that one of the reasons given for anti-nationalist sentiments among Jamaican leaders surveyed was 'that graft and corruption would come' and there is strong evidence that this prediction came true and has been dominant since the 1990s. Attendant on the state-reducing role that defined decentralization of the 1980s was the absence of a state-building agenda. Fukuyama (2004) identifies this as a basic conceptual failure to sufficiently appreciate/ recognize the multi-faceted dimensions of stateness and its relationship to economic development. The resultant absence of capable states is witnessed through the inability to carry out even routine tasks, as characterized by the label 'incompetent government,' much less those requiring difficult or complex reforms.

Perhaps our assessment of Caribbean economic performance should be influenced by the penultimate paragraph of *The Theory of Economic Growth*, where W. Arthur Lewis writes:

...what is surprising is not how little good government there has been in human history, but, on the contrary how much good government there has been, having regard to the limitations of human wisdom, and to the innumerable temptations which lie in wait for unwary statesmen (1955, 418).

Notes

1. 'Although its roots can be traced deep into the past, nationalism, as we know it today, did not emerge until the middle of the eighteenth century when it appeared in North-western Europe and its American settlements. During the nineteenth century, it became a general movement throughout Europe. However, if one considers the dominance and geographical spread of political organizations based upon the priority of the nation-state, the 'age of nationalism' has not reached fruition until now, during the second half of the twentieth century' (Bell 1964, vii).
2. The Cement Marketing Company was the British firm that exported cement to Jamaica.
3. This Statement, the initial drafting of which was Hart's responsibility, is reproduced in Appendix 1, Hart (1998).
4. Transfer income from outside the country, such as remittances, can reduce the fall in consumption but since we are interested in economic development, such transfers are not of any real interest here although they would be if the focus was on consumption bundles of households. Here the focus is on the capacity of the country to produce.
5. The Central Bank of Ireland had a similar currency board component over 1943–79 and was also remarkably successful in managing the Irish pound. As Honohan noted: 'The evolution of Irish monetary arrangements towards comprehensive central banking took place very gradually, and without losing the financial stability that the original pure currency board arrangement has established' (Honohan 1994, 28). This very importantly paved the way for Ireland becoming a founding member of the European Monetary System in March 1979. In more recent times Estonia followed this example in seeking to satisfy the conditions for membership to the European Union (Gulde 1999).

References

Atkins, A and Derick Boyd. 1998. Convergence and the Caribbean. *International Review of Applied Economics*, 12: 3, 381–96.

Bell, Wendell. 1964. *Jamaican Leaders: Political Attitudes in a New Nation*. Berkeley and Los Angeles: University of California Press.

Bernal, Richard. 1998. The Great Depression Colonial Policy and Industrialization in Jamaica. *Social and Economic Studies* 37: 1 and 2 (March–June 1988), 33–64.

Best, Lloyd. 1999. Economic Theory and Economic Policy in the 20th Century West Indies: The Lewis Tradition of Town and Gown. The 4th Sir Arthur Lewis Memorial Lecture, Basseterre, St Kitts, 3 November 1999.

Blackman, Courtney. 2006. *The Practice of Economic Management: A Caribbean Perspective*. Kingston: Ian Randle Publishers.

Boyd, Derick and Ron Smith. 2006. *Monetary Policy, Central Banking and Economic Performance in the Caribbean*, forthcoming. University of the West Indies Press.

———. 2006. Monetary Regimes and Inflation in Twelve Caribbean Economies. *Journal of Economic Studies* 33: 2, 98–107.

Boyd, Derick. 2006. *Monetary Institutions and Economic Performance in the Caribbean*. Paper prepared for the Sir Courtney Blackman Conference and Book Launch, The Commonwealth Secretariat, London, Thursday, 11 May 2006.

D'Loughy, Mickey. 2001. *Colonial and Postcolonial Literary Dialogue – The Black Jacobins*, http://www.wmich.edu/dialogues/texts/blackjacobins.html.

Downes, Andrew S. 2004. Arthur Lewis and Industrial Development in the Caribbean: An Assessment. Paper presented a conference on The Lewis Model after 50 years: Assessing Sir Arthur Lewis' Contribution to Development Economics and Policy, University of Manchester, 6–7 July 2004.

Ghosh, Atish R., Anne-Marie Gulde and Holger C. Wolf. 1998. Currency Boards: The Ultimate Fix? *IMF Working Paper*, WP/98/8, Washington DC.

Fukuyama, Francis. 2004. *State Building, Governance and World Order in the Twenty-First Century*. London: Profile Books Ltd.

Grindle, Mirelee S. 1996. *Challenging the State: Crisis and Innovation in Latin America andAfrica*. Cambridge: Cambridge University Press.

———. 2005. Good Enough Governance Revisted, A Report for DFIF with reference to the Governance Target Strategy Paper, 2001, http://www.odi.org.uk/speeches/states_06/29thMar/Grindle%20Paper%20gegredux2005.pdf

Gulde, Anne-Marie. 1999. The Role of Currency Board in Bulgaria's Stabilization. *Finance & Development* 6: 3.

Hart, Richard. 2004. *Time for a Change*. Kingston: Arawak Publications.

———. 1999. *Towards Decolonisation – Political, Labour and Economic Development in Jamaica 1938–1945*. Kingston: Canoe Press, University of the West Indies.

———. 1998. Changing Perspectives on Development in the 1940s & 1950s. Paper presented at the Caribbean Intellectual Traditions Symposium, 31 October–1 November 1998, Department of History, University of the West Indies, Mona.

———. 1990. An Historical Approach to Industrialisation in the English-Speaking Caribbean Area (seventeenth century to 1970), Mimeograph in Richard Hart's collection, unpublished.

International Monetary Fund. 2003. *International Financial Statistics Yearbook*, downloads from *www.esds.ac.uk*.

Phillips, A. W. 1958. The Relationship between Unemployment and the Rate of Change of Money Wages in the United Kingdom, 1861–1957. *Economica* 25:100, 283–99.

Quah, D. 1996. Twin Peaks, Growth and Convergence in Models of Distribution Dynamics. *Economic Journal* 106, 1045–55.

Schuler, Kurt. 1992. Currency Boards. PhD Dissertation, George Mason University, Fairfax, Virginia. http://users.erols.com/kurrency/webdiss1.htm.

World Bank. 1978. *The Commonwealth Caribbean: The Integration Experience*. Baltimore: The Johns Hopkins University Press.

6 | Alexander Bustamante and Constitutional Government in Jamaica, 1944-47

Robert Buddan

Introduction

Major studies of constitutional reform in Jamaica and the West Indies, such as Munroe (1969) and Spackman (1975), concentrated respectively either on the politics of negotiation between the parties involved and the terms of constitutional settlements reached or document the constitutional progress made. None have studied the operation of government under these constitutions. This chapter builds more precisely on Richard Hart's (1998; 1999; 2004) accounts by going *inside* the working of the system of government in Jamaica under the constitution of 1944, the first to grant adult suffrage and a wholly elected House of Representatives. It discusses the contradictions and controversies of what may be considered a colonial type system of separation of powers.

This separation of powers differentiated the colonial members of the executive from the elected Jamaicans in the Lower House of the legislature and preserved a privileged position for that colonial executive. At the same time, it undermined the power of the elected representatives of the people because government was neither accountable nor responsible. This was justified by the arrogant colonial philosophy of tutelary democracy whereby the colonials presumed that Jamaicans were not fit and proper to govern themselves and required a period of tutorship in Westminster governance before they could be allowed self-government.

Hart's central point was that the social and political movements fighting for constitutional reform enjoyed progress and encountered reversals at different times reflective of the maturity of progressive forces on the one hand, and the conservative and repressive forces of colonialism on the other. Although from 1944 repression gave way to progress, this progress was a deliberately gradualist and politically frustrating one compounded by the new phenomenon of party rivalry in the House of Representatives. Colonial authorities also exploited that rivalry.

In this regard, one can argue that:
- a constitution based on a type of colonial separation of powers frustrated government between 1944 and 1953, particularly in failing to provide accountable and responsible government;
- party rivalry in the House of Representatives during this period centred on frustrations caused by tutelary democracy and the failure to make the constitution work;
- politics revolved around competing visions of constitutional models, including one reflecting the political ambitions of the leader of the Majority Party, Alexander Bustamante;
- the constitutional formula for governing defeated hopes for comprehensive policies that could bring social and economic development; and
- by 1947, the Majority Party had begun to openly criticize the constitutional model and a new constitution (of 1953) began to release many tensions as the political system emerged towards a parliamentary model.

Social, economic and political conflicts in the period of the 1930s and 1940s culminated in Jamaica's first modern constitution in 1944. Hart (1998, 198) identified three cornerstone principles of the constitution proclaimed by Order-in-Council in October of that year – universal adult suffrage, representative government, and semi-responsible government. Under this constitution, the House of Representatives was wholly elected, and the nominated Legislative Council had delaying powers only. The Executive Council had five nominated members and five elected ones with the Governor having a casting vote.

It was not satisfying from the start. Norman Manley, leader of the movement for self-government and President of the People's National Party (PNP) had preferred a constitution of self-government in which the elected representatives had a majority in the executive and where the executive was the principal instrument of policy (Hart 1999, 41).

Manley's main criticism was that the Governor needed to consult only with the Executive Council and could reject the advice of that Council for any number of vague reasons (Hart 1999, 244–43). Furthermore, experience would show that there were more divisions of powers than was apparent. Power was divided between legislature and Executive Council and then between Executive Council and Governor. This was the true meaning of the term, Governor-in-Council. This Executive, and particularly the Governor-in-Council, would be the chief instrument of policy, not the elected majority of the legislature-in-executive, as Manley felt had been promised.

It was a colonial distribution of powers; power was more colonial than democratic. The hierarchy extended all the way to Britain. On matters to do with the police, the civil service and external affairs and trade, the Governor had to consult with the Colonial Secretary, who in effect, constituted an expatriate arm of government.

The fundamental problem with this constitution was that it represented a contradictory duad of power. Government was colonial and responsible to the British Monarch. But it was also (partially) elected and theoretically representative of the people. The constitution of 1944 was neither one nor the other, but sought to be both and was frustratingly unsuccessful. Worse, it stymied development. The elected representatives did not have power in the executive to engage policies that could produce the social transformation necessary at the time. Jamaica's experiment with democracy was a test of government's credibility with the people. Its failure to secure this credibility did lead to a change of constitution in 1953 and a change of government in 1955.

Throughout this period, the Jamaica Labour Party (JLP) was the majority party in the House of Representatives. By a constitutional paradox, however, its five members on the Executive Council constituted a governing minority. The party's leader, Alexander Bustamante, was leader of the majority party in the executive and the legislature. Bustamante's politics manifested the contradiction of the 1944 constitution. He rejected self-government without tutorship, but found cause to continuously complain about the lack of real power for the elected members and their consequent inability to do more for the poor.

The PNP was the minority party. Its leader in the House between 1944 and 1949 was Dr Ivan Lloyd. The party's President, Norman Manley, had failed to win a seat in 1944. However, having gained a seat in 1949, he assumed the role of Minority Leader. The PNP's leaders in the House had the advantage on two points of opposition. They attacked both the separation of executive and legislative powers, as well as the JLP for its failure to effectively pressure government to make the awkward system work for the people who elected it. They reminded the JLP that it had created its own dilemma by rejecting self-government.

One can only speculate whether an independent member of the House, Sir Harold Allan, appointed Minister of Finance and General Purposes, was the pivot on which the power of the Governor and Bustamante was expected to turn since Allan represented both. Probably Bustamante had thought this would allow him the best of both worlds – fending off the PNP's demands for self-government while enjoying power in the executive through Allan. He got the worst of both worlds instead. Bustamante and the JLP were to learn that power was separate and unequal with a distinct bias towards the Governor's executive.

Executive-Legislative Relations: 'Attack upon Myself'– Bustamante

The House first met in January 1945 and a curious form of politics between executive and legislature became noticeable within weeks. Bustamante and his four elected colleagues were concurrently members of the Executive Council and the House of Representatives. They were obligated to take to the House for debate motions proposed by the Governor's executive. They found themselves critical of certain motions of the executive, which as members of that executive they were nonetheless obliged to bring to the House as motions proposed by them. Being members of both arms of government they felt compelled to oppose some executive motions as members of the legislature causing them to appear to be attacking themselves.

By April 1945, the situation had become clear to Bustamante. When he rose to debate a resolution on land settlement proposed by the House, he explained:

> Perhaps, Mr Speaker, I will be making an attack upon myself because I am part of the government today. The government is divided into

two sections – one that is elected by the people, and that should be the true government. The other...is selected or nominated by His Excellency, the Governor. I divide the government into two sections because there are two distinct sections.[1]

Bustamante won the House's applause when he reasoned that the section elected by the people should be the true government. He did not win the sympathy of the PNP, however. The PNP felt he had brought this dilemma on himself by rejecting self-government.

If somehow this was good government it was not good politics. The two sections of the House existed on different principles of legitimacy, one nominated and one elected. The authority of the nominated executive to make policy in opposition to the elected legislature was therefore dubious. It did not produce good policy either. Bustamante said that the executive had the power to vote money for whatever it decided to be priority spending. But the executive, he charged, preferred law and order policies and wished to spend money on prisons and police stations rather than on land settlement. His party preferred increased spending for social and economic improvement. But when it asked for this, the executive – the Governor – often made the excuse that government did not have enough money.

Recognizing his dilemma, Bustamante conceived of a strategy of playing one arm of government against the other. He said:

> I am sorry to have to attack myself in this way as I am part of the government now, but I make myself stronger in another place than here by attacking myself here.[2]

He surmised that by using his majority in the House he could strengthen his influence in the executive. He would play off the stronger power on his side against his weaker one, which lay on the governor's side. The truth is that he was not able to do this successfully and this was precisely the point used later against him by the PNP.

Separation of Powers: 'I am in a Humiliating Position' – Bustamante

The division of powers led to the fragmentation of responsibility and accountability in a different way. House members in the executive had to face the fact that they were answerable for decisions for which they were not responsible because information available to them was not verifiable. As Ministers-in-Embryo, they did not have control over departments for which they had to answer to the House. On one occasion, Bustamante confessed to the humiliation of being in such a position.

He was required to respond to certain questions raised in the House during parliamentary Question Time. When a member of his own party asked him to clarify his explanation about why a certain road project had been suspended, Bustamante found himself having to grapple with the unaccountable system of expatriate government. He was frank enough to say:

> I am in a humiliating position because in spite of the fact that I was the same person who replied to the question, I never did understand how the Secretary of State for the Colonies could have remained in England and could have known what particular work should be suspended...The Secretary of State scarcely knows the geographical position of Jamaica, much more to know a road. Although I gave the reply, it is very humiliating to stand up now and condemn my own reply.[3]

Parliamentary questions are best answered when a member of the executive has full responsibility for his department with access to the information that covers the administrative details of projects under the portfolio on which he is required to report. But while Bustamante had the responsibility to answer questions under his assignment, he did not have administrative control and access to the information by which he could sufficiently know about his department's projects. The answers were simply handed to him on behalf of a Colonial Secretary who was distant and even more ignorant.

Bustamante confessed that he himself had not been comfortable with the reply to the parliamentary question even while he had been giving it. He had nonetheless hoped, by flattery of his executive position, to 'deceive' his colleague as he wryly put it. The kind of detailed knowledge required, if parliamentary Question Time is to be of any real value and for responsible government to be more than a farce, can be garnered from this exchange. In the particular case, Gideon Gallimore (JLP) asked his leader:

> Mr Gallimore: How much money was spent cutting a road from Watt Town to Cascade?

Mr Bustamante:	864 Pounds.
Mr Gallimore:	How many drivable miles were cut?
Mr Bustamante:	97 Chains.
Mr Gallimore:	How many miles were left to complete?
Mr Bustamante:	Approximately eight.
Mr Gallimore:	Will the project be completed?
Mr Bustamante:	Inadvisable.[4]

Bustamante had no idea if any of this was true. Colonial officials had provided the answers. He sarcastically wondered how the Secretary of State who resided overseas could then know such things. He mocked the process this way: someone recommended to the Governor that the road be suspended and he passed the recommendation on to the Secretary of State for the Colonies, who in his ignorance agreed.

The real problem was that the Governor needed the approval of the Secretary of State overseas for such a minor matter as the completion of a rural road whose construction had, at any rate, been suspended eight years before. Whether he intended to do so or not, Bustamante was also drawing attention to the fragmented and unaccountable structure of government, which divided power so bureaucratically, incoherently and irresponsibly. In such a system, the elected members in the executive did not have the level of control and kind of information needed to be properly accountable to the House. The power lay in the Heads of Departments who were colonial officials and were not members of the House and so not directly accountable to it.

This system of Government, relying as it did on a distant and ignorant expatriate arm, the Secretary of State for the Colonies, was open to ridicule. It was indeed comically exposed when it transpired that a decision had been referred to the Secretary of State and taken in his name even though the member of government acting in the Secretary's name did not know who the Secretary was and probably did not even know if there had been one at the time. The PNP saw an opportunity to embarrass the government (and the constitution) on one such occasion and did not hesitate to do so.

The important matter of the sale of the Island Telephone Company had come up in August 1945. A motion had been submitted to the House assuring that the Governor's proposal had been sent to the

Secretary of State who had made no objection to it. Ivan Lloyd (PNP) had been aware that Colonel Stanley had resigned that position and no successor had yet been named. He asked the JLP members of the executive, 'To which Secretary of State were these particular proposals and the particular documents submitted?' Frank Pixley (JLP) coyly replied, 'The Secretary of State for the Colonies.' Lloyd pressed further: 'I want to know who he was.' Bustamante confessed, 'I don't know.'[5] The leader of the majority party in the Executive had no idea who was the British authority in whose name he acted.

No Secretary of State had actually approved the Governor's motion to sell the telephone company. Florizel Glasspole (PNP) had complained about the haste in which the decision was being made. Probably the Governor had wanted to take advantage of this particular lapse in expatriate checks and balances. However, this was not a matter as minor as completing a rural road. On this occasion, Bustamante, who approved of the sale, must have once again seen the irony of responsibility without accountability in a system of government of which he was humiliatingly a part.

When the PNP's turn came to contribute to the budget debate in June 1945, William Linton (PNP) launched a three-part attack on that system of government and the JLP's role in it.[6] He reminded the House that the PNP had done all the fighting for self-government without support from the JLP and that the JLP was now paying the price of governing under a constitution that undermined the party's effectiveness in government. He pointed to the record of relative legislative impotence. The legislature had been largely marginalized and nearly emasculated. Over the first six months it had passed some 55 resolutions but none had been reflected in the estimates for the 1945–6 financial year. This was enough evidence for Linton to conclude that the constitutional model had been misconceived.

Even so, and this was the third and most politically potent line of attack, the JLP did not have the will to prevail over policy. It lacked the necessary control over the executive because it was not the 'principal instrument of policy.' More to the point, Linton argued that the JLP was not an effective majority party. Despite being hamstrung by the constitution it had a two-thirds majority in the House of Representatives by which it could 'force' the executive to adopt its policies.

Faced with a situation difficult to defend, Bustamante had to address Linton's point that the elected members needed to be more forceful in the executive. One month later, Bustamante had to exhort his ministers to do as Linton had pleaded. Under the pressure of criticism that Government was not acting fast enough, he joined Linton in making his own plea:

> I am calling on every Minister in the House to be strong up there in the Executive Council...because unless the Members in the House open their mouths wide up there and let the administrative side of government realize that you are part of Government you all will fail...It is not enough to go up there in Executive Council and murmur; it is only enough to let others realize that you are men like they are, and if there is any inferiority complex you should forget it. I have no use for men who cannot open their mouths wide and speak to the King, for the King is a man too.[7]

The elected members of the Executive Council, Bustamante continued, should make the administrators know that they were to be treated as men equal to the administrators.[8] Bustamante of course, would have had first-hand knowledge of the confessed timidity of his executive colleagues. He put it down to a possible inferiority complex, but we can rest assured that Bustamante did not suffer this cultural malady.

'Giving Something with One Hand and Taking it Back with Another' – Bustamante

Linton's budget contribution opened up a direct exchange relevant to the constitutional politics of the period and the contradictions being experienced in governing. The PNP wanted to know why the JLP had accepted the 1944 constitution in the first place and why it had opposed self-government. Bustamante's response to Linton's charges played into the hands of the PNP.

When Linton accused the JLP of timidity and lack of forcefulness, Bustamante resorted to an attack on the 1944 constitution. That constitution, he said, was guilty of 'giving something with one hand and taking it back with another.' This 'something' of course was power. He meant that his party had been given the power of the people but the constitution had taken away its power over government. If not for this deception, Bustamante ventured, his party would have been able to prove to the people that it had the ability to run the business of the country. Bustamante claimed, 'I told the public from my platform that the Constitution meant nothing.'[9] This only deepened the mystery more. Why did he accept the 1944 constitution, or more to the point, why was he opposing self-government? What followed is best reproduced *verbatim*. Florizel Glasspole asked, if Bustamante felt the constitution meant nothing, 'Why you opposed us then?'

Mr Bustamante:	I am not opposing. I don't oppose anyone with an honest mind. (Laughter).
Mr Glasspole:	You opposed self-government.
Mr Bustamante:	I oppose communism. I oppose atheism.
Mr Glasspole:	You opposed self-government for Jamaica.
Mr Bustamante:	I did not oppose self-government.
Mr Glasspole:	You did.
Mr Bustamante:	I oppose self-government right now.
Mr Glasspole:	Then what more responsible government can you have right now?
Mr Bustamante:	I oppose immediate self-government and I oppose moreso those who are clamouring for self-government now, why? The reply is this: Most are atheists who do not believe in God.
Mr Glasspole:	Rubbish.
Mr Bustamante:	Most are persons who believe, or try to lead the people to believe that if they get self-government they would be able to go to the man who had property with ten cows and say: 'Now I will divide your ten cows, giving five to the self-governing sea cow who is a lazy man and won't work. (Laughter).
Mr Glasspole:	Rank stupidity.
Mr Bustamante:	The day will come when these envious socialists who do not want to work and believe they can divide with others will not even get a hearing anywhere....[10]

Bustamante's rambling did not make things any clearer. Did he have personal ambitions and a model of his own in mind and was that the better explanation of why he opposed self-government?

The Bustamante Model: 'I Want to be the First Governor of the Colony' – Bustamante

Bustamante would declare in 1945 that he should be governor of Jamaica. His justification was, he declared, 'I know as much about the science of Government as any of the geniuses that have been sent from abroad to govern us.'[11] He kept his ambition in check while working with the constitutional model of 1944. But two-and-a-half years in government had been frustrating for him. By 1947 he appeared to have edged ever closer towards the PNP's position, a position the party continued to hammer home between 1945 and 1947.[12]

Having accepted in 1945 that the constitution had given something with one hand and taken it away with the other, Bustamante was ready with a new appeal:

> We want to have a majority on the Executive Council. We want to be in truth and in fact the instrument of policy. And as for the Upper House, which is called the Legislative Council, it should be annihilated…If we had full ministerial powers as we should have in our own country, we would have improved things more rapidly than it is being improved today.[13]

A relieved and probably incredulous Florizel Glasspole commented across the floor, 'You have opened up at last.'[14] Then, turning the British argument of 'fit and proper' on its head, the apparently converted Bustamante declared that this philosophy only caused him to suffer in the executive:

> I am in Executive Council. I suffer more than you do, more than I can tell you. We tell the Secretary of State for the Colonies point blank that England or no other country is a fit and proper nation to govern us.[15]

Bustamante had now broadened his argument. Jamaicans were not only fit and proper to govern themselves, but it was necessary that they do so to alleviate the poverty of the people since colonial policy had failed to do so.

The question remains, why had Bustamante really opposed self-government and agreed to the constitution of 1944? The answer involves some speculation but I believe Bustamante had a model of his own in mind. It lay somewhere between self-government and the constitution of 1944. But it was better accommodated by the constitution of 1944. There were probably two versions of this model.

In Model 1, Bustamante seemed to have felt that he could enjoy real influence in the executive by agreeing to bring Harold Allan into his side of the government. Allan was an independent who had enjoyed the confidence of the Governor. He had been a member of the Legislative Council before 1944 and had been knighted Sir Harold Allan, testifying to his anglophile pedigree. Bustamante, for his part, had arranged a political accommodation for Allan.

Hart (2004, 8–9) notes that Bustamante instructed his party not to oppose Allan's election in his St Mary constituency. He then appointed Allan one of the five elected members to the executive even though he had many others in his own party from which to choose. Allan was assigned the most important portfolio of all, Minister of Finance and General Purposes. Allan, I speculate, was to be the pivot on which Bustamante hoped his influence in the executive, especially over the Governor, would turn.

It is a matter worth researching further. However, the arrangement did not work to Bustamante's expected advantage. If Bustamante had expected to trade political opportunism for British favouritism, it did not happen. In others words, if he had expected the Governor to allow him broad freedom in the affairs of government in exchange for Allan's conservative balancing act against populism, he found instead that he had to do with the actual constitutional system designed to restrict the legislature and the representatives elected by the people, much as the British had expected tutelary democracy to do.

In the first two years of the new House of Representatives, Bustamante and his men complained of restrictions on their power. Even then, Bustamante never actually demanded in one of the many House resolutions, a proposal for a new constitution or an amendment that would increase the number of elected members on the Executive Council. For those two years, Bustamante apparently hoped to obtain more influence through private understanding and informal power arrangements. When this did not materialize, measures to compensate by using his strength in the legislature against the executive and mandating his men in the executive to speak up did not produce the results he wanted either. Still, he would not accede to self-government.

This was because Bustamante, it seemed, had another possibility in mind. As early as mid-1945 he had hinted at Model 2. He had exclaimed, 'I want to be the first governor of the colony.'[16] His ambition became more evident two years later, in 1947, when he expressed disgust with the 1944 constitution. By that time his patience with the constitution had run out. Model 2 envisioned Bustamante as Jamaica's governor with only minor adjustments to the system of government otherwise. He would become the chief executive under a colonial constitution that would be short of self-government. Any more far-reaching change to the existing constitution would apparently upset his personal ambitions and conservative vision.

Bustamante maintained that he should be governor of Jamaica and that the Legislative Council be abolished since it represented an unproductive colonial policy of 'delay and delay.' However, still distrusting national self-government, he preferred that financial matters remain the responsibility of the colonial Secretary of the Treasury. This was a curious, if not self-defeating model. To separate fiscal responsibility from elective power would obviously undermine responsible government. It would not solve the problem of the separation of power and responsibility.

Nevertheless, this was the model he offered. He insisted that he could govern Jamaica better than any British governor. He was correct to say that British governors did not understand the people because they did not come from the people. He was critical of the separation of powers under colonial bicameralism because the Legislative Council was annoyingly consumed with delaying legislation. He was correct that, under living conditions at the time, government could not always put off for tomorrow what needed to be done immediately.

However, Bustamante's enlightenment stopped there. He did not advocate independence but argued for an elected national governor and a Jamaican colonial secretary. His model, it seems, was for Jamaicanization within the empire. He wanted to be Jamaica's governor and he wanted a Jamaican-appointed colonial secretary. In his own language, he explained:

I am saying that some of us here have a perfect right to take the Governor's place and govern our own country...I am not saying our good Colonial Secretary should not be here. But are you going to tell me that we cannot find a man here to be Colonial Secretary?[17]

Bustamante had only appeared to have moved to the PNP's position. But he had really only moved away from the 1944 constitution to his own model.

Conclusion

Alexander Bustamante pursued three tactics as Majority Leader and Chief Minister under the 1944 constitution. He fended off the PNP's demands for a constitution of self-government; hoped nonetheless to gain influence over government through an informal alliance with the Governor and the Minister of Finance and Planning; but when this failed, reiterated his view that he should be governor of Jamaica.

Events were to show that all of these tactics failed. The constitution was reformed in 1953 and Bustamante lost his majority in the elections of 1955. He did become Prime Minister, not Governor, but only after political independence had been achieved in 1962.

Bustamante, however, shrewdly operated within the political balances of the constitution to side with the colonial authorities against the PNP when it suited him, and to use the PNP's support on social and economic reform when that suited him as well. Glasspole summed up the game plan of the JLP:

> I noticed on occasions when it suits the Honourable Ministers they display a great deal of agility and ability in getting certain things done but when it doesn't suit the ministers then just nothing is done. Copious excuses are presented in the House.[18]

Indeed, typical of separation of powers systems, representatives were confused over where responsibility and blame really lay. Some like Frank Pixley (JLP) thought that the constitution provided enough power for ministers to properly serve executive policy. It was a defence of the constitution. Glasspole felt that, if this was so, then the executive and the JLP members on it were guilty of a great dereliction of duty.[19]

There seemed no escape for the JLP. While some felt that most of the blame should fall on the executive, others like Burnett Coke

(Independent) suggested, quite logically, that since the constitution caused both Houses to pass the blame to and fro, power and responsibility should properly reside with elected members.[20]

The PNP's position was that government did not suffer from 'gridlock,' since the executive had commanded enough power to make law and policy. The problem was 'lockjaw' because the voice of the people who elected the JLP was not being heard in the executive.

Notes

1. Jamaica Hansard, House of Representatives, 10 April 1945, 126.
2. Ibid.
3. Jamaica Hansard, House of Representatives, 16 May 1945, 135.
4. Jamaica Hansard, House of Representatives, 2 May 1945, 94.
5. Jamaica Hansard, House of Representatives, 2 August 1945, 361.
6. Jamaica Hansard, House of Representatives, 20 June 1945, 169–71.
7. Jamaica Hansard, House of Representatives, 24 July 1945, 352.
8. Ibid.
9. Jamaica Hansard, House of Representatives, 19 July 1945, 175.
10. Ibid.
11. Ibid.
12. Jamaica Hansard, House of Representatives, 13 August 1946, 298; 9 July 1947, 390.
13. Jamaica Hansard, House of Representatives, 9 July 1947, 393.
14. Ibid.
15. Ibid., 395.
16. Jamaica Hansard, House of Representatives, 19 July 1945, 177.
17. Jamaica Hansard, House of Representatives, 9 July 1947, 393.
18. Jamaica Hansard, House of Representatives, 9 July 1947, 399.
19. Ibid.
20. Ibid., 400.

References

Hart, Richard. 1998. *From Occupation to Independence: A Short History of the Peoples of the English-Speaking Caribbean Region*. London: Pluto Press; University of the West Indies: Canoe Press.

———. 1999. *Towards Decolonization: Political, Labour and Economic Developments in Jamaica, 1938–1945*. University of the West Indies: Canoe Press.

———. 2004. *Time for a Change: Constitutional, Political and Labour Developments in Jamaica and other Colonies in the Caribbean Region, 1944–1955*. Kingston: Arawak Publishers.

Munroe, Trevor. 1972. *The Politics of Constitutional Decolonization*. Kingston: Institute of Social and Economic Research.

Spackman, Ann. 1975. *Constitutional Development in the West Indies, 1922–1968: A Selection from the Major Documents*. Barbados: Caribbean Universities Press.

7 | Seaforth in the Eye of the Storm: The Role of Rastafari in Major 1938 Events

Louis E.A. Moyston

Introduction

This chapter examines the role of cane cutters and loaders at Serge Island, Seaforth, St Thomas and their challenge to the plantation order from 26 December 1937 to 6 January 1938. It is argued that this event formed a most important forerunner to the mass revolts of May 1938. Additionally, it posits that the 'new awareness' created by Leonard P. Howell and the early Rastafari may have 'guided' the activities and actions by the cane cutters and loaders in Seaforth, St Thomas.

A Great Year for Sugar

Planters and factory owners entered 1938 in a very good financial condition regarding the economic soundness of sugar. A report in the *Daily Gleaner* (5 January 1938) praised the London office representing Jamaica's sugar interests for its satisfactory operation and noted the large increase of profit from the sugar industry of Jamaica, the first increase in sugar price in five years. The Legislative Council in the spring of 1937 had witnessed Mr Barnes giving an extensive presentation, praising the work of Mr H. G. DeLisser for his role in the recent World Sugar Conference in London at which Jamaica was permitted an increase in quota of 8,000 tons for the 1937–38 production year. However Mr Ehrenstein made an insightful response to Mr Barnes. He thought 'it should be well circulated and broadcast, (but) that people who are in the cane industry should maintain what they have, but do not increase otherwise there will be trouble' (Legislative Council Report, Spring 1937, 716). This statement may have been the source that inspired Carnegie's (1973) account of Mr Ehrenstein's statement, inferring the 'fears of social revolution.' This is indeed a fair assessment since Mr Ehrenstein, an immigrant from

Czechoslovakia, may have observed the growing militancy of the labourers in western St Thomas. He saw trouble. He was the first victim. It was at his sugar estate, Serge Island, that the cane cutters and loaders, from 27 December 1937 to 6 January 1938, started a strike that progressed into an uprising involving the labourers and the police.

The *Daily Gleaner* (7 January 1938) reported that 'Any history of the strike must begin from 27 December [1937] when cane cutters on Serge Island Estate struck for more pay. They were receiving 10½ d [pence] per ton for cutting cane which is 1½ d more than what they have been paid for a long number of years.' The workers were demanding two shillings per ton while Mr Ehrenstein, the owner of Serge Island, the Member of the Legislative Council and the Banana agent, was offering one shilling per ton, 1½ pence more that what they were receiving. Another *Gleaner* article (6 January 1938) reported, 'St Thomas District in Restive Mood as Estate Labourers Strike,' and noted that 'city police [had] rush[ed] to the scene of disturbance as fourteen hundred labourers at Seaforth District yesterday and last night seriously menaced the peace of the parish of St Thomas. Armed with machetes and sticks they staged a hostile demonstration which forced the Hon. R. Ehrenstein, owner of Serge Island to leave the district under police protection, and also turned on Mr Alexander Bustamante, reputed labour leader, at whom shouts of traitor were hurled.' The report continued,

> It is learned that apart from the actual show of hostility, the labourers, chiefly those who cut cane in Serge Island Estate [were] conducting house to house propaganda inducing other labourers and even domestic servants to start a general strike in St Thomas. For weeks there had been smouldering unrest in St Thomas and it appears that yesterday the situation swiftly move towards a climax. The police, however, have the situation under control and are prepared to meet any eventualities (*Daily Gleaner*, 6 January 1938).

In the meeting with Mr Ehrenstein the 1,400 workers had shouted 'away with Ehrenstein…we want two shillings.' The strikers blocked roads and stopped drivers of trucks and carts with sugar cane and sent them home.

The following day (January 6) there was a confrontation with the police. Thirty-four workers were injured and sixty were arrested while three policemen were injured. 'Nightly since the 27th December the police at Seaforth supplemented somewhat from other stations in St Thomas have had to be on the lookout for incendiarists, and as many as three attempts [daily] to set afire cane fields' (*Daily Gleaner*, 7 January 1938). The report indicated that the 'strikers' were organized on what appeared to have been on a parish level, and their activities became threatening to the families of the planter elite in the parish. It continued: 'On Wednesday evening the strikers raided the grocery and provision stores in three of the estates-Serge Island, Coley and Font Hill…Kingston constabulary…had to look on hopelessly, as breaches of the law were committed' (*Daily Gleaner*, 7 January 1938). This event took on national and international proportions as it featured on the BBC's broadcast of Empire and foreign news. It read, 'In St Thomas in the East of Jamaica police today made baton charges on labourers on strike on a sugar estate.' The BBC had 'globalized' the event.

Seaforth is a major town in Western St Thomas, and Serge Island was the major centre of production in that town. Trinity Ville, Petersfield, Coley and Cedar Valley are smaller towns within a reasonable radius from the sugar factory, areas which provided the bulk of the labourers for the sugar factory and the surrounding plantations.

While the strike was primarily about wages, the role of racial consciousness played a significant part in the uprising against oppressive conditions. This indicated a 'new awareness' associated with the early Rastafari movement and Leonard P. Howell, its founder. This was observed by the reporter of the *Daily Gleaner* (7 January 1938):

> Cane-cutters on Wednesday…appear to have veritably over-run sections of St Thomas. At Coley Estate they staged a hostile demonstration that resulted in a clash and injury of two or three persons, and at Petersfield property they invaded banana fields and coconut groves and wrought havoc. The colour question appears to have been drawn in, and dire threats were uttered against any and every person in St Thomas who was not black.

The 'colour question' had been evoked by Paul Bogle in the 1865 uprising in Morant Bay. Decades later, Cedar Valley and Trinity Ville were associated with the development and expansion of early Rastafari. Indeed, Trinity Ville and Seaforth were the two earliest sites from which Leonard P. Howell began his street meetings, preaching Haile Selassie as 'Messiah returned to earth,' and it was in Seaforth that Howell made what was considered a 'seditious' speech on a December night in 1933. Against this background he was arrested in January 1934.

Constabulary Office memoranda dated June 5 and 9, 1933 informed police in St James and St Elizabeth to look out for Howell and 'keep an eye on him' (Sedition File CSO No 1130). In a letter dated May 1933, Inspector W.C. Adams informed the Inspector General of Howell's bad influence on the 'less educated' in a report based on police observation of Howell's street meeting, as well as comments from Mr Robinson (JP), an official associated with the Bowden wharf. Robinson expressed his concern about Howell, that 'it is getting beyond a joke, he has told the people not to work for the white man etc. A stop should be put to it.' Sedition-Report re activities of Leonard Howell / Abyssinian League' (23 December 1933) has an interesting summary of interviews: Mr Thomas, Wharfinger of the Jamaica Producers Association at Port Morant, shared similar fears to Mr Robinson regarding the influence of Howell on the labourers in Port Morant. In the same report, Revd Surgeon of the Wesleyan church described Howell's utterances as 'Rank atheism and breaking down morality of the people, direct teachings against Ministers and established religion, extremists exciting to rebellion and bloodshed, movement spreading and growing-despicable, effort to undermine authority of Church and State.' Another letter by Elder W.E. Barclay of the Church of God states that Howell and his men 'are holding meetings and teaching several things contrary to the laws of the country' (CSO No. 1130/33).

By the next year, in an attachment to the Colonial Secretary's Office Minute Paper No. 5063/31 dated 5 September 1934, under the heading, 'Rastafari followers arrested in Seaforth,' one finds the story of a brutal attack on Delrosa Francis by Robert Powers, District Constable and planter in Seaforth on 4 August 1938. A letter dated 1 September 1934 by Rachel Patterson, one of the witnesses arrested and charged, reported that Robert Powers, describing himself as the 'King' of Seaforth and the 'master of Bellview Estate,' was out on the town and was 'out for all Rastas tonight.' Powers brutally assaulted Delrosa Francis in the presence of all who were present. Delrosa Francis and her 'associates' were tried and charged for disorderly conduct (CSO No. 5073/31). So not only was there a presence of Rasta elements in that town, but there was also an influence that was adequate enough to elicit such a brutal offensive from a member of the planter class. Another article, 'Sequel to Rasta Fari cult in District of St Thomas,' published in the *Daily Gleaner* of 19 August 1936, informs of the arrest and trial of 'exponents of Rastafari' in Cedar Valley (CSO Minute Paper No. 5073/34). The article notes that there was an increase of Rastafari in the upper areas of (West) St Thomas. But the expansion and sustained presence of early Rastafari was not restricted to St Thomas. An article, 'Ras Tafari cults excite Portlanders' published in the *Daily Gleaner*, 30 July 1935, speaks of the expansion of the early Rastafari movement in that parish and the 'rising courage of the misinformed and less intelligent.' The editorial: 'Danger Signals' published in the *Daily Gleaner* (31 July 1935) charges that Rastas were abusing the 'liberty,' that is, abusing the freedom of expression. The editorial presents a sharp picture of the elite perception of the activities of the early Rastafari Movement. It predicted 'trouble brewing around the corner,' and called for the 'canker' to be destroyed. These conflicts between Howell and the planter class, the church and the commercial class particularly from 1933–37 are important indications of the growing significance of the political influence of the early Rastafari movement in St Thomas.

Perceptions of the Early Rastafari Challenge

Phelps (1960) notes that in assessing the 'uprisings' of 1938 Governor Richards blamed events in Barbados, Trinidad and Serge Island for the widespread strikes, road blocking and other forms of protests. According to the writer the Governor commented that 'the strike at Serge Island is the forerunner to the recent disturbances.' But he also saw the possibility of the role of agitators. Phelps also says that N.W. Manley rejected the idea that the widespread disturbances resulted from the work of agitators but agreed on the role of events abroad and the events of January 1938 at Serge Island, Seaforth, St Thomas as forerunners to the mass protests of 1938.

Among academic assessors, Lewis sees the 1937–38 period of the Frome Riots as the 'catalyst for the new political and social phases in the history of imperial policy' (1968, 178); 'the story of modern Jamaica, starts of course, with the upheavals of the 1930s' (1968, 168). He shows that once the 1937–38 politico-economic drama started in Frome, it spread to the City of Kingston, but he neglects the events at Serge Island. The 1930s produced a 'moral earthquake' and Austin-

Broos (1997) goes further by recognizing the role of the early Rastafari in setting a new order. In *Main Currents in Caribbean Thought*, Lewis also examines the role of race in the emergence of twentieth century struggles for political independence (1983, 15, 19, 20). Lewis (1968), Post (1969; 1970; 1978) and Carnegie (1973) all describe the period in terms of labour organization and the role of race groups in the emergence of race consciousness and the development of a national society in Jamaica.

George Eaton Simpson (1985 and 1993), the pioneering scholar on the topic of Rastafari, raises an important question as it relates to the early political role of Howell and the early Rastafari Movement and its relationship to the rural struggles of the 1930s. Simpson (1993) notes that in the formative period of the Rastafari movement 50 years previously, the basic struggles of rural Jamaicans were over rent and taxes and that these struggles and pressures from the police 'gave rise to the millennium visions of the early Rastafarians.' In his 'reflections' the author suggests that the 'idea of domination by blacks' may have been an important factor in occasioning the labour uprising of 1938. This thinking is similar to Lindsay (1978) who cites George Beckford's insistence that 'race' is critical to the struggles against the colonial situation in Jamaica.

Hill (1981) linked Howell and the early Rastafari to the activities of 1938 by reference to anonymous letters to the Colonial Secretary warning about the dangers of the Rastafari Movement and the threat of 'war.' According to Hill, Major B.F. Cawes, the proprietor of Garband Hall Estate in Trinity Ville, read Howell's *The Promised Key*, published under an alias, in May 1938, the same month of the events of Frome and the docks of Kingston. In May 1938 construction workers on a new sugar factory for Tate and Lyle in Frome, Westmoreland (*Daily Gleaner*, 2 May 1938) went on strike for a dollar a day. Despite the 'stern warning from the Governor' the dock workers in Kingston (*Daily Gleaner*, 25 May 1938) followed suit. According to Hill, Cawes gave his views in his column in the *Jamaica Times* newspaper, under his pseudonym Ginger, that 'having read it (the book) twice (and) very carefully, I can well understand the race and bitter hatred which is now so clearly manifested in certain of our lower strata here' (cited from 'Dangerous Myths...Dodging Starvation,' *Jamaica Times*, 28 May 1983). Major Cawes attempted to link the 'bitter hatred' of the lower class to the 'mass revolts' of 1938.

In *Arise Ye Starvelings*, Post (1978) was concerned about the workers and peasants in Jamaica and the action which they took in May and June 1938. He provides important information regarding the rural activities of the labourers in Clarendon, St Mary and St Thomas and their responses to the plantation system and the realities of the colonial experience. Importantly, he also observes, 'We have seen that Ethiopianism has its greatest impact in the 1935–37 period among the poorest Jamaicans' (1978, 239). He elaborates on this in 'The Bible as Ideology: Ethiopianism in Jamaica 1930–38' (1970) where he traces the emergence of Ethiopianism in Jamaica as a radical doctrine; and made the distinction between the Ethiopian orientation and the Christian doctrine. The former is a breakaway from the latter. Furthermore, he writes that 'by March 1938 the Ras Tafarian was becoming significant enough to provoke a judge to remark on the "undoubted nuisance the Ras Tafarian people were becoming" and that in the same month [citing from *Jamaica Standard*, 15 March 1938, 3–4; 16 March, 4] there were police raids on cult members in different parts of the island' (1969, 387). In 'The Politics of Protest in Jamaica, 1938' Post (1969) pays careful attention to rural resistance, citizens associations and early trade union leaders such as H.C. Buchanan, Allan G. St Claver Coombs and St William Grant. However, he admitted that 'at present I know only of one instance of explicit (or Rastafarian type) participation in the events of May–June 1938.' He concedes, however, that 'there is no doubt that this aspect of the consciousness of the masses requires careful study' (1969, 385).

Post (1970) relied heavily on Hegel and Marx in describing Ethiopianism as a form of 'false consciousness,' this was so 'because it was based on imaginary motives and not from necessity.' Post (1969, 1970 and 1978) failed to see the Jamaican reality, in that the history of the country was not one of class struggles but one of struggles against slavery, black inferiority and exploitation. Lindsay, however, cites George Beckford's 'repeated insistence' that the Caribbean reality constituted a 'labour regime based on race' and that 'Race is the specific element…instituted in both the mode of production and the mode of exchange' (1978, vii). Following this position, it is reasonable to conclude that the element of race was critical to the struggles against the colonial situation in Jamaica.

In his book *Rise and Organise: The Birth of the Workers and National Movement in Jamaica*, Hart notes that '1938 was to be a decisive year for the working class struggle in Jamaica.' The events of 1938 provided the spark for the social conflagration that occurred in Westmoreland, in the western end of the island. In spite of this assessment, Hart made an important note that 'at the end of December 1937 the unrest at Serge Island by unorganized workers,' resulted in a strike in which the workers rejected Bustamante's role as mediator; and that police from outside of the parish had to be employed in quelling the resistance (1989, 36). But the writer's Marxist orientation might have prevented him from seeing the importance of the role of Howell and the early Rastafarian movement in the heart of the events in January 1938.

On the other hand, in *The First Rasta*, Lee makes an interesting link between the events of 1938 in Seaforth, St Thomas and the role of Leonard P. Howell. Critical of Post's work, she notes that his Marxist orientation and his reliance on published literature did not allow him to get into the 'actual facts' that triggered the January event in Serge Island. She writes, '...a big labour strike began at Serge Island, a plantation between Seaforth and Trinityville, right in the middle of Howell's preaching territory...[T]he strike began a campaign... that rolled through Jamaica like a social hurricane in 1938 and subsequently transformed the old colonial system' (Lee 1999, 117, 118). The writer then links the Serge Island strike with that of the Kingston dockers: 'workers all over Jamaica shared their concern.'

So contrary to the work of Post (1969, 1970, and 1978), Hart (1989), Campbell (1987) and Lee (1999) others were more direct in their association of Howell and the early Rastafari with the events at Serge Island in January 1938. Campbell described the uprisings in 1938 as the revolt of the poor; he argues that 'though the Rastas did not play a central role in the rebellion, the idea of black consciousness...by the Rastas helped to instill confidence necessary to confront the British State' (1987, 81). Against this background, Campbell agrees with the idea that the event in St Thomas in January of 1938 set Jamaica ablaze with militant uprisings. He writes, 'It is not insignificant that the 100th anniversary of the abolition of slavery began with a workers' revolt in the parish of Paul Bogle...and in the largest concentration of Rastafarians...The rebellion in St Thomas set a pattern which was replicated throughout the length and breadth of Jamaica'(1987, 81).

The author's position regarding the association of black consciousness with confidence-building and a guide to act against the 'British State' was indeed a reasonable assessment of the event and the contribution of the awareness created by Howell and the early Rastafari in Jamaica and in Seaforth, St Thomas in particular.

Conclusion

Sherlock and Bennett (1998) note the importance of Norman Manley's and Alexander Bustamante's association with the rise of the new national society in Jamaica between 1938 and 1962; the writers also put emphasis on the events of May 1938 in Frome as the hallmark of the 1938 uprisings island-wide and the forerunner to the ensuing development on the waterfront in Kingston.

A few weeks after the uprising at Serge Island, Seaforth, the *Daily Gleaner* (2 February 1938) published a Commission Report on the 'labour' uprising led by Uriah Butler in Trinidad in 1937 which was rooted in a major dissatisfaction among the labourers given high increases in the cost of living and very low wages; in all, the sugar industry had shown a 'lack of regard for the well being of the labourers.' The Sugar Industry in the West Indies, according to the report, survived by paying exploitative wages in an environment within which the people throughout the West Indies lived in squalor. The Report on Trinidad was followed by another report on the general conditions in the West Indies as discussed by the members of the House of Lords; it was published in the *Daily Gleaner* (24 February 1938). The members of the House of Lords expressed grave concerns about the conditions in the West Indies while the British public was paying cheaply for sugar. For instance, Lord Oliver said that 'recent labour troubles in the West Indies were due to the fact that the British public did not pay enough for their sugar to enable decent wages to be paid for labour.'

The struggles of the peoples, from Trinidad to Serge Island, St Thomas were not just about wages, but were general struggles against exploitation, poverty and squalor, led by the lower class labourers. In the case of Serge Island, the struggle involved 'race matters.' In all cases the people were courageous; they put their lives on the line and were determined in pressing their cause. Michael Manley, in *A Voice at the Workplace*, writes that the country was never the same after 1938. For the first time the idea was rife that all men in the society had rights, since the workers – grass weeders, cutters, loaders, shop assistants, dock workers and factory hands – had little idea of their economic rights (1975,47–48). They existed at the pleasure of that system in which the employers had absolute rights. There was also a new awareness of human rights, economic rights, of self and the role of community organization that triumphed in 1938.

References

Austin-Broos, Diane. 1997. *Jamaica Genesis: Religion and the Politics of Moral Orders*. Kingston: Ian Randle Publishers.

Campbell, Horace. 1987. *Rasta and Resistance: From Marcus Garvey to Walter Rodney*. Trenton, NJ: Africa World Press.

Carnegie, Jimmy. 1973. *Some Aspects of Jamaican Politics, 1918–1938*. Kingston: Institute of Jamaica.

Hart, Richard. 1989. *Rise and Organise: The Birth of the Workers and National Movement in Jamaica*.

Hill, Robert A. 1981. Dread History: Leonard P. Howell and Millenarian Visions in Rastafari Religions in Jamaica. *EPOCHE- Journal of History of Religions at UCLA*. Vol. 9: 31–71.

Lee, Hélène. 2003/1999. *The First Rasta: Leonard Howell and the Rise of Rastafarianism*. Trans. Lily Davis and Hélène Lee. Chicago: Lawrence Hill Books.

Lewis, Gordon K. 1968. *The Growth of the Modern West Indies*. New York: Monthly Review Press. 2004. Reprint. Kingston: Ian Randle Publishers.

———. 1983. *Main Currents in Caribbean Thought*. Kingston: Heinmann Educational Books Caribbean Ltd.

Lindsay, Louis. 1978. Methodology and Change. Working Paper #14. Mona: Institute of Social and Economic Research.

Manley, Michael. 1975. *A Voice at the Workplace*. London: Andre Deutsch.

Maragh, G. G. 1988/1935. *The Promised Key*. Clarendon: Iyabinghi Press.

Phelps, O.W. 1960. Rise of the Labour Movement in Jamaica. *Social and Economic Studies*. Vol. 9:4, 22–35.

Post, Ken W. 1969. The Politics of Protest in Jamaica, 1938: Some Problems of Analysis and Conceptualization. *Social and Economic Studies*. Vol. 8 (1969): 374–90.

———. 1970. The Bible as Ideology. Reprint from *African Perspectives*, eds. C. H. Allen and R. W. Johnson. London: Cambridge University Press.

———. 1978. *Arise Ye Starvelings*. The Hague: Martinus Nijhoff.

———. 1981. *Strike the Iron*. The Hague: Humanities Press.

Sherlock, Philip and Hazel Bennett. 1998. *The Story of the Jamaican People*. Kingston: Ian Randle Publishers.

Simpson, George Eaton. 1985. Religion and Justice: Some reflections on the Rastafari Movement. *Phylon* Vol. XLVI:4, 286–90.

———. 1993. Some Reflections on the Rastafarian Movement: West Kingston in the Early 1950s. *Jamaica Journal* Vol. 25:2, 3–10.

Archival Sources

Constabulary Memo dated June 5 and 9, 1933 to Police in St James and St Elizabeth: look out notice for Leonard P. Howell. Sedition File Colonial Secretary's Office No. 1130. 1B/5/79. Jamaica Archives IB/5/79/87.

Letters written by Delrosa Francis, McNish, Patterson and other charged in the 4 August 1934 event in Seaforth CSO Minute Paper No 5073/31. Jamaica Archives IB/5/79/87.

Letter from Rachel Patterson to the Colonial Secretary, dated 3 September 1934. Jamaica Archives IB/5/79/87.

Legislative Council Proceedings, House of Parliament (Jamaica) Library. Spring, 27 June 1937, 716.

Report of Inspector W. C. Adams on Howell's Activities : letters from Mr Thomas; Minister M. C. Surgeon and Mr R. Robinson. CSO No. 1130. Jamaica Archives 1B/5/79

Report by Mr Barnes in Proceedings of Legislative Council of Jamaica. Spring Session. 23 June 1937, 716.

Report from Inspector General to the Colonial Secretary re: Police reports of Pocomania meeting in Cedar Valley, St Thomas. CSO Minute Paper No. 5073/34. Jamaica Archives 1B/5/79/642.

8 | *The 1930s Labour Rebellions in Barbados and Jamaica: Considering Violence and Leadership in Decolonization*

Maziki Thame

Caribbean mythology has constructed the personalities of African Barbadians and Jamaicans as polar opposites. It represents Jamaican slaves and by extension personality, as aggressive, unbreakable and violent and Barbadians as the counterpoint, the good, passive, civilized Negro. The contemporary states are similarly conceived. Jamaica is seen as violence-filled, close to the state of nature and ungovernable. Barbados on the other hand is perceived as a well-ordered, civilized, peaceful, idyllic isle, the exemplar for the region and even more far-reaching – the most well-governed black society on the globe. On the slave plantation, the European civilizing mission associated passivity with civility as a means of curtailing the behaviour of the African population, of ensuring their submissiveness. The logic of civilization said that the opposition of the slaves to their condition and their resort to violence were marks of their savagery. In the Barbadian case then, the discourse of civilization raises the reputation of the African but evokes and invokes their passivity. On the other hand, in the Jamaican case, the slave was not sufficiently transformed and is therefore perpetually inclined to violence, barbarity and ungovernability. I wish to explore the meaning of violence in the 1930s labour rebellions in Jamaica and Barbados and to suggest that in both cases, it was liberating, even in the context of expectations of their behaviours. This was so because, despite expectations, the moments were part of a Diasporic consciousness rooted in anti-colonialism and anti-racism. Despite this conclusion, it is clear that the labour riots did not result in decolonization, even while they set these nations on the path to independence. Decolonization here is taken as being meaningful both in the mindsets of people of African descent and in terms of the ordering of their material worlds. I also wish to reflect on the role of leadership in diminishing the capacity for decolonization, largely given that they were out of sync with the liberatory ethos of the labour riots.

Fanon on Violence in the Colonial Context: Lessons of 1937–38

For Frantz Fanon, violence is necessary to decolonization because colonialism embodied violence. The nature of this violence in the Caribbean colonial context was threefold: it involved physical violence against the oppressed; it was an oppression of the mind, particularly based in racism; and it included structural violence through the systematized exclusion and impoverishment of the masses of African descent. Indeed, in the Caribbean case, psycho-racial violence and economic deprivation served as major substitutes for overt violence.

Fanon's *Wretched of the Earth* (1963) is concerned with the psychoses of the colonial subject – how it is that the oppressed internalizes ideas about themselves and their inferiority, how they deal with their oppression and how the 'natives' may shed their inferiority complex. For this reason, the Fanonian project of emancipation involves both redemption of the mind and a reordering of the social world that justifies ideas of native inferiority. He says that these can be achieved through violence against the colonizer. Anti-colonial violence must therefore be understood as aimed not only at ridding the nation of the colonizer, but also at restoring the personhood of the colonized. If colonialism is depersonalizing, decolonization must involve reclaiming humanity. It is when the colonized becomes aware of his condition, when there is self-recognition, that he must arm himself in defence against the violence of the colonial situation. Fanon argues that psychological and physical liberation are intricately linked to the process of desubjugation and that violence is needed to undo the original violence that inflicted the alienation in the first place.[1] It is liberating at the individual level in that it frees 'the native of their inferiority complex, despair and inaction and makes them fearless and restores self respect'[2] and hence reverses colonialism's assumptions about the native as childlike and submissive.[3] How do we understand the absences and presence of violence in the process of creating independence in Jamaica and Barbados, particularly in the context of the identity constructs I begin with?

To begin from the assumptions of 'Barbadianness' and 'Jamaicanness,' the violence of the 1937 labour riots of Barbados should be seen as an anomaly, having no bearing on the manner in which the African would seek to free himself from oppression. Further, since he was civilized, or at least more capable of civilization that his Caribbean neighbours, his condition required no special attention. Clearly this was not the case in Barbados in the colonial years. Of essence then are the questions, why did violence occur in 1937 and what did it mean for the process of decolonization? In the Jamaican case, not only would violence be expected, we can assume that since the Jamaicans were already inclined to violence and barbarity, the formula that Fanon poses had no relevance to explaining their condition in terms of its potential for revolutionary change.

According to Louis Lindsay, true independence did not come in Jamaica because there was neither struggle nor mobilization for independence.[4] I would argue, that while decolonization was not the specific aim of the rioters in the 1937/1938 labour riots in Barbados and Jamaica respectively, they were anti-colonial moments and further, represented creation moments – the foundations of independence in Jamaica and Barbados. In the Fanonian context of praxis, the fact of violence perpetrated against the system constitutes an aspect of the process of liberation. If decolonization occurs on the level of being, if what is at stake is the minds of the colonized, the uprisings of 1937 and 1938 can be read as a departure from the expectations of paralysis and deference towards white authority in the period, even in the Jamaican case. The potential of those moments was however problematic on two levels: the underdeveloped consciousness of the masses and the character of the leadership that emerged.

Considering the Meaning of Violence in Barbados in 1937

The 1937 labour riots were momentous in Barbados specifically because the entire population was supposedly committed to upholding the characterization of African Barbadians as passive. Presumably, the civilizing mission had been a complete success and when in 1937 ex-slaves challenged the plantocracy, both African and European Barbadians claimed to be in shock. The Governor was of the view that the entire country wholeheartedly condemned and deplored the disturbances.[5] So convinced were whites of the obedience of the African Barbadian that they ignored the Governor's pleas for an improvement in the conditions of the workers and his concern regarding the establishment of Universal Negro Improvement Association (UNIA) divisions following the return of First World War veterans in 1919. Similarly, despite police surveillance of the Garveyite activist Clement Payne, they did nothing to curtail his movements.[6] According to W. A. Beckles, 'the lid was blown off before a shocked and dumbfounded community.' He says it was even more surprising because it occurred in 1937, the year of coronation, when 'Barbados patted herself on the back on possessing possibly the most law-abiding and the most peace-loving people in the world.'[7]

The riots therefore seemed to represent a break with traditions of passivity. I wish to pause here on the idea of Barbadian passivity. I would argue that it should not be taken as conclusive. Indeed, in 1923, the Governor of Barbados, reflecting on the UNIA chapters there, claimed that, 'the Barbadians are generally a quiet well-behaved body of men, but they are very excitable and easily roused.'[8] Barbadian passivity must be seen as partly predicated on fear inclusive of the threat of violence against Africans. George Belle compares the response of the Barbadian state to the rioters with the riots in Jamaica in 1938 and highlights that while the strikes in Jamaica lasted two and a half weeks and killed eight persons, the two-day[9] strike in Barbados left 14 dead.[10] A further example of the resolve of the authorities in putting down the riots is highlighted by David Browne. He points out that when a crowd at the African Methodist Episcopal Church at Collymore Road readied themselves with stones for battle, 'the police fired at the crowd near the church until they ran out of ammunition.'[11] Official reports say that other than the 14 dead at the end of the riots, 21 were injured and hundreds awaited trial for their involvement, but according to Cecil Gutzmore, the official records may be a gross underestimation of the numbers dead and injured. He points to the travel logs of Keith and Jefferson Bowan, representatives from Trinidad who were involved in putting down the riots. They indicate that 1,800 bullets were fired by reserves. This represents a major discrepancy between those figures and the numbers dead and wounded.[12] The fears of the African population also has to be appreciated in the context of the powers of whites over the fate of blacks. As a settler colony, the white community had more at stake than elsewhere in the region and for that reason put in place greater measures to keep Barbadian blacks at their mercy. According to Hilary Beckles, Barbados was the only colony where planters used wage reductions to increase profitability.[13] Workers were also unable to take advantage of opportunities abroad given restrictions on emigration, faced heavy rents for small plots of land next to the plantation, where they were forced to work in exchange for land rental, and were 'barred in all efforts to achieve a meaningful emancipation.'[14] Further, the geography of Barbados aided in the control of the population. Perpetrators of offences were easily identifiable because there was nowhere to hide in its relatively flat landscape.

Fear is of concern to Fanon. It is this fear of the colonizer and the settler that he wished the native (here taken as the colonized) to shed. The labour riots and its violence have to therefore be seen as important. Barbadians' attitudes to violence are ambiguous. They are not strictly given to docility as myths about their passivity propound. Clues about Barbadian attitudes to violence are reflected in the fact that, when given the opportunity, that is, when they believe they will not be caught, when the geography permits, Barbadians exercise violence. In fact, Barbadians developed a reputation as badjohns/ruffians in the rest of the Caribbean for their ferociousness and skill in stick fighting.[15] They also developed a reputation for misbehaving once they left Barbados, once they gained space. Bonham Richardson advises that in the early twentieth century, 'when some of these "good" Barbadian workers travelled to British Guiana for seasonal cane harvests, they were often identified as troublemakers.'[16]

The year 1937 may have been perceived as an opportunity, as a creation of space because in the confusion of the moment, there was room for cover. It is very plausible therefore that the community was not shocked when violence broke out in 1937 and that they wilfully misled the Deane Commission in order to maintain the reputation of Afro-Barbadians as civilized and to diminish the punishment to be meted out in the aftermath. At the same time, there remained an overriding deference to whites and commitment to ideas about Barbadian civilization that would have informed Barbadian blacks. Barbadian construction of memory around the riots illuminates the extent to which Barbadians wished to reproduce ideas of themselves as good Negroes. The fact of Clement Payne's belated acclaim for his contribution to the nation has to be seen against the memory of the riots. Beckles points out that the riots were presented as a mistake, an act of political vandalism, a riot by rabble-rousers and social misfits. He argues further that Barbadians have apologized for the event, which inspired in 1937 and today, feelings of shame and guilt.[17] Belle notes that opposition to the riots and the rebel forces built up even before they were expended.[18] Some workers armed themselves to defend white planters and they quickly returned to the plantations with little or no improvement in conditions. In that vein, Belle suggests that despite their rising consciousness, Payne would not have had success over the eventual 'hero' of the day, Grantley Adams, because of the conservatism of the working class.[19] It may be surmised that while they were roused by Payne, they were also fearful of him. This ambiguity led one of the informants to the Deane Commission, Herbert Bourne, to declare that Payne was too advanced for Barbados, 'he wanted us to do something drastic.'[20] On the other hand, Adams was pleasing not only to the Colonial Office but also to the mass and subsequently became the spokesman for the people.

If there were expectations of passivity, what was different about 1937? Belle argues that emphasis on economic factors in explaining the riots is misplaced. He points out that though the Deane Commission stressed economic motivations for the riots, this was not an adequate reading of the situation since Barbadians had been living under perpetual and severe deprivation and rarely revolted. Belle accredited the riots to a consciousness imparted through Clement Payne and hence they amounted to revolts of the mind rather than spontaneous responses to economic hardship.[21] Payne was able to build on a consciousness already in Barbados. According to Bill Schwarz, the presence of Garveyism was decisive. He notes that throughout the 1920s, there were many hundreds of Garveyite activists and when Payne arrived in Barbados in March 1937, they became his allies.[22] He argues further, that from March onward, Payne and other agitators articulated popular discontent, elevating what had been an inchoate mood into a codified public voice. The movement identified its enemy as the traditional white plantocracy.[23] Race was central to their consciousness but not all whites were targeted, rather white racism was the target. Rioters were selective in their attacks against agents of oppression. While they waged war against most businesses on Broad Street, the hub of commercial activity of the merchant/planter class, they avoided businesses such as Fogarty store, known as a bargain centre for blacks and among the only stores to extend credit to them.[24]

Racial consciousness was, like elsewhere in the African Diaspora, inspired by events in Ethiopia. Schwarz indicates that 'in Barbados, when news of the invasion of Ethiopia reached the island, mass prayer meetings were organized.'[25] Grantley Adams agreed in his testimony to the Deane Commission, that racial consciousness informed the mass. He noted that the Abyssinian War had a great deal to do with the riots and proclaimed that it was the first time he saw people beginning to talk of white against black.[26] Similarly, one of the respondents to the Commission, Roland Edwards, said that the rioting was inspired by 'racial prejudice and oppression of the poor,'[27] an indication that a racial and class consciousness had played out in the actions of the Barbadians.

Jamaica: Contradictory Consciousness and a Spoiled Rebellion

The resort to violence as a response to problems with the management at Frome was not out of sync with a history of violent uprising against the oppressive conditions of work and living in slavery and colonialism. Nonetheless, Jamaicans too toiled under desperate working conditions and lived in desperate times without engaging in sustained violence against the colonial state. Consequently, according to Ken Post, the 1938 labour rebellions in Jamaica were sudden. He argues that they were also total, when 'between May 23 and 31, 1938 the social order was shaken by a full scale rising of the black masses.'[28] Post's assertion indicates the potential of the black population for violence but not any automatic predisposition for it. It was not out of character with the Jamaican personality that even while the workers gained reputations of militancy, the riots did not lead to the creation of liberation armies destined to free the nation from colonial domination. Nonetheless, they were inspired by anti-colonial and racial feeling.

At the May 3 demonstrations, following from and in support of the workers at Frome, in response to St William Grant's appeals for calm, the workers angrily shouted 'down with imperialism.'[29] They associated their conditions with a global system of racial oppression and companies like Tate and Lyle were seen as representatives of the system. When asked about their feelings on Tate and Lyle, workers indicated that they saw them as agents of low wages, who employed discriminatory practices against blacks. According to a stenographer interviewed, 'they are hiring Europeans to do jobs of consequence. To my mind, they are an octopus trying to get everything out of Jamaica and they do not want to employ coloured Jamaicans at decent salaries.'[30] Even while they held ideas about a benevolent Crown, they understood the collaboration between local and metropolitan whites. An editorial in *Public Opinion*, in response to the Frome riots, argued that the state was an employers' state since 'every weekend labourers are defrauded of their pay and no bullets fly on their account.'[31]

In Jamaica, the riots had as a core element a race consciousness that explained reality through coloured lenses and pointed to the experience of slavery and a thwarted emancipation. Among the problems giving rise to the riots was that of limited access to land. The peasantry was encouraged by the belief that after emancipation planters had been allowed to maintain their holdings only by lease from the Crown for a hundred years at which point lands were to revert to descendants of slaves.[32] The centenary had arrived. In the post-emancipation period, ex-slaves were able to carve out space for themselves mainly through squatting and farming on Crown lands. This created not merely economic space, but mental space that was not as evident in Barbados. To a degree free of the control of local whites, black Jamaicans had greater room for economic and mental liberation, even while the colonial state and the church continued to teach attitudes of submissiveness to whites and whiteness. In the 1930s, however, land ownership was steadily declining and there was an increase in rural tenantry. Room to manoeuvre was increasingly diminished and the feeling that emancipation was unfulfilled, great.

A view of the worker's consciousness is proposed in a *Public Opinion* article, which states:

> a hundred years ago Jamaican slaves were freed. A hundred years later they feel that their freedom is a mockery…They notice that for white residents and tourists, life in Jamaica is as delightful as human life will ever be anywhere. But they themselves see all these joys from the outside…Labourers toil from dawn to late evening to secure a wage on which they cannot live…Kingston slums yield in point of foulness to none in the world, on certain sugar estates whole communities of workers live in huts like dog-kennels, some have even sold their roof coverings to pay their taxes.[33]

Blacks' increasing assertiveness was noted by a visitor to the island in 1938. Mrs Charlotte Cameron commented to the *London Star* that, 'the Kingston Negro is insolent. He thinks he is as good as any white man and he is convinced that Jamaica belongs to him and not to us.'[34] According to Obika Gray, the movements occurring among workers at this time had the potential for a radical anti-colonial movement that could demand a break with the British Empire. At the same time, he argues that though peasants were inclined towards anti-colonial consciousness and activity,

> other influences disposed them neither to revolt nor to develop a coherent oppositional ideology. Slavery and colonialism had produced a peasantry whose psychic structure was riddled with mutually contradictory impulses. Thus, in addition to producing a rebellious peasant, slavery and colonialism also produced a figure victimized by inhibiting beliefs and self suppressive sentiments.[35]

Similarly, Post argues that the contradiction of 1938 was that black Jamaicans, 'in a mood of self-deprecation, often expressed the dominant views on race.'[36] There was an urge therefore to seek good graces from whites as expressed for instance at Frome, when a 'rustic hero,' Rufus Jones, saved the general manager and office staff of the plantation from the armed workers storming the offices by hiding them under barrels.[37] Even while Garveyite ideas affected how African Jamaicans explained their poverty, Post argues that the image of quashie continued to be projected on poor blacks, was accepted by them and they also expressed preference for browns.[38] These attitudes accommodated the rise of the light-complexioned Alexander Bustamante and Norman Manley and affected the extent to which the unrest of the late 1930s could directly attempt to change the social order.

The challenge of 1938 did not lead to an agenda to reorder society in the interest of blacks. The strikes did not throw up accepted black leaders who could develop that agenda and therefore had no far-reaching effects in that regard. Rather, browns emerged from the strikes with programmes for the future of the nation. Brown collaboration with whites began to be institutionalized during this period, with the main effect of securing white wealth and the future of browns in the politics of the nation. They served as the buffer between the mass of the Jamaican population and the white economic and political elite.

The Matter of Leadership

If the labour riots had revolutionary potential, why did they fail to reorder the nation and the minds of the colonized? The answer, I believe, rests partly in the character of the leadership that emerged. Fanon prophesied the response of colonial intellectuals and leaders to the outbreak of violence in their midst. He advanced that 'the elites and nationalist bourgeois parties will be seen rushing to the colonialists to exclaim, "this is serious! We do not know how it will end; we must find a solution – some sort of compromise."'[39] Brown and white reaction to the strikes in Jamaica, as with whites and the black middle class in Barbados, coincided in their desire for a swift return to normalcy. The emerging leadership eschewed revolutionary violence and its potential to reorder the world but not violence itself, since it later became the means of partisan mobilization. Leadership acted as agents of the authorities in their mediation to quell the rebellions,[40] doing their utmost to stop strikes where they arose. They expected the workers to depend on them as buffers rather than take independent action. They especially condemned strikes when they included any pretensions to violence. There was no consideration of the potential of violence as a strategy against colonialism or how it could be mobilized in the interest of the mass. While Manley pledged himself to advocate the workers' cause he did so on the condition that they curtail their behaviour. In response to the May 23 and 24 riots he declared:

> while every person in Jamaica who belongs to it and believes in this country's future and must realise that it is putting the clock to progress backward, nevertheless if legitimate labour grievances are to result not in the putting forward of a proper case for their remedy but in creating complete confusion and disorder endangering innocent people's lives, destroying property and compelling government to call out armed forces, a thing which every Jamaican must see with the greatest sense of regret, the fact remains that what is wanted is training and leadership and responsible assistance. The workers themselves will have to recognise that what they have been told before…the putting of garbage tins in the streets, pulling out of trees, the smashing of windows and being shot at and killed is not going to give them better wages or better hours or better conditions of employment. It has been rumoured that I have advised the activities of the past four days. It is sufficient to

say that nobody who knows me would possibly believe that I could think that Jamaica's interest would be served by letting loose the irresponsible pandemonium of the past two days....[41]

Similarly, Bustamante sought to de-emphasize revolutionary thought and action by the workers. He is remembered by Frank Scott as proposing instead of Garveyism, a revolution in the thinking of the workers so that the discipline under which they existed in slavery could be converted to their advantage: a theory not entirely removed from his 1938 call to the workers that only if they demonstrated discipline and restraint in a mental revolution could he successfully espouse their cause.[42]

Throughout the riots, Bustamante turned up 'as soon as violence escalated to preach' this message.[43]

In Barbados, Grantley Adams saw his duty as labour leader to keep the workers in check seeing the right to strike as stupid and criminal.[44] Adams entered into a politics of accommodation and alliance with the government and merchant and planter class, condemning future strikes led by the Garveyite Herbert Seale. His alliance with white Barbadians was part of an alliance with the larger project of global white supremacy. Adams' view of whites was consistent with his view that colonialism was a benevolent force. According to his Permanent Secretary of many years, he 'had the greatest respect for white people, for what they had done for Barbados.'[45] If Adams could not see the problematic of white power, he could not be expected to seek to challenge it. In 1948, at the United Nations General Assembly, Adams advanced the idea that:

> colonial exploitation is a thing of the past...there may have been a time when colonialism was synonymous with exploitation. There was undoubtedly such a time. But today we are living in the twentieth century...[S]peaking therefore on behalf of the people of the British colonial empire I reject categorically the notion that the outlook for us is one of grim relentless struggle for freedom against reactionary colonial oppressors.[46]

Like Grantley Adams, Bustamante did not oppose colonialism nor did he oppose the white oligarchy. Instead, he saw himself as a potential Governor under the Crown Colony system. Further, according to Richard Hart, the contradiction of Bustamante's leadership of the labour movement was his involvement with the capitalist project and his collaboration with the white capitalist elite. Hart points out that as a moneylender in the period before his ascension to leadership, Bustamante taxed creditors (workers) up to 260 per cent interest per annum and often lent on behalf of Charley Johnson, one of the founders of the Jamaica Fruit and Shipping Company.[47] While he discontinued his money lending as labour leader, he did not do so immediately.[48] Sugar manufacturers and big planters felt that Bustamante would have been amenable to inducements and be disposed to take their interests into account and as a result they supported his bid for leadership in the 1944 elections. Harold Lindo, owner of the Bybrook Sugar Estate in St Catherine and agent of British motor cars in Jamaica was influential in persuading his peers to support Bustamante.[49] Bustamante saw his role as somehow balancing capitalism with the workers' needs. In a letter to the Executive Committee of the Jamaica Workers and Tradesmen Union (JWTU), Bustamante asserted that his 'desire [was] not alone justice to the workers but justice and fair treatment towards capitalists.'[50] In addition to their efforts to temper the workers' behaviour, was the question of the leadership's commitment to the white supremacist colonial project. Manley and his People's National Party (PNP) had a more advanced view of self-government and sought independence but under pressure from the popularity of Bustamante and his assertion that self-government would mean brown man rule, they retreated from this position. There was some truth to Bustamante's assertion that the PNP most represented this group and saw themselves as natural rulers of Jamaica. Their competition with Bustamante and involvement in electoral politics pushed an even greater conservatism in that the PNP sought to diminish its association with any forms of radicalism, eventually expelling leftists from its core. Further, the PNP had the utmost respect for British constitutionalism and British culture which they felt underlined their own sense of Jamaicanness.[51]

Conclusion

The labour riots were defining moments in the history of the Caribbean, but what did they mark? The most important development following the riots was the move for greater involvement of the whole nation in the processes of governance. However, the revolutionary potential of the riots was undermined by leadership's attempt to restore order and in effect also, the status quo. The new 'nationalist' leadership achieved the workers' return to relative passivity after the 1940s. They sought to quell the workers into obedience and ushered them into a process of decolonization that did not seek to reorder the nation or deconstruct coloniality and slavery's ideation systems. The mass of African descendants continued to experience desperate conditions and the society's colour complexes remained firmly in place. While the leadership was not revolutionary, it is also important that they were able to draw on the people's inclination to submissiveness to white authority and a lack of faith in their self-redemptive capacities. These are the qualities that they sought to manipulate.

The agenda of decolonization became one in which white rulers would be substituted by brown ones in Jamaica and by the black middle class in Barbados. While changes would occur on the political stage, the economic power structure would remain intact. Indeed, when independence was achieved, as prophesied by Fanon, the new leadership merely replaced colonial authority. In Jamaica, independence concretized the transfer of the nation from white British rule to 'brownman government.' In Barbados, space was created for the emergence to leadership of sections of the black middle class but in a compromise of fateful dimensions, whites were allowed to maintain their control over the economy. In fact, this became the character of a lasting compromise between blacks and whites in Barbados that may have occurred as a result of a belief that it was impossible to unseat white power. At the same time, there were benefits for blacks in the economic arrangement in that the resources of the state were used to make provisions for free education, health care and other social services.

What are the lessons in relation to the question of violence? While the labour riots were important moments, particularly in the confidence displayed in raising arms against white authority, how far could this take blacks in effecting meaningful emancipation? The nationalists did not follow on the bid to remove colonial and white authority in the two nations under consideration and as a result independence did not come until over 20 years hence. Even in the fact of independence, Lindsay reminds us that this did not mean that these nations were decolonized. Should we consider violence in its destructive sense as contradictory to the process of restoring personhood? While it may have use in curtailing the powers of the offending force, the work of reordering the mind must involve another process of detoxifying the individual of violence. Indeed Fanon is aware of this and speaks to the need for reconciliation in the aftermath of revolution. This process of reconciliation only came to the agenda in the post-colonial era. It came to Barbados in what I would argue was a failed attempt by the state at airing racial grievances through its Committee for Reconciliation in 2005, without any attendant programme for reordering the social world of the racial state. In the Jamaican case, reconciliation has come in terms of projects of self-repair, through Black Power, Rastafari and the recuperative forces of the cultural domain, through especially reggae and dancehall. Seeing these processes as reconciliatory may be optimistic since they have not had success in treating with social fissures and high levels of horizontal violence among the poor. Indeed, the nation has turned in on itself.[52] Nevertheless, Jamaicans have sought to establish for themselves spaces of freedom that challenge racial stereotypes that sought to subjugate Africans even while there are contemporary reversals in their efforts at self-repair. This project of decolonization occurs on the Fanonian level of being. In the case of Barbados, this project has faced significant challenges and will surely re-emerge in the collective consciousness.

Notes

1. Alice Cherki, *Frantz Fanon: A Portait*, trans. Nadia Benadid (Ithaca: Cornell University Press) 2008, 174.
2. Frantz Fanon, *The Wretched of the Earth* (Presence Africaine, 1963), 73.
3. For a companion discussion, see Maziki Thame, 'Reading Violence and Post-colonial Decolonization Through Fanon: The Case of Jamaica,' *Journal of Pan-African Studies*, Special Issue: 'Veneration and Struggle - Commemorating Frantz Fanon, Vol. 4, no. 7, 2011, 83.
4. Louis Lindsay, *The Myth of a Civilizing Mission: British Colonialism and the Politics of Symbolic Manipulation* (Kingston: ISER, 1981).
5. Barbados Archives, Legislative Council Debates, Vol 49., 3 August 1937.
6. David Browne, 'The Rumblings of a Social Volcano: Precursors to the Disturbances in Barbados,' *Bulletin of Eastern Caribbean Affairs* 21. 1 (1996): 10–11, 13–14.
7. W.A. Beckles, *The Barbados Disturbances, 1937* (Advocate News, 1937), i.
8. Governor Charles Bain to Secretary of State, Colonial Office, 16 January 1923. Cited in Tony Martin, *Race First: The Ideological and Organizational Struggles of the Universal Negro Improvement Association* (USA: First Majority Press, 1986), 50.

9. David Browne argues that the rebellion should be seen as lasting for 2 weeks given a general climate of industrial upheavals between July 26 and August 9. Browne, 'The 1937 Disturbances and Barbadian Nationalism' in *The Empowering Impulse: The Nationalist Tradition of Barbados*, ed. Glenford Howe and Don Marshall (Kingston: Canoe Press, 2001), 160–61.
10. George Belle, 'The Struggle for Political Democracy: The 1937 Riots' in *Emancipation III: Aspects of the Post Slavery Experience in Barbados*, ed. Woodville Marshall (Kingston: Misutose Printery, 1987), 82–83.
11. Cited in Browne, '1937 Disturbances,' 154.
12. Cecil Gutzmore, *Gossip as Evidence in Two British Colonial Hammerings: An Exploration and Comparison of Responses to the Morant Bay (1865) and Barbados (1937) Uprisings*. Paper Presented at the Richard Hart Conference, UWI, Mona, 8–10 June 2006.
13. Hilary Beckles, *Chattel House Blues: Making of a Democratic Society in Barbados, From Clement Payne to Owen Arthur* (Kingston: Ian Randle Publishers, 2004) 1.
14. Ibid., 5–6.
15. Examined in Elton Elombe Mottley, 'Cover Down Yuh Bucket: The Story of Bajan Stick-licking,' unpublished ms., 2004.
16. Bonham Richardson, 'The Impact of Panama Money in Barbados in the Early 20th Century,' *New West Indian Guide* 59.1, 2 (1985), 5.
17. Beckles, 157–58.
18. George Belle, *The Political Economy of Barbados, 1937–1946, 1966–1972* (MA thesis, 1974), 74.
19. Ibid., 72.
20. Report of the Commission Appointed to Enquire into the Disturbances which took place in Barbados on the 29th July 1937 and Subsequent Days, in W.A. Beckles, 1.
21. Belle, 'Struggle for Political Democracy,' 21, 63.
22. Bill Schwarz, 'C.L.R. James and George Lamming: The Measure of Historical Time,' *Small Axe* 14 (2003), 48.
23. Ibid., 55.
24. Browne, '1937 Disturbances,'151.
25. Schwarz, 48.
26. Testimony of Grantley Adams to the Commission, in W.A. Beckles, 4.
27. Ibid., 9.
28. Trevor Munroe, *The Politics of Constitutional Decolonisation: Jamaica, 1944–62* (Kingston: ISER, 1972), 21.
29. 'Hundreds of Men and Women Stage Demonstrations in City Yesterday Forenoon,' *Daily Gleaner*, 4 May 1938.
30. Our Enquiring Reporter, 'What are the Reactions in Westmoreland to Messrs Tate and Lyle's Advent Here,' *Public Opinion*, 23 April 1938.
31. 'A More Forceful and Practical Leadership of the Middle Classes is Necessary if we are to Prevent Worse Things than the Frome Riots,' *Public Opinion*, 7 May 1938.
32. Abigail Bakan, *Ideology and Class Conflict in Jamaica: The Politics of Rebellion* (Montreal & London: McGill-Queens University Press, 1990), 119.
33. 'Why There is Trouble in Jamaica,' *Public Opinion*, 9 July 1938.
34. The Philosopher, 'Views the Passing Show,' *Public Opinion*, 7 May 1938.

35. Obika Gray, *Radicalism and Social Change in Jamaica, 1960–1972* (USA: University of Tennessee Press, 1991), 21.
36. Ken Post, *Strike the Iron – A Colony at War: Jamaica 1939–1945*, Vol. 1 (The Hague: Institute of Social Studies, 1981), 41.
37. 'Rufus Jones Tact: Barrels Saved Their Lives! How a Rustic Hero Saved the General Manager and Office Staff,' *Daily Gleaner*, 4 May 1938.
38. Ken Post, *Arise Ye Starvelings: The Jamaican Labour Rebellion of 1938 and its Aftermath*, (The Hague: Martinus Nijhoff, 1978), 144.
39. Fanon, 49.
40. Ken Post, 'The Politics of Protest in Jamaica, 1938: Some Problems of Analysis and Conceptualisation,' *Social and Economic Studies* 18. 1 (1969), 381.
41. Manley Pledges Himself to Advocate Labourers' Cause,' *Daily Gleaner*, 25 May 1938.
42. B. St J. Hamilton, *Bustamante: Anthology of a Hero* (Kingston: Times Printery Ltd, 1978), 8.
43. Ibid., 22.
44. Belle, *Political Economy*, 76.
45. Sir Donald Wiles, Adams' Permanent Secretary for many years makes this claim. Cited in Karl Watson, 'Sir Grantley Adams as Seen by Others: Oral Histories of the Private Man' in *The Empowering Impulse: The Nationalist Tradition of Barbados*, ed. Glenford Howe and Don Marshall (Kingston: Canoe Press, 2001), 189.
46. Cited in Horace Campbell and Rodney Worrell, *Pan-Africanism, Pan-Africanists, and African Liberation in the 21st Century* (USA: New Academia Publishing, 2006), 104.
47. Richard Hart, *Towards Decolonisation: Political, Labour and Economic development in Jamaica, 1938–1945* (Kingston: Canoe Press, 1999), xiii.
48. Ibid., xiv.
49. Ibid., 299.
50. Letter to the JWTU Executive Committee, 15 October 1937. B. St J. Hamilton, *Bustamante: Anthology of a Hero* (Kingston: Times Printery Ltd, 1978), 27–29.
51. For a discussion, see Lindsay's *Myth*.
52. For a discussion of contemporary violence in Jamaica, see Thame, 'Reading Violence', 75-93.

9 | The Early Political History of Wilfred A. Domingo, 1919–39

Margaret Stevens

This chapter traces the intellectual history of Wilfred A. Domingo's political development for several reasons. First, Domingo's own politicization in the interwar period circulates between Kingston and Harlem, reflecting the fluid and indeed reciprocal process that so many black radicals and Marxists experienced during these years from 1919–39. New archival evidence on the history of Domingo's pre-Second World War activism suggests that there are larger questions about the interplay between black transnational radicalism and Bolshevism in the region that spans the Caribbean and New York City which in fact forms the basis for much of the global anti-colonial upheaval that emerges during and after the Second World War.

Second, the history of Domingo's transnational political development uncovers a whole series of networks of Caribbean diasporic figures and organizations, of 'race men' and 'organization men,' whose politicization was inextricably linked with the actions, motivations and undertakings of one another as well as with those of the Third International then headquartered in Moscow. Many of these same figures identified with the cause of Bolshevism, much like Domingo. Indeed, his correspondence with Jamaican Marxist and labour organizer Richard Hart illustrates the extent to which both men, while non-card carrying Reds, both supported the Soviet Union, and both placed the political and economic empowerment of the Jamaican 'mass' at the forefront of their activism. If Domingo was very important to Hart's early political development, and Hart remains iconic in Jamaican radical history, then Domingo's influence indeed comes full circle and returns to Jamaica itself.

Domingo and the Jamaican Movement for Self-Government, 1910–17

Born in Kingston, Jamaica on 11 November 1889, Wilfred A. Domingo came of age in the early 1900s in the wake of a movement for self-government in Jamaica that challenged the hegemony of British political and economic domination over the island. In short, local intellectuals and activists were engaged in a struggle to determine the extent to which the British would control the internal political affairs of the island. In this context other islands in the British West Indies, such as Grenada under the leadership of T.A. Marryshow, were also instrumental in leading movements for self-government. As a young radical student in Jamaica, Domingo would join a similar movement in Jamaica under the leadership of S.A.G. Cox called the National Club. This anti-colonial movement against the British Empire, however, was not confined to the West Indies alone. On a larger scale, this was a process that challenged the entire empire and included movements from Ireland and India, chiefly. In the West Indian context this movement, took on a racial character defined by black subjects in opposition to their white colonial authorities and the 'mother' country herself but, taken in conjunction with the Irish and Indian struggles, anti-colonialism within the Empire crossed racial boundaries in a unified struggle. The internationalist dimension of this struggle, crossing racial lines, was to become a chief basis for Domingo's long-term commitment to socialism in the years to come.

Thus Domingo began his activist career as an anti-colonial – though not distinctly anti-capitalist – champion. His relatively middle class family upbringing notwithstanding, Domingo evinced a strong tendency toward organic intellectualism with his grassroots advocacy for the 'struggling mass.' Notably, he embarked on this anti-colonial journey with a quintessential organic intellectual, Marcus Garvey – Jamaican compatriot and imminent founder of what would soon become the largest international organization of black people in human history: the Universal Negro Improvement Association. Domingo utilized a relatively advanced formal education that was denied to the majority of his fellow black brethren on the island in order to co-write with Garvey 'The Struggling Mass,' a pamphlet espousing the cause of Jamaican self-government that was put forward by Cox. On Domingo's account it was a pamphlet that, 'in a sense, we both wrote in Kingston and he [Garvey] published.'[1]

But Garvey's independent publication of the pamphlet in 1910 rendered him the ostensible sole author. This certainly helped to propel Garvey forward as an up-and-coming anti-colonial leader of the mass black population in Jamaica. Domingo's ghostwriter status as the unnamed co-author suggests that he might have differed from Garvey around the notion of cult-of-personality leadership. The former did not insist upon casting his name into the political spotlight even though his political wits – at a minimum – matched those of the latter.

Domingo's political activism in Jamaica abated when he was prematurely orphaned and left under the supervision of his uncle. His uncle finally secured Domingo's passage to Boston, Massachusetts in 1910 where he stayed in his older sister's boarding school for Jamaican youth. Upon arriving in the United States Domingo brought with him the typical 'American dream' of social mobility evident in his goal to pursue medical school.[2] Yet, like so many black youth, US and foreign-born alike, he awakened to the American nightmare of Jim Crow racism that made such high hopes little more than pipe dreams. With his goal of becoming a doctor unfulfilled in Boston, he headed to New York City in 1912.

Domingo took to networking with Harlem's burgeoning black radical population and commenced with the cause of Jamaican self-government. On 25 July 1917, Domingo was one of seven members to found the British-Jamaicans Benevolent Association (JBA), an organization apparently based out of New York City which advocated universal adult suffrage, civil service reform, free labour unions and political self-government. In 1922 it became incorporated in the State of New York, and its membership by then had grown to include Reverend Ethelred Brown, a Unitarian who arrived in Harlem post-First World War and later became a paid organizer for the Socialist Party.[3] The JBA's early goals anticipated, if not precipitated, those of the Jamaica Progressive League nearly 20 years later which was based out of Harlem, also advocated for Jamaican self-government, and was partially founded by the stalwart radicals Brown and Domingo.

While the JBA was in the process of formation, Garvey and Domingo had sustained their comradeship across the Atlantic. Domingo was working concurrently with Garvey who was building his UNIA forces in Kingston and fast expanding throughout the Caribbean region. In 1916 Garvey had written to and immediately sought out Domingo when he arrived in Harlem to begin the work of building the UNIA in the United States. Domingo introduced him to local radical black leaders such as Hubert Harrison and supported Garvey in his earliest appearances as a public speaker at Liberty Hall in the Harlem scene, even though Domingo privately dismissed 'the amount [of] horn tooting and tom-tom beating that had preceded' one of 'the most amusing [memories] that I have ever seen,' after observing Garvey speak in Harlem.[4]

Domingo in Hubert Harrison's Harlem

If Domingo was poised to help lead the anti-colonial movement for Jamaica from his Harlem base, then his foundation in this new land was cemented by his ties to Hubert Harrison, the leading 'New Negro' in Harlem. Domingo's efforts to thwart colonial domination were to join forces with the movement to overturn Jim Crow in the United States. Hubert Harrison, the pre-eminent 'New Negro' responsible for this US-based politicization of Domingo and many other aspiring young black radicals in Harlem, was also an immigrant from the Caribbean – St Croix of the Danish West Indies – and therefore he could serve as 'glue' to conjoin these struggles.

However, Harrison's own political development, which took him from leading member of the Socialist Party (1911–14) to founder of Liberty League in 1917, was primarily grounded in his interests of advancing the cause of African American labourers suffering from racial discrimination and melding this with the trade union and Socialist labour movements. Therefore there were two streams of Harrison's political praxis which impacted the political development of Domingo and other young black radicals in Harlem: a class-based critique of the capitalist economic system that sought to deny workers the 'fruits of their labour;' and a race-based critique of institutions and organizations – Black, White or Red – that relegated the cause of black people's social and economic uplift to the periphery or 'talented tenth.'

Domingo's relationship with Harrison was also important because his political tutelage was under someone who was at one time an avid Socialist Party (SP) member but later defected, a trajectory which Domingo himself would mirror. Perhaps Domingo's scepticism of political organizations in general and parties with white radicals in particular was at least initially influenced by Harrison who was of this same persuasion.

Though Harrison founded the Liberty League in Harlem, it was Garvey who harnessed the energy generated from Harrison's political teachings and the general atmosphere of Black discontent with Jim Crow discrimination, all of which Garvey channelled into the creation of the UNIA in the United States. Domingo observes that, 'Garvey came at the psychological moment. There had been the East St Louis riot, he visited the scene and then came back here. However, before him there was Hubert Harrison. He was a brilliant man, a great intellectual, a Socialist and highly respected. Garvey like the rest of us followed Hubert Harrison.'[5] Though the exact chronology is unclear, it was during the first half of 1917 when Domingo not only helped co-found the JBA, but was also active within the Liberty League itself. And yet, only months later, another world-historical movement would arrive on the scene to expand Domingo's horizon of what was possible in terms of anti-colonial and class emancipation: the Bolshevik Revolution in Russia.

Whither the 'New Negroes'? Domingo and the Garveyite/Bolshevik Matrix

In 1917 Wilfred Domingo elected to join the Socialist Party. Domingo had a particular affinity for the Russian Bolsheviks who, in his eyes, were the first class-based litmus test for abating colonialism. In short, he subscribed to the political theory of socialism and – at some point in the post-First World War period – became an actual member of the Socialist Party in the United States. Under Lenin's leadership, the Russians were (in this same period) in the process of granting social and political autonomy, i.e., national liberation, to their own colonial minorities such as Jews and many of the semi-colonized subjects of the tsar around the Caspian and Black Seas stretching east to Mongolia! Insofar as Russian-born Jews were fairly prominent in the ranks of the Socialist circles that Domingo was in while in New York City, the Bolshevik Revolution of 1917 fundamentally altered Domingo's approach toward radical transformation and laid the basis for a new conception of the historical possibilities of black people as members of a multi-racial and international class of workers.

He co-wrote *Negro Worker* with Chandler Owen, Fort-Whiteman and Randolph in December 1918, the title alone suggesting an attempt to base a periodical around the class interests of black labourers.[6] Their collaboration portended the later publication of a periodical with the same name by black communists. Several of the latter would later come to collaborate with Domingo in the Harlem radical scene. Quite plainly, Domingo was positioned at the nexus of political developments between the JBA, Liberty League and the incipient UNIA, while the recent Bolshevik overthrow of the tsarist regime in Russia added a qualitatively different political spin to the race-based approaches toward the anti-colonial struggle and toward Black workers from across the Diaspora. Notably, in the revised edition of the Liberty League founding statement originally written in summer 1917 and revised in 1920 by Harrison, the end portion praises the 'Jews in Russia' for their liberation from ethnic persecution and struggle for national liberation within the empire, suggesting that much of Domingo's initial sympathies for the Russian Revolution was born within the Liberty League under the tutelage of Harrison.

But Harrison, like Garvey, initially seems to have defended the Bolshevik cause only to later retract such support by early 1920. Garvey, too, had initially invoked a sense of solidarity with Bolshevism by declaring his own struggle in the name of 'red,' black and green in order to show UNIA's sympathy with the 'Reds' of the world. But the question of race versus class solidarity placed New Negroes such as Domingo at the centre of an inescapably antagonistic contradiction. How was he to explore and finally position himself in all of these intertwined, though not necessarily non-antagonistic, movements?

When Domingo agreed in 1918 to become the chief editor of Garvey's incipient newspaper entitled *Negro World* and even facilitated this chapter's existence by introducing Garvey to his first printer in New York,[7] this was hardly proof that Domingo was a sworn Garveyite. But involvement with the Garvey-led UNIA was instrumental in providing Domingo with an opportunity to engage in an all-black political organization modelled after the Liberty League with a political base that extended well into the Caribbean.

As the first editor of *Negro World* Domingo was in a position to disseminate anti-colonialist and also pro-labour ideals to a mass audience, potentially of millions – an opportunity hitherto unforeseen for black radicals in Harlem, much less anywhere else in the world. Also, it was a vehicle through which to continue the type of critique of 'Old Crowd' black leaders such as Du Bois that had been possible through involvement with the Liberty League. In April 1919, Domingo played a key role in a meeting denouncing W.E.B. Du Bois who, during his participation in the first Pan-African Congress in Paris, ruffled the feathers of many black radicals in the US by lauding black soldier participation in an 'imperialist' war while others, such as Garvey, were denied passports to attend the conference. Dismissing Du Bois as a 'mouthpiece of the government,' by operating as a functionary of US imperial aggression during the First World War, he charged that UNIA followers 'repudiate any kind of selected leadership,' and instead 'continue in the great movement with impartiality and self-interest.'[8]

And yet, it was precisely around the question of how to understand the problem of racism in the United States and, furthermore, 'what was to be done,' that laid the basis for Domingo's imminent departure from the UNIA and fissure with his long-time ally, Garvey. Insofar as Booker T. Washington was included in this 'Old Crowd' coterie, and Garvey was a sworn follower of Washington, Domingo's own collaboration with Garvey would have required that Domingo reconcile his emergent disaffection with capitalistic economic ventures, which was a cornerstone of the UNIA's economic development, with his angst towards white people as a race, or else a split was inevitable. Unable to make this reconciliation, his break with the *Negro World* and UNIA was complete by September 1919.[9] On Domingo's retrospective account in 1925, 'I didn't boost his ideas...he had me "tried" before the executive committee of the UNIA, for writing editorials not in keeping with the programme he outlined.'[10] In other words, Domingo was utilizing his editorial position in the earliest issues of *Negro World* in order to work his way through 'race first' and 'class first' ideologies as he became increasingly more militant in Harlem.

In any case, expunging Domingo from the ranks of UNIA was no simple political task for Garvey. First, Garvey could not dismiss Domingo as a blood-tainted, assimilationist 'mulatto'– a rhetorical attack he would repeatedly utilize with the likes of such rivals as Du Bois – because Domingo's complexion was comparable to that of Garvey himself. Second, he could not establish that Domingo had failed to make his political contribution to the black liberation struggle, i.e., supporting the UNIA, since after all, Domingo had helped jump-start the organization's leadership base in Harlem and its periodical. Finally, Garvey could not accuse Domingo of abandoning his Jamaican roots simply because no evidence seemed to suggest that Domingo was any less interested in conditions in Jamaica as a result of his emergent affinity toward the worldwide socialist movement. Domingo's political development demonstrates, therefore, the ways in which Garveyism and Bolshevism became antagonistic movements; and yet, his lived political experience also shows how their development was mutually dependent. In point of fact, there was unity in their opposition. Expunging Garvey's political platform of race unity and black business enterprise – including economic co-operatives – from his political consciousness was, conversely, no simple task for Domingo.

This was all to occur in the tumultuous period now referred to as the 'Red summer' of 1919. In this time, Red radicals and black people – overwhelmingly though not solely black workers – faced the violent backlash of state repression and lynch law after the First World War in the United States. The question of black and white unity in the face of racist, anti-Bolshevik terror was therefore placed squarely before radicals in both races. Moreover, the October Revolution and the First World War changed the way many black people thought about white people since, in the international context, there were 'white' Russians declaring the right to self-determination of colonial minorities, in the name of 'international proletarian solidarity.'

Socialism Imperilled!

At the time of his departure from the editorial board of *Negro World*, Domingo had already begun to meet with leading Socialist Party members and anti-colonialists at the Rand School of Social Science in lower Manhattan. In addition to Harrison's variety of Socialist training, Domingo was mingling with a multi-racial crowd, an international community of Socialists, in which anti-colonialism took the form of Leninism. In addition to a number of people who would later become vital members of the international Communist movement, such as Elizabeth Gurley Flynn and Sen Katayama at the Rand School, Domingo also developed alongside black young radicals from the US and Caribbean – particularly A.P. Randolph and Chandler Owen of the United States, Richard Moore of Barbados and Otto Huiswoud of Dutch Guiana.

It was with Huiswoud and Moore that Domingo would remain closely linked, both politically and personally, for the duration of the interwar period. Indeed they would help form the core of black militants in Harlem that later emerged as an important nucleus of Black Reds in

Harlem. Though Domingo became an active member of the Socialist Party approximately in this period, by 1923 his ties to the Socialist Party had been altogether severed and his primary political alliances were to lie with those black revolutionaries who formed the nucleus of the Workers (Communist) Party – Richard Moore and Otto Huiswoud in particular.

Domingo, a Messenger

Domingo went from the Socialist Party-backed *Messenger* to the African Blood Brotherhood-backed *Crusader* all within the years from 1919–23. In fact, months before *Emancipator* dropped in March 1920 Domingo had begun writing for *Messenger*, though he was still chief editor of UNIA's *Negro World*. Evidence of his sustained sympathies to race-based ideologies was evident in an early *Messenger* article where he asserted that black people 'give prestige to the word Negro, first, by capitalizing it and next by deeds that any race would be proud to have connected with its name.'[11] Race pride still remained a social and political imperative to Domingo as he transitioned into utilizing an anti-capitalist perspective in the *Messenger*.

Evidently, Domingo's political transition was not without its own internal tensions; chief among them appears to have been his internal reservations about the potential for socialism to appeal to the black masses. The editorials in *Messenger* written by Domingo suggest ambivalence and possibly even opportunism in his approach to questions of race and class. At a minimum, they demonstrate his uncanny ability to pragmatically delimit the relationship between the fight against racism and the fight for socialism depending on the political venue. Though he was in two minds, he wrote his last editorial in November 1920 and by 1923 had made up his mind to officially break with *Messenger* because he was disgusted with the African American editorial board's incessant anti-Caribbean diatribe against Garvey, specifically their characterization of him as a 'Jamaican jackass.'[12] But this did not signal his break with Bolshevism; rather, it was the beginning of his deeper affiliation with that movement.

Wilfred A. Domingo: The Emancipator

His paper, *Emancipator*, represents the most striking attempt to provide a black transnational circuit of information, ideas, and struggles using the framework of a class-based paradigm which was to emerge in this post-First World War period of 'New Negro' radicalism. Indeed, Domingo in many ways, though never an official Communist, would help lay the basis for the Black-Red campaigns such as 'Scottsboro Committees' and the defence of the 1929 'Haitian Revolution' that conjoined Communists and Black radicals from New York City across the Caribbean basin.[13] *Emancipator* discussed developments in the Francophone, Anglophone, Spanish and even the Dutch Caribbean. Wherever the African Diaspora was located and waging rebellion Domingo's periodical covered it. That this paper has been given such minimal attention in current discourse on the 'black Atlantic,' transnational studies, and Black Diasporic radicalism, suggests a huge oversight in the relationship between New York City and transitional movements influenced by Bolshevik and Black radical politics across the Caribbean. Domingo was in the 'vanguard' of this historical development.

On the first page of the first issue, *Emancipator* featured articles on Harlem, South Africa, Trinidad, Panama and Jamaica. 'Negro Workers Strike in Panama' discussed the problem of differential pay between white and black workers in the Canal Zone in gold and silver respectively. Though UNIA had been protesting this racist situation vigorously,[14] *Emancipator* put a class spin on it by asserting that the pay differential was a 'subtle device to separate the workers.' Ironically, however, Domingo did not censor the article's intimation of the superior physiology of the 'black workers' whose 'mighty brawn made the Canal a reality when all other kinds of labor – Greek, Chinese and Spanish – had failed under the fierce vertical rays of the equatorial sun.'[15] These biases notwithstanding, there was an article on the same page about political developments in Johannesburg with a sub-headline 'Negro Workers Breaking Through to Freedom With Help of White Radicals' in which the case was made that South African workers under the leadership of the International Socialist League were breaking previously unforeseen barriers on the colour line in South Africa.[16]

By featuring South Africa as a beacon of black–white worker unity, Domingo came ahead of many subsequent Communists around the world who would also look to developments in South Africa as a litmus test for Communist vanguard leadership in the multiracial class struggle. Finally, on this first page was also a headline that 'Black

Workers of Jamaica, BWI' were rising up in Kingston. 'All grades of labour' such as 'nurses, cab-drivers, railway employees...and, wonder of wonders, Policemen,' were 'passing thru [sic] a period of strikes,' and '[s]teps are being taken to affiliate with the workers of Great Britain.'[17] Years later, Richard Hart, a prominent Marxist and labour activist in Jamaica, recalled that Domingo was influential in Jamaican politics as a political more so than a labour radical in the 1930s and '40s.[18] In post-First World War Harlem, however, Domingo appears to have focused overwhelmingly on international labour campaigns and particularly championed the cause of striking workers everywhere, including those in his beloved Jamaica.

The focus on Black Diasporic labour uprisings in *Emancipator* was not at the expense of covering topics of a theoretical, political, cultural and even personal nature. One article lauded the radical content in the poetry of Claude McKay, fellow Jamaican compatriot, friend to Domingo, 'full-blooded Negro' and, at that time, Communist. It stated '[m]any of his poems were charmingly composed satires upon the present capitalist order' and wished 'the young poet every success in the land of fog' while 'working with English radicals.'[19] Another article praised the leadership of Rothschild Francis, 'Socialist, freethinker and member of the local legislature,' in St Thomas, which was one of 'Uncle Sam's newly acquired tropical nephews' in the Virgin Islands.[20] After brief but significant experiences with the Communist International, both McKay and Francis – the former a delegate to a Communist International (Comintern) convention in Moscow and the latter an ally of the Comintern-led Anti-Imperialist League – would become estranged from the Communist movement.

Under Domingo's editorship the paper incessantly brought the international movement to the local Harlem scene and, conversely, propelled Harlem's radical militancy onto the global stage. But his commitment to building a political climate that would invoke a sense of class reciprocity amongst the black masses in America – the Caribbean and United States together – was not reciprocated by his readership. His internationalist vision was not enlightening enough to overcome the blind eye that many leaders, organizations and everyday people turned toward concerns that were seemingly out of their territory, literally.

In short, the reception of and support for *Emancipator* was also lukewarm. The paper quickly yielded to economic distress; it appears that Domingo had not built a base of political support within the movement around his brand of Bolshevik-Diasporic-transnational journalism and, as such, he was ill-positioned to ensure its continued existence in the face of mounting intrigue. He noted that the paper was being 'held up,' and that 'for some reason or other bundles of The Emancipator (sic) have been unreasonably delayed in transit through the mail,' with the inevitable result of an 'increase of publication expenses up to the point of forcing us to cease production.' The weekly's survival depended 'entirely upon the support' from 'those whose cause we champion.'[21] But Domingo was no Garvey. In fact, *Emancipator* was sued by Garvey, and it succumbed shortly thereafter.

African Blood Brothers – from the Caribbean

The United States-based chauvinism of the *Messenger* crew quite understandably rendered Domingo more willing to express his own regionalist tendencies, especially given his history as an advocate for Jamaican self-government. Since on the question of West Indian pride he was hardly dispassionate, he found fraternal refuge with his Caribbean brethren – including one woman, Grace Campbell – in the nucleus of the short-lived African Blood Brotherhood (ABB) and its organ, *Crusader*. But more profoundly Domingo aligned himself with a fledgling body of Black Diasporic radicals who were to soon become affiliated with, and indeed part of the Workers (Communist) Party based in New York City.

In the aftermath of the bloody Tulsa race riot in 1921, Domingo was at an ABB gathering at 57 West 138th Street in Harlem characterized by the *New York Times* as advocating solely 'race retaliation.' Domingo reportedly said 'Our aim is to allow those who attack us to choose the weapons,' and '[i]f it be guns, we will reply with guns. If the attack is made through the white press, the negro press will defend us.' Such sentiment pre-dated by 40 years the 'self-defence' ethos of the Black Power movement of the '60s: 'By any means necessary' was to be declared by Malcolm X; 'Negroes with guns' was the call to arms from Robert Williams. But unlike X and Williams, Domingo simultaneously asserted cross-racial unity with the need 'to take advantage of class differences among whites.' He ended his speech at this gathering by quoting Karl Marx's nineteenth-century dictum 'You have nothing to lose but your chains' and adding his own rendition, 'You have your liberation to achieve.'[22] In effect, Domingo was at once organizing for black-led and multiracial working class solidarity in order to combat Jim Crow racism in the United States. In so doing he capitalized on the slippage of Marxist doctrine since the 'you' whose liberation was to be achieved could have been interpreted as both a race and class-based community. But why did he not transition into the Harlem branch of the Communist (Workers) Party formed in 1922 by Otto Huiswoud and later joined by his ABB comrades, Cyril Briggs, Grace Campbell and, finally, Richard Moore, by 1923?

Domingo and the Workers (Communist) Party: The Road Not Taken

In Harlem, Domingo would come across radicals who compounded their anti-colonialist viewpoints with anti-capitalist struggles aimed at furthering the cause of the 'international proletariat.' Yet during certain periods more so than others, Domingo, an owner of a business that imported West Indian produce, was obligated to elicit some degree of support for 'capitalistic' business relations. If the Domingo of 1916 was fearless, single, broke, and poised to take over the world, the Domingo of 1922 – hounded by federal investigators, still fearless and still financially strapped – was now with wife and firstborn (named Karl Marx Domingo!). Joyce Moore Turner, historian and daughter of Richard B. Moore, surmises that Domingo's retreat from politics after the dissolution of the ABB into the WP was the result of his personal responsibilities as a breadwinner; thus, he delved into his importing business.[23]

When Domingo was to return to the 'New Negro' scene, he would do so in the realm of literature and culture rather than overt politics, much less Bolshevism. This demonstrates the way in which, in his early political development, Domingo made a conscious effort not to align himself solely with his Black-Red Caribbean partners. His article entitled 'The Tropics in New York' in the January 1925 issue of *Survey Graphic,* as in his prior work 'If We Must Die,' was named after a McKay poem of the same title that was conjoined with Domingo's essay, though by now McKay had broken with the international Communist movement. This would make it all the more significant that Domingo aligned his 1925 piece with that of McKay. Later that year,

Domingo re-worked this essay into his piece entitled 'The Gift of the Black Tropics' in Alain Locke's *The New Negro*. 'The Gift of the Black Tropics' was hardly the direct action against lynching and Bolshevism led by black and white workers that Domingo had trumpeted several years prior. Instead, he spoke of black 'folk' and the fashion in Harlem under the vanguard cultural leadership of the West Indians. Since the beginning of his Red affiliation, Domingo had maintained a dual, though uneven, commitment to region-oriented race pride and international-based class solidarity. But as opposed to his earlier writings, his 1925 publications seemed to stress regional and cultural pride over class and international solidarity.

In *Spectres of 1919*, Barbara Foley explains how Domingo's Locke essay was a culturalist re-appropriation of the radical militancy and socialist internationalism of 'Socialism Imperiled.'[24] But even in 'Socialism Imperiled' Domingo declared, albeit in passing, that the few Black people in the United States who were 'radicals' happened to be 'foreigners,' (i.e., himself and other West Indian 'New Negros' like Moore and Briggs). That is, he was always a staunch advocate for placing his Caribbean people in the vanguard of the conceptual map of radical Black Americans. Furthermore, in *Emancipator* there was also an article entitled 'West Indians in New York' which Domingo edited, if not authored, claiming that West Indians as a 'people' were both 'great' and 'intelligent' and must refrain from 'hero worship' and 'emotionalism.' Strikingly similar to his subsequent articles in both *Survey Graphic* and *The New Negro*, this piece relegated West Indian immigrants' status as labourers to the periphery while focusing on their regional origin as the essence-determining factor in their existential experience in New York.[25]

Even in this Bolshevist phase, essentially, Domingo was inclined toward a form of West-Indian exceptionalism regarding the uniqueness of his 'people.' Therefore, in the period between 1920 and 1925 when Domingo's relationship to the Red parties in Harlem became increasingly estranged, he correspondingly reified his perception of West Indians, at first considering them radical 'foreigners' and later 'West Indians in New York,' then as the 'tropics' in New York, and, finally, as the 'Gift of the Black Tropics.' Perhaps his intentions were simply to make a quick dollar in the cultural literature that was emerging from the Harlem Renaissance since his political literature with the newspapers bore little monetary fruit, in which case he would have quite pragmatically chosen to minimize his class politics for acceptance of his writings in cultural venues.

But it would stand to reason that he was making a political point aimed at the Communists when he allied artistically with the now Comintern foe McKay at the very moment when he himself had chosen not to join the WP with his Harlem comrades. Too, the WP was to become the employer of these Black Reds. Not only had he survived a stabbing attempt from a Garveyite in his 1919 days, but he had also survived the repercussions associated with the raid of the Lusk Committee in the same period. In plain fact he had to create as little friction with State Department as possible if his import business was to be allowed to succeed. Domingo, therefore, still had to answer to Uncle Sam in a way Richard Moore, Huiswoud, and Briggs did not. Domingo was clearly not wedded to the Party as a card-carrying member of a political organization though he would forever self-identify as a socialist.[26]

A Fellow Traveller: Domingo and the American Negro Labour Congress

His literary ventures into the 'culturalist' dimensions of the Harlem Renaissance notwithstanding, Domingo's prevailing allegiances remained with the Reds as evidenced through his affiliation with their mass organization, American Negro Labor Congress (ANLC). In September 1926, Moore, then leading the ANLC, organized a lecture conducted by Hubert Harrison entitled 'World Problems of Race' in which Domingo, seated prominently front and centre in the audience, was poised to give Harrison a gift at the lecture's closing. Among the other attendees at the event were Huiswoud and Williana Burroughs, a leading Black female Communist in Harlem. Also in that year Domingo, along with Otto Huiswoud and Grace Campbell, his old pals from the ABB and current members of the WP, was on the executive board of the 'Joint Committee of the Harlem Educational Forum, Institute for Social Study, American Negro Labor Congress' that had drafted a letter designed to garner political and legal defence for Moore after his arrest for ANLC organizing.[27] In short, Domingo was in a subsidiary body of the ANLC itself. If he might have been a 'fellow traveller' of the WP, he was not so far removed from the mass,

Red-led work of this WP offshoot. His alliance with McKay in *Survey Graphic* in 1925 notwithstanding, Domingo had apparently stuck closely with his comrades in the ANLC well into the imaginable future.

Mass evictions throughout Harlem were becoming increasingly brutal by the late 1920s. In 1929 with the onset of the World Depression the ANLC took leadership in organizing militant direct action to defend the black residents. At one meeting of the Harlem Tenants Association in which the goal was to plan for a 'huge mass rent strike, [q]uite a number of tenants took the floor, among them: W.A. Domingo, Solomon Harper, George Padmore...all of them giving militant support to the call for immediate organization toward calling a rent strike in Harlem.' But rather than abstractly philosophizing about the need to take action, they '[a]ll emphasized the tenants' task as to organize house and block committees and generally prepare the ground for a rent strike.'[28] There is slim chance Domingo was there merely to prevent his own eviction. Alongside George Padmore, a fairly young Trinidadian radical who was on the brink of becoming a pre-eminent international black communist organizer and chief editor of the *Negro Worker*, Domingo was engaged in what was, in fact, a global movement of workers against evictions particularly in China, Latin America, and the United States under the leadership of local Communist party branches. As astute and 'worldly' as he was, Domingo must have understood full well the political implications of advocating such militant, anti-capitalist tactics at a moment when his immediate political allies were in the thick of a Communist organizing campaign that had international significance.

From Harlem to Kingston: Domingo and the Jamaican Movement for Self-Government, 1936–39

From 1923–35, Domingo did not simply confine himself to concerns with his West Indian imports company only to re-emerge in 1936 with the Jamaica Progressive League. But his political activism did take a back seat in these years. This makes it all the more intriguing that those times when he did appear to address political matters, he did so in connection with Communist organizations.

By 1936 Domingo's concern with the situation in Jamaica itself was intensifying, but was this at the expense of a weakening bond with the Comintern? A look into the mission and goals of the organization founded in Harlem by the writer W. Adolphe Roberts, the Jamaica Progressive League and National Reform Association (often shortened to the Jamaica Progressive League, or JPL), helps answer this question. Though they focused primarily on the question of universal adult suffrage and self-government within the British Empire, the coterie of Jamaicans living in New York City that created the Jamaica Progressive League in 1936 initially began their transnational campaign in 1935 with a fundraiser in response to a tuberculosis outbreak on the island. Important too is the fact that once again the development of radical politics in both the Caribbean and Harlem was a reciprocal process.

A look at the coterie of black radicals whose transnational radicalism was conjoined to give voice to a common cause is also telling. Roberts, JPL president, left Jamaica as a youth and travelled as a 'war correspondent,' finally landing himself in Greenwich Village in the radical literary scene during the late 1920s and early 1930s. Ethelred Brown, Domingo's longtime ally from the Benevolent Association of 1917 and longtime member of the Socialist Party, was secretary of the JPL. James O'Meally, a former UNIA member and delegate to the League of Nations in the late 1920s, who would increasingly lean toward Marxist politics, was also a founding member along with Wilfred Domingo.[29] In short, this group of Jamaicans in Harlem who were among the most militant advocates for the colony of their birth were operating within a transnational circuit of black radicalism, infused with Red alliances, that developed as the result of reciprocal political developments between New York City and Jamaica. That is, these 'Caribbean Militants in Harlem' would also then turn around and impact the political climate back in Jamaica.

The JPL emerged on the scene in Harlem precisely at the moment when Jamaica and islands throughout the British West Indies were engaged in the fiercest labour revolt of the black masses that the British had ever confronted. At the same time, the JPL was almost immediately incorporated into the ideological apparatus of Jamaica's growing radical community. In the pages of the Jamaican radical newspaper *Public Opinion* under the editorial supervision of O.T. Fairclough, it is clear that the official position of JPL centred on the demand for 'bourgeois democratic' rights for the Jamaican people; this was a far cry from the demands of a revolutionary party. As expressed by its president, W.A. Roberts, the organization was designed chiefly to act as a proponent for the 'immediate founding of a political party in Jamaica, pledged to work for self-government' within the British Empire.[30]

Ethelred Brown was featured in several issues of the newspaper making the case that the civil service in Jamaica had systematically shut out 'lower strata' Jamaicans from employment; hence, the need to re-open the service to all qualified candidates.[31] No doubt the political demands of Brown and Roberts paled in comparison to the direct action labour uprisings that spread like wildfire throughout the island – better still, the entire West Indies – under the spontaneous leadership of the Jamaican workers in this period. And yet, Roberts' call for a Jamaican political party preceded that very same demand that was soon to be heralded by the People's National Party, and Brown's interest in securing a decent living for the island's 'lower strata' was a sure sign of his concern for the struggling mass.

But even more progressive was the wing of the JPL that went further and critiqued the capitalist mode of production itself as the basis of the Jamaican and British economies that were so detrimental to everyday Jamaicans. Quite appropriately, Domingo was one such member. James O'Meally of the JPL wrote a pamphlet entitled 'Why We Demand Self Government' in which he verbally assailed the colonial 'ruling class' for failing to meet the needs of the Jamaican people.[32] In *Public Opinion,* he went on to criticize fascism as a specific type of capitalism in contradistinction to socialism which was an 'almost complete break with capitalist economy while fascism is an important continuity of its precursor.'[33] While O'Meally's political characterization of fascism was rejected at the 7th congress of the Comintern in 1935 in favour of a 'Popular Front' approach to fascism, it demonstrates that on some level he was interested in querying the pitfalls of a nationalist movement that did not put forward a class-based, anti-capitalist challenge to colonial domination and global fascism.

For her part, Eulalie Domingo, Wilfred's wife, praised the work of the women's clubs in Jamaica because of their 'social uplift of the poorer and unemployed girls.' In particular she applauded the intellectual accomplishments of the Jamaica Women's Liberal Club which sought the following: 'To foster a National Spirit among the women of Jamaica; To encourage women to take an active and intelligent interest in Local and World events' and 'to form a Study Circle, including Politics,

Economics and Government.'³⁴ Much like her husband, Eulalie was intent upon drawing the political linkages between the local and the global while still insisting upon an independent, national Jamaican programme for change. Moreover, she advocated that this women's movement up the ante by participating in 'sit down' strikes at home such that Jamaican wives would 'lay your cards face upwards on the table first to the men'³⁵ since the home was the point of production for so many economically and socially oppressed wives. Contemporaneous with Eulalie's sit-down proclamations was a whole wave of sit-down strikes around the world in the mid-1930s, especially based out of the United States, Latin America and Europe and often under the direct leadership of Communists. In this manner, Eulalie was indirectly linking a class-struggle technique that was operative on an international level to the empowerment of Jamaican housewives. This was hardly the work of a political amateur.

Domingo's intervention in *Public Opinion*, however, reflects this radical stance within JPL more than anyone else. 'As I See My Country' was Domingo's regular column in the paper where he waged a series of relentless denunciations against British colonialism, a system that oppressed darker peoples 'whose countries are to be regarded as so much territory reserved for exploitation by British capitalists.' In this debut column he seized the opportunity to berate the colonial *Daily Gleaner*, which '[r]ather than inoculating its readers with imperialistic hunkum' ought to 'become truly Jamaican and try to build up an intelligent love of Jamaica by Jamaicans.' Convinced that this national pride was not antagonistic toward building a sense of international solidarity of the exploited, he continued '[t]hat does not mean hating any other country, but it does mean loving Jamaica best of all just as a normal individual loves his or her mother above all other mothers.'³⁶ In this column Domingo elicited the same dual affinity toward internationalism and nationalism that he expressed as far back as his own *Emancipator*. One crucial difference, however, is that by 1937 Domingo had placed significantly more emphasis on the question of Jamaican independence and cross-class solidarity than in his earlier years when international class struggle against capitalist exploitation was his primary concern.

All the same, one would be remiss in failing to consider the significance of a Jamaican-produced radical journal agreeing to feature a column from a citizen who had been, and currently was, residing in New York City for over 20 years. In itself this stands as a testament to Domingo's persistence as an advocate for the country in the face of British colonialism. It also points to the sustaining impact of his Harlem radicalization on his transnational networking with his homeland. The 'I' and 'My Country' emphasize the public persona he had built for himself – that is, his opinion was of prime significance to the Jamaican radical ideologues, for surely many people had opinions about Jamaica but few were worthy enough for a column. In this column he still attacked anti-Communist slander in the *Daily Gleaner*, thus implicitly defending the Soviet Union.[37] Still, he was insistent upon connecting the struggles in both the United States and the West Indies by decrying American-style Jim Crow and by bringing to Jamaican attention the racist practices of United Fruit on vessels in the West Indies. The ideological mix that served as the JPL's public face in Jamaica ranged from advocating parliamentary power through a political party on one hand to defence of the Soviet Union and radical labour militancy on the other.

So too did Domingo's 'public opinion' remain valuable in the eyes of another political coterie with whom he remained in contact: the black communists of Harlem. Concurrent with *Public Opinion's* features of Domingo in 1937 was a front-page headline entitled 'Letter from W.A. Domingo' in *The Negro Worker*, the monthly periodical of the Communist-led International Trade Union Committee of Negro Workers. In this January issue, Domingo took several pages to give the final word on a debate within 'your-our-magazine' between the Communist editor, Charles Woodson (pen name of Otto Huiswoud), and long-time Garveyite from the island of Dominica, J.R. Casimir.

Recalling his own bitter rivalry with Garvey in the pages of *Emancipator*, *Messenger*, and *Crusader* from nearly 20 years before, Domingo both thanked the editor for challenging the critique put forward by Casimir and advocated for the class-based approach to black liberation put forward by Woodson.[38] Many of those same black communists from the inner circle of the ABB after the First World War remained involved in the production of *The Negro Worker* in the 1930s – Briggs and Huiswoud in particular – and the use of Domingo as an authority on the Garvey question years later suggests the continued legacy and respect Domingo maintained for the International, and vice versa. Though he was not the editor as McKay had suggested as early as 1922, he was given a prominent place as late as 1937.

Close scrutiny of the letter reinforces one other premise upon which this essay is based: Domingo was a political chameleon, possibly to the detriment of the dual anti-colonialist/pro-working class goals to which he aspired. For example, in this same *Negro Worker* op-ed letter he recommended international solidarity with those who used violent force in self-defence to oust colonial powers. Further still, he stated plainly the need to 'try to weaken the capitalist forces at home by organizing labour unions, by forming co-operative societies, and by demanding self-government everywhere.' As if this were not demanding enough, he expected this to be accomplished 'while cooperating with all the forces of the world that are opposed to and fighting against Fascism which is the most vicious form of imperialism and capitalism.'[39]

This critique of fascism was more radical than much of the Popular Front rhetoric of the Comintern that focused mostly on the problem of fascism in Western regions because Domingo was primarily concerned with its manifestations in colonized territories such as Ethiopia. Once again, though not in a party, Domingo seemed to be in the political vanguard. But also once again, this was hardly equivalent to the position he took in *Public Opinion* in his own column which, though very radical, did not place his anti-capitalist sentiments so prominently at the centre as did this letter for the Communist *Negro Worker*. His Jamaican compatriots who did not subscribe to the *Negro Worker* did not, therefore, have equal access to his most radical visions for international solidarity.

With the onset of the Second World War by 1939, Domingo had made it his mission to help create a West Indies National Emergency Committee that was designed to challenge the impending threat of American imperial domination in replacement of British colonialism. As the escalation of fascism entailed the intervention of British forces in the Second World War, however, Domingo found himself in the political contradiction of defending the political sovereignty of the Soviet Union on one hand and challenging a Comintern policy that opposed British and American intervention in the war on the other. Ironically, however, the Comintern itself would later adopt Domingo's same position once the Soviet Union had entered into an alliance with the Western powers against Germany, Italy and Japan. On a personal level, he found himself at odds with long-time comrade Richard Moore with whom he had collaborated in political ventures since the days of *Emancipator* and into Moore's years as a Communist. Speaking in confidence to what was apparently an informant for the United States government, Domingo surmised:

> You probably learned of the debate I had with a Communist friend of mine as to the attitude British colonial Negroes should take in the present war between Great Britain and Germany. I took the affirmative that we should support the former, not because we love her but as between the two evils we should prefer the former...I am opposed to all imperialisms, that I am for the only anti-imperialist country in the world; and that my support of any country stops the moment the USSR is involved. Russia, as I see it, is the hope of all colonial peoples, especially those of the colonial races. Hence my unconditional support of Russia now and in the future.[40]

Apparently Moore 'won' the debate which, quite remarkably, was of such interest that it became a travelling conversation across the United States. In the West Indies, too, Domingo would also have found himself at odds with a number of those who were partial toward Nazi aggression against their British colonial rulers. There had arrived a moment in history where Black people were now considering their participation in inter-imperialist rivalry as an optional rather than mandatory matter. In no small sense, Domingo and Moore were helpful in facilitating that sentiment. One was a Communist, the other not, but both proclaimed defence of the Soviet Union. This story ends, though, precisely where Domingo's new political activism from within Jamaica begins.

Both Richard Moore and Cyril Briggs had been expelled from the Communist Party USA (CPUSA) in 1939, but the former remained active in Domingo's WINEC-turned West Indies National Council. How could a non-Communist defend 'the only anti-imperialist country in the world,' declaring Russia 'the hope of all colonial peoples, especially those of the colonial races'? Perhaps this question is precisely to the point: how does one define what it has meant to be a Communist, particularly when looking at the early political career of a figure such as W.A. Domingo? Indeed, some of the most international, anti-capitalist figureheads of the class struggle in the interwar period such as Langston Hughes and W.A. Domingo were never officially card-carrying Communists.

Domingo and Hart, Full Circle

Richard Hart himself never formed a Communist party in Jamaica, though he was a self-identified Communist for the duration of his radical career in Jamaica. In fact, a series of exchanges between Domingo and Hart from New York and Kingston indicate that Domingo, from his headquarters in Harlem, was critical in helping to shape the political climate and destiny of the radical labour movement on the island. In one letter to Hart, he observes that:

> I have followed the developments growing out of the recent strikes in JA to the extent that they can be gleaned from the daily and weekly press of the country and am gratified to note...that Buchanan is working with Bustamante and that they propose organizing the workers along industrial (CIO) lines. However, it is regrettable that there should seem to be hostility between Busta and Coombs, but I know that those things are sometimes unavoidable. Despite everything, or because of everything, it is clear to me that Jamaica is moving forward ideologically; that no longer will the people take it 'lying down.'[41]

Particularly noteworthy in this exchange for the purposes of this exposition is Domingo's reference to the CIO, or Committee of Industrial Organization-style of union organization under the leadership of Bustamante and Buchanan that he adamantly condones. Such a form of centralized union bureaucracy, with a strong emphasis on direct action at the point of production, was precisely the method of mass Communist labour organizing in the United States in this very period, indicating that Domingo was consciously attempting to, at least partially, mould the labour movement in Jamaica after this very model in the US. Again, the flow of Red-Black radicalism was reciprocal.

He continues, 'Like you I have no illusions about constitutional means being capable of "turning the trick"...However, as you say, we must exhaust every constitutional means, and their failure to achieve the desired result will be the most eloquent and effective propaganda in steeling the souls of our not-sufficiently-political people....' In this context, both Hart and Domingo, operating as non-card carrying Marxists in the movement for self-government and labour organization, were sharing their views on the 'stages' method to 'steeling the souls of our not-sufficiently-political people,' as a means toward finally achieving revolutionary unity. That is, even Domingo's participation in the JPL was a calculated tactic, a means to furthering his larger radical ends, insofar as he had no 'illusions,' like Hart, of the 'constitutional means' in which his organization was implicated. He confides that his 'personal views on the best programme for Jamaica' included the political demand for self-government in addition to the 'fight to democratize the country and transfer power to the workers and producers of the country,' along with organizing labour 'at the point of production through labour unions and at the point of consumption through the organization of Consumers Cooperatives,' and finally in the social realm wherein 'forms of sec[ular], racial and other discrimination must be checked, then abolished.'[42]

Apparently Domingo's counsel was not in vain. In the last issue of the leading labour magazine in Jamaica, *Jamaica Labour Weekly*, the editors noted that '[w]ith some of our comrades dead, some wounded and some imprisoned…in the political field stands the Jamaica Progressive League and the People's National Party worthy of our closest attention.'[43] Here we see the manner in which Domingo's legacy of political and labour leadership in the late 1930s, conducted from Harlem, would remain recorded in the public consciousness by way of the JPL. And Richard Hart, the Jamaican Marxist without a party, was Domingo's counterpart that helped direct this transnational circuit.

Therefore, in examining Domingo's political development from 1919–39 we must consider what the Soviet Union *meant* to Domingo. For even when he was interned as a result of the dual forces of British and American political persecution upon arrival to Jamaica in 1941, he was purportedly carrying a photograph of Lenin in his possession. At a minimum, Domingo's approach to the anti-colonial project in Jamaica cannot be properly understood when separated from his engagement with Bolshevism. Perhaps a similar case can be made for many others.

Notes

1. 'Report of a Pamphlet by Marcus Garvey,' in *The Marcus Garvey and UNIA Papers*, vol. 1, ed. Robert Hill (Berkeley and Los Angeles: University of California Press, 1983), 22.
2. W. Burghardt Turner and Joyce Turner, eds., *Richard B. Moore: Caribbean Militant in Harlem* (Bloomington: Indiana University Press, 1988), 34.

3. 'Personal Papers,' Box 1, Ethelred Brown Papers; Interview with Joyce Moore Turner. Schomburg Center for Research and Culture, New York.
4. 'Account by W.A. Domingo of Marcus Garvey's St Mark's Church Hall Lecture,' *The Marcus Garvey Papers*, vol. 1, 190.
5. Jeffrey Perry, *A Hubert Harrison Reader* (Middletown, CT: Wesleyan University Press, 2001), 6.
6. Ibid., 298.
7. The printer was Henry Rogowski who at the time produced the Socialist Party's paper, the *New York Call*. See *The Marcus Garvey Papers*, vol. 1, 528.
8. 'Address Denouncing W.E.B. Du Bois,' *The Marcus Garvey Papers*, vol.1, 400.
9. 'Withdrawal of W. A. Domingo from the *Negro World*.' Ibid., vol.2, 40.
10. Ibid.
11. W.A. Domingo, 'Who Are We, Negroes or Colored People?' *Messenger*, vol.1, no. 5/6, 1919.
12. 'The Police of the Messenger on West Indian and American Negroes,' *Messenger*, vol. 4, March 1923.
13. 'Scottsboro Committees' refer to the groups of Caribbean activists in Haiti, Cuba and Mexico which were formed in response to the threat that nine African American young men would be subject to lynching if convicted of the [false] crime of raping two girls while aboard a train in Scottsboro, Alabama. The arrest of these youths and the subsequent campaign, largely led by the International Labor Defense, a mass organization directed by the Communist Party of the United States, all began in 1931. The ILD helped bring about the formation of Scottsboro Committees in said Caribbean locales, among others. The 'Haitian Revolution' refers to the late 1929 rebellion in Haiti initially led by Haitian students discontent with what they considered an American, anti-Haitian chauvinism reflected by a prominent faculty member, subsequently spilling over into mass protests and armed resistance to the American Marines stationed in Haiti at the time. In New York City, American Communists, primarily under the leadership of black communists such as Richard Moore and Otto Huiswoud, and through their Red-led organization called the American Negro Labor Congress, called protests across New York which reverberated across the country, in solidarity with the 'Haitian Revolution,' as it was denoted. (See Desulmé in this volume).
14. Theodore Kornweibel, ed., *Federal Surveillance of African Americans, 1917–24*, reel 23, (Microform, Library of Congress) 1985, documents attempts from Marcus Garvey and the UNIA to challenge the racial discrimination in gold and silver differential pay and also the segregation that Black workers in the Canal Zone were subject to in public facilities and housing.
15. 'Negro Workers Strike in Panama,' *Emancipator*, 13 March 1920, 1.
16. 'Blacks and Whites Coming Together in South Africa,' *Emancipator*, 1.
17. 'Black Workers of Jamaica, B.W.I. Strike,' *Emancipator*, 13 March 1920, 1.
18. Richard Hart to Barrymore Bogues, interview, London, 1978.
19. 'Negro Poet Working With English Radicals,' *Emancipator*, 13 March 1920.
20. 'Clean Up in Virgin Islands Put Up to Congress,' *Emancipator*, 13 March 1920.
21. *Emancipator*, 7 April 1920.

22. 'ABB Accused of Fomenting a Tulsa Riot,' *Crusader*, vol. 4, 12.
23. Interview with author, August 2007.
24. Barbara Foley, op. cit., 229.
25. 'West Indians in New York,' *Emancipator*, 21 March 1920.
26. Interview, Joyce Moore Turner with author, August 2007.
27. Box 1, Folder, 'Communist Party Years,' Letter, 4 October 1926, Richard B. Moore Papers, Schomburg Center for Research and Culture, New York.
28. 'Plan Harlem Rent Strike,' *Liberator*, 7 December 1929, 1.
29. James Carnegie, *Some Aspects of Jamaica's Politics, 1918–1938* (Kingston: Institute of Jamaica), 141.
30. *Public Opinion*, Vol.1. no.1, February 1937, 12.
31. Ibid., Vol.1, no.7, 27 March 1937, 10.
32. James O'Meilly (sic), *Why We Demand Self Government* (New York: Jamaica Progressive League), 11.
33. *Public Opinion*, Vol. 1, 3 April 1937.
34. *Public Opinion*, 1 May 1937, 10.
35. Ibid.
36. 'As I See My Country,' *Public Opinion*, vol. 1, No.9, 26 June 1937.
37. Ibid., 2.
38. 'Our Letter Box,' *Negro Worker*, January 1937, 15.
39. Ibid.
40. West Indies National Council Papers, FBI File NY 100–11857, Schomburg Center for Research and Black Culture, New York, 8.
41. Richard Hart Papers, National Library of Jamaica, Box. 3 Folder 3, letter, 13 July 1938, Domingo West Indies Produce Corp. from NYC, 1692 Park Ave. to Hart.
42. Ibid.
43. Richard Hart Papers, 'The New Year,' *Jamaica Labour Weekly*, 31 December 1938, Box. 3, Folder 3.

10 | Black Marxist: Champion of the Negro Toilers

Rodney Worrell

It is my contention that no discussion on Marxism or trade unionism in the Caribbean or in Africa in the first half of the twentieth century can be complete without some reference or mention of George Padmore. Between 1927 and 1933, Padmore was one of the main promoters of Marxism and trade unionism when he worked inside the International Trade Union Committee of Negro Workers, an important arm of the Communist International. Therefore it is fitting that as we place the lens on Richard Hart, a noted Marxist, champion of working people, and anti-colonialist, we should also examine the contributions of one of his ideological predecessors, George Padmore. Padmore was a tireless advocate of the need for black workers to become organized in order to engage the capitalists and imperialists and bring about some betterment in their wretched conditions, which were being exacerbated by the one of the greatest challenges that capitalism faced in its history. This chapter therefore examines Padmore's role in championing the cause of black toilers internationally.

Early Marxism

George Padmore was born on the island of Trinidad in 1903. He left Trinidad in December 1924 to pursue tertiary education in the United States. Padmore enrolled at Fisk University in 1925 to study medicine. After two years at Fisk, he terminated his studies and headed to Howard University to pursue law. At both universities Padmore became heavily involved in student activism. The racist, unjust, discriminatory Jim Crow system contributed to Padmore's radicalization; while he was aware of racism existing in Trinidad 'there was no official segregation.'

Padmore the militant student activist soon abandoned his academic studies and became a full time revolutionary so that he 'could render in a fuller way some aid to my Negro brothers in Africa.'[1] He became a member of the American Negro Labor Congress (ANLC), an auxiliary of the Communist Party and subsequently became a member of the Communist Party of the United States in 1927. Padmore believed that the communist party presented the best available programme for the liberation of the black working class in the United States and the toiling masses globally. He was a very active, dedicated, committed and hardworking communist although there were some concerns about his total commitment to Marxism-Leninism orthodoxy because of his strong attachment to racial issues. Padmore was an energetic member of the Harlem's Tenants League, a communist front organization, and he edited and wrote articles for the *Negro Champion*, the organ of the ANLC. Additionally, Padmore served on national committees on Negro work during 1928 and 1929 and actively campaigned for William Z. Foster to become president of the Communist Party of the United States of America. He also attended the Second Congress of the League Against Imperialism in Frankfurt, Germany in July 1929.[2]

First Trip to Russia

Shortly after returning from the Second Congress of the League Against Imperialism, Padmore attended the Trade Union Unity League convention in Cleveland. This conference was of great significance as it witnessed the dissolution of the Trade Union Educational League and the creation of the Trade Union Unity League (TUUL) in keeping with a directive that was issued at the Sixth Congress of the Comintern in 1928. The Communist Party of the United States of America was instructed to 'launch revolutionary unions' to challenge the floundering American Federation of Labor (AFL) and to meet the demands of an envisioned revolutionary crisis.[3]

Padmore accompanied William Z. Foster to Russia where he was asked to deliver a report on the implications of the new trade union initiative. In his report, Padmore noted that millions of Negro workers in the United States were brutally exploited, and were 'the targets of police terrorism, lynching, Jim Crowism, disenfranchisement and peonage.' Padmore further explained that the Negro toilers had been betrayed by the AFL. He charged that the AFL, despite its declaration of non-discrimination, 'practices a deliberate policy of Jim Crowism.'[4]

Therefore given the discriminatory practices of the AFL, Padmore argued that Negro workers would have to turn to the left wing section of the labour movement for leadership, because they were the 'only ones who expose the corrupt policies of the so-called "champions of the working class"– the socialists and Musties.'[5] He pointed out that the left unions led by the Trade Union Educational League (TUEL):

i. not only fight for the admission of the Negro Workers into the existing unions, but also advocate full equality for Negro as well as White;

ii. demand equal pay for equal work for the Negro;

iii. demand the right of Negroes to hold office in unions, thereby helping to shape the policies of the organizations and protecting the rights of Negro members;

iv. fight against separate unions for Negroes and Whites realizing that this Jim-Crowism policy pursued by the AFL weakens the united front of the working class.[6]

Padmore further elucidated that blacks were already occupying leadership positions in some of the left wing unions. In the racist South, the left wing controlled National Textile Workers Union was advocating 'equality in the union for Negro and White alike.' However the United Textile Workers Union controlled by the AFL and the socialists refused to admit the Negro Textile Workers; and when the left-wingers protested against the policy of racial discrimination, they were expelled as 'Reds' and 'Nigger lovers.' He identified two major challenges the black working class had to overcome: on the one hand they would have to unite with the class conscious white workers to wage a merciless fight against white chauvinism; and on the other hand they would have to struggle against the treacherous, sycophantic petty bourgeois Uncle Tom Negroes who would attempt to discourage the coloured workers from joining in solidarity with the left wing unionists.[7]

Padmore was also invited to speak about a labour struggle that was of great interest to the Comintern, the 'famous' Gastonia strike. Harvey Khler contends that 'even though it was a small unsuccessful strike and not even the largest in the textile industry that spring, Gastonia became famous, the Communist Party was able to transform a failed strike into a symbolic victory.'[8] He further maintained that the communist party received 'an important psychological boost' from its involvement in the Gastonia strike – 'for however brief a moment, the Party had led American born workers from the south.' A party plenum declared: 'the struggle in the South symbolized by Gastonia is the best proof of the growing radicalization of the working class in the Third Period.'[9]

In Padmore's view the Gastonia strike 'symbolises in a far-reaching and significant way for events making for the emancipation of millions of oppressed and brutally persecuted Negroes in the South.' He predicted that Gastonia was the first of many class battles which were going to take place in the newly industrialized centres in the South. These struggles would be energized by the process of 'capitalist rationalization' caused by the crisis of capitalism. Padmore believed that the class conflicts would force the Negro and white workers to come to the realization that although there were racial differences among them they were 'both members of the proletariat.' He was quite optimistic that proletarian unity '[would] be the most powerful force in breaking through the age long prejudices between the workers of both races.' Padmore recognized that the 'eradication of race prejudice' would not take place instantaneously, but 'must come about as a result of the social forces propelling both groups in the same direction and throwing them in the struggle against the class enemy – capitalism.' For many years the 'capitalist oppressors' had used the race card as their 'most effective instrument to maintain their privileged position.' However, the Gastonia conflict demonstrated 'that workers [would] no longer be fooled by the deceptive propaganda of their oppressors.'[10]

Padmore posited that several valuable lessons could be deduced from Gastonia in relation to the working class in general and the Negro in particular:

i. Race prejudice is not a geographical feature of American capitalist society. It is everywhere, although more bitterly entrenched in the South, because of its semi-feudal remnants. As the process of industrialization proceeds and the Negroes and poor whites are drawn from the rural communities into the industrial centres they will be forced to discard the ideology of the past and to orientate themselves into their environment. This process of urbanization will bring them together and out of these contacts they will learn to recognize that both groups are the slaves of the bosses. They will further learn through their everyday experiences that the employers foster race prejudice in order to keep them apart, and thereby exploit them more easily.

ii. The new class battles which will increasingly break out will necessitate the application of new methods of class warfare. We have already realized that the antiquated Jim Crow craft unions fostered by the AF of L must be displaced by new industrial unions under the militant leadership of the Communist and the left wing TUEL. Every battle will present us with new lessons in class tactics and methods of struggle. We must therefore be always on the alert to recognize our weak and strong points. Rigid self-criticism must be indulged in, in order to immediately correct our mistakes and steel our fighting forces so that all advantageous positions gained by workers will be consolidated.

iii. A systematic ideological campaign against white chauvinism must be carried on among the workers as well as within the Party ranks. There is still a tremendous underestimation of Negro work among some comrades. Up until now too little serious attention has been given to this phase of our activities. The TUUL convention marks a new effort, which, however, must not end merely in resolutions...These Negro workers, as pointed out by the Comintern over and over again, represent revolutionary potentialities which it will be criminal for us to neglect for the social revolution. We must therefore intensify our work among them, and draw them not only into the new unions but also into the ranks of the Party.

iv. We must popularize our slogans of full social, political and economic equality for Negroes more than we have done in the past. The most effective means of doing this is through our Press, especially the *Negro Champion* which should be developed into the mass organ of the Negro workers. In districts and centres of the basic industries special leaflets and bulletins dealing in a concrete way with everyday problems should be distributed at regular intervals. The Negro Press can also be utilized to a greater extent than some of our comrades recognise. In order to do this the Crusader News Service should be subsidized.[11]

Padmore's presentations greatly impressed the members of the Communist hierarchy and he was made 'a manager of the Negro Workers Committee.'[12]

Conference of the Negro Toilers

Padmore played a major role in organizing the first International Conference of Negro Workers in Hamburg, Germany in 1930. The Red International of Labour Unions created an International Bureau of Negro Workers headed by James Ford to 'prepare and convene an International Conference of Negro Workers at the end of 1929.'[13] At the Second Congress of the League Against Imperialism, Ford called all the black delegates together to inaugurate plans to make this conference a reality. Padmore travelled 'over half the globe' seeking to recruit delegates to attend this conference. However, the white capitalists tried to prevent this conference from becoming a reality. The British, French, South African and other imperialist governments refused to grant passports to the delegates. They even threatened to arrest and imprison those who attended the conference.[14]

At the conference, about 17 delegates from Africa, the United States and the Caribbean discussed trade union issues and problems affecting their socio-political condition. The delegates from Africa spoke about the system of forced labour and slavery that was widespread throughout Africa. They also pointed out how the imperialist governments oppressed Africans by compelling them to pay exorbitant taxes and how they lived under some of the most oppressive legislation. They also noted how the European capitalists exploited the workers in the factories, mines, the railways and the docks by paying them less than a liveable wage, whilst giving them a pittance for their crops and charging them exorbitant prices for manufactured goods and food items. The representatives from the USA highlighted the terrible oppression black workers and farmers faced. They described how 'the white capitalists and landlords rob[bed] them of their wages through long hours of toil.' They also mentioned being beaten by the police and mobs and revealed that a wave of lynchings was taking place. The Jamaica delegate described the misery and hardships faced by Jamaican and Haitian workers who went to Cuba to work on the sugar estates and were treated like slaves. He noted that most of them were now out of work and unable to return home. The situation in Antigua, Barbados, St Vincent and the Grenadines, Grenada, Dominica, Trinidad and Tobago, and British Guiana was just as bad with thousands of workers unemployed without any relief from government. This situation was compounded by the fall in sugar prices and severe drought that had literally ruined the peasants.[15]

Life and Struggles

Padmore, in the *The Life and Struggles of the Negro Toilers,* extended the discussion that was started at the Hamburg conference and fashioned a pioneering text of the Black International of Negro Toilers. This work looked closely at the conditions of workers on three continents and the potential of these workers to overthrow the oppressive, exploitative system of capitalism. Padmore argued that the oppression of Negroes takes two distinctive forms: i) they are oppressed as a class, and ii) they are oppressed as a race. He observed that black workers in Africa are more brutally exploited than the white proletariat in Europe because of their colonial status. Moreover, 'their racial subjugation assumes the most barbarous forms of oppression.' In Padmore's opinion racial oppression was most conspicuous in the Deep South of the United States and in South Africa. However, 'the general conditions under which Negroes live, either as a class or as a race, form one of the most degrading spectacles of bourgeois civilization.' What was particularly apparent to Padmore was that the crisis of capitalism had exacerbated the stark economic, political and social status of Negro workers.[16]

Padmore noted that because of the racial discrimination in South Africa, European workers were paid a higher wage than black workers. Black workers had to work long hours in some of the most 'demoralizing and devitalizing conditions' and a large number of them suffered from tuberculosis and other social and industrial diseases.[17] In West Africa, Padmore observed that the agrarian crisis had led to the universal pauperization of the peasantry. This situation was further compounded by the fall in the prices of farm products, rising costs of manufactured goods and foodstuffs, additional taxation and the application of more ruthless methods of usury by the banks and the moneylenders.[18] In the United States, black workers were feeling the effects of the economic crisis 'more severely than any other section of the working class' with millions of them 'faced with the spectre of starvation and death.'[19] In the West Indies Padmore noted that the Negro masses were exploited as viciously as the African and the black toilers in the United States. He posited that throughout the West Indies one was confronted with the 'shocking spectacle of whole populations living on the verge of starvation.'[20] In Latin America Padmore observed that there was widespread unemployment in the banana, coffee, cocoa and rubber industries, and black workers were faced with a situation where they were the last hired and the first to be laid off.[21]

Padmore called on the black workers to support the Red International of Labor Unions (RILU) because it was the first Trade Union that actively sought to promote the development of trade unions among the colonial peoples. Moreover, it was the only trade union which 'conduct[ed] a consistent and permanent struggle against white chauvinism, for equal rights for the labour movement in the colonial and the semi-colonial countries.' Padmore acknowledged that the problem of racial equality 'ha[d] not been sufficiently appraised even by many of the Profitern supporters.' However, Profitern had charted the correct route for solving the race problem. Profintern had struggled against racial chauvinism, against racial discrimination and 'for uniting the workers of all races and nations.'[21]

According to Padmore the national race policy of the Profintern was best manifested in its fight for strengthening and extending the trade union movement among the Negro workers. Moreover, Profintern had raised the Negro problem before its affiliated sections in the USA, South Africa, England, France, Belgium, Portugal and had sharply condemned all 'manifestations of white chauvinism and underestimation of winning the black workers for the class struggle, pointing out the necessity of paying the most serious attention to the organisation of workers into revolutionary trade Union with the Whites.'[23] Padmore contended that the white workers must take the initiative of bringing the Negro workers into the revolutionary unions and the movement of the unemployed, while giving them every opportunity to 'actively participate in shaping the policies of the workers' organizations and leading the united front struggles of the working class against the offensive of the capitalist.' He also advised the Negro worker to take a more active role in the 'revolutionary struggles of the working class as a whole and make a decisive break with all bourgeois and petty bourgeois reformist movements.'[24]

Editor of the *Negro Worker*

Padmore was appointed the Executive Secretary of the International Trade Union Committee of Negro Workers (ITUCNW). This organization emerged out of the Hamburg Conference of Negro Workers. According to Padmore:

> After hearing all of these reports of misery, hardships and oppression of the toiling masses, the Conference passed a number of resolutions and decided to establish a permanent organization so as to enable the Negro Trade Unions and other working class organizations in the different countries to keep in contact with each other. In this way it is hoped to develop a spirit of international solidarity among the black workers in their common struggle with the workers of other countries against imperialism.[25]

The ITUCNW was, therefore, charged with the responsibility of leading the fight of the Negro Workers in Africa, the West Indies and other colonies. The ITUCNW sought to i) carry propaganda and agitation, ii) call upon the Negro workers to organize themselves into revolutionary trade unions in order to fight for higher wages, shorter hours of work, and iii) help the millions of workers who were then unemployed and organize councils in order to demand relief from their government, free rent and non-payment of taxes.[26]

Padmore became the editor of the *Negro Worker*, the organ of the ITUCNW. As soon as he became the editor he changed the name of the journal from the *International Negro Workers Review* to the *Negro Worker*. In Padmore's view the title *Negro Worker* was shorter and therefore should enable it to be better popularized among the masses of Negro toilers. Padmore further explained that the name *Negro Worker* communicated more clearly and definitely the central objective of the committee and that only by the organization and leadership of the workers could the Negro toilers successfully carry on the struggle for their freedom and emancipation. He also gave the journal a new cover design: a picture of a Negro worker breaking his chains of enslavement that bound the black masses in the United States, West Indies and Africa. This strong Negro 'symbolises the power and the strength that lies in the great masses of Negro toilers for the class struggles and through which we must join hands with the workers of the world.'[27] In his first editorial, Padmore let his intentions for the journal be clearly articulated:

> This journal is the official organ of the International Trade Union Committee of Negro Workers. But it is our aim not to make this a

sort of theoretical journal to discuss resolutions, opinions, etc...It is our aim to discuss and analyze day-to-day problems of the Negro toilers and connect these up with the international struggles and problems of the workers. It is therefore necessary that we receive the fullest cooperation of Negro workers. This means that articles, letters, points of view and pictures of your daily life must be sent to us. It is only in this way that we can build a much needed popular journal, taking up the broad international problems of Negro Workers.[28]

C.L.R. James informs us that the *Negro Worker* gave 'tens of thousands of Negro Workers in various parts their first political education.' The journal gave:

information, advice, guidance, ideas about Negro struggles on every continent...A movement...needs an ideology. It needs a body of ideas and information in the light of which the daily grind can have some significance beyond that which is immediately visible...This the *Negro Worker* gave to hundreds of thousands of active Negroes and the millions whom they represented...Uriah Butler and workers in the Trinidad oilfields were nourishing themselves on illicit copies of the *Negro Worker* and preparing the great outburst to launch the new West Indies upon the paths of nationalism and democracy.[29]

One must mention that the colonial officials sought to prevent this journal from reaching their shores. Padmore sought to capture the reaction to this development. He stated:

...the capitalists are getting frightened and are trying to prevent the *Negro Worker* from reaching the native masses in Africa and the West Indies, because they know that if the workers and peasants read the militant paper they will wake up and fight for their rights... For without a fighting paper we cannot build a real revolutionary movement.[30]

Edward Wilson informs us that vessels coming from Europe to British West Africa were searched regularly for copies of the *Negro Worker* and the British colonial government reportedly imposed lengthy prison terms on natives in whose possession it was found.[31]

In an article entitled the 'Fight for Bread,' Padmore outlined a strategy for Negro workers in the colonies to follow in order to get food, clothing and shelter during the capitalist crisis. He stressed that the solution to protecting themselves and their families was to organize and demand social relief. Padmore felt that in Africa and the West Indian colonies, where labour unions existed, the unions must call a series of meetings of all unemployed persons. In the territories where trade unions were non-existent, 'the most active and intelligent workers in the community should call the meeting.' These meetings should be advertised as widely as possible. The leading members of the union should explain the purpose of the meeting and call upon those assembled to elect from their midst a small Committee of Action to draw up a programme to demand:

i. introduction of obligatory unemployment insurance for all out of jobs, whether men, women or youth;

ii. unemployment relief to be paid out to part-time workers;

iii. no rent or taxes to be paid by the unemployed. Reduction on house rent and taxes for those only working part-time;

iv. food, clothing, medical and dental treatment for the children of the unemployed free of charge, books and a hot midday meal for all school children;

v. funds for relief to be provided by a special tax levied on big business enterprises and capitalists and by cutting down the high salaries of the European government officials; and

vi. the introduction of old age pension; a 40 hour week and compensation for injuries on the job.[32]

Padmore anticipated that the imperialist rulers would not readily agree with these demands. However, he felt that the demonstrations by the British Guiana Labour Union provided an example of what was possible, as the Governor of British Guiana was forced to grant some very small concessions to the trade union. In the Gold Coast, widespread protest forced the Governor of that colony to withdraw his schemes for additional taxation. In the United States and in Europe, the gigantic hunger marches of the unemployed workers prevented the implementation of many contemplated anti-working class measures in these countries. These examples of 'proletarian mass action should serve as an inspiration to the unemployed colonial toilers to do likewise.' Padmore felt that the employed workers must show their class solidarity with their unemployed brothers by taking an active part in all meetings and demonstrations of the unemployed. Those workers who were still lucky enough to have a job must recognize that the bosses would play the white and coloured workers against each other. He insisted that only the common struggle of the employed and unemployed could prevent the bosses from further lowering the standard of living of all workers, and could help them to gain a human existence for themselves, their women and children.[33]

In an article 'Hands off Liberia' Padmore wrote that Liberia 'had become an economic colony of American imperialism and the peasantry the slaves of the Government and Firestone Company.' A story appeared in the major newspapers in the United States of America and Britain which accused the Liberian government and some influential Americo-Liberians of practising slavery, recruiting forced and indentured labour and exporting or selling migrant labour to the island of Fernando Po. As a consequence of these reports, the League of Nations sent a fact-finding Commission to Liberia. Padmore took issue with the recommendations of the Commission because they seemed to reflect the interest of American imperialism, moreover the report exonerated Firestone Company. He felt that the stage was being set for American imperialists with the support of the League of Nations to 'openly annex the only independent Negro country in West Africa.'[34]

Padmore felt that, given the danger which threatened Liberia, Negro workers and their white brothers should organize protests, mass meetings and demonstrate their solidarity with the Liberian working class against American imperialism, the League of Nations and their black lackeys. He further explained that the seamen and dockers in Liberia should organize themselves into trade unions as the basis for the development of a broad mass anti-imperialist movement. He argued that this was the only way that the Liberian workers would be able to defend their economic interest and carry on the struggle for improving their political and social conditions.[35]

In his 'Notes and Comments' with subtitle 'African Slave Dealer Hitler's Guest,' Padmore attacked the South African Minister Oswald Pirow who was visiting Berlin as a guest of the German government. Padmore described Pirow as one of the greatest Negro haters in the world, because of the brutal fascist methods he employed against the black masses in South Africa. He contended that Pirow wanted to study Hitler's methods and introduce new devices of terror when he returned to South Africa. Padmore also criticized Piet Grobble, the Minister of Native Affairs, for refusing to allow two black boy scouts to attend the International Boys Scouts' rally in Hungary, because they would socialize with white boys from other parts of the world and think that 'Negroes were the equals of white people.' Padmore contended that the entire psychology of these uniformed 'white tyrants' is that: 'all people with a dark skin are inferior and ordained by God to be hewers of wood and carriers of water for white men.' He argued that this kind of thinking was also evident in England among the leading politicians, but they 'do not realize that the day has gone for ever when the colonial peoples can be kept down with impunity.'[36]

Comintern Operative

In addition to the utilization of his organizational, propagandistic and journalistic skills, Padmore was a Comintern operative of some note. Part of his mission involved securing African recruits to be trained in Moscow, to return to be in the vanguard of the embryonic trade union movement and political parties. It was estimated that Padmore recruited over 60 students to go and study in Moscow.[37] While one does not know if that figure was accurate, it is common knowledge that he visited London in 1932 seeking recruits to take to Moscow. He also sought the assistance of Kobina Sekyi of the Aborigines Society in the Gold Coast in a 'scheme to send African workers from the Gold Coast to study in Europe to help the toiling masses in the Gold Coast in organizing themselves for better economic and social conditions.'[38] Padmore also visited Gambia in 1930, and 'had undertaken suspicious activities' which linked him 'to trade union activism and to the publication called the *Gambia Outlook.*'[39] Padmore, as stated before, was also responsible for bringing some of the delegates that attended the First Conference of Negro Workers, where he used his skills as a conspirator, 'a specialist in decoys, codes and stratagems.' James stated that:

> ...George himself travelled and there were agents and representatives from various units with whom he was in constant communication... [T]here were difficulties to be smoothed out, advice to be given, programmes and policies to be outlined...George acquired an extraordinary skill of understanding a situation from the slenderest data and writing a programme, outlining a policy and indicating

a line of action by which untaught and inexperienced Negroes in a particular situation could direct themselves.[40]

Conclusion

George Padmore utilized all the skills, tools and resources at his disposal to assist the Negro toilers in the struggle against the oppressive capitalist and imperialist systems. While his efforts did not realize the numbers he hoped would join the trade unions or the level of trade union development in the colonies, the seeds he planted bore fruit with the rapid development of the trade union movement and political parties in the post-Second World War period. Padmore throughout his Comintern career was an uncompromising warrior on behalf of the Negro toilers throughout the world. He became a communist because he felt that this organization would allow him to work for the liberation of his African brothers and he worked assiduously with this objective in mind.

Notes

1. George Padmore, 'An open letter to Earl Browder,' *Crisis*, October 1935.
2. Joyce Moore Turner, *Caribbean Crusaders and the Harlem Renaissance* (Urbana: University of Illinois Press, 2005), 158.
3. Mark Solomon, *The Cry was Unity: Communists and African Americans, 1917–1936* (Mississippi: University of Mississippi Press, 1998), 103.
4. George Padmore, 'Trade Union Unity Convention and the Negro Worker and the Negro Masses,' *Daily Worker*, 27 August 1929.
5. Ibid.
6. Ibid.
7. Ibid.
8. Harvey Klehr, *The Heyday of American Communism: The Depression Decade* (New York: Basic Books, 1984), 29.
9. Ibid.
10. George Padmore, 'Gastonia: Its Significance for Negro Labour,' *Daily Worker*, 4 October 1929.
11. Ibid.
12. Moore Turner, 158.
13. Solomon, 59.
14. George Padmore, *What is the International Trade Union Committee of Negro Workers?* (Hamburg: The International Trade Union Committee of Negro Workers, 1931), 4.
15. Ibid., 5–7.
16. George Padmore, *The Life and Struggles of the Negro Toilers* (California: Sun Dance Press, 1971), 5–6.

17. Ibid., 12.
18. Ibid., 27–28.
19. Ibid., 47.
20. Ibid., 57.
21. Ibid., 62–63.
22. Ibid., 121–22.
23. Ibid., 122–23.
24. Ibid., 123–24.
25. Padmore, *What is the International Trade Union Committee of Negro Workers?* (Hamburg: The International Trade Union Committee of Negro Workers), 10.
26. Ibid.
27. 'The Change in the Name of our Journal,' *Negro Worker* 1 (3) (March 1931), 2.
28. 'Our Aims,' *International Workers Review* 1 (1) (January 1931), 3.
29. C.L.R. James, 'Notes on the Life of George Padmore,' Undated typescript, Schomburg Center for Black Culture, 16–17.
30. Padmore, *What is the International Committee of Negro Workers*, 10.
31. Wilson, 219.
32. George Padmore, 'The Fight for Bread,' *Negro Worker* 3 (6/7) (June–July), 1–4.
33. Ibid.
34. George Padmore, 'Hands off Liberia,' *Negro Worker* 1 (10/11) (October–November 1931): 6.
35. George Padmore, 'Notes and Comments,' *Negro Worker* 3 (8/9) (August–September 1933): 9–16.
36. Ibid.
37. Roi Ottley, *No Green Pastures* (New York: Charles Scribner's & Sons, 1951), 62.
38. Samuel Rhodie, 'The Gold Coast Aborigines Abroad,' *Journal of African History*, 6 (3) 1965, 393.
39. Brent Edwards, *The Practice of Diaspora: Literature, Translation, and the Rise of Black Internationalism* (Cambridge, Mass. and London: Harvard University Press, 2003), 248.
40. James, 18.

11 | Self-Liberation: The Cases of Occupied Haiti and the Anglophone Caribbean's Labour Rebellions

Myrtha Désulmé

Haiti fought for 12 heroic years to win her independence from France in 1803, but was effectively re-colonized economically in 1825. During the revolution, Haitians valiantly struggled, bled, and died, but did not yield. Unable to subdue Haiti on the battlefield, France resorted to holding her ransom – through an odious, illegal, and extortionary indemnity – in exchange for recognizing her independence. The economic repercussions of this financial burden wreaked havoc on the Haitian state, stifling the growth of the infant nation.

This first era of Haiti's quasi-independence came to an abrupt end in 1915, when the United States, anxious to enforce its Monroe Doctrine in the Caribbean, invaded and occupied Haiti for 19 brutal years, through a military dictatorship. This chapter will compare and contrast Haitian resistance to the Occupation with the Labour Rebellions of the 1930s in the British Caribbean colonies, as documented by Richard Hart.

The ostensible goal of the US occupation was to impose order, and to remove the 'threat' of European loans and investment.[1] It was, in effect, a physical American colonization, to replace the French economic recolonization, and to thwart growing German interests in Haiti. Incredibly enough, the occupiers went as far as to brazenly seize Haiti's National Gold Reserve, which they transferred to National City Bank in New York, in order to ensure complete financial control.

An integral part of the programme, in fact perhaps the key, was to create a secure environment for US investment in railroads and plantation agriculture. This meant ensuring access to land, labour, and favourable financial policies. However, despite US formal and military control of the country from 1915–34, these goals were never achieved. The American Occupation led to a second Haitian revolution of self-liberation, comparable to the Labour Rebellions of the 1930s in the British Caribbean colonies. Haitians responded to US control with the twin phenomena of migration and resistance, and frustrated US efforts to establish a favourable field for investment. Control of labour was fundamental to the US agenda, but control of their own labour was also fundamental to Haitians' efforts to resist US domination of their country.

Haitian independence in 1804 had combined political sovereignty with emancipation from slavery, and both were racial victories of blacks against white domination. US political control, with all of its economic aspects, continued the connection, in Haitian political reality, of foreign imperialism, racial domination of whites over blacks, and foreign/white control of Haitian/black labour.

However, a social consciousness based on race and nationalism, and a national identity intimately tied to liberation from slavery and anti-imperialism, as well as class issues, led to a coherent and strong reaction to the US occupation, which systematically undercut US plans for the island. In fact, when US forces invaded the country in 1915, peasant fighters stayed in the field long after their supposed leaders had surrendered, turning what US policymakers called 'Haiti's ignorant and half-educated peasants,' into the spearhead of anti-imperialism in the country.

Crushing this resistance was the first stage in facilitating US investment in Haiti. In 1915, there was a continuous flow of correspondence from US businesses to the State Department regarding the necessity of a full occupation of the country, and from the State Department to business interests, assuring them that the conditions for investment were being implemented.

What US officials celebrated in particular were Haiti's low wages. Labour was of no use to US investors, however, if they could not get access to land. Dessalines' 1805 Constitution prohibited foreign property ownership, as he believed that that would lead back to slavery. One of the Occupation's first tasks was therefore to 'regularize' land tenure, by forcing the Haitian government to revise the Constitution, in order to allow foreign land ownership. This they accomplished by dissolving Haiti's elected National Assembly, thus giving the occupying forces absolute power over the Haitian President. That done, the occupying authorities instituted a system of *Corvée* or forced labour, which was used for public works, like roads and irrigation systems, that provided the infrastructure necessary for plantation agriculture, and sometimes also provided workers directly for the plantations. The *Corvée*, an old discredited nineteenth century statute dug up from Haiti's law books, confirmed Haitian peasants' primal fears that the Occupation would bring a revival of slavery. This fear led to the first major uprising of the Occupation.

In 1918, two years after the *Corvée* was instituted, a rebellion erupted, led by Charlemagne Péralte, a former Haitian officer. Péralte had been demoted for his fierce anti-Occupation views shortly after the invasion, and later resigned his commission as Military Chief of the city of Léogane. He was arrested for assaulting the home of an American Officer and was sentenced to five years of forced labour. Escaping his captivity, he fled to the mountains, from where he called for a popular uprising 'to drive the invaders into the sea and free Haiti.'[2] By the end of the year, the country was in a state of insurrection. Péralte formed a provisional government, and thousands of armed peasants, nicknamed 'Cacos,' flocked to his standard. The 'Cacos' were comparable to the rural troops which historically had provided the manpower for warring political parties in the nineteenth century. These guerrilla warriors proved to be such strong adversaries that the United States was forced to upgrade the US Marine contingent in Haiti, and employed airplanes for the first time, for counter-guerrilla warfare against unarmed peasants.

Characterized as an outlaw bandit by the American Occupiers, Péralte would soon become Haiti's premier twentieth-century martyr. He was eventually betrayed by one of his officers, who led a squadron of 22 American Marines into Péralte's camp. The invaders crept up and shot him before he could escape. Péralte was, however, just one of the 3,250 Haitian 'bandits' killed by the Marine Corps, based on their own estimation. But unlike his followers, Péralte would become an iconic legend.

The American authorities carried the dead guerrilla leader's body to his hometown of Hinche, tied it upright to a door, and photographed him. Copies were circulated throughout Haiti as an illustrated lesson in what would happen to those who rebelled against the Occupation and the 'best interests' of the Haitian people. Instead of having the desired deterrent effect, the image of the Christ-like Crucifixion was seared

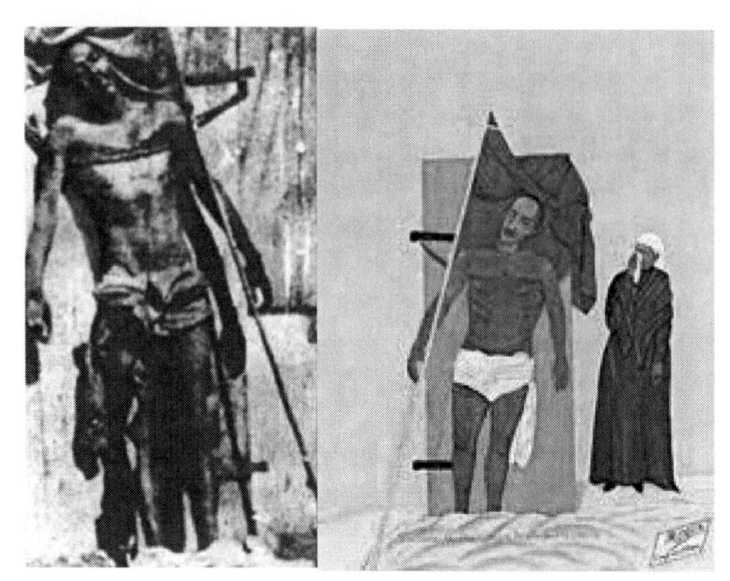

Charlemagne Péralte's photograph was later immortalized by Philomé Obin

into Haitian consciousness, and Péralte is to this day still considered one of Haiti's greatest heroes.

One of Péralte's Lieutenants, Benoît Batraville, would take up the torch of the struggle. A few months later, betrayed in turn, he would be arrested by US soldiers, and summarily executed. After the death of these guerrilla leaders, the revolutionary movement weakened and was eventually eliminated in 1921. The defeat of the rebellion opened northern Haiti as a field for investment, and several important contracts were signed with US companies shortly thereafter. American investors made it clear that they considered the Marines' presence crucial to their ability to run their businesses. Be that as it may, the Haitian peasants actively manoeuvered to maintain their independence under occupation, and ultimately succeeded.[3]

The stolid domination of the Occupation, which effectively controlled Haiti for the next eight years, with little overt resistance, was broken again by explosive political and economic forces, which converged in the fall of 1929. Economic distress caused by a poor coffee crop in 1928, and the collapse of the coffee market in 1929, due to the Great Depression, which ravaged America and Europe from 1929–39, were compounded by the Occupation's policy of constantly pressing new tax collections. These factors exacerbated the latent hatred of the Occupation, inspired by American racial condescension, and boorish military dictation. By the fall of 1929, unbeknownst to complacent officials and the State Department, popular discontent in Haiti needed only a rallying point to develop into another major uprising against the Occupation. This rallying point was provided by a series of student strikes against the Service Technique (a US-sponsored technical training programme).

On 3 December 1929 US High Commissioner in Haiti, John Russell reported to the State Department that politicians and businessmen were aligning themselves with the strikers, and that the loyalty of the Garde d'Haiti, a Haitian auxiliary force created by the Marines to replace the Army they had disbanded, was very questionable. He requested an additional force of 500 Marines immediately, to protect American lives.

The following morning, the expected uprising began with a strike by customs employees in Port-au-Prince. A large, angry mob gathered at the site of the strike. By the end of the day, the streets of Port-au-Prince were filled with agitated crowds stoning the Marine patrols, who had been called out to reinforce the Garde.

High Commissioner Russell reacted to the uprisings by reinvoking curfews and martial law, by interdicting the opposition press, and by cancelling the independent status of the Garde d'Haiti, incorporating it as a regiment of the Marine Brigade.

In the town of Cayes, 1,500 angry peasants, armed with stones, machetes, and clubs, surrounded a detachment of 20 Marines, armed with rifles and automatic weapons. The Marines had gone out to meet the peasants, who were advancing on the town, intent on securing the release of strikers arrested the day before, and on airing various grievances against the Occupation, including complaints about onerous taxes on alcohol, tobacco, and other basic goods.

This encounter culminated in the disastrous 'December 6 Cayes massacre.' The High Commissioner informed the State Department that the final hospital list totalled 12 dead and 23 wounded, and that it was possible that other deaths occurred in the hills from contaminated wounds, as all of the wounded were not brought in. Casualty lists published in the Haitian press in January 1930 totalled 24 dead and 51 wounded.

The general insurrection spread quickly throughout the country. As we will see later in the British Caribbean labour rebellions, each insurrection fed on the previous one. The *Manchester Guardian* of 9 December 1929 published the following dispatch from a British reporter in Haiti, three days after the Cayes massacre:

> The situation in Haiti, where almost the entire population is in revolt against American control...comes as no surprise to those in close touch with the affairs of the Negro Republic. Resentment against the American Occupation has long been smouldering, and needed only some minor dispute to cause it to burst into flames.

The uprisings, especially the sensational Cayes massacre, were as great a disaster as President Herbert Hoover cared to face. Hoover, in dispatching a special commission to Haiti in February 1930, declared: 'The primary question which is to be investigated, is when and how we are to withdraw from Haiti...' Subsequent American policy was to avoid further popular demonstrations at all costs, and to get out of Haiti as quickly as could be done in an orderly fashion.

While the United States government's commitments to American bondholders persisted as a source of contention until the bonds were fully paid, the withdrawal of American military and civilian personnel proceeded smoothly according to the Haitianization agreement incorporated in the accord of 7 August 1933. In the accord, the United States agreed to withdraw the last marines in October 1934. As an extra goodwill gesture, President Roosevelt, on a personal visit to Cap Haitien on 5 July 1934, announced that the last marines would leave by August 15.[4] Haiti had won its second independence.

The Case of the British Caribbean

As illustrated in the case above with the complacent US administration in Haiti, Richard Hart tells us in *Labour Rebellions of the 1930s in the British Caribbean Region Colonies*, that the Colonial Authorities in the British colonies were also lulled into a false sense of security, by what appeared on the surface to be a picture of general working class subservience and docility, while sullen resentment and dissatisfaction were swelling steadily among the working people and the unemployed in all of the British colonies in the Caribbean area, exactly as it was in occupied Haiti. Hart asserts that:

Despite the lack of inter-colony contacts, the labour rebellions of the 1930s were an inter-colony phenomenon, sweeping like a wave across the region, because the principal causes of working class unrest and dissatisfaction were the same throughout the region: low wages; high unemployment and under-employment; arrogant racist attitudes of the colonial administrators and employers in their relations with black workers; lack of adequate, or in most cases, any representation; and no established structure for the resolution of industrial disputes by collective bargaining.

Another factor increasing general distress and dissatisfaction regionally was the world economic crisis, which had started in the USA in 1929, and by the early 1930s was having a residual effect internationally. The grievances caused by these factors existed in all of the British Caribbean Colonies.[5]

As we have seen above, the grievances caused by these factors also existed in Haiti at the same time as in the British Caribbean.

We also learn from Hart, that the earliest manifestations of the growing unrest occurred in Belize, Trinidad and Tobago, Guyana, and Jamaica. In Belize, Antonio Soberanis Gomez, who had been holding public meetings expressing popular dissatisfaction, emerged as the most popular leader. Soberanis organized mass meetings in various parts of the country, and played a decisive part in channelling the growing unrest into mass action. The Governor described his speeches as 'offensive and inflammatory.' New legislation prohibited processions without police permission, and a Seditious Conspiracy Law was enacted so that, as the Attorney General explained, 'Soberanis could be successfully prosecuted for sedition.'[6]

Just as the Americans rewrote the Constitution in order to be able to seize the Haitian peasants' land, so the British enacted tailor-made, self-serving, expedient and retroactive laws in order to prosecute agitators. Like their hegemonic American counterparts, the British colonial forces resorted to censorship, the suppression of the freedom of expression, police brutality, and even murder, as illustrated in Jamaica in the Frome sugar factory strike where four people were killed and twenty-five were reported injured. Again, just as in Haiti, all parties assumed that the wounded may have been more numerous, as there was a widespread belief that anyone who sought medical treatment would thereby be identifying himself as a participant, and inviting arrest.

Hart also tells us that, in the 1930s, although legislatures existed in the British colonies, few if any workers enjoyed the right to vote in elections. The franchise was available only to persons who possessed property or income qualifications, which limited the size of the electorate to approximately 10 per cent of the adult populations. The colonial constitutions provided that effective political control remained in the hands of Governors appointed by the British Government.[7] Similarly in Haiti, the US administration dissolved the Haitian National Assembly, and rewrote the Constitution, in order to ensure that effective political control remained in the hands of the occupying forces. Hart concludes by telling us that:

> What occurred in the 1930s was a series of spontaneous uncoordinated uprisings. There had been no advance planning. Neither the leaders who emerged, nor the participants, had any premeditated conscious objectives. Nor, during the course of the rebellions, did the workers or their leaders develop any revolutionary demands, such as the expropriation of property, the seizure of political power by the working class, or the achievement of political independence. But this does not in any way detract from the historical significance of what had taken place.[8]

On the other hand, we know that in Haiti, though the uprisings were spontaneous, the workers, like the former slaves in 1804, did indeed make revolutionary demands, such as the expropriation of property, the seizure of political power by the working class, and the achievement of political independence. They not only demanded it, but in an ultimate act of self-liberation, they actually achieved it. The end result, however, was ultimately the same, if not worse, for the colonizers and the occupiers were replaced by a local elite, which replicated the pattern of the foreign oppressors vis-à-vis the masses.

As a result of the cumulative effect of the labour rebellions in the region, the British Government appointed the West India Royal Commission to investigate the causes of the rebellions. Hart relates that:

> The principal immediate benefit that the workers derived from the rebellions was that they forced upon the Royal Commission, and through its recommendations the British Government, a realisation of the need to bring trade union legislation in all the colonies into

line with legislation in Britain. Trade Unions were made lawful in those colonies where they had previously been unlawful. In all the colonies, legislation was amended or introduced, making peaceful picketing of employers' premises lawful, and giving trade unionists immunity from actions for breach of contract as a result of strikes. The organisation of trade unions followed in all the colonies, and the foundations were laid for the modern trade union movements, which continue to contribute to the struggle for an improved standard of living.[9]

In Haiti, President Hoover's Forbes Commission studied and reviewed the prevailing conditions under the Occupation, and negotiated the four-year withdrawal process of the US Marines from Haiti, which ended the Occupation.

Hart further mentions, that there were three islands – Dominica, Grenada and Antigua – where, in the 1930s, although plantations and distressing poverty existed, no labour rebellions occurred. How can this be explained?

We are told that a relevant factor in Dominica and Grenada may have been that in those islands, independent peasant farmers comprised a larger percentage of the working population than in the other islands.[10] That is, in fact, the same solution the Haitian peasantry resorted to, for a peaceful, albeit, precarious life.

In the early nineteenth century, while fighting to maintain the integrity of the national territory, and live free of outside interference, the Haitian military and landed gentry hijacked the freedom and democracy the masses had fought for alongside them, and tried to bind the peasantry to the plantations once more. Having inherited a plantation economy, the prosperity of the minority continued to depend on the exploitation of the majority. The former slaves, however, would have none of it. Rejecting the perpetuation of the plantation economy, they fled to the hills, determined to survive on their own subsistence farming.

In his brilliant essay, 'Locating Haiti in the Caribbean,' distinguished Trinidadian scholar Lloyd Best tells us that:

> At the time of Independence in 1804, 50–60 percent of the slaves were African-born, and called *negs bossales*, the rest being Haitian creoles. Freedom in the rest of the Caribbean was achieved at a later date with an overwhelming number of slaves creolized over an

extended period. In Haiti, however, the fact of this enormous mass of Africans, suddenly acquiring independence, and creating their own country, constitutes a very special situation, which has existed nowhere else. It played a determining and unique role, revolving around the African-born, who became creolised only under conditions of freedom, and who formed the core of a peasantry that did not consist of mere footloose cultivators, creatures of the plantation, but who satisfied the Aristotelian condition of organised householders, engaged on autonomous production for domestic consumption, and only after that, for export trade, and international investment.

Best quotes French anthropologist, Gérard Barthélemy:

> The most important thing about the Haitian case is the very profound economic and social revolution made by the Haitian people, when they repudiated the system of plantation slavery. Everywhere else in America, the system of slavery and the system of the large plantations were preserved. Until official abolition in the Caribbean, Haiti was the only country which achieved this fundamental revolution.[11]

This revolution resulted in the phenomenon of the two Haitis, with an isolated and independent peasantry, which the government, the oligarchy, and later the American occupiers, nevertheless found the means of exploiting through unjust and disproportionate taxation on the exportation of their production, and on the importation and consumption of primary goods. This exploitative taxation without representation inhibited the independence and autonomy sought by the hardworking peasantry, the backbone of the country's productive sector, hence the rebellions.

In Antigua, on the other hand, we learn from *Sources of West Indian History*, that the opposite circumstances prevailed, ironically resulting in the same inhibition of labour rebellions as in Dominica and in Grenada. The Antiguan experience was one of 'utter dependence' of the slave labourer 'on the proprietor and the capitalist for the means of procuring food'; due to the 'peculiarity of climate and the absence of unoccupied lands, except those of absolute sterility.'

A large portion of the population, whether bond or free, could not hope for the means of subsistence, except by some labourious occupation in one of those frequent periods of long drought, especially to which [Antigua is] almost annually subject.[12]

Black Nationalism: The Common Denominator

The sheer brutality of the US Occupation elicited a tremendous nationalistic movement. It galvanized nationalistic pride and black consciousness amongst all classes of Haitians. Emerging from those harrowing years of overt reaction, virulent racism, and stifling oppression, the nascent Garveyism of the 1930s in the British Caribbean would be mirrored by the rising *Négritude* movement in the Franco-African world. This *Négritude* movement known as *Indigéniste* in Haiti would lead to the emergence of a Black Nationalist movement in 1946, resulting in Haiti's third Black Revolution: 'La Révolution de '46.'

After 30 years of US-enforced mulatto rule, culminating in the ineffective administration of President Élie Lescot (1941–45), which installed mulattoes in virtually every post of the government, black voters turned out en masse and elected a sympathetic National Assembly. Following much radical social agitation, the 1946 presidential election, often referred to as the Revolution of 1946, was contested by three black candidates. Dumarsais Estimé (1946–50) won the election, garnering especially strong support from the emerging middle class of blacks in the northern region of the country. An analogous Black Power movement would reach Jamaica in the '60s and '70s.

According to Richard Hart, one of the problems confronting the pioneers of the popular movements of the 1930s was the formidable historical legacy of a widespread lack of racial self-respect. 'While many peoples who have been subjected to alien domination have been able to draw strength and inspiration from their own legends and history, the Jamaican people were at a disadvantage. The imperial power had largely succeeded in erasing from their memory their African cultural heritage. Jamaica had no legends, but it did have a history...which, if brought to the people's attention, could provide abundant inspiration for future struggles against oppression.'[13]

One hundred and eighty years before Hart's writings, the enslaved Africans of Haiti had risen up, and struck a historic blow against white supremacy, demolishing the myth of white superiority and invincibility, as well as the fiction, 'sedulously disseminated, that the enslavement of Africans was part of the natural order of things....'[14] The Haitian revolution of 1791 defied the global racial order, and in so doing, changed the course of humanity. In Dessalines's 1805 Constitution, the first ruler of independent Haiti declared that: *'All Haitians shall hence forward be known only by the generic appellation of Blacks.'* Black is thus de-racialized in terms of skin colour, and becomes the appellation for Haiti's liberators, no matter their colour. *Black denotes the Lovers-of-Liberty*, who stood for freedom and human dignity, and were willing to live free or die. Haiti becomes the first Western nation founded on universal freedom and racial self-respect, as its starting point.

Despite our differing languages, religions, customs, and other cultural traits inherited from the colonizers, the people of the Caribbean have faced a similar history of slave rebellions and labour uprisings. In order to transcend the socio-politically constructed race paradigm, in which white supremacy established itself as a determinant of moral and social hierarchies, racial self-respect has had to be one of the pillars of inspiration for the advancements achieved by Caribbean people.

Notes

1. See Aviva Chomsky, 'Migration and Resistance: Haitian Workers under US Occupation, 1915–34,' Unpublished manuscript, Bates College, 1995.
2. Robert Debs Heinl Jr and Nancy Gordon Heinl, *Written in Blood: The Story of the Haitian people, 1492–1971* (Boston: Houghton Mifflin Co., 1978), 452.
3. See Chomsky.
4. Hans Schmidt, *The United States Occupation of Haiti, 1915–1934* (New Jersey: Rutgers University Press, 1971), 229–30.
5. Richard Hart, *Labour Rebellions of the 1930s in the British Caribbean Region Colonies* (London: Caribbean Labour Solidarity and the Socialist History Society, 2002), 5–6.
6. Ibid., 7.
7. Ibid., 5.
8. Ibid., 24.
9. Idem.
10. Ibid., 21.
11. Lloyd Best, 'Locating Haiti in the Caribbean,' Paper presented at the Haitian Bicentennial Conference, University of the West Indies, St Augustine, July 2004.
12. F.R. Augier and Shirley C. Gordon, *Sources of West Indian History* (London: Longman Caribbean Ltd., 1962), 147.
13. Richard Hart, *Slaves Who Abolished Slavery: Volume 1. Blacks in Bondage*. (Kingston: Institute of Social and Economic Research, University of the West Indies, 1980), i–ii.
14. Richard Hart, *Slaves Who Abolished Slavery: Volume 2. Blacks in Rebellion*. (Kingston: Institute of Social and Economic Research, University of the West Indies, 1985), iii.

12 | *Imagining Freedom: Afro-Jamaican Yearnings and the Politics of the Workers' Party of Jamaica*

Obika Gray

My interest in this topic began with my own earlier effort to assess the social power of the urban poor in relation to the politics of the dominant political parties. The result of that inquiry was a book in which I explained an oddity in the status of the rebellious urban poor: they existed as social pariahs, yet managed to display awesome social power.[1]

The argument there was that sections of the Afro-Jamaican inner city poor experienced not just economic marginalization, but also massive social dishonour and a violent political parasitism by the two dominant political parties, the People's National Party (PNP) and the Jamaica Labour Party (JLP). That party parasitism from above, combined with both violent repression and cultural solicitation of the black poor, helped spawn a species of social power that had massive negative repercussions – not just for party politics, but also for the fate of democracy, the rule of law, civil liberties and moral culture in Jamaica. Indeed, negative social power by militant alienated blacks in urban Jamaica has thrown in doubt the very idea of Jamaica as a civilized society.

A concern with the politics of the Workers' Party of Jamaica (WPJ) sprang, therefore, from an interest in seeing how communists would fare in such a setting. I wanted to assess what would happen when a Marxist-Leninist vanguard party and its middle class leaders made a bid for power and for labour's support in Jamaica's violent clientelist democracy. It should be emphasized that this democracy could accommodate personalities, parties and organizations that championed the cause of the poor, even as it repudiated communists' presence within the political mainstream and inside the two dominant political parties.[2]

Complementing this interest, I also wanted to assess how these communists would respond to the urban poor's sweeping cultural influence and massive presence in the country's political life. How did the WPJ relate to the subaltern politics of this group at once inured to outlawry and uncivil forms of expressing discontent? After all, the alienated poor had long been engaged in plaintive rioting, banditry and social predation, extortion rackets, and readiness to employ menaces, intimidation and violence. This not just against the state and against better off classes, but also, stunningly, against other members of the poor! Such outlawry from below therefore contained both an anti-system animus as well as self-destructive impulses harmful to the poorer classes. Indeed, this horizontal violence among the poor was all the more terrifying since the main political parties, the JLP and the PNP, had a role in facilitating it while keeping it within certain boundaries.

Thus, neither the Jamaican state nor the communists in the WPJ could afford to ignore this outlawry and its moral underpinnings. Indeed, even as such uncivil behaviours and anomic sensibilities threatened the status quo, it is arguable that they also posed particular problems for the leaders in the WPJ. This was so because the most alienated section of the urban poor typically repudiated not just conventional norms and the moral authority of civic and political leaders, but they also rejected the very idea of political tutelage and moral leadership from any source but themselves.

Because WPJ left-wing political activists in the 1970s hoped to mobilize and organize popular disaffection under radical middle class leadership, the potential for sharp conflict between the moral culture of the alienated urban poor, and the political culture of dissident middle class leaders and their organizations becomes apparent.

This contradiction would prove especially acute for the radical intellectuals who formed the Workers Party of Jamaica in 1978, since they unapologetically subscribed to the organizational culture, leadership style and the mass-elite relations associated with orthodox communist parties. Above all else, this political culture affirmed the importance of the communist elite as leaders of the working class and as the indispensable agents of revolutionary political change. Moreover, as communists committed to this kind of political orthodoxy, WPJ leaders justified the right to lead not just by dint of education and class membership, but also by conceited command of a difficult political technique: the theory and practice of Marxism-Leninism.

Even more important, as persons acutely aware of politically motivated violence that was sometimes directed at them, and anxious not just about the island's violent political culture, but fearful also of surveillance by state security agencies and the police, WPJ leaders early on adopted both a bunker mentality as well as the severe, sacrificial style typical of an embattled revolutionary elite, despite the fact that Jamaica was not in the throes of social revolution. By resorting to clandestine politics and encouraging recruits to think of themselves as communists under siege, the WPJ broke decisively with the post-colonial left's generally open and informal orientation.

While admirable in many respects, this overarching commitment to organizational norms and rules with their iron logic and insistence on deference came up against a long-held disposition among the alienated Afro-Jamaican poor: That political life should express powerfully held cultural concerns, and that the search for an alternative politics should not diminish Afro-Jamaicans' sense of themselves as free persons. In sum, for Afro-Jamaicans, the search for freedom had to reinforce and be consonant with their cultural identity, their jealously guarded ethnic pride and inborn sense of liberty.

Afro-Jamaicans' pride in their long-standing sense of birthright freedom expressed this sentiment well. In fact, it would not be too much of an exaggeration to say that by the 1970s criminal and non-criminal social action among the Afro-Jamaican poor became increasingly defined in terms of this deeply held ethnically inflected sense of freedom. To be sure, that sense of inborn liberty was complemented by desire for inclusion and social reconciliation on the basis of equal identity and equal competence inherent in capability for personal and group achievement and a mastery of social life the Afro-Jamaican poor knew they possessed.

Could the WPJ find a meaningful foothold in a Jamaican political setting in which both parties had not only bid up distribution of handouts in exchange for votes, but were also hailing the Afro-Jamaican population with a political language that emphasized not just disputes over the uses of power, but also contentions over cherished notions of freedom and liberty and their possible link to ethnicity?

I hope it is no longer controversial to say that then, in the 1970s, as now, substantial political freedom existed in Jamaica and that the idea of freedom – no matter its violation in this same period by the state and by its victims among the poorer classes – remained a cherished ideal and a widely shared value.

More than that, the Jamaican constitution, its laws, public policies and most of Jamaica's social and political institutions have, in the main, affirmed these democratic values. The 65-year-long durability of Jamaican democracy attests to the importance of the value of political freedom and to the population's effective enjoyment of social freedoms more broadly.

Indeed, it is arguable that in Jamaica's class and racially divided society of the 1970s, all classes generally sought some form of freedom for themselves. Moreover, there was not just a single notion of freedom abroad at this time, but rather several competing versions of it.

I shall argue below that there were four versions of imagining freedom that were deeply held across the class system in this period. I call these birthright freedom with Eric Foner, capabilities freedom with Amartya Sen, and rule of law and political freedom with liberal theorists.[3]

The first two ideas of freedom – birthright and capabilities freedom – were held and given great emphasis by the popular classes, while the latter two – rule of law freedom and political freedom – were accorded great significance by political and economic elites, and by a majority of Jamaicans who subscribed to both conventional norms and to the juridical principles associated with the modern democratic post-colonial state. These other ways of imagining freedom collided with the other two, birthright and capability freedom.

To be sure, concerns for social justice, economic want, and the standard of living remained important to the poorer classes. However, in the 1970s and after, there can be little doubt that a majority of the Jamaican population was powerfully imagining and contesting rival versions of liberty, rights, power, and yes, freedom! Why there should be this acute concern across the class system with the idea of liberty at this time no doubt had to do with how conflicting classes viewed the ongoing social struggle at the time and their stake in its outcomes.

Delayed Destiny: Political Domination in Jamaica and the Emergence of a Communist Vanguard Party

Commentators on class and political domination in post-colonial Jamaica have rightly identified violent political clientelism and manipulative middle class populism as highly effective mechanisms of class control.[4] Despite the fact that these forms of control are now collapsing, it is indisputable that they successfully blunted, co-opted or harshly repressed every form of popular resistance that emerged since political independence.

More than that, the operation of this structure of domination blocked all efforts by dissident middle class intellectuals and other activists of every political stripe to subvert it. All attempts by these intellectuals to create and build durable alternative organizations that could win popular support ended in abject failure. Such was the effectiveness of this form of domination over the years that it has not only blocked change from below, but won support for various projects of political reform from the same dissident middle class intellectuals who had opposed such reforms.

The post-war Jamaican political landscape is therefore littered with the wreckage of these failed movements and related organizations. That landscape is identified with the bitter frustrations of university-trained political intellectuals as well as grassroots popular intellectuals who have seen their own repeated bids for power come to naught. Thus, in the 20 years between 1950 and 1970, a succession of these anti-systemic movements and leaders emerged and quickly passed from the political scene.

Among them were: The People's Freedom Movement led by Richard Hart; the Rastafarian Movement at the forefront of which was Claudius Henry; the Workers Liberation Union led by Hugh Small; the Young Socialist League in which Denis Daley and Hugh Small played leading roles; the Marxist-oriented Unemployed Workers Council led by Ben Monroe; the Jamaica Congress of Labour led by Chris Lawrence; the Independent Trade Union Advisory Council; the university-based New World Group in which Lloyd Best and others played a significant role; the anti-social rude bwoy phenomenon; the contraflow of black nationalist sentiment in reggae music that made Bob Marley its herald; the Jamaica Council of Human Rights; the breakthrough black power intervention of Guyanese historian and political activist, Walter Rodney; and the black power Abeng Movement.

These movements, organizations and leaders were expressions of the rich variety of outlooks that comprised a protean tradition of radicalism in the country. In the 1950s and after, it contained sentiments and forms of activism by orthodox and independent-minded communists, trade unionists, and socialists. This tradition also included the contributions of secular nationalists, as well as religiously-minded, prophetic black movements like the Rastafarian phenomenon. Though labourist and Marxist-oriented ideological currents held a significant place within this tradition, it was militancy based on race-consciousness that became truly national and popular in the '60s.

This other militancy was rooted in a long tradition of black radicalism in which racial identity assumed pride of place. It was a decisive force for change in the '50s and after. In fact, as the decade of the '60s came to a close, it became clear that a distinct, popular current had moved to the fore: this in the form of a racially informed rebellion by militant, primarily youthful sections of the urban poor, at whose head stood radical contingents of the lumpenproletariat. Of course, militant labourism and national concerns rooted in feelings of impugned racial honour together defined the period, but in Jamaica, as elsewhere, it was mostly culturally defined animus, not exclusively class concerns, that proved subversive.

Individually, none of these organizations or movements possessed sufficient capability to topple Jamaican governments or to seize state power. But cumulatively these organizations, movements and personalities undermined the legitimacy of authoritarian state power, and while not rendering it impotent, such movements at least limited the destructive impact of authoritarian power. By the late 1960s and early 1970s then, a broad opposition in Jamaica that saw the conjunction of militant and orthodox labourism, as well as affirmation of African-civilization identity and demand for democracy, succeeded in eroding the legitimacy of authoritarian democratic power.

In this respect, the Jamaican anti-systemic social movement echoed non-Western peoples' epic resistance to an exploitative capitalist world order. After all, in the sweep of twentieth-century radical resistance to despotism elsewhere, and especially in the heyday of the so-called 'revolutions in the third world,' autocratic regimes were toppled by socialist revolution, by left-wing army officers, by armed guerillas, as well as by mass popular movements affirming a democratically-inspired 'people power.' Broad popular movements combining both national and social concerns therefore succeeded in routing dictators like Fulgencio Batista in Cuba, the Shah of Iran, Anastasio Somoza in Nicaragua, Ferdinand Marcos in the Phillipines, and more recently, the Duvaliers in Haiti.

Likewise, in this high period of post-war popular revolt, both armed insurrectionist movements and the strategy of 'people's war' successfully challenged and even overthrew dictatorial regimes across the globe. From the '50s right through to the '80s in all areas of the Global South, then, myriad forms of popular resistance emerged to confront regimes deemed to be oppressive. Socialists, communists, populists, as well as nationalist leaders headed up these movements and while the majority of them failed to win power, a minority succeeded in taking power with destabilizing contagion effects for the international system.

For instance, one can hardly think of revolution and upheaval in Latin America in the 1960s and after without taking into account the impact of a Fidel Castro; nor can the late 1970s rise of political Islam in the Middle East and elsewhere be appreciated without the leadership of the Ayatollah Khomeini.

In each instance, both national and social concerns combined to topple autocratic regimes. But it must also be said that in each case it was the national dimension that assumed pre-eminence, since what was being challenged was partly an affront to the 'nation,' – to an imperilled national culture, and to a sense of sovereignty violated. How else to explain the felicitous role of Islam in the Iranian revolution, the significance of impugned national dignity in the Cuban revolt, or the role of Catholic identity in the Nicaraguan revolution? In each case, the popular movement came to identify foreigners as being in charge of the destiny of the people-nation, whether in the form of an invasive American imperialism, or in the incumbency of a culturally foreign native elite.

To be sure, while the working class participated in these upheavals, they were neither demographically dominant, nor morally and ideologically pre-eminent in this insurgency across the so-called Third World. The dominant ideological discourse in these movements was not expressed in the worker-labourist accent, but rather in the popular-democratic idiom. In these non-Western settings, orthodox labourism as challenger, pitting bourgeoisie and proletariat at the barricades, was displaced by something more complicated: Namely, emergence of a variegated grassroots opposition that drew labour and other social forces to it, yet dominated the latter in the name of hegemonic national interests.

For Jamaica, however, successful challenge to abusive power came neither by socialist revolution, nor by seizure of power by reform-minded army officers, nor by means of a broad popular revolt. Rather, power in Jamaica during the '60s was undermined by means of capillary forms of dissidence, reflecting a protean democratic culture among the Jamaican people that cumulatively called into question the Creole nationalist project of accommodating a dependent sovereignty in which the Afro-Jamaican majority was economically marginalized, culturally demeaned, and politically victimized.

As we now know, the momentous 1972 victory of the PNP began the process of making important adjustments in this dependency. Yet despite this political breakthrough, the PNP success antagonized and inflamed sections of the far left in Jamaica, many of whom saw in the PNP victory, and especially its 1974 declaration of Democratic Socialism, only the permanent cunning of class and political domination since the emergence of modern party politics in Jamaica in 1944.

It was this core belief that PNP and JLP politics represented an unbroken record of manipulation and blunting of popular aspirations along with the Left's memory of defeat which drove a tiny minority of political intellectuals at the University of the West Indies to make a momentous break with their own tradition of open political organizing.

Thus, unbeknownst to most Afro-Jamaicans joyously celebrating the 1972 PNP victory, a fateful mutation had already occurred in the ranks of the very left wing opposition that had helped secure the PNP's triumph over the JLP.

Three years prior to the PNP's victory, the Abeng Newspaper Movement had collapsed in acrimony, as a small contingent within it pressed for a shift from the Abeng movement's black culturalism and black nationalist politics, to the adoption of scientific socialism.

Although the Abeng movement was ideologically diverse and

included radical Catholics, patriotic liberals, as well as Rastafarians and Marxists of various persuasions, it was the nationalist contingent organized around racial concerns and cultural identity politics that became hegemonic. Unfortunately, however, despite its unparalleled ideological dominance, 'black culturalism' and its exponents were unable to transform its appeal into a viable political practice that posed a real alternative to the status quo.

As several left wing forces looked for a way forward and searched for organizational vehicles and ideological means to transcend indirection and political uncertainty on the left, advocates for scientific socialism and for a shift to organizing the working class pushed hard for their cause. In the aftermath of the collapse of the Abeng Newspaper Movement these intellectuals from the university scored important political victories over their demoralized black nationalist opponents. As champions of activist politics and direct political engagement with the working class, they wrote biting critiques of black culturalism, and in time scored a significant victory against their major opponent, the advocates of Black Nationalism.

This socialist group maintained that black nationalism, for all its popularity among the people, was exhausted as an ideology and as a social force. The socialists insisted on a turn not just to a materialist viewpoint and class-based approach, but also to a Marxist-Leninist politics that could conceivably win power. Led by Trevor Munroe, Derek Gordon, Don Robotham and other academics, this contingent, against fierce opposition from nationalists and other leftists, began to restructure the collapsed Abeng movement along Marxist-Leninist lines. The on-campus organizing vehicles for these initiatives were the Paul Bogle League and the Socialism Group that was formed in 1972. Both were small study circles devoted to studying scientific socialism, although the League was the earlier vehicle for recruiting students and sympathetic activists on the campus and elsewhere.

This evolution was by no means straightforward or unproblematic. Indeed, between 1969 and 1971 radical activists and organizations including those forming the post-Abeng group were consumed with figuring out where next to take the popular opposition, considering which social force might lead the movement, debating what organizational form the movement should now assume, and the ideology it should adopt. Black nationalists from the former Abeng movement and elsewhere also searched for options that could embrace their culturalism, while taking them beyond it into revolutionary politics. For many of these nationalists, however, scientific socialism was not the way forward. Others of their ilk, however, had observed a reinvigorated PNP that was now championing the people's cause. And notwithstanding bitter knowledge of repeated PNP betrayal of its own radicals, a few of these activists looked once again to the PNP as a source of radical change.

Notwithstanding a distrust for the PNP's newfound radicalism, this group – the so-called revolutionary nationalists – were persuaded by Michael Manley, the PNP's new charismatic leader. He sought their support for his restructuring of the PNP's politics and won it when several activists from the Abeng Movement joined Manley's new movement for social change. Still, the PNP leader was not entirely successful in winning middle class radicals to his cause. Holding a long-standing animus for the PNP's well-known reformism and tendency to incorporate radicals and then to expel them, activists like Trevor Munroe drew the appropriate lessons from the PNP's history with the left and with popular movements and firmly rebuffed Manley's invitation.

It was amidst this contention and debate inside the Abeng in the wake of its collapse, that a clandestine Leninist formation – the so-called Paul Bogle League – made its historic appearance on the Jamaican political scene. Dismay with the political status quo in Jamaica among this tiny minority of university-trained political intellectuals had once again led members of the middle class to create yet another dissident political formation. This time, however, the small group operated clandestinely, hiding from public view its growing commitment to Marxism-Leninism as this sect's new approach to politics and organization.

At this early stage, it is clear that not just anyone could join this special group. It was Trevor Munroe who appeared to have been the gatekeeper and severe monitor of recruits' ideological fitness. In fact, one did not join the Paul Bogle/Socialism Group, but entered them by secret invitation only. This siege mentality seemed strikingly at odds, then, with the democratic political opening ushered in by the PNP's victory.

A wave of popular protest had swept the authoritarian JLP regime from power in an electoral floodtide in 1972, and a new militancy was afoot. Firstly, this expressed a demand for participation, equal citizenship and for the redistribution of power and rights. Secondly, the new militancy was captured in the people's unceasing desire for material betterment and economic uplift in the form of jobs, better pay, and the need for housing, healthcare, education and welfare. Thirdly, and perhaps most importantly, the new militancy affirmed deep ontological values of African cultural provenance.

In them, cultural familiars to Afro-Jamaicans such as affirmation of the right to an honourable identity, acknowledgement of African-civilization membership, right to be treated with dignity in the workplace, as well as yearning for moral infrangibility in the society were given pride of place. The new militancy of the Afro-Jamaican people was captured therefore in the protean character of a durable, but comparatively mild, martial tradition of making huge sacrifices for a just cause by engaging in protracted warfare with those deemed to be oppressors.

This tradition was comprised of working-class labourism, grassroots black nationalist culturalism, religiously-based prophetic movements, and a fugitive insurgency designed to both thwart state power and to recover that power for the people. Racially inflected concerns for more power and more rights were core features in the new militancy.

Meanwhile, the search for an independent politics in which left-wing radicals sought to link themselves to the working people had begun in earnest from 1970–72. By the latter year, it was clear that these university-based radicals had identified the working class as the leading force for change, and had made orthodox Marxist-Leninist politics and ideology their guide. Indeed, the decision of the small band of Marxists at UWI that had sought links to labour and had looked to the working class to build a new movement was vindicated. The proof came when disaffected unionized workers at the Mona campus sought out these same radicals to represent them in a labour dispute. In a stunning and fortuitous development, a small group of academics who had long been isolated from the black working class and who had now become Marxist-Leninists saw their bold voluntarism and theoretical option for the working class confirmed with this summons. In a hard-fought and sometimes violent battle for representation, these Marxists formed the University and Allied Workers Union (UAWU) and won the representational poll in 1971 against determined and violent activists and organizers from the Bustamante Industrial Trade Union.

Fortune had smiled on these Marxists, and their victory seemed a vindication of the approach they had championed against determined opposition. The creation of the UAWU was certainly reproof to their nemesis, the black nationalists, that much more than ideology-critique of power, and more than militant culturalism were required of dissidents seeking to improve the lives of the Jamaican people.

The UAWU's unprecedented triumph against perhaps the most powerful trade union in the country could not but embolden these campus-based leftists and give a fillip to their bold voluntarism. Between 1971 and the PNP's 1972 electoral victory, this tiny group of UWI academics continued their recruitment, while deepening the study of Marxism with an eye not just to its relevance for Jamaica's political experience, but more importantly, for its ability to help these self-identified revolutionary intellectuals to win political power!

Two developments were especially striking in this early period. The first was Trevor Munroe's and others' ability to recruit the best and brightest talents from among students and lecturers on the Mona campus. The League and Socialism Group attracted continuing students and leading graduates from the university. Both these tiny formations on the UWI campus drew freshly minted UWI graduates, middle class professionals, as well as returning Jamaican leftists with advanced degrees from leading American universities to their cause. The core group, however, came from the departments of sociology, government and economics at Mona.

Presence in the university, therefore, afforded these fledgling Marxists unparalleled access to high-level talent hitherto unavailable to socialist movements in the post-war period. At a time when students, professionals and the alienated intelligentsia in the country were giving their support to the reformist PNP and to other political initiatives, leaders of the Socialism Group managed to snare many of them.

Hence while it is arguable that the PNP's 'Better Must Come' campaign for office between 1969–72 had snapped up the lion's share of talented youth, intellectuals, professionals, and other personnel with scarce cultural capital, the tiny Paul Bogle League and the Socialism Group got more than their fair share of radically-oriented personnel with university training. This happened precisely because of these left wing organizations' presence on the campus, and more importantly, because of these left-wing leaders' class and personal ties to each other and to their recruits.

The Leninists meanwhile held to a sectarian politics and belief that Marxist-Leninist mobilization of the working class was the right strategy. Nor was this thinking tempered by the PNP's November 1974 declaration of democratic socialism. Rather than seeing this development as a further political breakthrough that sharpened the contradictions between the people and the domestic and international ruling class, the UWI Leninists early on set their face firmly against this development. In fact, the declaration spurred the UWI radicals to action. Within two months of the PNP's declaration, therefore, the UWI Leninists announced the formation of the Workers Liberation League (WLL). The group had thus moved from clandestine recruitment and study to open agitational politics in mid-December 1974. Four years later, a political party – the Workers' Party of Jamaica (WPJ) – had replaced the WLL. This new party formalized and intensified the Leninism and conspiratorial tendencies carried over from the Paul Bogle League and the WLL.

UWI Leninists and Democratic Jamaica

It is arguable that the group of socialistically-inclined middle class intellectuals that emerged in the '60s nursed a political wound that the creation of the Paul Bogle League, the Socialism Group, the WLL and the WPJ were meant to repair.

That wound was created from the memory of defeat. This record of defeat, which this post-independence left mournfully took as its own, is substantial and shockingly protracted. The long list includes: Alexander Bustamante's sundering of the national movement in 1942; the PNP's 1952 expulsion of the 4Hs; the failure of Richard Hart's People's Freedom Movement; the routing of Hugh Small's Workers' Liberation Union in the sugar fields of Westmoreland; the frustrations of the Young Socialist League and bitter memories of PNP sanctioning of their leaders in the 1960s; the meager political yield of the Walter Rodney's Black Power intervention; the failure of the New World Group and the subsequent acrimonious collapse of the Abeng Movement. If the organizationally deficient and seemingly pyrrhic gains of post-war black culturalism and Rastafarianism are included, then this left's agonism for its own fate and for that of the Jamaican people is understandable.

What seems problematic about the anxiety of post-independence middle class leftists that turned to Leninism, however, are the lessons they apparently drew from the experience of defeat. Those lessons were informed by a dark, pessimistic conception of power and of the bankruptcy of middle class nationalist leadership in Jamaica. For these leftists, the Jamaican political order was despotic, violently repressive, and headed by a venal, manipulative political elite. This view reflected this left's interpretation of its difficult political experience. But their views were also stirred by the imbibing of a potent blend of Fanonist and orthodox Marxist views of the national bourgeoisie in peripheral formations as irredeemably venal and corrupt.

In scholarship, pamphleteering and in failed activism, the narrative that this left recited for all to hear was one of PNP and JLP betrayals; of the need for an independent mass politics based on the working class; and the insufficiency of a popular black nationalism shorn of organizational rigour and effective political leadership. In all this, not much was said with any specificity about the political and cultural traditions of the Jamaican people, since these traditions were regarded as the puppeteered effects of decades of elite misrule. In sum, this group regarded the people's tradition as throttled and contaminated with bourgeois values and this disaffected left blamed a Jamaican statecraft that was despotic, and even cruelly repressive for these outcomes.

In the view of these newly-minted Leninists, Jamaican power holders brooked no challenge and showed no compunction in crushing dissent. The authoritarian '50s and '60s appeared to confirm this dark view of power since, in truth, radical organizations were infiltrated, books and literature banned, dissenting party members expelled, and violence employed to deny expression of political opinion and curb democratic choice, though more so in the urban slums than in middle class precincts.

While the adoption in Jamaica of a Leninist form of the vanguard party with its closed structure, hygienic approach to membership, and celebration of a knowledge elite may be rightly criticized for its unapologetically elitist model of political leadership, it is also true that this vanguard did secure a breakthrough in one major respect. This was its searing induction and socialization of radicalized sections of the middle class intelligentsia into the rigours of sacrificing much for an uncertain political cause.

By the time the WPJ was created in 1978, a tiny minority of Jamaica's political intellectuals was experiencing, for the first time, that arduous process of doing exhausting political work; of engaging in round-the-clock rituals of intense party work; and participating in a myriad of political activities to the neglect of all else.

As Alvin Gouldner usefully reminds us, the Leninist vanguard party is as much a vehicle for socializing middle class intellectuals into these rituals – the better to calm their anxieties as they engage in perilous political work – as it is a mechanism for training the working class in revolutionary politics.[5]

In another respect, despite its undoubted faults, adoption of the Leninist vanguard model in Jamaica might have had another salutary function. Notwithstanding the fact that holding fast to a hygienic approach to recruitment and holding firmly to an unchangeable class-driven political line cost the WPJ dearly, its leaders' fear of moral contamination and anxiety for ideological pollution might have actually saved the WPJ from the worst crudities and excesses that the lumpen and other unemployed strata brought with their incorporation into the two dominant political parties.

In the worst cases, these parties actively recruited, trained and funded the grasping, piratical and over-loyal partisans from the slums whose motivations were less about defending grand utopian ideals, than about whetting their appetites with the parties' bounties. WPJ circumspection regarding who could join its ranks and WPJ scrutiny of potential members for their ideological fitness, personal habits and moral traits, was not just a routine attempt to guard against infiltrators and saboteurs, but more importantly a valuable corrective to the then-prevailing tendency that popular culture, no matter its expression, should have unchecked sway within political parties.

Thus, while the PNP and the JLP encouraged and recruited participants from the most morally corrupt sections of the working class and abided the presence of a venal lumpenproletariat, the WPJ's vanguard party model of excluding potential recruits on the basis of their moral and ideological fitness greatly relieved the WPJ of the trap of adding, in the name of the people, this dissonant and anomic culture to an otherwise morally stringent party culture.

Dismissing and excluding the lumpen on the basis of their venality, moral turpitude and ideological unfitness was one thing; to ignore their instructive role as the leading force for the idea of black freedom in Jamaica, a value itself nested inside the Jamaican people's commitment to an expansive, general notion of freedom and liberty, was quite another. The WPJ's neglect of this general and broad idea of freedom, its association with class concerns and contestations about its meaning as a premium value for all Jamaicans, would, in time, cripple the WPJ.

Correlatively, these anxious leftists also held to a conception of poor and working class Jamaicans as a long-suffering people if not ripe for revolt, then certainly starved of firm revolutionary leadership. Antecedent forms of protest and modes of organizing were seen as having failed in large part because of their porousness, their ephemeral character that allowed no institutional continuity, and their lack of organizational capacity that could allow them to seize political opportunities and transform them into meaningful political gains. Equally important was the judgment that earlier protest movements were deficient in their ability to withstand sustained intimidation, and incapable of surviving punitive violence and infiltration by the Special Branch. As the 1970s wore on and as violent partisan attacks mounted, there was indeed need for security not just for the WPJ itself, but also more importantly for its leaders and personnel. As the politics of the gun came to define the era, a Leninist party alert to security concerns was not all that outlandish.

Imagining Freedom in Jamaica: Variants of a Multi-form Democratic Spirit

Freedom has remained a premium value for all Jamaicans. As numerous commentators have reminded us, enslaved and colonized peoples have cherished this ideal and the value of freedom for them has been amply documented in the myriad slave revolts and national liberation movements to throw off colonialism.

In the era of political decolonization, freedom meant political self-determination, national sovereignty and the elimination of racial dishonour. Jamaica's nationalist movement, like others, successfully prosecuted the battle for freedom that resulted in political independence.

But, beginning in the '50s, this version of freedom as self-determination entered a major crisis, as that notion of freedom was subject to biting critique by scholars and activists and grassroots political movements who bemoaned 'flag independence' and the limits of this freedom in a world economy dominated by huge multinational corporations and by powerful actors like the United States, who could flex their economic, military and political power against weaker actors like Jamaica. And where freedom as self-determination for Jamaica was being disputed in the international system, that dispute overlapped with disputes about freedom on the domestic scene.

It is possible to identify a broad democratic spirit among Jamaicans that is expressed in a commitment to freedom. All groups express their commitment to this ideal. What this identity consists of is debatable, but there are four possible ways in which Jamaicans have imagined freedom. As indicated, these are: Rule of Law Freedom, Political Freedom, Birthright Freedom and Capability Freedom. All four capture a general commitment to freedom as an ideal and this commitment is apparent in the vaunted democratic spirit of the Jamaican people, and more narrowly in the popular-democratic sentiments of poor Afro-Jamaicans.

Jamaica's multi-form democratic culture includes several freedom components that movements, parties, groups and classes emphasize differently.

At the broadest level, both propertied and elite groups, as well as property-less Jamaicans celebrate the importance of the rule of law and the freedom it provides. This is the generic idea of freedom as understood in the West, a civilization to which the Caribbean people belong: legal-constitutional protection of the rights of persons and their property from unreasonable infringements and abuses.

In Jamaica, this rule of law freedom helped secure the island's democratic credentials, even as the changing conception and formulation of the constitutional law of Jamaica and the actual practice of freedom cast doubt on the effective reach and application of these principles to all Jamaicans. Loving freedom is one thing; enjoying its fruits is quite another. Still, within this broad framework, political freedom has held pride of place for the many law-abiding Jamaicans of all classes who subscribe to its tenets. Thus political freedom consists of the unconstrained expression and right to political participation, representation, and organization.

As should be apparent from the emphasis on law in this version of freedom, it is shot through with concerns for the maintenance of social and political order; it is hemmed in with claims regarding respect for the legitimate power of the authorities and institutions; and it is freighted with protections against threats to the security of the state and the people-nation. The enjoyment of this freedom is therefore highly circumscribed as the imperatives of statecraft, the dynamics of public regulation, the impulse to bureaucratization and the application of political technique justify themselves in the name of providing the conditions for the enjoyment of freedom.

Political freedom in Jamaica, then, understood as the right to free expression, to voice, association and dissent cannot be imagined without the corresponding protection for society and for the authority of the state.

This image of freedom with its disciplinary politics and its politics of state-building has typically impelled state elites in ex-colonial societies like Jamaica to invariably choose 'order' over freedom as their first, and often only priority. This latter version of freedom – so jealously guarded by the middle class, the business elites, the professional strata and political elites in Jamaica – competes with another rival notion of freedom, namely birthright freedom.

This ideal celebrates innate rights of persons who possess, as the saying goes, inalienable rights – rights that are not subject to surrender or negotiation. For natural rights liberals, these rights are inborn, they come naturally; they come with being born a human. So too for intellectuals from the African prophetic grassroots tradition that also affirms an unapologetic racially-grounded rights claim. Thus for former African slaves and the defenders of pre-colonial African communities, innate rights are more than that: they are contextual, historical and relational. That is to say, for pre-colonial African societies and in former slave societies in the African diaspora in contact with the white West, innate rights are ethnicized, are racially embedded, and civilizationally implicated.

So this 'innateness' – this form of recognition of group and self qualification – is not racially neutered and not abstract, as in natural rights theory, but rather is explicitly historicized and linked to a redemptive memory of the possession and enjoyment of a first, original, unspoilt freedom as member of a non-white civilization.

In the Jamaican context, such rights have been given only weak recognition by political and economic elites and by many among the general population, but these rights are held to be most precious by the most militantly defiant among the poorer classes – the alienated workers, landless peasants, the unemployed urban poor and especially the Rastafarian minority among the Afro-Jamaican population.

The watchword of this birthright freedom group is aptly captured in the Afro-Jamaican riposte to unwarranted claims and encumbrances by an authoritarian state and a repressive society: man free! By which is meant – the African-Jamaican worker-peasant is sovereign in personhood because of culture and because of belonging to a cultural group that was originally born free. It is an assertion of non-submissiveness before all authority claims on black persons. It is the defence of volitional rights before any authority! Fierce defence of this version of freedom against all unwarranted claims has led both to emancipation for Afro-Jamaicans and to their immolation. Such claims to an untrammelled exercise of liberty, understood as personal agency, collides with that other very different valuation of freedom celebrated from above – rule of law freedom.

The last and related, but distinct image of freedom imagined by many Afro-Jamaicans is capability freedom. This is the yearning for and even the declaring of a right to the achievement of social competence by means of developing one's capabilities. This is the freedom that that is achieved when know-how (expressed as optimal social functioning and doing) is matched with appropriate spiritual-psychological capacities (being) that make use of practical skills.

The value of this freedom cannot be underestimated, because, as Amartya Sen reminds us, it goes to the very heart of the development project. That is, for economically poor countries, national development in the broadest sense is linked to a people's sense of moral well-being that comes not from the populist or Marxist assurances of the people's virtue, or from the leaders' benevolence, but rather from policies and practices that allow citizens to acquire capabilities and skills that enhance their independent functioning. These would include acquiring the ability to organize, plan and mange both persons and things; to make decisions and to exercise choice. In Jamaica, moral well-being for the Afro-Jamaican majority remains elusive, where it is not being actively denied.

Because poor Afro-Jamaicans have always asserted a claim to this form of freedom and because the Jamaican state and society have been unable to provide the black poor with the fruits of this freedom – black competence with superior moral-psychological functioning – they have sought it elsewhere and through different, often deviant routes.

The WPJ and the Four Freedoms

From the foregoing, it is arguable that this variant imagination and sharp contestation around the meaning, worth and realization of these four freedoms, along with the social action they produced, form the basis for an understanding of modern Jamaica's political and social history, particularly in the period after political independence.

This is clearly an issue that goes way beyond the WPJ and into the character of Jamaica's political parties and Jamaica's social institutions. For now, however, I want to relate the problem to the politics of the WPJ. To be fair to the WPJ, there can be little doubt that in the 1970s, the party and its activists recognized the powerful, vital democratic spirit of the Jamaican people. Like the PNP in the 1970s, the WPJ leaders also tried to draw on this great spirited motivation for fair play, for social justice, power and rights. As good communists, the WPJ understood this motivation to liberty as a species of militancy to be put at the disposal of the class struggle and to be paced by the working class.

But why the working class came to be identified as the only group that best expressed this spirited motivation for justice and fair play was merely justified on the basis of Marxist dogma: the working class is always the most advanced subordinate social class by dint of its relation to the mode of production and to the bourgeoisie. Yet as Jamaica's social relations in the 1970s clearly demonstrated, it was not the working class, but the lumpenproletariat that, by dint of its demographic weight, hegemonic moral culture and extremisms, showed that it was more the herald and icon of the popular Afro-Jamaican democratic sentiment – far more so than the working class.

But the WPJ misread the zeitgeist. The conjuncture belonged not to the left and the working class in Jamaica, but was far more complicated. It did not favour organized labour so much as it established two simultaneous and clashing trends: on the one hand, increasing demand for democratization from below; on the other, anarchic collapse of the norms and institutional pillars of liberal democratic rule, as the economic foundations of that form of power began to give way.

One trend opened the way to a brief political spring and it was this democratic current in the zeitgeist that led communists in the WPJ to think the era belonged to them. The other trend – collapse of faith in liberalism, erosion of state authority and legitimacy, and onset of normlessness that fed crime and social anarchy – also led Jamaican communists astray.

To be sure, these developments fitted nicely with a Leninist politics in which a trained, closeted elite readied itself for the collapse of the ramparts of power. But anarchy does not necessarily lead to revolution; it can instead consume the whole society and threaten the very communists that hoped to profit from it. This was precisely the fate of the WPJ from the 1970s until their demise.

Suffice to say that this anomic social force became agents of a new militancy that swept all before it, confounding liberals and Marxists alike. In its role as both rogue actor and avatar of liberation, the lumpenproletariat showed by mostly negative example and highly destructive acts, that cultural needs such as respect and racial honour may be dismissed only at this society's peril.

Alongside this concern, there is abundant evidence for a majority and mainstream Afro-Jamaican celebration of the worth and value of both law and political freedom. This is apparent from high voter interest in democratic elections; in high turnout rates in elections, especially after 1972; in the vigour and proliferation of a myriad of civic-minded organizations, and in the explosion of unconstrained public opinion in new media as various as vox pop radio and television programmes, or in a raft of newspaper and magazine publications with their politically combative editorials and 'op-ed' commentary on public affairs.

Certainly, the politicization and mobilization of the Jamaican people especially after 1972, intensified rather than weakened concern for democracy and the rule of law among the law-abiding majority of Jamaicans. Similarly, their widespread condemnation of violence and crime and the public outcry and broad public censure of rampant moral decay in the society confirm the vigour of the Jamaican democratic spirit during a time of great trial.

But for the communists, rule of law freedom was merely the ideology of the bourgeoisie, and such freedom as was available existed only for the capitalist class. This left-wing contempt for this brand of freedom actually converged with militant Afro-Jamaican contempt for this kind of freedom and WPJ dismissal of 'bourgeois democracy' as a sham, may well have given a fillip to vigorous affirmation of birthright freedom claims from below.

Freed of Marxist cant, however, 'dictatorship' has always been reserved for regimes that eliminate, not merely constrain political choice. Where political choice exists, and where the population can reasonably exercise meaningful choice in mostly unconstrained balloting, as well as enjoy independent political activity, a modicum of political freedom exists.

Indeed, that way of organizing power is called a democracy. Placing the epithet 'capitalist' or 'bourgeois' in front of the noun, merely begged the question and muddied the waters. Such rhetorical gestures only seemed to justify the suffocating and unedifying discourse about competing political systems that was the hallmark of political rivalry during the Cold War.

Beyond that, there is no denying that Jamaica's democracy is exercised autocratically. Prohibitions, censorship, expulsions of expatriates, beatings and killings on a small scale by or at the behest of the state, capture the brutality of power in Jamaica. In the orgiastic violence of the party wars, in the exterminist hunt for criminal and political gunmen, this corrupted democratic state has long been accustomed to drowning challengers from the slums in blood.

The UWI Leninists were right to call attention to this odious feature of Jamaican power. The sustained, wanton snuffing out of life and the dashing of hopes that political victimization produced across the decades since 1944 were worse than unconscionable; it was criminal and deserving of not just communist censure, but international condemnation.

However, to conclude from these facts, as the UWI Leninists did, that power in Jamaica was, in the main, routinely tyrannical and brutally repressive, is simply untrue. Power in Jamaica has dictatorial traits, but without their fullness. This is so because power is restrained by meaningful democratic structures and by deeply held liberal political values, among which the defence of freedom, especially for economic and political elites, holds pride of place.

Unlike dictatorships and forms of despotic rule elsewhere, power in Jamaica exhibits deep and often genuine affection for the people. Thus unlike typical dictatorships that seek to expel the people and keep them at a distance, statecraft in Jamaica nuzzles the people democratically, shows them cultural affection, even as it reserves the right to kill and maim them over the spoils that power brings.

And here is the distinction that undercuts the claim to despotism in Jamaica: violent power used against the people has, in the main, been spoils-driven. Competition for turf, the race for booty, battle for shares of influence among the people – not desire for political monopoly – provoke brutality here. The spilling of middle class socialist blood on the docks in 1974 when Munroe and others were chopped in their heads with machetes did not come from the JLP or the police, but from a hitherto friendly source – the National Workers Union and its thuggish recruits, jealously guarding their turf from interlopers. This is merely one example where paradoxically, it was democratic competition that spawned the violent curtailment of democracy in Jamaica – not quest for political absolutism, as the Leninists implied.

State power in Jamaica is therefore Janus-faced; it censures and it is solicitous. It employs the 'politics of affection,' defers to law and democratic constitutionalism, but in the race for spoils, votes and influence, it wages bloody war against competitors of whatever ilk or political persuasion.

Of course, the Jamaican left was counted in this roll call of competitors. In the 1960s right through the early 1980s, middle class activists were harassed, but received mostly a political cuffing. What happened to them was child's play compared to the bloodletting in the slums brought about by violent political clientelism.

The related complaint that communist identity encouraged violence and repression in the 1980s has more validity. The early-to-mid '80s did see a resurgence of anti-communism in the region, as the US and the JLP tried to regain lost political ground. The PNP defeat in 1980 and the debacle in Grenada in 1983 did briefly embolden anti-communists at home and abroad. After the Seaga administration returned to power in 1980, it did begin a political witch-hunt. WPJ leaders and middle class supporters were harassed; they were fired from their jobs in public agencies across the country because of their communist affiliation; their homes were searched and numerous WPJ activists were briefly detained. Moreover, residents in WPJ strongholds like Greenwich Town in South West St Andrew testified to being tortured by the police, and one or two WPJ sympathizers there were shot and killed, allegedly by partisan policemen. Indeed, top WPJ leaders felt sufficiently fearful for their lives that they sought and got police protection for their rallies. So serious was this problem of potential assassination, that WPJ security were also given police-approved gun licences to guard the leader, Trevor Munroe.

All this occurred in the context of the JLP smear that communists were engaged in armed insurgency, terror and mayhem in a plot to overthrow the government. As political and other forms of violence spiralled out of control in the 1980s, the disorder encouraged rogue elements of all kinds, and the WPJ was moved to desperately petition Commissioners of Police for protection against these elements in the police force.

In post-independence Jamaica, then, the Edward Seaga administration produced what was perhaps the most severe bout of anti-communism yet. But this allergy, like others before it that were used mainly for political gain, was confined to the JLP leadership, had little support among most Jamaicans, and in time the contrived panic subsided.

The Communist complaint about constraint on political freedom, and the charge of anti-communism at home, was therefore partly justified. After 1980, the JLP had succeeded in whipping up anti-communist hysteria in the media and among anxious members of the political and economic elite. It is debatable, however, whether this hysteria found much support among ordinary Jamaicans.

Still, the suggestion that anti-communism manifested itself as an entrenched and hard-bitten antipathy for Jamaican communists seems less convincing. JLP anti-communism brought no pogrom against communists that resulted in the round up, jailing or disappearance of top leaders and their supporters. Indeed, the WPJ was neither proscribed nor banned, but permitted to pursue its brand of politics during this period.

Indeed, across the years, PNP socialism – no matter Leninists' dismissal of it as 'half-wayism' and 'mouth water socialism' – afforded WPJ communists political space and legitimacy. This favour inoculated WPJ supporters against hard-bitten Cold War prejudices and the

Jamaican people increasingly shared this guarded tolerance for communists. After all, WPJ labour militancy and anti-capitalist invective easily converged with known traditions of race and class militancy on the island that carried a historical animus for the ills of capitalism.

It may not be an exaggeration to say that because of this PNP validation, and because of the resonance of left-wing politics with popular idioms and aspirations, Jamaicans tend to view communists not as mortal threats to the society, but rather as part of the political flora and fauna, persons who are perhaps misguided and impractical in making unwise use of their time and talents – people who are not alien to the political community, but politically familiar and part of the family.

Put another way, when Trevor Munroe or Don Robotham encounter their nemeses in the ruling parties, meet with the middle and upper class, and with ordinary Jamaicans, then as now, they are greeted not so much as sworn enemies, but rather as brainy prodigals gone astray, but still kith and kin! For the Jamaican middle and upper class clan, therefore, allegiance to Marxism-Leninist ideology did not disqualify them from middle class membership, did not bar them from return to the political fold or deny them national belonging. Among that other clan – the Jamaican workers and the black poor – communists are also admired as fighters for the small man, viewed as 'one of us,' belonging to the group, but not necessarily because they held similar political opinions and ideological outlooks.

In sum, WPJ communists enjoyed and were granted full moral membership by both the top and bottom of Jamaican society, though both sectors concurred that these communists ought not be trusted with power.

WPJ sectarianism led to other distortions about the nature of political freedom in Jamaica. For example, WPJ activism employed crude stereotypes of political adversaries and resorted to cartoonish images of Jamaican politics and politicians. WPJ depictions of the JLP and of Edward Seaga, its leader, typified this distortion. Depicted by the WPJ as the embodiment of far-right reactionary politics, the JLP was described not as one branch of a two-party establishment competing for power, but foolishly as an alien force in the land, politically and culturally foreign to the Jamaican people. Correlatively, JLP leader

Edward Seaga, because of his Lebanese ancestry, was portrayed as the political face of this supposedly alien organization, and his ethnicity was used to stir latent ethnic chauvinism among the people. But JLP supporters of all classes and ethnicities did not believe this abominable smear, and backed their leader and party in the continuing exchange of political violence and in the sharing out of spoils,

On the other hand, WPJ attitudes to the PNP were more complicated, but even after the WPJ changed its political line and adopted a policy of 'critical support' for the PNP, that party too was reduced to its cartoonish role as another puppeteer of the Jamaican people. An unfortunate consequence of such sentiments on the far left was a reductive view of the people as completely robbed of their own power and bereft of meaningful political freedom. In this distorted far-left view of Jamaican power relations, then, Afro-Jamaicans were caricatured as mere pawns in a grand political game organized by capitalists and mediated through their class-dominated political parties, the PNP and the JLP.

In addition, both the vanguard party model and the General Secretary's eventual slide into the Stalinist brand of authoritarianism arrested any meaningful development of capability freedom in this party. This throttling of capability freedom applied across the entire party, to both the middle strata that comprised the top leadership, as well as to the rank and file. In practice, this meant quiet acceptance of censorship and imposition of self-censorship; it meant curbing the freedom to think and to criticize for the sake of the revolutionary cause, and in the name of building the party. In time, the strain of self-censorship and arrest of capability freedom proved too much for dissenting elements among the middle strata in the WPJ's leadership and the Faustian bargain collapsed amidst bitter recrimination.

As for the minority of Afro-Jamaican students, workers, peasants and the unemployed who joined the WPJ, party membership placed massive limits on their capability freedom. Besides curbs on freedom to think, WPJ party life and culture took their toll on these groups' sense of fair play.

Former members of the WPJ narrated to this author, commented in published interviews, or wrote retrospectively about a party culture and a style of leadership by the General Secretary and others that throttled rank and file members' capability freedom. For example, former activists recall that when some members sought self-improvement by trying to leave the party to pursue advanced study, their desire was sneered at and their ambition dismissed as an indication of incorrigible petty bourgeois traits.

WPJ loyalists and leaders' use of the epithet, 'petty bourgeois' to both name the infraction and to dismiss the claims of the culprit, appears to have been the weapon of choice in dealing with attempts at independent thought or initiative inside the party. Thus, one UWI student and party member who wrote for 'Struggle,' the party newspaper, later commented on the hostile reception that greeted his article in the newspaper because it gave fulsome praise to Bob Marley's cultural significance, amidst the outpouring of Afro-Jamaican grief during funeral ceremonies for the singer. Succumbing to petty bourgeois values was again the indictment that silenced this WPJ writer's enthusiasm for popular music culture and its political significance.

Similarly, the party's gross disrespect for its cadres' personal and family life became a major sore point and fetter on these members' functioning. Leaders' adoption of a siege politics and insistence on non-stop, round-the-clock party work by its cadres, physically exhausted its personnel, destroyed careers, and tore families apart.

Many more examples of this abuse and stifling of capability freedom could be cited here. The point, however, is that at the very moment when claims for this particular brand of freedom were being given full-throated expression all across the land, and especially among downtrodden Afro-Jamaicans, WPJ party life and culture degraded its expression and sharply opposed its fruition.

Indeed, the model of tight political control from the top was not so much a non-Western and alien implantation in Caribbean politics, as it was a variation on existing structures of authoritarian leadership in the region. While autocratic leadership would prove to be a problem for the WPJ, as well as the two dominant political parties, it is fair to say that the WPJ model of leadership was fairly typical of contemporary political organizations in Jamaica, and even beyond to the major social and economic institutions in the country and the Caribbean region. In sum, hierarchy, top-down control and taint of authoritarian values were not peculiar to the WPJ, but were shared by existing institutions, both public and private.

Conclusion

The leaders of the Workers Party of Jamaica belong to an honourable tradition of struggle by reform-minded intellectuals in the Caribbean who – often at great personal risk and sacrifice to themselves – joined the poor and working people in their historic bid to achieve complete emancipation.

Looking back from the perspective of some 34 years since the founding of the Workers Liberation League, and exactly 30 years since the founding of the Workers' Party of Jamaica, we can better appreciate the serious flaws that handicapped its effort to engage and mobilize the Jamaican people.

As the foregoing has indicated, the WPJ's leadership devised a politics wholly at odds with a core feature of the Jamaican identity: spirited motivation for fair play, justice, power and rights. The WPJ tried to harness this militancy to its search for power. Yet, in summoning this militancy, the WPJ only caricatured, trivialized and suppressed the dispositions and social actions that informed the broad Jamaican democratic spirit.

In particular, by being dismissive of the value of freedom and by ignoring the variety of ways in which the Jamaican people imagined and fought over their right to freedom, the WPJ's sectarian politics consigned the party to political irrelevance in the face of ongoing and often incompatible demands for liberty in the country.

Notes

1. Obika Gray, *Demeaned but Empowered: The Social Power of the Urban Poor in Jamaica* (Kingston: The University of the West Indies Press, 2004).
2. In a particularly notorious instance, the PNP – long known for its socialist ideology – in 1952 expelled four of its own labour organizers for holding communist sympathies. Likewise, in the 1960s, the PNP would discipline members of its youth arm – the Young Socialist League – for the same reasons. Because of its far greater antipathy for communists and for left-leaning intellectuals, the JLP experienced no such ruptures or expulsions.
3. See Amartya Sen, *Development as Freedom* (New York: Oxford University Press, 1999), and Eric Foner, *The Story of American Freedom* (New York: W.W. Norton, 1998).
4. For the most authoritative of these accounts, see Carl Stone, *Democracy and Clientelism in Jamaica* (New Brunswick, NJ: Transaction Books, 1980).
5. Alvin Gouldner, *The Future of Intellectuals and the Rise of the New Class* (New York: Sage, 1979).

13 | *Grenada, Once Again: Re-visiting the 1983 Crisis and Collapse of the Grenada Revolution[1]*

Brian Meeks

'If old truths are to retain their hold on men's minds, they must be restated in the language and concepts of successive generations.'

Friederich Von Hayek[2]

Remembering Grenada

The 25th anniversary in October 2008 of the tragic killing of Maurice Bishop and his associates and the subsequent invasion of Grenada, followed closely by the release on 5 September 2009 of Bernard Coard and the six remaining prisoners convicted of his murder, has been cause for a flurry of new conferences, papers, letters and communiqués on the Grenada Revolution and its tragic demise. The conference and remembrance activities on the 25th anniversary at the University of Toronto;[3] the April 2009 conference on the legacies of radical politics in the Caribbean at Pittsburgh University; Rupert Roopnarine's[4] reflective paper delivered at the Pittsburgh event; Shalini Puri's panel[5] at the 2009 Caribbean Studies Association (CSA) conference along with her graphic presentation of memory and the revolution first presented in Toronto, were among the most outstanding. Then, following the September release of the Seven, things picked up pace. Thankfully, many of the letters on the ubiquitous websites and email circuits, particularly those written by Grenadians, suggested wariness with the recriminatory monologues that have been typical of many reflections on the tragedy. Wendy Grenade's 'Beyond the Legal Chapter...,' for instance, suggests that the release of the Seven provides the opportunity for a genuine and open discussion on the strengths and weaknesses of the revolutionary period and calls for the assertion of humanitarian, socialist and democratic principles for the future.⁶ Patsy Lewis's intervention in similar vein, distinguishes the reaction of Grenadians as opposed to those of other West Indian nationals who attended the 2009 CSA panel. She suggests that Grenadians have moved further along the road of reconciliation, while others seem to have been suspended at the traumatic moment of crisis in 1983.⁷ Most tellingly, layperson Randall Robinson's letter to the Methodist Church's newsletter, suggesting genuine happiness over the release of the Seven, strengthens Lewis's conviction of a deep current of reconciliation on the island: 'This day will be a bittersweet one for us Grenadians, but if we don't learn to forgive we will all perish through hate and there is no place in Heaven for haters.'⁸

Countering Conventional Wisdom

Understandably, all commentaries did not comply with this tone. Jorge Heine, for instance, who had written one of the early, forensic studies of the collapse of the revolution, wrote in his short piece, 'The Return of Bernard Coard,'⁹ that the 'dual leadership' formula of the Central Committee (CC) was 'utterly impractical and unworkable' and, inter alia, in opposition to the common perspective that Coard and Bishop held distinct and contradictory ideological perspectives, that '...no differences existed among the party leadership as to the pace or general direction of "The Revo."' These observations I entirely agree with and shall return to look at in more detail anon, but it is with Heine's substantial claim as to the fundamental cause of the crisis with which I disagree. He suggests that the entire joint leadership proposal was merely a ploy, as he puts it '...merely one additional move in Bernard Coard's long-term strategy to gain full control of the party and state.'¹⁰ In relation to the underlying causes – the impetus for Coard's actions – Heine proposes a 'feeling of resentment' that the young Bernard had inherited from his father. Coard's father, Frederick, had written a book entitled *Bittersweet and Spice: Those things I Remember* in which he reflected on the fact that as a civil servant he was subordinate to people less qualified than himself. This led to resentment and by a process of transference Heine proposes that the son came to feel the same way about his seemingly perpetual number two position in revolutionary Grenada:

The son identified with the father. Both bureaucrats to the core, who loved statistics and files, the colonial civil service was to the father what the party was to the son. The complaints by father and son about their fellow clerks or party comrades are also similar. The father's frustration is that he never made it to the very top of the colonial civil service, the officer of comptroller of income tax. Thirty years later, for Bernard Coard, the prospect of spending the rest of his professional life in the relative obscurity below the very top of the political structure, doing the legwork for somebody else, was surely unbearable. To live in the shadow of Maurice Bishop, whose father was a martyr of the anti-Gairy struggle and who had once employed Bernard's father as a clerk, was unacceptable, as was working under somebody he considers his intellectual inferior.[11]

Heine's proposal is highly tendentious and eminently contestable. I am not equipped to delve into the claims of inherited psychological states and thus will leave that aspect of his argument for the experts to consider. However, the equation of the elder Coard's lowly status in the civil service with his son's number two position in the New Jewel Movement (NJM) begs an immediate response.

Since his return from Jamaica in 1976 until his resignation from the CC in 1982, Coard enjoyed inordinate influence in the Party and after the 13 March 1979 Revolution, in the state. This was in part the result of a special and peculiar symbiotic relationship between Maurice and Bernard, which was palpable and noted often in various commentaries. In what was a de facto form of joint leadership, they divided labour according to their respective talents and maintained a genuinely fraternal relationship. Thus, Roopnarine in his paper recollects speaking with Maurice at the first conference in solidarity with Grenada in St Georges in November 1981. Just before leaving the event, Maurice pulled him aside and said: 'If ever you come and I am not on the island, talk with Bernard. Talking to Bernard is the same as talking to me.'[12] Claremont Kirton, then a senior economist with the People's Revolutionary Government's (PRG's) Ministry of Finance told me in an interview in the '80s that 'I worked with both of them and each used to tell me, if I submitted documents to one, then ensure that the other had a copy. I had no reason to believe on the basis of what I could see that there was any kind of tension at all between them.'[13] I recall meeting Maurice for the first time in Jamaica in 1977 when he and Bernard were seeking support from the Jamaican government and subsequently, though without any success, from the Cubans. They were ebullient and almost romantically optimistic about their hopes for success in their struggle against Eric Gairy. What was most evident though, was the closeness between them. There was a distinct casualness that suggested friendship in their conversation and a naive willingness to share what seemed to me at the time, very dangerous details of the covert aspects of the anti-Gairy struggle. Coard, evidently, was no bureaucratic subordinate to Maurice. On the crucial decision to strike on March 13, Maurice was against it, but when the majority of the Political Bureau, including Coard, voted in favour, he supported the action wholeheartedly.[14] Maurice accepted Bernard's fine eye for detail, superior grasp of economics and, for the most part, political judgement. Bernard and, indeed, the entire Party understood equally that Maurice, while considered weak from organizational and theoretical perspectives, possessed a quality that was more valuable than any of these. He was the person with the common touch, with the ability to move crowds, to convert the PRG's policies into words that everyone could grasp and the timing to use them appropriately. He was the charismatic leader and everyone seemed to understand this. Both enjoyed tremendous prestige within the ranks of the NJM; but if one were asked who in 1983 commanded the greater respect, I would have to conclude that it was Coard. This in some respects was inevitable. After March 13, Maurice had an immense responsibility for state and diplomatic work. Bernard had the Ministry of Finance, but with his meticulous organizational abilities, he was able to manage this and also play the leading role in party organizing and building. Thus Coard's popularity grew among party cadres, while Maurice's consolidated and blossomed in Grenada as a whole and beyond.

On the question of long-standing conspiracy, I suggest that the Achilles heel in Heine's and most of the conspiracy-based arguments is exposed when asked to explain how Maurice became so marginalized within his own party. One school led by Fidel Castro, proposes that Coard and his clique were able, by subtlety and subterfuge, to eke out majorities in the CC and in the military leadership and this is how they eventually ousted Bishop.[15] This notion of a narrow majority primarily at the level of the leadership is a misrepresentation. In reality, when the crisis ripened, the overwhelming majority of the NJM was in opposition to Maurice as was the leadership of the People's Revolutionary Army (PRA) and also the rank and file. This is because they, unlike the rest of the population, were privy to the twists and turns of the joint leadership discussions, voted, in the main, in favour of it, and had collectively come to the conclusion that it was Maurice who had disrespected the Party by breaching a solemn promise. Herein lay the root of the tragedy of October 19; for if the NJM had been divided and the PRA split, Maurice would have rallied the 'loyal' sections to his side and with the populace overwhelmingly in his favour, the gig would have been immediately up for Coard and the recalcitrant minority. But with a united party and behind them a united army facing the largely unarmed and now hostile population, the door was open for dangerous and deadly solutions.

As an aside to the notion of conspiracy, I recall an incident in August 1983 during my stint with the Ministry of Mobilisation following Maurice's return from what would be his final visit to the United States. He had given an uncompromising anti-imperialist speech to an adoring New York crowd at CUNY's Hunter College,[16] belying the view expressed by many subsequent commentators that his trip to the US represented some sort of attempt to modify the PRG's previously unrelenting hostility to the Reagan regime. Selwyn Strachan, who at the time was Minister of Mobilisation, on the instruction of the Political Bureau (PB), called on me as coordinator of worker education classes to play the hour-long videotape of Maurice's Hunter speech at every class, as it was an excellent defence of the Revolution and showed the Comrade Leader at his best. A month later, divisions would become apparent and two months later, Bishop would be killed. This directive however, suggests that in August, Strachan, arguably at the time the third most powerful man in the country and someone who would spend the next 26 years of his life in prison convicted and accused of killing Maurice Bishop, was in August 1983 actively promoting him! This is a powerful piece of evidence and I am remiss, out of a desire to take my own story out of the narrative,[17] in not having used it in previous writings, for it throws significant amounts of sand in the engine of the conspiracy idea.

In preliminary summary then, in response to Heine's contention of Coard as being resentful of his second-best status as deputy leader, I advance the simple contention that there is significant evidence of a very comfortable and one might argue, fulfilling relation of mutual sharing of leadership between both men, certainly up until late1982. This questions, though in itself cannot dismiss, the notion of a power grab based on venal, long-term, psychologically fuelled factors. In relation to conspiracy, I advance the evidence of Strachan's position on promoting Maurice in August and ask for consideration whether the entire Party, bar a literal handful, was duped by Bernard Coard's magic, or whether the overwhelming suit of majority votes in the Party opposing Maurice on pivotal decisions suggests a different, more complex story that needs to be told, beyond the tattered notion of a long-standing conspiracy based on the will to power.

The second comment that I wish to contest is that of Barbadian lawyer and political activist Robert 'Bobby' Clarke. In a sketchy letter,[18] though significant for its reflection of commonly held perspectives, Clarke makes a number of assertions, three of which are worth mentioning:

1. *Bernard Coard was not made Deputy Prime Minister by Maurice Bishop's government but by an announcement made by his wife Phyllis on the radio*. This argument is new to me and I cannot recall seeing evidence of it in any of the numerous documents stolen from the country as spoils of war by the US military in 1983. Taken on its own it is preposterous. The NJM was an aspiring Leninist Party, which as tragic events would prove, actually believed in the notion of democratic centralism as the best way to organize a party to lead a revolution. Phyllis Coard was on the CC, but she was not a member of the all powerful Political Bureau (PB) and as such simply did not have the kind of influence to get away with such a manoeuvre. She would have been roundly condemned and the results of the enquiry would have surfaced in the captured and extensive Party minutes.

2. *The OREL Conspiracy Proposition*. The pre-party Organisation for Revolutionary Education and Liberation (OREL) which Bernard Coard helped to guide before the revolution and which included key proponents of joint leadership like Liam 'Owusu' James and Ewart 'Headache' Layne, was never dissolved into the NJM, but remained as a conspiratorial clique, guiding the plot and eventually displacing Bishop for Coard. This is also a part

of Fidel Castro's[19] argument, but it is equally fallacious. Again, there is simply no evidence of OREL in any of the minutes or the numerous microfiche documents. Elsewhere I have argued that on Grenada's physical and demographic scale, it is impossible to hide a conspiratorial organization for four and a half years of revolution in which virtually everything was public and social. Inhabitants of larger, small countries like Jamaica or Trinidad and Tobago, with populations in excess of a million are beyond a certain minimal threshold for an easy grasp of the phenomenon that it is impossible to keep an organization secret for very long in a micro-state with roughly 100,000 inhabitants. This applies not only to the OREL contention, but to the general theory of a long-standing conspiracy. Further, the overwhelming demand on time which the Party and Revolution imposed on leading individuals would have made it virtually impossible for front-line cadres like Coard, Ewart Layne, Leon Cornwall, Owusu James and John Ventour to maintain a parallel set of meetings, minutes etc. The OREL argument, I suggest, is simply not true. The subset of this contention, however – that Coard manoeuvred people on to the CC, so in the end his people were on board and Maurice's were ousted – needs also to be addressed. The pattern of promotions and demotions, while on first glance persuasive, ultimately belies this argument. Layne, James and Ventour, formerly members of OREL, all found their way on to the PB after the revolution, while long-standing militants like Kendrick Radix and Vince Noel were demoted. But on closer examination, it was the Chairman of the PB – Maurice Bishop himself – who was in charge and he never once expressed doubts about this process. Indeed, on closer examination, the pattern is simply not consistent. George Louison who had risen fastest in terms of state and party responsibilities was never a member of OREL and ended up on Maurice's side in the final dispute; among the members of the PB who had been severely reprimanded by Coard at an earlier date for showing militaristic tendencies was Ewart Layne, an ex-OREL member and one of the final Seven convicts; and also among the Seven and in favour of joint leadership in the crucial September meetings were Selwyn Strachan and Hudson Austin who were with Maurice from the foundation of NJM and definitely not a part of OREL group.[20] Louison himself, hostile to Coard and the other prisoners until his death, in an interview with me in the '80s, put the nail into the coffin of this argument when he said 'I think that over the years there were certain people who earned their position on the CC and there were certain people who could not function or pull their weight in the last days.'[21]

3. *Bishop was ideologically different from Coard.* Clarke asserts that Maurice's position '...differed completely in that the Grenada Revolution should take the path of a combination of Marxist economics and Caribbean based cultural philosophy.'[22] Bernard Coard, on the other hand, 'was influenced by his mentor Dr Trevor Monroe (Munroe) of the Workers Party of Jamaica, a devout Stalinist at the time'[23] and 'he advised (Coard) on all the actions he should take to bring about a USSR style government.'[24]

My own residency in Grenada between 1981–83, consultations with Maurice Bishop on the editing of the weekly newspaper *The Free West Indian*, meetings with Bishop, Coard and Strachan on planning the worker education classes and subsequent extensive reading for my PhD thesis of many of the available documents on the Grenada Revolution, lead me to the conclusion that there were few, if any, substantial differences on critical ideological matters between the two. Both had been nurtured in the Black Power and anti-war movements of the '60s – Coard and Bishop in Britain, Coard subsequently in Trinidad and Tobago and Jamaica, and Bishop in the cockpit of action in Grenada itself. Both had subsequently passed through that transitional phase between 1970 and 1975 when a significant part of a generation of radical intellectuals shifted from various Black Power streams to an equally varied potpourri of 'Marxisms.'[25] Both had settled on a particular version of the doctrine that we might call, for want of a better coinage, 'Caribbean Marxism-Leninism' and the available evidence suggests that on the key markers of ideology, theory, party strategy and government policy there were no discernible differences between them before 1983.

Caribbean Marxist-Leninists cannot simply be folded into 'Stalinists,' though they were subject to potentially dangerous authoritarian tendencies that derived in part from ideology but also from indigenous regional traditions of authoritarianism. From this perspective, to describe Trevor Munroe as a 'Stalinist' or even more startling a 'Pol Potist' is as wrong and equally mechanical as was Munroe's highly flawed praxis as applied by the WPJ. Stalin was a product of one of the worst forms of state oppression in the nineteenth and twentieth centuries – Czarist Russia – and he became its even more terrible alter ego. Despite the WPJ's propensity for dogmatic interpretations of Marx and its failure to gain political traction in Jamaica, to equate Munroe with Stalin is a travesty and a failure of imagination in not sufficiently understanding Caribbean politics and its inhabitants on their own historical foundations. The irony is that Coard, Bishop and Munroe were all part of the same post-independence, radical Caribbean middle class intellectual stream. Neophytes in Marxism, the overarching problem is that they had all launched into the big league of revolution while attempting to master instruments that they had barely begun to comprehend. When crises overtook them, the answer, rather than seeking creative solutions, was sought in exegesis – the doctrinaire adherence to scripture. The peculiarity of the Caribbean turn to Marxism of the intellectual generation of the early '70s then is its immaturity and the dangerous implications that this held for popular movements that were advancing at a faster pace than were their intellectual leaders. This approach is more fertile ground for an enquiry as to the collapse than the worn notion of a 'moderate' or a 'cultural' Bishop versus a 'Stalinist' Coard.

Much work, however, still needs to be done on the WPJ's involvement in the Grenada events. There is a view held in Jamaica and elsewhere and evident in Clarke's comments that the WPJ was the intellectual and ideological mentor – the *eminence grise* – of the NJM. This was not the case, but there was WPJ involvement and again, a more complex picture needs to be painted. Coard had read Marxism-Leninism with a Worker's Liberation League (WLL)[26] study group during his sojourn in Jamaica from 1973–6 and was therefore very close to the Jamaican party. An interesting footnote to this is that when Trevor Munroe who was seeking to win port workers away from the traditional unions and organize them in the University and Allied Workers Union

(UAWU) and was attacked and seriously injured along with a group of students and union workers on the Kingston waterfront in 1974, Bernard Coard was physically present. He narrowly escaped injury by being further away from Trevor who was the main focus of the attack. This story, to my knowledge, has never been told and I speak from personal experience. I travelled to Grenada for the first time in July 1981 at a request from the PRG to come and help build the media there. After the 1980 Jamaican elections, the entire News and Current Affairs Department at the Jamaica Broadcasting Corporation had been made redundant by the newly elected right-wing Jamaica Labour Party (JLP) Government which had considered us adversaries in the hotly contested 1980 election campaign. George Louison visited Jamaica in March 1981 and among his requests was that Maurice and Bernard wanted me to come and work. I packed my bags and left in July, without a contract and quite willing to work for 'free' if that were the arrangement. I was somewhat surprised to discover that I had a rented house that I shared with another WPJ comrade and a salary. This was a far cry from the bleak future that I faced in Jamaica as an unemployed television producer in a country with one government-owned television station and a hostile government that had just kicked us out of work. There were seven WPJ comrades in Grenada when I arrived, with an additional two coming sometime after. Four of us worked in the media, two in the commercial sector and one in the Ministry of Justice. Aside from the Cubans, whose numbers, boosted by hundreds of construction workers on the airport, far exceeded other 'international workers,' WPJ comrades were the largest group and the only one to my knowledge with an organized cell. We participated fully in the life of the 'Revo' – attending rallies, conferences, budget debates etc., and all members of the group interacted regularly with the leadership of the PRG, though this was more in the nature of tiny Grenada than any special favour extended to us.

What was immediately evident was that the Grenadians had their own distinct organizational standards and a keen sense of national pride. During the Julien Fedon army and militia manoeuvre a friend had loaned me a green army jacket which I was wearing with some pride on the steps of Butler House, when I was spotted by Ewart 'Headache' Layne, then a Colonel in the PRA. He approached me discreetly and indicated that as an international comrade it would be damaging to the revolution if I were photographed in even a partial army uniform. I removed the jacket immediately. It is difficult to know the details of party to party relations beyond the material in the minutes reproduced in the Grenada Documents, Grenada Papers[27] and the original papers and microfiche documents in the National Archives in Washington DC. However, this much is evident. In the weeks leading up to the October crisis, Trevor Munroe did visit Grenada, as did leaders of other 'fraternal' parties, including Michael Als from Trinidad and Rupert Roopnarine from Guyana. What Munroe said and what effect this might have had on the NJM leaders is difficult to discern, but I suggest that the crisis had its own dynamic, rooted in the tension between the two logics mentioned above. The WPJ almost certainly supported the idea of joint leadership, but it was not their invention, and any notion of the WPJ giving directions to the NJM simply fails to understand Grenadians in general and the enhanced sense of pride and self-determination that blossomed with the Revolution.

As to which side the WPJ stood with in the end, I recall a poignant moment on October 19 – the day of the killings on the Fort. I had returned to Jamaica to pursue doctoral work at the University of the West Indies on the political economy of the Revolution. News of the crisis had traumatized the entire country but it was particularly acute for me and the few Grenadians on campus, including my close friend and later wife Patsy Lewis. I had gone down to the WPJ office on Lady Musgrave Road, because I knew that there would be a close monitoring of events. News of Maurice's death was not yet confirmed when a female comrade on the WPJ Central Committee emerged and said quietly 'Maurice is dead. The CC is in charge.' For my part, there was just a deep and bottomless sadness. For at least a year, I was unable to put pen to paper to write about Grenada. Gradually, with Patsy's help, I emerged from depression. Over time, I started to do research and the act of writing became cathartic. I finally finished the thesis 'Social Formation and People's Revolution: a Grenadian Study'[28] in 1988.

In summary then, in 1983 the WPJ sided with the NJM's Central Committee (CC) on the matter of joint leadership though its influence on the peculiar dynamic of events was, I suggest, limited. In the sweep of history, however, it paid the price for this as the Party and many of the other left-leaning groups in the Caribbean failed to survive. I propose that while the WPJ did not instigate the joint leadership proposal, their support for the majority on the NJM CC gave the latter greater confidence in the decisions that had been taken and thus contributed significantly to the hardening of positions and the slide that eventually led to the collapse of the Revolution and the discrediting of radical politics in the Caribbean for a generation or more.

Alternative Explanations

Having tried to counter some of the flaws that seem to be re-emerging in the new round of debate, it is only reasonable to propose even the outlines of an alternative explanation. If Coard was not power hungry whether via Freudian or Nietzcheian explanations; if OREL was not planning to overthrow Bishop; if Bishop and Coard did not have measurable ideological differences; then why was he placed under house arrest and subsequently executed in the most brutal militaristic manner? I have tried to explain this twice before, in my doctoral thesis and in my book on Caribbean Revolutions, but time provides new information and as Hayek in the epigraph suggests, a new generation demands that old truths be restated. I restate my argument as a series of theses:

Authoritarian Social Formation

At its fundamental level, the crisis of 1983 was rooted in traditions of authoritarianism and arbitrary rule that the Grenadian Revolutionaries inherited from Eric Gairy and the colonial regime that preceded independence. Gairy, in his hostility to the local elites and desire for effective power, abandoned many of the tenets of liberal democracy including notions of *habeas corpus*, individual security and free and fair elections. The British, despite the active opposition of tens of thousands of citizens, granted independence in 1973 in the full knowledge of Gairy's predatory capabilities and what he was likely to do if given greater autonomy. Indeed, it is Gairy's arbitrary rule, fixing of elections and terror, particularly from 1972–79 which undermined his initial legitimacy and laid the foundation for popular support for extra-constitutional activity.[29] The NJM therefore came to power with an ideological predisposition that disparaged 'bourgeois' constitutional electoral government, but also in a social and political moment in which these forms had already been savaged by Eric Gairy. Nonetheless, it is the failure of the imagination[30] of the NJM leaders as a whole not to recognize that after having promised early elections at the birth of the 'Revo' that the longer they held on to power without restoring democratic rights and freedoms was the more they came to mirror the regime that they had toiled so hard to overthrow. An early election, say in 1981, when anti-Gairy feelings still ran high, would undoubtedly have been won by the NJM, would have undermined the internal opposition to the regime, would have blunted the effectiveness of the US and regional conservative opposition to the process and would have given the PRG breathing space to consolidate its authority as it strove to complete the programme of infrastructural development. Elections, however, are uncertain things and they hold, inevitably, the possibility of defeat. The straightforward lesson derived from the Grenada tragedy must be that revolutionary and reforming regimes must be prepared to lose. If democrats believe that the people ultimately are sovereign, then they must be willing to concede governmental power when the voters are fed up with them, return to the hustings and live to fight another day.

This, some might argue quoting Lenin perhaps, is a form of parliamentary cretinism and fails to take into account the overwhelming power of capital, the poisonous nature of the media, the machinations of the CIA etc. These, as in Allende's Chile in 1973 or Sandinista Nicaragua, all work together to ensure that reforming regimes are isolated, excoriated and never return to power. All of these are substantial points, but the stark alternative is to hold on to power in the absence of the perceived wishes of the majority and this must, in the end, lead to the erosion and destruction of any notion of popular rule.

The Role of Vanguardism

The vanguard party, or 'small group of highly trained and committed comrades leading and guiding,'[31] was a critical element in the success of the March 13 overthrow, but became its dialectical opposite afterwards. In 1973 and 1974, when the newly formed NJM was able to put a significant part of the population on the streets and help shut down the country in opposition to independence under Gairy, it was still unable to remove him from power. The Party was capable of bringing people into the streets, but it did not possess the capacity for clandestine work, nor did it have a military capability. In the new, more repressive conditions that emerged after independence, both of these were critical requirements for political survival and, with the erosion of free and fair elections, were vital for possible military victory over the regime.[32] Both of these features were incorporated after 1975 and served the Party well as it built a small but effective armed force and planned for the possibility of insurrection. At the same time, NJM vanguardism led to a rapid fall in the number of active cadres and a highly hierarchical top-down system of command, both inimical to popular democracy and empowerment. Inevitably too, the NJM became a somewhat schizophrenic organization, with the full members reading Marx and seeking to build a 'real' Marxist-Leninist party, while the popular base remained largely ignorant of all this, supporting the Party mainly because of its history of standing for popular causes.[33] In hindsight, the best solution after 1979 would have been a rapid transition from a clandestine 'vanguard' structure to a mass organization, allowing all supporters to join with minimal requirements. This would naturally have to be accompanied by elections to posts in the Party at all levels, conventions and all the paraphernalia of democratic mass parties. This to the Grenadian 'Leninists' and their wider Caribbean compatriots was heresy, but consider what would have been the result of a joint leadership dispute that went before a convention with – based on the crowds the NJM was able to mobilize from its birth – 10,000 party members. Coard would have had his fulsome say and so would Bishop. Which one of them could oppose a decision for joint leadership, carefully considered, if the vast majority of that 10,000 supported it? Which one could have even considered calling on the PRA for support if the overwhelming majority of the 10,000 party members and quite likely the majority of the soldiers felt that it was a bad idea? This, of course, is wishful thinking, but it is sobering to consider that such a discussion was entirely off the agenda of the Party for four and a half years, only to be raised, ironically, by Bernard Coard in the dying weeks of the revolution when he proposed that there should be popular selection of members to the Party.[34] Finally, the small and narrowly constituted nature of the NJM was taking a terrible toll on the health of its membership. Faced with the daunting task of running a state, maintaining an army, building a revolution, projecting tiny Grenada on to the diplomatic stage and building the party, by 1983 most of the leadership and many of the members were groggy, sick or demoralized from overwork and sheer exhaustion. This as a factor in the final demise cannot be overstated for it undergirds the evident lack of judgement that prevailed among all the leadership in the final days.

Rethinking the Cuban Connection

What brought Grenada sharply into the crosshairs of the United States was its extraordinarily close relationship with Cuba. The Cubans played a central role in the building of the Grenadian airport, new housing construction facilities, medical care and the education of hundreds of Grenadian professionals among many other gestures that went far beyond the boundaries of generosity.[35] Most urgently, the Cubans provided critical military support in the form of small arms and equipment in the uncertain days after Gairy's overthrow and the months and years that followed. In exchange, Grenada gave Cuba and her strategic ally the USSR diplomatic solidarity, most egregiously, by supporting the Soviets in voting against the condemnatory UN resolution surrounding the 1979 Soviet invasion of Afghanistan.[36] This was a dangerous game as it served to focus unnecessary attention on Grenada and strengthen the view of the hawks in Washington that in a military standoff, Grenada would be a reliable and valuable asset for the Soviets in the middle of a presumed American sphere of influence. This to the resurgent right under Ronald Reagan was intolerable and underlined their expressed fear as to what the airport meant. As Assistant Undersecretary of Defense Dov Zakheim said after the invasion: 'It mattered little whether the airport at Point Salines would be used primarily as a tourist facility, as the NJM claimed. It was the potential that the airport offered to the Soviets that worried American analysts.'[37] In retrospect, it is difficult to see how the PRG would have survived without a modicum of military assistance and Cuba was the only regional force able to provide it. But a more tactical diplomatic relationship with Cuba might have blunted the arguments of the US policy hawks. The vote on Afghanistan certainly was entirely unnecessary. Would the Cubans have stopped assistance to Grenada because of an abstention on this issue? It is unlikely. In the end, this is a moot question, as the murder of Bishop so utterly tore down the last defences against invasion that the subtleties of diplomatic manoeuvring were made redundant.

Crisis and Collapse: Coard's Resignation from the Central Committee

If long-standing conspiracy, secret cells and ideological differences are to be ruled out of the equation, then the crisis of 1983 can best be understood as a series of vignettes, each causally connected to the previous and each contributing to an accumulation of uncertainty and misunderstanding that was eventually irrecoverable.

The first stage was the October 1982 resignation of Bernard Coard from the Political Bureau, Central Committee and Organising Committee (OC) though retaining his public positions as Minister of Finance and Deputy Prime Minister. Coard claimed that he was tired, that his influence had intimidated other comrades and that they would now have a chance to develop. More pointedly, he outlined that the CC was 'slack'[38] and in order not to have personality clashes with its chairman Maurice Bishop, he would rather resign. What had undermined the carefully developed synergy between Coard and Bishop to the point that Coard felt he would rather withdraw than clash with the leader? I suggest elsewhere that this was part of a divergence that had been present from the taking of power in 1979, in which two logics competed against each other.[39] One was the logic of the vanguard party, in which collective CC decisions, arrived at by democratic discussion and then applied downwards in an authoritarian manner (democratic centralism) prevailed. The other logic was that of the national, charismatic leader, in which, typically, the leader is responsible only to himself and the crowd. Bishop through the years in opposition adhered faithfully to the notion of democratic centralism as most strikingly illustrated in the previously mentioned decision to seize power. But as the months and years wore on, the influence of the second logic became overwhelming. It was he and not the NJM whom the crowds saw as the embodiment of the 'Revo.' He was the individual who more often than not interfaced with heads of state and prime ministers. While the Party remained the creaky, increasingly overworked but necessary instrument that held everything together, outwardly, to the general population of Grenada, it barely existed. The very exclusivity, clandestine nature and secrecy that had served it well in the preparation for insurrection, was returning to haunt it. Bishop was also prompted by his new Cuban associates, particularly in the diplomatic and military spheres who, in elevating their own particular experience of a single powerful leader almost to a law, encouraged him to act independently without reference to the Party. This was the cause of the clear spat – to my knowledge, the first between Coard and Bishop – in mid-1982 when military comrades who should have attended an Organising Committee (OC) meeting chaired by Coard were told that they were instead to attend an army meeting under Bishop's direction.[40] Yet, Coard's absence from the leadership in this period seemed to have done nothing to assuage the tension between these two competing logics. Faced with his resignation the CC, now entirely under Bishop's leadership in conceding to Coard's reference to slackness, sought not to rapidly increase membership by loosening entry requirements, but to place the Party on a more rigid Leninist footing by increasing study times, tightening membership requirements and intensifying disciplinary measures for supposedly recalcitrant comrades. Alongside these, plans were also put in place to project the image of the leader more effectively in public events and in the media – undoubtedly the basis for the aforementioned directive to use Maurice's Hunter College speech in worker education classes. Thus in late 1982, notably under Bishop's sole leadership, but with the full assent of all the CC members, vanguardism was intensified while simultaneously the tendency to imbue the leader with a heroic national profile was accelerated by the Party itself.

The Nature of the Crisis

The Revolution was approaching a crisis and that became evident early in 1983. The US military manoeuvres of March 1983, in which elements of the US fleet carried out activities in the Atlantic off the coast of Barbados, was for the first time met with a lukewarm response from Grenadians. A subsequent Party survey of support for the NJM and PRG came out with frighteningly low figures,[41] which suggested significant disenchantment with the process. My own experience in teaching worker education classes (primarily Caribbean and Grenadian history)[42] in a number of workplaces in this period supports the contention that support was tepid, though I had no basis to assess whether it had decreased over time or had always been low. I taught classes in the nutmeg factory in Grenville, to the road building crew on the Eastern Main Road, the Grenada Electricity Company workers and civil servants in the Ministry of Finance. In all instances, attendees were polite and I developed over time an easy camaraderie with many of the participants. But many others, particularly in the Ministry, did not attend and among those that did there was a handful that were clearly hostile to the idea of spending an hour each week talking about Caribbean history and politics. At the time, it struck me that for a country in the midst of revolution, the atmosphere was far less militant than I had expected, indeed far less militant than the average trade union meeting that I remembered in Jamaica. My own perceptions, blurred by the intervention of a quarter century may be skewed, but they are echoed in the documents of the CC, where the dominant opinion, including that of Maurice himself, felt that the Party had come close to losing its mass base.

This perspective was conveyed to a meeting of the entire party in July, in which the state of the deteriorating links with the people was raised.[43] The CC in keeping with its earlier positions used the opportunity to blame Party comrades for indiscipline and called again for a further intensification of Leninism as the only required solution. This time they were met with solid opposition from the members, led by the women who argued that they were doing the best for the Party and sacrificing care and attention to their children in the process. Members demanded and succeeded in getting the CC to reconvene and review its assessment. When the CC reconvened on August 26, there was extensive debate followed by the sobering conclusion enunciated by Chairman Maurice Bishop and noteworthy for its effect on the course of subsequent events. He said, in concluding, 'We are faced with the threat of disintegration.'[44] Jorge Heine, Gordon Lewis[45] and others have argued in effect that the revolution was going well in 1983 and that elements in the Central Committee argued that it was doing badly in order to promote their solution of joint leadership, effectively to elevate Coard and demote Bishop. This argument is predicated on the notion that Grenada had recently obtained IMF loans, many of the infrastructural programmes were advancing and that when the Point Salines International Airport was completed it would have led to significant improvements in the country's economy. This assessment is largely true, though it misses the effects of the international economic downturn of 1982–83 and the resultant fallout of loans which even then had started to adversely affect employment. However the cutting edge of the crisis was not the economy, but rather, the effective collapse of the Party and the implications therein for the collapse of popular support and the revolutionary base. This was a point understood by the entire leadership and enunciated by Bishop, above all. It required creative solutions; but the one that was eventually sought was fatally flawed, exacerbated the latent tension between the two logics of the Party and of the leader and eventually contributed to the catastrophe of October 1983.

The Joint Leadership Debates

On 16 September 1983 the Central Committee of the NJM reconvened to consider the crisis that, under the chairmanship of Maurice Bishop, it had previously recognized in August. Liam 'Owusu' James started the meeting by criticizing Maurice's leadership style and calling for a new model of joint leadership, marrying the qualities of the two men, Coard and Bishop. Unlike the earlier meeting there was no unanimity. After much discussion, nine voted in favour, Bishop, Unison Whiteman and Hudson Austin who had arrived late abstained, while George Louison voted against.[46] Bishop was obviously wavering and expressed the view that the masses might interpret this as a power struggle in the revolution. Despite the vote, however, he was asked for time and he granted it to consider the implications. Nine crucial days elapsed until the party general meeting on September 25. What happened in that period is difficult to piece together. I recall being asked seemingly out of the blue by two party comrades in the corridors of the Ministry of Mobilisation on Lucas Street, what I thought were the qualities of a leader. I found it odd and don't recall what my answer was, except that they seemed pleased with whatever it was I had said. I was preparing to head back to Jamaica at the time of the full Party meeting on September 25 and recall hearing from my house next to the St George's lagoon, muffled sounds from the gathering further up the hill in Butler House.

The meeting itself appeared to be a decisive turning point. Bishop at first expressed his reservations couched in the notion that there was a distinction between the Party's Leninist perceptions of what a leader should be and that of the masses, who, he mooted, tended to build up a cult around a single individual. In this, he was expressing in his way the tension between the two logics of the party and of the leader. Then, member after member spoke from the floor, expressing overwhelmingly support for joint leadership, but also love and respect for Bishop and Coard. Maurice was clearly overwhelmed and conceded to the views of the majority. The meeting ended with embraces between the two now joint leaders and the singing of the Internationale. Later, members of the CC gathered at Maurice's house for what seemed like completely convivial drinks and reflection.[47] It is important to pause for a moment and take stock of the events up to this point. Only Louison and Whiteman aside from Maurice Bishop on the CC had expressed reservations about the policy of joint leadership. The Party members were overwhelmingly in favour and Bishop himself was genuinely swayed by the show of solidarity. Had he not been scheduled to travel the next day to Hungary with both Whiteman and Louison – the two leaders most opposed to the proposal – as part of his entourage, things might have turned out differently. I am certain that both worked to convince him that he should change his mind. However, the decisive moments occurred on his way back from Hungary, when the plane stopped over unexpectedly in Cuba. Maurice met with Fidel Castro and something emerged from that meeting which changed the mood entirely. Bishop's personal security chief Cletus St Paul is reputed to have called Grenada and threatened the overall head of Security that blood would flow on their October 8 return.[48] In response to this ominous threat, Coard did not go to the airport and meet Bishop as was the custom and indeed did not see him for four crucial intervening days.

Then on October 12 rumour hit the street that Phyllis Coard and Bernard[49] (in that order) were trying to kill Bishop, heightening tensions and leading to the first physical clash when a militia group in Bishop's community, St Paul's, sought to mobilize in defence of their leader and one member was shot. When the Party, now in full emergency mode, met on September 13 to consider the source of this damaging rumour, Bishop denied knowing anything about it. He was immediately followed on the floor by Errol George, the second person in his security unit, who testified that the rumour had been given to him by none other than Bishop himself. When asked to respond to George's report, Maurice refused to answer. There was deep emotional distress and many comrades started to cry.[50] It is at this moment on September 13, when the integument between Maurice and the Party was severed. From here onwards, the overwhelming majority of the vanguard were convinced that their adored, if still only human, leader who had despite his reservations stuck with the Party over its desire to improve the profile and substance of leadership, had betrayed them in the worst possible way. For not only had he seemed to be retreating from the joint leadership agreement, but had opened the door to division and actually caused bloodshed by what they perceived to be his dangerous and unprecedented rumour-mongering. This is the setting within which the CC took the precipitous measure of detaining Bishop, which brought the inner party conflict – without any prior warning – to the people for the first time and rang the death knell of the revolution. The critical factor at this juncture is not the overwhelming support of the masses for Bishop; this was a relative constant throughout the process. He was the leader and was revered then as he is in death today by many Grenadians of a certain age and beyond. Who, after all, to the man in the street, were these interlopers who were mere shadows in the wake of the great leader? What is critically new is the unity that now prevailed in the Party and by extension the PRA, whose officer corps was composed almost entirely of Party members and candidates. Without the people, the NJM could not rule; but Maurice equally could not easily assume power in the face of a fully mobilized PRA and a Party convinced that he had betrayed their trust by reneging on his own solemn commitment of September 25. This is what I have referred to as the 'gridlock of events'[51] in which each element on its own contributes to a traffic jam of consequences, leading beyond these to his release on October 19; the decision to capture the fort; the clash with the troops sent to retake it; the capture of Maurice and his small contingent; and then their bloody execution.

Conclusion

To attempt therefore to move beyond 'conventional wisdom' and try to understand the crisis, I suggest that three critical decisions need to be brought to the fore:

1. **The Fatal Choice of Joint Leadership**. Joint leadership was not something entirely alien to Grenadians. Bishop and Unison Whiteman had been joint leaders when the two movements JEWEL and MAP merged in 1973 to form the NJM. Coard and Bishop were in effect joint leaders though informally so

at the time of Gairy's overthrow. There were therefore some resonances in recent Grenadian history, but the time for such an approach had been eclipsed by the transformation in Bishop's role and standing after the seizure of power and the very nature of the NJM which in its mechanical approach to the vanguard severely restricted membership and thus damaged its organic connections with the people. The average Grenadian who revered Maurice but knew little or nothing about the Party could not be expected to understand that out of the blue, for no apparent reason, Coard was now to be elevated to equal rank with Bishop. This, some have argued disingenuously, was an internal party matter and did not affect the profile of the state. Such a fine distinction could only be expected from persons who were fully aware of the Party and its relationship to the state and this was by definition only known to senior party members. In the end, the perception was inevitable that Coard was being promoted, while Bishop's sole leadership of both party and state was being reduced.

2. **Reneging on Joint Leadership.** Those responsible for opening up suspicions and hostilities on the trip to Hungary and on the way back in Cuba must take their full share of the blame. Whether it was Fidel Castro, George Louison, or Unison Whiteman, or all three and others unnamed, the question in retrospect must be asked, what were they thinking? Anyone who attended or was given reports of the September 25 meeting, the show of solidarity and the sense of relief when Bishop consented to the sentiments of the majority, should have thought twice about the implications of convincing Maurice to renege on his initial agreement. This could only have been met by hostility and the closing of ranks, which is exactly what eventually happened. Was the plan to execute a military coup with the support of Cuban construction worker/militia-trained contingents as Ventour and Coard,[52] writing from behind bars, intimated? This is a possibility, but would a seasoned tactician like Fidel Castro and the other members of the Cuban leadership have advised Bishop to resist the agreement on joint leadership if they knew exactly how united and determined the Party was at this moment? I suspect not, supported by the

fact that the at best lightly armed Cuban construction workers would have been heavily outgunned by the PRA with their artillery, light armoured vehicles (BTRs) and heavy machine guns. The only feasible context for a military victory by Maurice over the Central Committee, supported by the Cubans, would be in a context where the Party was divided and a significant section of its members and their comrades in the military had supported or been won over to Bishop's side and this was never the case. One distinct possibility then is that Whiteman and Louison convinced the Cuban leadership that the Party was an insignificant force and/or that support among its membership and crucially, in the military, was split. This is a consideration as it would be a means of boosting their own image, when the alternative point is mooted that you have no support whatsoever in the party beyond your own small contingent. I shall return to this argument in the postscript.

3. **The decision to hold power after the popular rebellion.** The CC had one final option when they became aware that the crowd had freed Maurice from house arrest. They could have called it a day. Indeed Bernard Coard had made it clear that he was packing and preparing to leave. This would effectively have ended NJM rule in Grenada, though whether Bishop would have been able to piece together a new party and resume power in the fluid situation in which the United States had already begun to mobilize its assets in and around Grenada, is moot. It might however, have avoided the worst possible outcome, the terrible events on Fort Rupert. Had Maurice headed to the Market Square, mobilized a general strike, cut off power and called for the resignation of the entire leadership, this new Maurice without the Party might have had a fighting chance to succeed. But when the crowd headed for the Fort, entered the compound, stripped female soldiers of their clothes and weapons and threatened NJM members present, the die was cast for a military confrontation.

Over the past quarter century I have thought long and hard about the Grenada revolution, about my time in that wonderful, little island and about those sad and tragic days of October. I stand in utter revulsion to the all too real image of soldiers putting Maurice Bishop, Jacqueline Creft, Fitzroy Bain, Norris Bain and their supporters up against the wall and riddling them with bullets. Whether Maurice's supporters had fired first and were responsible for the deaths of the four soldiers who were killed in the approaching BTRs or not, all conventions of war assert that combatants, once hostilities have ceased, have the right to be treated humanely. The execution of Maurice Bishop thus put the final nail in the coffin of the Grenadian Revolution. The US invasion, despite the fierce resistance from the PRA and elements of the militia,[53] was its inevitable reprise. The story of what happened, however, is still to be fully told and as a partial result what I consider to be old misunderstandings keep recurring. I have tried to address these and to re-think and restate what I know to the best of my ability for a new generation and a completely different world.

Postscript: The Turn to Fort Rupert

Much has been made by the many commentators on the events of October 19, including myself, on the decision taken while marching to the crowd in Market Square to turn towards Fort Rupert.[54] The common wisdom as intimated here is that had Maurice and the group who freed him gone to the Square to meet the very large throng waiting there, then he would have lived. The military would have found it difficult to fire on an unarmed crowd as was the case when they had come to force his release only moments before at his home in Mt Weldale. From this tactical place amidst his natural mass support base, he would have been able to follow a variety of tactics, including, most potently, calling for a general strike, as was the case against Gairy in 1974. Why the decision to confront the military by going to the Fort? Did Bishop, Vince Noel, Unison Whiteman, Einstein Louison and the others who led the group (Einstein in particular, George's brother and the only senior PRA officer to break with the CC) expect that the show of popular force would divide the army and give them at least a fighting chance of success? If this were the case, the tactics followed once the Fort was occupied should surely have been aimed at appeasement, discussion and an attempt to win over potential converts who were wavering among the troops, militia and party cadres who were present. Instead, the opposite was the case. Soldiers were forcibly disarmed, female soldiers in particular were treated badly and at least two were stripped.[55] Party comrades who were present were forced to lie prostrate and were told that they would soon be 'dealt with.' Meanwhile, a small contingent of armed men led by his press secretary, Don Rojas, had travelled the short distance to Grentel, the telephone company located on the Carenage, and gave instructions that all telephone lines to the homes of CC members and the other St George's military installation at Fort Frederick be cut.

This is powerful evidence to suggest that Bishop and his closest supporters had made the clear decision that a military solution was the only possibility. The implications of this are clear. The Party and PRA in turn were fully aware of the events on the Fort and it was now a matter of survival. Having conceded to the Crowd at Mt Weldale, they were unlikely to concede again as in their minds it was a matter of life and death. But did Maurice genuinely think that a largely untrained group of people off the streets of St George's could bring the small, but reasonably well trained PRA, with its BTRs and light artillery to its knees? Bernard Coard and John Ventour, writing from their time in prison, suggest that at this stage Bishop and his supporters were depending on Cuban support. The some 800 Cuban construction workers – a sizeable counterforce by any measure – in typical Cuban fashion were all trained militia and were prepared to be mobilized into a battalion led by Cuban officers who were present in Grenada to train the PRA. If indeed the Bishop-led group expected such a force to rally to their side, then it would explain not only the turn to the Fort, but also the uncompromising behaviour once it was occupied. It might also explain the fact that once crowds had started to come on to the streets before October 19 and the CC sought to negotiate terms with Unison Whiteman, they were met with the sole response 'no compromise.'[56] So why in the end didn't the Cubans mobilize? I suspect, to return to a point made earlier in the chapter, that whatever discussions which occurred in Cuba (vehemently denied by the Cubans to this day) were predicated on a split party, or at minimum a split army. The Cubans understood that the united PRA was a small but committed force and certainly a match for a lightly armed Cuban militia. The likelihood of the decimation of their own units when it was known that they would face the PRA at full strength would have caused the Cubans to pause, thus settling the balance of military forces for the tragedy that was about to unfold.

Notes

1. This chapter is dedicated to Richard Hart and in honour of his indomitable spirit and lifelong struggle on behalf of the working people of the Caribbean at home and abroad; and for being one of the few voices to mine below the surface in seeking to understand the reasons for the fall of the Grenada Revolution.
2. Friederich von Hayek, *The Constitution of Liberty* (London: Routledge, 1990), I use Hayek as epigraph somewhat ironically, as I am critical of much of his argument, justifying continued hierarchies based on wealth and property. And yet, having taught *The Constitution of Liberty* for the better part of two decades, the constant, critical engagement with his work suggests that there is much to be learnt from his assertion that voices of difference and opposition need to be heard and there can be no genuine progression of ideas without dissent. Thus, the above quote, in which he is making a case for the reaffirmation of liberal principles, is entirely appropriate, though deployed here to different purposes than he might have been comfortable with.
3. Under the leadership of Professor Alissa Trotz of the University of Toronto's Caribbean Studies Programme, a remarkable series of events was hosted in October 2008, among them: an audio visual presentation by Shalini Puri entitled 'Operation Urgent Memory: The Grenada Revolution and the US Invasion Twenty Five Years Later'; a lecture by Brian Meeks on 'Pan-Caribbean Futures 25 years after Grenada' and two cultural presentations reflecting on the Grenada Revolution, one at the University of Toronto and the other at the Jamaican Canadian Association building, featuring writers Merle Collins, Jacob Ross and Dionne Brand among others.
4. See Rupert Roopnarine, 'Resonances of Revolution: Grenada, Suriname, Guyana,' paper presented at the colloquium 'Remembering the Future: The Legacies of Radical Politics in the Caribbean,' Center for Latin American and Caribbean Studies, Pittsburgh University, 3–4 April 2009.
5. Entitled 'Thirty Years Later: The Regional Legacy of the Grenada Revolution,' Caribbean Studies Association xxxiv Annual Conference, Kingston, 1–5 June 2009, 50.
6. See Wendy C. Grenade, *Beyond the Legal Chapter: an Opportunity for Rebirth*, email courtesy the author.
7. See Patsy Lewis, 'Grenadian Reflections,' *Stabroek News*, www.stabroeknews.com, 14 September 2009.
8. Randal Robinson, 'Forgiveness Day?' *Stabroek News*, www.stabroeknews.com, 14 September 2009.
9. See Jorge Heine, 'The Return of Bernard Coard,' *Jamaica Gleaner Online* http://gleaner-ja.com.
10. Ibid.
11. Ibid.
12. Roopnarine, 2009, 14.
13. Brian Meeks, *Caribbean Revolutions and Revolutionary Theory: an Assessment of Cuba, Nicaragua and Grenada* (London and Basingstoke: Macmillan, Warwick University Series, 1992), 172.
14. See Meeks, 1992, 155.

15. See Fidel Castro, *Nothing Can Stop the Course of History*, interview with Jeffrey M. Elliott and Mervyn Dymally (New York, London, Sydney: Pathfinder, 1986).
16. See Maurice Bishop, 'Maurice Bishop Speaks to US Working People, 5 June 1983,' in *Maurice Bishop Speaks: the Grenada Revolution, 1979–1983* (New York: Pathfinder Press, 1983), 287–312.
17. I owe many thanks to the late Jamaican Prime Minister Michael Manley, who in his very generous speech at the launch of my 1992 book on Cuba, Nicaragua and Grenada made the mild critique that he would have wished for more of my personal narrative, as a 'participant,' in the historical record. This paper attempts in part to redress that earlier failure. See Meeks 1992.
18. Robert 'Bobby' Clarke, 'Statement on Grenada by Robert "Bobby" Clarke,' (email document) 14 October 2009.
19. See Castro 1986.
20. See Meeks 1992, 169–70.
21. See Meeks 1992, interview with George Louison, 170.
22. Clarke 2009, 4.
23. Idem.
24. Idem.
25. See for somewhat different approaches to this period, Perry Mars, *Ideology and Change: the Transformation of the Caribbean Left* (Detroit: Wayne State University Press) and (Barbados, Jamaica, Trinidad and Tobago: The University of the West Indies Press, 1998); and Brian Meeks, *Radical Caribbean: from Black Power to Abu Bakr* (The University of the West Indies Press, 1996).
26. The WLL was the pre-Party organisation that became the Worker's Party of Jamaica (WPJ) in 1978.
27. See Departments of State and Defence, *The Grenada Documents: an Overview and Selection*, Washington D.C., 1984; and Paul Seabury and Walter A. McDougall, eds., *The Grenada Papers: The Inside Story of the Grenadian Revolution and the Making of a Totalitarian State – As Told in Captured Documents*, Institute for Contemporary Studies, San Francisco, 1984.
28. See Brian Meeks, 'Social Formation and People's Revolution: a Grenadian Study,' PhD Thesis, The University of the West Indies, 1988.
29. See ibid. which seeks to understand long-term instability as a peculiar feature of the Grenadian 'social formation.'
30. I borrow this turn of phrase from George Lamming's reflections on the 1983 crisis. See George Lamming, 'The Plantation Mongrel' in *Conversations: Essays, Addresses and Interviews, 1953–1990*, ed. Richard Drayton and Andaiye (London: Karia Press, 1992), 248.
31. This was expressed most vividly in the infamous 'Line of March of the Party' Speech delivered by Bishop himself. See Maurice Bishop, 'Line of March of the Party' in *Grenada Documents*, 1984.
32. See Meeks 1988, especially chapter 3, 'The Revolutionary Situation.'
33. See Meeks 1992, for a more detailed discussion of the transformation to a vanguard party and some of the resulting political effects of this.
34. See Meeks 1988, 485–86.

35. See, for an accounting of the relationship, John Walton Cottman, *The Gorrion Tree: Cuba and the Grenada Revolution* (New York: Peter Lang, 1993).
36. See, for a discussion, Frederic Pryor, *Revolutionary Grenada: a Study in Political Economy* (New York: Praeger, 1986), 63–64.
37. Dov Zakheim, 'The Grenada Operation and Superpower Relations: a Perspective from the Pentagon' in *Soviet/Cuban Strategy in the Third World After Grenada: Toward Prevention of Future Grenadas: A Conference Report*, ed. Jiri Valenta and Herbert J. Ellison, Kennan Institute for Advanced Russian Studies and the Wilson Center, Washington DC, 1984, 21.
38. 'Minutes of Extraordinary Meeting of the Central Committee, NJM, 12–15 October 1983,' in *Grenada Documents*, 1984, 105–1.
39. See Meeks 1992, 177–78.
40. Ibid., 173.
41. See 'TAWU Balance of Forces Assessment, August 19, 1983' in Meeks 1988, 460.
42. The primary text, in the absence of easily available histories of Grenada, was the EPICA task force book in celebration of the Revolution. See EPICA Task Force, Cathy Sunshine ed., *Grenada: The Peaceful Revolution*, EPICA, Washington DC, 1982.
43. See Meeks 1988, 462–63.
44. 'Minutes of Emergency Meeting of Central Committee, NJM, 26 August, 1983,' *Grenada Documents, 1984*, 111–1.
45. See Gordon Lewis, *Grenada: The Jewel Despoiled* (Baltimore: Johns Hopkins University Press, 1987).
46. See Meeks 1988, 473.
47. Ibid., 485.
48. Ibid., 488.
49. Richard Hart, *The Grenada Revolution: Setting the Record Straight*, SHS Occasional Paper No. 20, 39.
50. Meeks 1988, 493.
51. Meeks 1992, 176.
52. See John 'Chalky' Ventour, *October 1983: The Missing Link*, self-published, 1999 and Bernard Coard, *Summary Analysis of the October 1983 Catastrophe in Grenada*, self-published, 2002.
53. Maurice Paterson's self-published book is still the best source as to the real extent of Grenadian involvement in defending their small island despite the political catastrophe that had occurred in the days before the invasion. It belies the myth of a Cuban resistance and asserts unquestionably the agency of Grenadians acting in defence on their soil. See Maurice Paterson, *Big Sky, Little Bullet: a Docu-Novel*, Maurice Paterson, St George's, 1992.
54. See, for instance, Hart 2005, 40–42; Lewis 1983, 53–55.
55. See Coard 2002, 68.
56. Ibid., 62.

14 | Grenada, Education, and Revolution, 1979–83

Anne Hickling-Hudson[1]

Introduction

Grenada's New Jewel Movement, led by Maurice Bishop, was the first indigenous political grouping in the history of the English-speaking Caribbean to overthrow an existing government by armed force. Yet most of the four and a half years of the Revolution (1979–83) were characterized by considerable popular support for the new People's Revolutionary Government before it came to its tragic, unexpected and shocking end in October 1983. Social, economic and political change seemed possible in the 1970s and '80s. People in newly decolonizing countries were encouraged by the beginnings of the Non-Aligned Movement of Third World nations demanding a new international economic order that would win them some economic justice after the ravages of colonialism. People also saw that some radical regimes, such as that led by Michael Manley in Jamaica and the Sandinistas in Nicaragua, were articulating and implementing basic rights that held the promise of countering the social and political oppression that they had endured throughout the centuries of colonial history. A majority of Grenadians committed themselves to fighting by the side of the People's Revolutionary Government for such new goals.

This chapter will analyse how the Grenada Revolution reconceptualized education, planned new goals, and implemented bold new educational policies. It will discuss the extent to which the government and people were able to reshape education as a tool for national reconstruction and the raising of national consciousness.

The Grenada Revolution and its Effect on Educational Goals

The People's Revolutionary Government (PRG) consisted mainly of members of a socio-political alliance of young people known as the New

Jewel Movement (NJM), which had developed close links in solidarity with disaffected Grenadian workers and peasants. In the pyramid structure of Grenadian society, the mass of peasant, wage-labouring and unemployed poor, almost all descendants of African slaves who had been transported to the region by the French, and subsequently the British colonizers, lived at a subsistence level, socially, politically and economically at the base of society. As in other Caribbean countries, their lives were characterized by 'extreme poverty, high malnutrition, illiteracy, backwardness, superstition…and massive migration' (Bishop 1979, 41). At the apex of society were the small elite groups who ran the institutions that kept the pyramid structure intact. These elite groups included the salaried, educated middle class and an even smaller minority consisting of those who owned substantial land and business enterprises most of which were tied to powerful, privately owned British and North American firms.

The impact of the Grenada Revolution on the political culture of the society had significant implications for education. As the NJM analysed it, post-colonial societies suffered from a psychological dependence which made it difficult for them to challenge and emerge from their dependent economic status. This analysis was in accordance with the observation of Michael Manley that 'post-colonial societies inherit the gross inequalities of the colonial system along with a view of the world that tends to the acceptance of this arrangement and an education system which works to perpetuate it' (Manley 1974). It was the dependent and imitative pattern of thought and the divided social and political relationships, said Bishop, which kept the Caribbean 'wide open to domination. . . so drugged by the hypnosis of American television, American advertising and capitalist consumerism that some really have no objection to becoming the backyard of the US' (Bishop 1982, 196).

The growth of Grenada's economy as a result of the policies of the Revolution also contributed to changing educational policy and practice. First, it made possible an increase in education spending, and secondly, it led to a demand for workers with higher levels of education. The People's Revolutionary Government pursued mixed economy within a path of 'socialist orientation.'[2] This was seen as being appropriate to Grenada's stage of development for a considerable time (Hart 1984, xii). In practice, a mixed economy meant that private sector ownership continued to dominate, but that its dominance was somewhat challenged by the growth of public sector enterprises. Traditional private business interests, both foreign and local, retained their dominant ownership and control of economic resources in tourism, agriculture, industry, transport, trade, commerce and banking. The PRG enlarged public sector ownership and enterprise from a negligible share to about 30 per cent of the economy, and encouraged the development of a small producer co-operative sector in small farming, fishing and restaurants (Ministry of Finance and Planning 1983). It also introduced structured government planning and leadership of the economy, which included new trade and aid agreements with socialist and non-aligned countries (Ambursley & Dunkerley 1984, 31–32; Payne, et al.1984, 22). This approach to economic development was flexible, gradualist and pragmatic, 'consonant with the broad character and appeal of the PRG' (Ambursley & Dunkerley 1984, 31). It had a bold, radical aspect in its rapid development of State economic activity, its militant support for trade unions,[3] and its negotiations with socialist countries, yet at the same time it cautiously encouraged the economic activity of the dominant private sector and maintained Grenada's traditional links with Western capitalism.

The new enterprises in the expanded public sector and the new government's ability to attract greatly increased sums in foreign grants and loans for infrastructural and social welfare projects provided several thousand new jobs. Unemployment, which was 49 per cent of the labour force in 1978, was cut down to 14 per cent by 1983 (Payne, et al. 1984, 24), at a time when most other countries in the region had an unemployment rate of 20–30 per cent. There was consistent economic growth measured in terms of the rise in GDP: 2.1 per cent in 1979, 3 per cent in 1981 and 5.5 per cent in 1982, and an inflation rate of 7 per cent. Per capita income increased, and, taking inflation into account, real living standards rose by 3 per cent. Contributing to this improvement in living standards was increased government expenditure on the social services. This led to more housing provision, more places in secondary, tertiary and adult education, and an expanded public health service which included a rise in the number of doctors from one per 4,000 people in 1979 to one per 3,000 in 1982 (see Ambursley & Dunkerley 1984, 9–10, 40–45; Payne, et al. 1984, 24, 26; Lewis 1987, Ch. 7).

This economic development had a profound effect on education. Increased expenditure made possible an expansion of places and a granting of subsidies for food, books and clothing to many students who needed them. Even more importantly, the thousands of new jobs which grew out of economic expansion required much higher levels of general education and technical and vocational skills in the workforce. By 1982, it was clear that without such education, progress would be severely constrained in the many new projects in construction, in the hotel industry, in craft design, in food technology, in scientific agriculture, forestry and fishing, in economic and environmental planning and in financial and administrative management (Creft 1983).

The PRG also aimed at providing for the development of higher levels of cultural skills: for example, in the recording and use of folklore and traditional music for drama, dance and literary development, and in book publishing. A new type of education and training was needed to 'produce the producers' in all of these areas. Grenadian leaders and technocrats frequently stressed the connection between education and economic development, and urged the people both to take advantage of, and to contribute to, new opportunities for educational advancement.

Some Problems of Post-colonial Development and Education

The PRG's goals of expanding education and refashioning it into an instrument that would help Grenada to achieve its aspirations for a better life were similar to those of other post-colonial Commonwealth Caribbean governments. These governments have done what they perceived to be possible in building schools and providing scholarships to expand primary and secondary places, training more teachers, developing new curricula and examination formats, and providing increased opportunities for technical and university education at the tertiary level (Miller 1984, 36). Such changes, however, although expanding educational provision compared to the colonial system, did not effectively alter the stratification of colonial education which selected out an elite for the minority of well-endowed schools and consigned the majority of young people to a much larger number of poorly-endowed schools, thus perpetuating the socio-economic pyramid and economic underdevelopment (Persaud 1975, 40). Similarly, although adult literacy campaigns were carried out in some countries, they had little impact on the access of the newly literate to improved economic opportunities. It has become increasingly clear to most Caribbean countries that the hopes of universal education based on equal opportunity are unlikely to be achieved in the near future (Miller 1984, 31). The hopes of the majority of people to transform their life chances through educational achievement have been widely thwarted. The provision of more schooling has fallen short of achieving the social aims of equality, justice and the improvement of economic conditions for the majority. Some educational analysts argue that this situation has been caused by the problem of 'educational inflation.' Bacchus (1980, 250–51; 1981, 216–17) explains educational inflation as the situation in which increased educational opportunities are producing more and more educated people who will not be able to find in their country's economy the 'wage and salary' jobs that their education leads them to expect. This has led, in many developing countries, to the paradox of the 'educated unemployed,' large numbers of schooled young people without jobs, and without the capacity or chance to create jobs, in economies which have spent a significant proportion of scarce resources on their education. Miller, describing the size of this problem in the Caribbean of the 1980s, points out that 'Most pupils leaving school each year end up unemployed, and the unemployment rate in the 15–24 year old category in almost every Caribbean state is over 50 percent' (1984, 37). The situation gets worse as unemployment increases. As Dore (1976, 4) has observed, 'the worse the unemployment situation gets...the more useless education certificates become and the stronger grows the pressure on an expansion of educational facilities.' In so far as the education sector continues to grow in response to this pressure, it absorbs funds which might have been more productively invested in the kind of economic development which significantly expands job opportunities. This can, therefore, further inhibit development and add to the growing unemployment problem.

Another problem, bound up with educational inflation, has to do with curriculum content. In many post-colonial countries, much of the content of the education offered in their schools and even in some of their tertiary institutions is unsuitable to their development needs. Curricula have tended to remain theoretical, inadequately technical or scientific, and with an expository focus which discourages local investigation and experiment. Nyerere's classic critique of the traditional school set up by colonial regimes is still applicable to many developing countries. He points out the tendency of schools to continue to stress urban, consumerist and anti-manual work values, to ignore the realities and problems of local communities and to perpetuate the escapist orientation which can lead students to develop attitudes of over-reliance on imported solutions and the desire for migration. All of this contributes to rural and national poverty (Nyerere 1968, 275–79).

In 1979, Grenada had been independent for only five years. In this short post-colonial period, there were no signs that the problems of educational inflation would be avoided. Places in the educational system had been increased, but this had little impact on improving socio-economic opportunities. Unemployment had not been reduced from the high level of 49 per cent of the workforce. The continuing unsuitability of the curriculum did not suggest that people were being trained to improve the economy. Curriculum content tended to be bookish, largely imported from Britain, expository, impractical and scarcely relevant to local conditions. Coard (1985, 10) commented that 'we inherited an education system that...was totally disconnected to the requirements of earning a livelihood, building an economy, improving the material standards of living of the working people, and generally improving the economic and social welfare of the people.'

Grenada's education system was dysfunctional for economic development, in that it resulted in waste, underachievement and a poorly educated, largely unskilled labour force. In 1980, the primary and all-age schools held approximately 21,922 children aged five to 16 (Ministry of Education 1982, 35), the vast majority of them from poor peasant and working class families. The elementary education received in these schools left many of the pupils barely literate and numerate, as was illustrated by their very poor performance in examinations and by the high rate of minimal literacy among the adult population. Repetition of grades and dropout rates were high (see Brizan 1981, 12–13, 44–45). Secondary high schools, based on the model of the British 'grammar' school, provided secondary education for 4,660 students in 1979 (Ministry of Education 1982, 66). These high schools, financed partly by private fees and partly by government subsidies, had limited success in training their students for the British General Certificate of Education (GCE) school-leaving examinations. The minority who passed were qualified to obtain the small number of high-status white-collar jobs in the society. Most students, however, failed the British examinations: in 1978, for example, the pass-rate for Cambridge GCE Ordinary Level subjects was 33 per cent (Brizan 1981, 44) and in 1980 there was a 20 per cent pass-rate for GCE Advanced Level subjects (Ministry of Education 1982, 93). Thus, even the more privileged high school system was unable to provide the majority of its students with academic success seen in terms of passes in the British examinations. One important factor underlying the poor quality of schooling as evidenced by poor performance and high dropout rates was that a large proportion of teachers had no teacher training. In 1980, some 500 (67 per cent) primary, all age and junior secondary schoolteachers had no post-school education (Ministry of Education 1982, 101) and very slim chances of entering the Grenada Teachers' College to obtain it, since this institution could only take up to 50 students a year in its two-year Teacher Training Certificate programme. Of the 218 teachers in secondary (grammar) schools, 126 had no post-school education, 32 had Primary Teachers' Certificates and 60 were university graduates, only 29 of these having postgraduate training in education (Ministry of Education 1982, 68). Thus, some 72 per cent of secondary teachers were not suitably educated or qualified for the profession.

Since opportunities for tertiary education were few, Grenada had no way of producing the numbers of skilled and professional personnel needed for the development of the economy and of the educational system. Although some 352 Grenadians had been educated at universities abroad between 1946 and 1970 (Jacobs & Jacobs 1980, 94), most of them were privately financed by their families. On graduation, many of them stayed abroad. By the mid-1970s, only two or three students per year could hope for government scholarships to pursue university education abroad (Coard 1985, 8). The combination of few educational and economic opportunities led to massive migration. Some 300,000 Grenadians lived outside Grenada, particularly in the United States, Britain and Trinidad and Tobago, compared to the 110,000 who lived in Grenada (Coard 1985, 11). In circumstances of economic stagnation, this large migration of people each year may have been desirable in terms of reducing pressure on inadequate resources, and contributing to foreign-exchange remittances that helped the economy. With the anticipated development of education and the economy, however, a reduction in migration would be desirable so as to harness the skills and commitment of people to national reconstruction.

The PRG repeatedly committed itself to providing 'mass education' in Grenada – the educational development 'of all our people, not just a few' (Creft 1982, 52). The aims were to counter the past educational neglect of the majority, and to produce a system in which an educated and politically-aware working class would join with trained and progressive professionals and administrators to reshape production and socio-political practices. Two questions should be considered in examining the educational developments that took place within the framework of these goals. How far did it appear that the quantitative expansion of education was remaining within the capacity of the economy to absorb the newly educated so that Grenada could avoid the educational inflation problem experienced by other developing countries? Secondly, how far did it appear that the government would be able to change the education system both by modernizing it and by encouraging school pupils, adult students and teachers to accept and work towards the qualitative goals of education for a new kind of development in the society and the economy? To assess these questions, it is important to consider the emphasis on tertiary and adult education, the type of developments that were initiated in the school system, the growth of the economy and the role of mobilization.

Policies and Priorities in Education

The educational reforms in Grenada were developed and carried out through a range of new policies and programmes. All the policies were instituted during the four-and-a-half-year period, but some took priority in emphasis and resource allocation, as will be discussed in this section.

Policy preparation
- Public meetings on the goals and restructuring of education
- Education sector survey – an analysis of the system which would prepare the ground for progress in planned stages
- Teacher conscientization through workshops led by Paulo Freire

Programmes and strategies at stage 1 (1979–83)
- NISTEP – in-service education for unqualified primary teachers (70 per cent of all primary teachers)
- Expansion of university education – overseas scholarships
- Establishment of local tertiary education (Institute for further Education, In-Service Training Unit)
- Adult literacy campaign
- Adult continuing education through the Centre for Popular Education (CPE)
- Expansion and systematization of vocational education and worker training
- Establishment of popular education in Mass Organisations
- Expansion of places in the early childhood and school system
- Reduction then abolition of school fees
- Provision of subsidies for uniforms, food and books for the neediest students
- Curriculum development and change
- Establishment in Primary schools of a practical weekly education programme through community-school links (The Community School Day Programme)
- Development of the library sector

Policies for second-stage development (1984–89)

Expansion of first-stage development, plus:
- Qualification of Secondary teachers through NISTEP
- Upgrading of Junior Secondary Schools into full secondaries
- Upgrading of All Age schools into vocational schools linked with worker training
- Replacement of British School leaving exams (GCE) with regional Caribbean exams (CXC)
- Establishment of a Grenadian university college

The PRG leadership was keenly aware of the dangers of the temptation to spend more on education than was wise, or, as Finance Minister Coard put it, of 'trying to do so much so fast that everything crashes' (Coard, 1982). Educational developments in the Revolution showed an attempt to prioritize certain programmes with roughly sequenced stages, with the aim of preparing the ground at one stage for progress in the next. This prioritization was worked out, not through formal educational planning of which there was very little in Grenada, but through considerable discussion in public meetings about the needs of education. This formed the basis of policy approaches drawn up by teams of leading educators, administrators and government representatives. For example, in 1979 and 1980, several meetings of a wide cross section of teachers and other interested people, including the revolutionary Brazilian adult educator Paulo Freire, worked out general approaches for immediate emergency training of the huge backlog of untrained teachers, and for literacy and post-literacy campaigns.

The PRG saw itself as leading the first, initial stage of developing the educational system. In this stage, envisaged as lasting for five years, budgetary increases and skill deployment were maximized on projects in tertiary and adult education, and minimized on other projects such as curriculum development and other needs within primary and secondary education and the library sector. The PRG's emphasis on tertiary education reflected the government's conviction that the education of adults would flow into developing not only the economy but also the schools in the second stage of educational development, which was envisaged to take place between 1984 and 1989. Spending on tertiary education, which included teacher training, technical and vocational education and payments to the University of the West Indies, increased from $1.2m to $2.5m Eastern Caribbean (EC) dollars, which was a jump from 14 to 21 per cent of the total recurrent budget in education. (In 1981, the exchange rate was: US$1 = EC$2.70. A British pound sterling was worth EC$5.90.) Spending on administration was also increased, from 7.8 to 9.7 per cent of the education budget, to facilitate more efficient management of the education system. The newly established adult education sector was assigned 2.6 per cent of the budget. However, although monetary increases of just under $1m each went to primary and secondary education, their per capita and percentage share of the recurrent budget rose very little (Ministry of Education 1982, 177, 181).

Apart from the recurrent budget, the PRG successfully negotiated overseas grants for education in the form of university scholarships abroad (mostly from Cuba and other socialist countries), Cuban assistance with the printing of textbooks, and funding provided by multi-lateral agencies such as UNESCO and the Organisation of

American States. Grants such as these increased the ability of the government to initiate the expansion of tertiary education, and enabled it to improve pre-school provision and primary curriculum development to a greater extent than the recurrent budget allowed. A look at the PRG's efforts to expand school capacity and start curriculum change suggests that they were more in the nature of initial indications of the direction to be taken rather than the large-scale problem-solving thrusts which characterized the effort to provide tertiary and adult education.

Developing Tertiary Education

The PRG's emphasis on tertiary and adult education was a bold policy contradicting prevailing wisdom by international institutions such as the World Bank that government funding should maximize the rate of return by investing mainly in primary schooling and minimizing investment in tertiary education. Traditionally, this minimal spending on tertiary and adult education had been the norm in Grenada. The other countries in the English-speaking Caribbean which were more developed in this respect than Grenada were nevertheless seriously underdeveloped with no more than five per cent of the 18–25 age cohort in tertiary education, and two per cent or fewer completing university.

The PRG made these areas a priority because it saw the educational development of the nation's adults as the key to improving both the social service aspects of the economy (for example health care, teaching and administration) and the major productive economic sectors of agriculture and fisheries, tourism, construction, light manufacturing and craft. Tertiary education was assigned not only the largest percentage of the recurrent education budget, but also the highest per capita expenditure in the education system (Ministry of Education 1982, 177, 181). The tertiary sector was assigned 21 per cent of the recurrent education budget compared to the 14 per cent which had been spent in 1978. Adult education (that is, the literacy and basic education programme) was established as a new sector receiving 2.6 per cent of the recurrent budget (Ministry of Education 1982, 177). The PRG hoped that when there was no longer the need for programmes of adult literacy and basic education, all adults at a certain standard would have the opportunity to enrol in tertiary education. A step-by-step process was envisaged and initiated by bringing about this situation.

The tertiary education system was organized to expand significantly the number of places in degree, certificate and diploma programmes, both at home and abroad, which prepared people to work in fields that needed high levels of training. The starting point was the establishment of the Institute of Further Education (IFE), which began with a sixth form college. This centralized the preparation of young people for the Cambridge GCE Advanced Level examinations which matriculated them for entering the University of the West Indies and other tertiary institutions. Previously, small sixth forms, with insufficient teaching resources, had been scattered throughout the nation's high schools. By 1982, the IFE had over 200 studying in the two-year Advanced Level programme (Ministry of Education 1982, 88–95). About 100 of these students each year could expect to get places in universities or tertiary institutes abroad.

University education was treated as an economic priority. When compared to the very few young Grenadians who had, in the years just prior to the Revolution, been assisted by the then government to study at university level, educational opportunities had greatly improved. By 1983, there were 319 students in university and higher education, most of them on scholarships. Of these students, 66 were studying in the Commonwealth Caribbean and 215 in socialist countries which had provided scholarships in fields requested by the PRG. In June 1983, there were 161 students at universities and higher institutes in Cuba, 18 in the GDR, 14 in the Soviet Union, 35 at the University of the West Indies, three at other tertiary institutions in the Anglophone Caribbean, five in the United States and four in Tanzania. The Cuban government had provided another 46 tertiary scholarships by September 1983 (Ministry of Education 1983).

Considerable investment in three senses underlay the provision of these university places. First, a relatively large annual financial contribution was made to the University of the West Indies to pay off by installments arrears of EC$1.1 m inherited from the previous regime, and to finance 35 places there for Grenadian students – a large increase. Secondly, aid from other countries was accepted in the form of hundreds of tertiary scholarships. Thirdly, there was an investment in terms of the temporary loss of the work and production of the nation's most highly educated young people who were given the chance to continue their studies abroad. Another section of the tertiary education system consisted of the local institutions and programmes that offered both full-time and part-time or in-service certificate level training to personnel in social welfare or technical fields. Some of these were existing institutions such as the Grenada School of Nursing and the Grenada Technical and Vocational Institute, in which few changes were made at this stage of the development of education. The PRG put resources into creating two new tertiary programmes, for workers in public administration and for teachers.

The In-service Training Unit was established to run regular short courses and seminars for upgrading the administrative and managerial skills of civil servants, 332 of whom attended the courses between 1980 and 1981 (Ministry of Education 1982, 114–19). The National In-Service Teacher Education Programme (NISTEP) was established in 1980 as an experimental and emergency approach to training all of the nation's 500 unqualified teachers in every government primary, all-age and junior secondary school. NISTEP, a high priority of the PRG, offered three years of on-the-job training at least equivalent in hours of lectures and supervision of practical teaching to the superseded full-time, two-year programme (Ministry of Education 1982, 100–10; Olliverre, 1982). The staff, recruited both locally and overseas, grew from 16 in year one to 28 in year three. Within the three-year target (October 1980–October 1983), NISTEP succeeded in providing a basic course of initial teacher education for 350 out of the original 500 students, about 150 having dropped out of teaching (Hickling-Hudson 1985, 11).

In October 1982, in-service teacher training was extended to 70 of the unqualified teachers in the pre-primary schools. It was planned that these student teachers would attain their qualifications as pre-primary teachers by October 1985. The first batch of 350 NISTEP trained primary teachers would have graduated in December 1983, were it not for the tragic events of October 1983 that brought about the collapse of the Revolution. In July 1983, plans were being worked on to start NISTEP Phase 2 in January 1984. This phase of NISTEP would have trained a second batch of unqualified primary teachers – the 150 who had replaced those who had dropped out of teaching to pursue other careers. It would also have provided three or four years of in-service teacher education for the 158 unqualified teachers in the secondary schools (Hickling-Hudson 1997). Through in-service teacher education, therefore, Grenada would have been able, within about seven years, to make professional training and certification the norm and a compulsory requirement for all of its teachers. This development had not then taken place either in policy or practice in most of the other countries of the Commonwealth Caribbean.

With the accession of a new government following the US invasion, it was decided that Grenada would return to the system of obtaining regional (Eastern Caribbean) qualifications for teachers, studying the certificate course coordinated by the Education Faculty of the University of the West Indies in Barbados. Since this programme accepted only limited numbers, the large-scale teacher training approach of the PRG was ended, and NISTEP was discarded. However, aspects of the in-service approach pioneered by NISTEP were continued in that student teachers were required to do two years of initial in-service and one year of full-time training at the Grenada Teachers' College in order to qualify for the regional teachers' certificate (Olliverre 1984). Those who had entered NISTEP without the normal matriculation requirements of passes in three British GCE O-Level examination subjects were required by the post-revolutionary government first to attain these passes before being allowed to complete one further full-time year of teacher education that would enable them to graduate with the regional teacher's certificate. Those who had the three O-Level passes could immediately complete the extra full-time year to earn their regional certificates.

Recognizing the inadequacy of relying entirely on overseas universities for degree-level education, and of having too great a variety of standards in the local in-service tertiary programmes, the PRG had two ideas which it hoped to put into operation in the future. One idea, which was sketched out in the Education Sector Survey, was to expand the Institute of Further Education so that it would coordinate and standardize all of the post-school education in Grenada (Ministry of Education 1982, 95–99). The second idea was to have discussions with an overseas university, perhaps a Canadian or an American one, with a view towards setting up a Grenadian university which would initially be a college offering associate degrees. Some government leaders and local businessmen reasoned that if Americans could establish the St George's University in Grenada as an 'offshore' medical school which trained students for medical degrees acceptable in the USA, there was no reason why such an institution could not be incorporated into a local university which both Grenadians and foreigners could attend.

Emphasizing Adult, Continuing and Vocational Education

Another high priority of the PRG was to develop new systems of adult education for workers who had not necessarily had any secondary schooling, and for adults who were illiterate or sub-literate. On-the-job training, usually in the form of six-month vocational courses, was provided for tourism workers at the Hotel School, craft workers at Grencraft, and farmers and fisherfolk at the new Farm Schools and Fisheries School. In these adult vocational courses, productive work and the management of co-operative business enterprises were an integral part of the education offered (Ministry of Education 1982, 145–55).

The PRG saw the education of adults with little or no literacy as not only a moral and ethical responsibility, but also as being vital to the more efficient functioning of the economy. Their view was in accord with the observation of Bacchus (1981, 221) that 'People with an education seem to display a greater willingness and ability to participate more actively in the political decision-making process and in community development efforts. Education also increases the predisposition of the population to try out new ideas and practices such as improved health practices, family planning and the introduction of new crops and cultivation techniques.' In 1980, the Revolution introduced the provision of adult education for 3,500 non-literate adults through a new community-based structure, the Centre for Popular Education (CPE). A literacy campaign was carried out by the CPE's small core of paid organizers, coordinating an initial number of 1,575 volunteer unpaid teachers who each took responsibility for teaching one or more adults to read and write by regular visits to their homes (Brizan 1981, 138–45).

Because of organizational and resource problems in the CPE, more than half of the teachers dropped out in the first year and fewer than half of the entrants, just over 1,000 adults, completed the basic literacy level of the programme. Efforts were made to reorganize and improve the programme, and by 1982 there were 1,500 adults studying at various levels of the CPE, which planned to bring them from basic literacy to the stage of the primary school-leaving examination within three years. The target was that the CPE would have expanded, within the five years of Stage 2 of the Education Plan, to provide these and more adults with a secondary level education which had a strong vocational component (Creft 1982). The CPE would therefore equip Grenada's traditionally most neglected adult workers with a primary and eventually a secondary level education. From this point the best would be ready to enter the Institute for Further Education where they could matriculate for university or pursue a local tertiary diploma.

In addition to adult education in the funded and structured institutions established by the Revolution, non-formal education was further provided to rural and urban communities all over the country through the new Community Organisations described earlier. These held regular sessions of political and general-interest debate and discussion which contributed to raising the general level of awareness of local and international issues affecting Grenada.

School Expansion and Curriculum Change

Inadequate capacity in both primary and secondary schooling, plus status-divided stratification of school quality for wealthy and poor families, are entrenched problems in Caribbean education. Even today they have not been overcome. A stratified education system of low capacity was in place in Grenada in the 1970s. The PRG's goal of modernizing and establishing some degree of equity in the system was even more difficult to implement than their goal of developing the tertiary and adult education sectors. Entrenched attitudes of conservatism had to be challenged to make curriculum and status changes in schooling.

The expansion of school capacity was an important long-term goal, the basis for equalizing education for rich and poor. The PRG made a start at stage one (1979–83) by providing subsidies and scholarships, upgrading school plant and building one new high school. The primary school system already had an enrolment of 98 per cent, but daily attendance was, on average, 3,277 fewer children than the 18,322 enrolled (Brizan 1981, 42). Since, in many cases, this was related to the problem of extreme poverty, the PRG, from the first year of the

Revolution, started a programme of subsidies for food, schoolbooks and uniforms for the neediest children. In 1983, a Child Care and Protection Unit was established to attend professionally to children with problems. It was hoped that in 1984 this Unit would be extended to the point where it could provide a full programme of counselling and material assistance to ensure regular and compulsory attendance at primary schools. Many primary schools had fallen into serious disrepair, and the government and mass organizations coordinated a community repair and repainting drive which was enthusiastically supported with voluntary contributions of cash, materials and labour (Coard 1985, 13). A structured system of child care centres and pre-primary or nursery schools was introduced to replace the existing situation of unregulated and unqualified private childminders. By 1982, some 250 infants under age three and 2,500 children aged three to five were benefiting from government supervised and subsidised child care and pre-schooling, and there were plans to develop and expand this provision with some 1750 additional places by 1985 (Ministry of Education 1982, 202–7). An in-service training programme was established for those who gave child care. Seven new pre-schools were established with UNICEF assistance, and many others were repaired and refurbished. It was hoped in Stage 2 of the Education Plan to extend nutrition and other subsidies in this sector.

In the secondary school system, the government gradually reduced then abolished school fees and expanded capacity. By 1981, secondary (grammar or 'high') schooling was free in all government subsidised schools. By 1983, the PRG had provided an additional 2,000 places by expanding existing high schools and building a second government high school. High school places were, therefore, awarded to some 32 per cent of the children who took the Common Entrance Examination at the age of eleven-plus to seek entry into secondary education, instead of the 10 per cent who were allowed to 'pass' it in 1978. There were no immediate plans to phase out the Common Entrance and allow all children of eleven-plus entry into high schools. This was not possible at stage one, since an additional 7,000 high school places would have been needed. It was regarded as unfeasible to put the increased resources of the education sector into providing this universal secondary education while the majority of teachers remained untrained.

At stage two of educational development (1984 and 1989) however, the PRG planned to provide at least 2,000 of the 7,000 additional high school places needed. This would be done by upgrading and expanding the four junior secondary schools with their 1,361 students, into 'full secondaries,' something which could only be done with the provision of increased plant, including additional library resources and science laboratories, and more secondary-trained teachers (Ministry of Education 1982, 228–32). Improvements were also planned at Stage 2 for the neglected 'senior forms' of the all age-schools with their 3,383 students (Ministry of Education 1982, 53, 58). In these schools, 12–15 year-olds received so rudimentary an education that fewer than 20 per cent of them passed the government school-leaving examinations specially designed to test the all-age curriculum, and, indeed, many left school barely literate (Brizan 1981, 44–45). The plan was that the all-age senior forms would become vocational skill-training centres, which would concentrate on preparing the students for apprenticeships and jobs while providing them also with a basic general education (Ministry of Education 1982, 230). It was envisaged that in the third stage of educational development, beginning in 1990, these vocational skill-training centres would become a part of a unified comprehensive secondary-school system which offered both technical/vocational and academic education to all of Grenada's young people (Ministry of Education 1982, 220–22, 247–51).

School curriculum reform was the educational area that remained least developed in the Grenada Revolution, because the majority of the resources were concentrated elsewhere at Stage 1 of the Education Plan. Qualitative change was started on only a small scale, and indeed proved much more difficult to implement than the expansion of school capacity. An attempt was made to initiate new projects and approaches such as modern 'child-centred' methods at the pre-primary level, and the writing by teachers and teacher educators of a new series of culturally relevant reading primers (the 'Marryshow Readers') for primary schools. The Ministry of Education continued the tradition of organizing several short methodology and curriculum development workshops for teachers. The political leaders constantly stressed the importance of integrating the school with the community and of developing a 'work-study' approach in the curriculum, whereby the practical work of students should inspire their studies and vice-versa (Bishop 1980, in Searle, 1984, 52, 60; Creft 1982). A Community School Day Programme (the CSDP) was launched, in which parents and other community volunteers helped to teach the children craft, farming and other skills each Friday (Coard 1985, 14) while the bulk of the teachers were being trained in the in-service teacher education programme. An agricultural 'work-study' programme was started in three pilot schools where there was suitable land for farming, but this remained rudimentary and not well understood. The CSDP, too, was so beset by organizational and other problems that it was only successful in a few communities. In 1983, the Ministry on Education sought advice on how to improve the planning and organization of work-study in the schools by inviting Cuban experts in work-study education to examine the CSDP and the agricultural pilot projects, and to hold discussions with the local teachers and organizers involved.

In secondary schools, students were given the beginnings of democratic involvement in school affairs through new Student Councils elected by secret ballot (Coard 1985, 18). As part of the plan to rationalize secondary curricula, it was decided that the British GCE Cambridge Ordinary Level examinations would be phased out from 1983. They were to be replaced with the regional secondary school-leaving examinations and 'continuous assessment' coordinated by the Caribbean Examination Council (CXC), a process of evaluation which had already been adopted by other Anglophone Caribbean territories. Secondary teachers were encouraged to form Subject Associations to launch the development of curricula which would more suitably prepare students for the Caribbean examinations. British GCE Advanced Level examinations would be maintained in the foreseeable future as they were the instrument of selecting students for entry to the University of the West Indies with its three campuses in Jamaica, Trinidad and Tobago, and Barbados.

However, most of the traditional weaknesses of the curriculum continued unabated. There was still very little technical education: planning for the expansion of this was just beginning. The humanities curriculum still had a virtually colonialist orientation in many schools. Literature and history, for example, were designed according to the Eurocentric perspective of the syllabuses for the British external examinations, with their focus on British writers, heroes and exploits, and often a negative portrayal of Caribbean people. The new Caribbean Examinations are regarded as the norm in the Commonwealth Caribbean today, but in that era, some teachers were reluctant to abandon the British exams and make the shift to the Caribbean ones. Mathematics and science teaching, and student performance in public examinations in these subjects, remained extremely weak, so weak that the government could not find enough qualified students to take up the increased number of university and technical education scholarships offered abroad (Bishop 1980a, 58).

If the Revolution had continued and had been able to implement its education plan along the lines envisaged, three vitally important areas of curriculum change would have helped to alter the unsuitable curriculum inherited from the past. The first change would have been to establish work-related technical, vocational and agricultural education as an important aspect of school learning. This would have been initiated by means of the interim plan to train students in the senior forms of all-age schools as skilled apprentices in a variety of trades. It would have been considerably more difficult to get all primary and secondary schools to offer vocational subjects as a normal part of the curriculum, but there were plans to pursue this goal through developing and systematizing the CSDP and other structures. The combination of production and study would have eventually become a compulsory component of the curriculum (Ministry of Education 1982, 245–49).

Secondly, the PRG stressed the importance of improving science and mathematics education, starting with the formation, in September 1982, of a Young Scientists' Association and the recruitment of more science lecturers in teacher education. A more controversial approach to strengthening science and maths education was the personnel loan, negotiated by the government from 1983, of several primary and secondary Science and Mathematics curriculum experts from Cuba and the Soviet Union. For example, two Cuban experts in primary curriculum planning (science and mathematics) visited Grenada in the summer of 1983. They worked together with teacher educators at the teachers' college, through a translator, to produce detailed analyses of the weaknesses in primary science and mathematics, and made recommendations as to how these could be tackled. Soviet curriculum experts in secondary school science and mathematics were to have arrived in the latter part of 1983 to help plan for and teach in the proposed Secondary In-Service Teacher Education Programme in 1984, but these plans came to nothing after the collapse of the Revolution and the US invasion in October 1983.

The third important area of curriculum change was that, with the introduction of the CXC curricula, the humanities would have become more Caribbean-oriented. Additionally, the PRG was discussing, with education officials, plans to allow students to take school courses in political studies. It was hoped that this would help to spread a more nationalist, regionalist and 'progressive' consciousness among school students although this would have been one of the changes likely to have attracted considerable hostility.

The Integration of Educational Development, Economic Growth and Mobilization

Because of the growth in the GDP that took place during the revolutionary period, Grenada was able to spend $23m on education by 1983 instead of the $8m spent in 1978. This together with assistance from abroad enabled the PRG to afford the educational expansion that it considered feasible and desirable in the first stage of its education plan.

Within the framework of educational growth, costs were held down and many programmes, especially in adult education, were made possible by the effective mobilization of people and resources. Many school buildings were used day and night for education and community purposes. Hundreds of people gave time and effort voluntarily to contribute to education, for example, the volunteer literacy teachers responding to the CPE's campaign slogan 'Each one teach one,' the parents who gave their labour, cash and materials to the School Repair Drive and the citizens who volunteered in the Community School Day Programme to help teach children on the Fridays when their teachers were attending NISTEP classes. Many trained educators not only willingly took on an increased workload, but also gave extra time and effort to do additional unpaid tasks in education – for example those who contributed their research to educational planning, their curriculum skills to the production of new materials and their organizational skills to coordinating zonal council meetings on the National Budget and the education programmes of other community groups. Professional administrators and project leaders in the Civil

Service devoted a regular part of their time to preparing material for public sessions in which Parish and Zonal Councils were informed about economic and social development policies as a basis for the discussions which followed. There is little doubt that an important factor encouraging this mobilization of voluntary work was the team spirit engendered by frequent consultative and planning meetings between educators at all levels – principals, teachers, department heads, Ministry of Education officers and others in the education field.

From the perspective of the 'socialist orientation' path, the type of economic development that was undertaken by revolutionary Grenada would have made it likely to avoid the problem of producing educated people faster than the economy could absorb them. The fact that a significant part of the economy (the public or state sector) could now be planned, and that new sources of international assistance were being utilized beyond the traditional ties with Britain and the USA, made it likely that the number of jobs would continue to grow. Related to the development of the public sector was the PRG's effort to increase local scientific and technical capacity so that still more jobs could eventually result from the opening up of new fields, for example, in the establishment of a mini hydroelectric power supply, of an improved water supply and telecommunications network, and of local geothermal energy. At the same time, the encouragement of the private sector by way of investment incentives also created new jobs, for example with the increase in the capacity of privately owned garment factories and the growth of privately owned producer co-operatives.

Grenada's economic development in this period made it almost certain that all those being trained at tertiary institutions would be immediately absorbed in the economy. Many would have the opportunity of helping to enlarge its productive capacity – using their professional skills in privately owned enterprises if they wanted, or in the enormously expanded public sector. The expansion of the economy also demanded more manual and middle-level workers with literacy and technical competencies: many of these would be school graduates. From the point of view of the adult student undergoing vocational training or attending courses in the CPE or in their Community Organisations, education would not just be for its own sake. It was the kind of education that would help them obtain a job, set up a co-operative or function more efficiently as enterprises became more technically developed. Given the rate of economic growth, it was highly likely that the country would be able to avoid the problem afflicting some other developing nations in which adult time and effort invested in acquiring literacy is largely wasted in terms of improving economic opportunity.

Several factors indicated the possibility of gradual success for the government's goal of laying the basis for acceptance of a new kind of socially conscious and development-oriented education. A most important factor was the enthusiasm with which much of the population supported the development goals and projects of the Revolution: as Lewis (1987, 33–34) points out, the extent and nature of volunteer participation in these programmes 'demonstrated that a whole population was serving the common cause with zeal and dedication, unaided by... material luxuries.' People increasingly saw the connection between developing these programmes and developing both the formal and the non-formal education system. The training of the country's teachers and the new opportunities for their participation in community work was to provide a basis for involving them in reorganizing the education system and developing more appropriate curricula in the humanities, science and technical education. The education, in socialist countries, of several hundred young people who would return to take up deliberately planned positions of professional expertise and leadership in the society would have underpinned administrative understanding of a path of socialist orientation.

Conclusion

The educational policies and strategies of the Grenada Revolution have important implications for developing countries. Historical evidence was used to show that the government was able to change the education system both by modernizing it and by encouraging students and teachers to work towards studying for a new kind of development.

A major focus of educational change in Grenada was the attempt to correct the nation's educational underdevelopment in a manner that was consistent with three factors: the general trends towards curriculum modernization in the Caribbean region, the political objectives of the

People's Revolutionary Government for the socio-cultural development of the nation, and the growth of the economy.

This transformation agenda is what makes educational change in the Grenada Revolution an important model to be studied and considered by other formerly colonial countries with the same kind of poverty and social deprivation that characterized Grenada in 1979. The revolutionary government set about pursuing its goal by restructuring the formal and the non-formal education system in a way that would both promote the cultural development of the people and serve the needs of an expanded economy. Many radical and unusual strategies were used in increasing quantitative provision in secondary and tertiary education, in establishing structures for combating illiteracy and sub-standard schooling, and in planning for an education future that would give the traditionally poor and neglected the opportunity for learning that had throughout Grenada's history been denied them. The government, in its determination to combine political and educational development, also gave thousands of people their first experience of active participation in the affairs of their country and nation, in itself an educative process. The target of establishing a qualitatively new type of education was delineated. Some initial steps were taken towards it, and further changes were systematically planned for future stages of national development.

This development of educational provision for the Grenadian people was likely to avoid the common post-colonial problem of educational inflation in the sense of producing more expensively educated graduates than the country could afford. Two factors suggested this. One was that, although educational expenditure was increased, it was kept within practicable limits by a variety of means such as the prioritization of programmes, careful budgeting, the mobilization of voluntary work, and utilization of both traditional and new avenues of overseas educational aid. The second factor was that, at the same time, the economy was being developed to an extent and in a manner which made it likely that it would absorb the increasing numbers being educated and for whom education was planned.

Notes

1. I was privileged to spend two years working in Grenada in teacher education and educational planning during this period of intense change. My family

developed a deep friendship with Richard and Avis Hart, who were in Grenada during the same two years.
2. The New Jewel Movement, which was the controlling party in the coalition People's Revolutionary Government, considered the Revolution to be 'socialist oriented,' meaning that 'while socialism was the ultimate goal, the government's actual policies were pragmatic and did not envisage any sudden transformation' (Sunshine 1985, 96). Ambursley & Dunkerley (1984, 32) further explain that the theory of socialist orientation 'holds that a direct transition to socialism is not possible in underdeveloped countries.' In the pre-socialist stage that must take place, the existing system of dominant private capitalism is usually retained but modified and controlled by the Revolution's assertion of the interests of wage-workers and peasants. The revolutionary government in the meantime builds public sector enterprises, often with the help of new foreign alliances, and implements social programmes to develop the traditionally neglected masses of the people. This establishes a 'mixed economy.' Theoretically, an important factor characterizing the subsequent socialist stage of development is the dominance, both proportionately and in terms of policy influence, of the public sector of the economy, controlled by the representatives of the working class.
3. The PRG legalized the right of Grenadian workers to select and join the union of their choice (Peoples' Law No. 29 1979), as a result of which 'some 70 to 80 percent of all workers on the island were unionised. The unions remained independent of the PRG and were encouraged to work for the best possible conditions for their members within a framework of free collective bargaining and the market economy... – There were eight trade unions in Grenada and most were led by NJM members' (Ambursley & Dunkerley 1984, 37).

References

Ambursley, F. & Dunkerly, J. 1984. *Grenada: Whose Freedom?* London, Latin American Bureau.
Bacchus M. K. 1980. *Education for Development or Underdevelopment?* Canada: Wilfred Laurier University Press.
———. 1981. Education for development in underdeveloped countries, *Comparative Education*, 17, 215–27.
Beckford, G. 1972. *Persistent Poverty*. Oxford: Oxford University Press.
Beckford, G. & M. Witter. 1980. *Small Garden. Bitter Weed*. Jamaica: Maroon Publishing House.
Bishop, M. 1979. Imperialism is not Invincible. Address to the Sixth Summit Conference of the Non-Aligned Movement, Havana, Cuba. 6th September In: D. Jules & D. Rojas (1982).
———. (1980a). Education is a must. Speech to inaugurate the National In-Service Teacher Education Programme, 30 October 1980, in *In Nobody's Backyard: Maurice Bishop's Speeches, 1979–1983: A Memorial Volume*, ed. C. Searle (1984). London: Zed Books.

———. (1980b). Learning Together, Building Together. National Broadcast to Declare the Literacy Campaign Open, Radio Free Grenada, 27th July, in: D. Jules & D. Rojas (1982).

———. 1982. For the Cultural Sovereignty of the Caribbean People! Address at the Caribbean Conference of Intellectual Workers, St Georges, Grenada, 20 November, In: C. Searle (1984).

Brizan., G. 1981. *The Education Reform Process in Grenada 1979–1981*, report. Grenada: Institute for Further Education.

Coard, B. 1982. Opening Address to the Education and Production Conference, Carriacou, Grenada. November (unpublished).

———. 1985 *Revolutionary Grenada: a big and popular school, 1983 speeches*. London: NJM UK branch.

Creft, J. 1982. The Building of Mass Education in Free Grenada, in: *Grenada is Not Alone*, speeches by the People's Revolutionary Government at the first International Conference in Solidarity with Grenada. November 1981. Grenada: Fedon Publishers.

———. 1983. *The Importance of the Centre for Popular Education. Phase 2*. National broadcast on Radio Free Grenada, January 1983 (unpublished).

Dore, R. 1976. *The Diploma Disease*. London: Allen & Unwin.

EPICA Task Force. 1982. *Grenada: The Peaceful Revolution*. (Washington, DC, USA).

Girvan, N. 1972. *Foreign Capital and Economic Underdevelop,nent in Jamaica*. Kingston: University of the West Indies.

Hart, R. 1984. Introduction, in: C. Searle (1984).

Hickling-Hudson, A. 1985. In-Service Models of Teacher Education in Developing Countries, In: *The Preparation of Teachers and Emerging Curriculum Issues*, Collected Papers of the Fifteenth Annual Conference of the South Pacific Association of Teacher Educators, Tasmania, Australia.

———. 1997. Caribbean Experiments in Education for Social Justice: the Case of Grenada, in *Social Justice and Third World Education*, ed. T. Scrase. New York: Garland, 133–62.

Hodge, M. & C. Searle. 1982. *Is Freedom We Making. The New Democracy in Grenada* Grenada: Government Information Service.

Jacobs, W. & R. Jacobs. 1980. *Grenada. The Route to Revolution*. Havana: Casas de Las Americas.

Jules, D. & D. Rojas, (Eds). 1982. *Maurice Bishop. Selected Speeches, 1979–1981*. Havana: Casa de Las Americas.

Lewis, G.K. 1987. *Grenada: the Jewel Despoiled*. Baltimore: Johns Hopkins University Press.

Mandle, J.R. 1985. *Big Revolution, Small Country. The Rise and Fall of the Grenada Revolution*. Maryland: North South Publishing Company.

Manley, M. 1974. Keynote Address at Sixth Commonwealth Education Conference, Kingston, Jamaica.

Miller, E. 1984. *Educational Research: the English-speaking Caribbean*. Canada: International Development Research Centre.

Ministry of Education, Youth and Social Affairs, Government of Grenada. 1982. *Education Sector Survey*, unpublished report, St Georges, Grenada. [This report was researched and written by Caribbean personnel, and should be differentiated from the *EducationSector Survey: Grenada* written by UNESCO personnel in 1982].

Government of Grenada. 1983. Survey of Numbers of Grenadian Students at Tertiary Institutions Abroad, unpublished report, St Georges, Grenada.

Ministry of Finance and Planning (Government of Grenada). 1983. An Overview of Economic Sectors in Grenada. An unpublished document prepared for classes in the National In-Service Teacher Education Programme, St Georges, Grenada.

Nyerere, J. 1968. Freedom and Socialism: a selection from writings and speeches. Oxford: Oxford University Press.

Oliverre, I. 1982. NISTEP, a Revolutionary Approach to Teacher Training in Grenada. Paper presented at the 'Education and Production Conference,' Carriacou, Grenada. November.

———. 1984. Interview on developments in teacher education, November.

Payne, A., P. Sutton, & T. Thorndike. 1984. *Grenada: Revolution and Invasion* Beckenham: Croom Helm.

Persaud, G. 1975. The socializing functions of teacher education: system maintenance or change? *Caribbean Journal of Education*, 2(1) June.

Searle, C. (Ed.). 1984. *In Nobody's Backyard: Maurice Bishop's speeches, 1979–1983: A Memorial Volume*. London: Zed Books.

Searle, C. & D. Rojas, (Eds). 1982. *To Construct From Morning: Making the People's Budget in Grenada*. Grenada: Fedon Publishers.

Sunshine, C.A. 1985. *The Caribbean: Survival, Struggle and Sovereignty*. Washington DC: Epica.

15 | Foreign Policy and Economic Development in Small States: A Case Study of Grenada

Patsy Lewis

Introduction

On 4 August 1998, Fidel Castro made a historic visit to Grenada to what the British Broadcasting Corporation (BBC) described as 'a hero's welcome' (BBC 1998). This was his first visit to Grenada despite his close relations with Prime Minister Maurice Bishop and his strong support for the 1979 Revolution. Castro's visit came 15 years after Cuba's expulsion from Grenada following the United States invasion; the erasure of its contribution to economic and social development; the general vilification of its role in Grenada, and in particular, a misrepresentation of its involvement in resisting the US invasion. Also significant was that this visit, which followed the resumption of diplomatic ties between the two countries and a previous visit by Grenadian Prime Minister Keith Mitchell, occurred in a period of consolidation of neo-liberalism as the exclusive development path which small states were being forced to embrace. Fidel's visit to Grenada was also symbolic of a broader turn in the Caribbean toward greater autonomy in foreign policy with the resumption of diplomatic relations with Cuba by most countries, the embrace of Venezuela's Hugo Chávez administration concretized in the PetroCaribe initiative, despite continued US hostility towards both governments, and a general shift from diplomatic relations with Taiwan in favour of China.

This chapter seeks to understand the factors underlying shifts in foreign policy in small states in general, through the specific lenses of Grenada's post-independence experience. It argues that Grenada's foreign policy, despite taking different turns, was driven by the same underlying imperative: the challenges that constraints of size and the structure of the global economy place on small states. It discusses this against the backdrop of different conceptual lenses used to analyse small states, foreign policy, from the geo-political lenses of the Cold War to vulnerability and post-vulnerability debates designed to fashion spaces for manoeuvre within the strictures of neo-liberalism. Grenada provides a good case study for discussing the interplay between economic challenges and foreign policy approaches and the constraints in foreign policy conduct imposed by the global political climate, because of the rupture which the Revolution represented, in what at first appears as consistency in foreign policy. The about turn in foreign policy direction seen in the mid-1990s not only in Grenada, but across the region, also provides an interesting point for understanding shifts when they occur.

Background

Grenada became independent in February 1974. Within a mere five years, on 13 March 1979, a new government had forcefully replaced the post-independent government of Eric Gairy with a self-styled 'people's revolution.' This government lasted a short four years before self-destructing in October 1983 with the killing of leading members of the government, including Prime Minister Maurice Bishop, followed by an invasion of United States armed forces on October 25. Since then, Grenada has seen four changes of government, the most recent in July 2008. The government with the longest reign was the New National Party (NNP) led by Keith Mitchell, between 1995 and 2008. The main foci of analysis are the period of the revolution which, though short, represented a radical shift in foreign policy and the 13 years of NNP rule which represented the most stable post-independence regime and thus provides a longer time frame from which to assess shifts or consistency in foreign policy approaches. The periods also provide interesting points for comparison as they capture shifts in international alliances that ultimately condition the economic policies available to countries, with implications for their foreign policy.

Grenada, with a population of just over 100,000 and geographic size of 345 km^2 is one of the smallest independent states in the United Nations system. While there are no accepted parameters for defining a small state, the World Bank (2007) identifies some 45 developing countries as having populations of below 1.5 million. Although the particular challenges of small states were first formally recognized in the 1960s with the UNITAR [United Nations Institute for Training and Research] 1969 report, their visibility was heightened during the 1990s, leading to an acceptance by the World Trade Organisation that they may well face special development challenges that require specific responses. On the economic front these include the constraints that small physical size and limited natural resources placed on achieving economies of scale, specialization and economic diversification, with implications for competitiveness and stable growth; a high degree of openness accompanied by a dependence on a few commodities and services; the relatively higher cost of transportation arising from their distance from major markets; limitations in human resources aggravated by high out migration rates and weakness in their capacity to absorb skills; the high cost of raising finances on the international markets; and their susceptibility to environmental hazards.

In Grenada, these features are clearly manifested. The country engages in a limited range of economic activities. The main contributors to GDP in 2007 were services, with the category 'other services' contributing 35 per cent, followed by transportation and construction, 14 per cent and 11 per cent, respectively. Government is the third largest contributor to GDP, accounting for 13 per cent. Tourism (hotels and restaurants), agriculture and manufacturing contribute equally to GDP, around 6 per cent (CDB 2007).[1] Because of the narrow range of goods and services produced the country relies heavily on imports, which increases the importance of its export sector as an earner of foreign exchange. The economy is highly open with a trade to GDP ratio of 111.7 between 2004 and 2006 (WTO Statistics 2007). The main contributors to export are tourism and agriculture dominated by cocoa and nutmeg, which are subject to deteriorating terms of trade. The income generated by the economy has proven inadequate to finance the imports of consumer and capital goods and fund government programmes, resulting in a chronic deficit on the current account which is financed by heavy borrowing. Grenada's foreign debt stood at 99.28 per cent of GDP in 2005, and this was after it was re-negotiated following hurricane Ivan (MOF 2008). Government thus relies heavily on tax revenue on imports, grants and loans from friendly governments and funding from International Financial Institutions (IFIs) to finance its programmes. It also borrows heavily on the domestic market and high cost private international sources.[2] Both the manufacturing and agricultural sectors were developed on the basis of access to protected markets in the US and Europe. However, erosion through successive rounds of liberalization in the WTO and the restructuring of trade agreements by Europe and the US have placed the competitiveness of the major economic activities in question. Given the weakness of the economy and the constant need to meet deficits between earnings and spending, the foreign policy concerns of the country, evidenced in an analysis of policy pursued across successive governments naturally turn on securing funding and favourable market access.

Another peculiarity which Grenada shares with many small states is difficulty with accessing funding from IFIs and donor governments because of its classification as a middle income country enjoying high human development, ranking 74 in 2009 on the UNDP HDI. Paradoxically, the country also experiences high levels of poverty and unemployment which belie measurements of high per capita income of $7,344 (PPP 2007) (UNDP 2009 HDI).[3]

Conceptual Lenses for Viewing Foreign Policy Approaches to Small States

Foreign policy concerns of states are largely determined by the particular challenges they face or goals they wish to achieve in economic or political spheres, conditioned by the international environment in which they operate. Thus, before the 1970s the literature on small states focused on European small states, such as Austria, Belgium, Switzerland and Luxemburg, and sought to explain their foreign policy behaviour in the context of the challenges they confronted within the broader European political framework of powers competing for territory and influence. The primary concern of small European states in this context was not economic development as became the analytical focus for small states in the post independence period, but the maintenance of territorial integrity.

The focus of debates shifted dramatically in the early post-independence period – 1960s to 1970s – to newly emerging states, many of which were in the Caribbean, whose considerably smaller size raised questions of their economic and political viability. In 1968, the UN had 16 member states with a population of one million or less. By 1997, the Commonwealth Secretariat had identified 49 independent states, 42 of which were in so-called 'developing countries' (Commonwealth

Advisory Group 1997, 18). Concerns with small states development generally formed part of a broader post-independence discourse on development embracing developing countries. In the Caribbean attempts to understand the development challenges can be found in three broad approaches: development economics, associated with Arthur Lewis; the New World Group, an offshoot of the dependency school; and a focus on the structural limitations of size, as developed by William Demas. Despite variations these were all grounded in an acceptance of modernization which centred industrialization as the prerequisite for development. Specific developmental concerns for the small islands of dependent and non-independent territories hinged on their viability as independent states.

The earliest attempts to understand the challenges that small size posed to newly independent countries include the work of UNITAR (1969) and William Demas's *The Economics of Development in Small Countries* (1965), which set the framework for later attempts to understand the role of size in development. The early focus emphasized the structural limitations small size imposed on economic development, which was viewed through the lenses of modernization. In particular, W.W. Rostow's prescription in his stages of growth thesis for achieving self-sustaining growth as the basis for economic development set the conceptual backdrop for understanding small states challenges. This led Demas to a focus on structural features that inhibited self-sustaining growth. These included small market size and weak resource base that limited scope for economies of scale in production, and inhibited economic diversification and specialization. Demas's focus on size as inhibiting self-sustaining growth represented an important oeuvre in attempts to understand the constraints affecting small economies. This was implicitly recognized in Arthur Lewis's work, which advocated integration as a way of circumventing size and resource constraints, including human resources, though it was not explicitly developed. Lewis's main focus, however, was on the role of the traditional agricultural sector in supporting a strategy of industrialization (Lewis 1955).

The New World Group, which had its genesis in the Latin American dependency school, focused on the structures of the global economy within which these states emerged. It centred the legacy of colonialism and the structural relationships which Caribbean states continued to maintain with formal colonial powers as the main factors inhibiting their development. Thus the New World Group saw the region's development challenges primarily as determined by the structure of the relationships they had developed under colonialism which persisted in the post-independence period and inhibited any real development. The Group rejected Demas's analytical focus on size privileging instead the structure of their economies and relationship to the 'metropole' (Best 1968, 1971; Levitt and Best 1984). All these approaches, however, appreciated the need for broader external markets and production structures, crucial given their small size, even when this was not the explicit focus of analysis.

These attempts to understand the nature of Caribbean development problems jostled for primacy with Cold War perspectives on development in the framing of small states' foreign policy. In Cold War terms, development was viewed more narrowly as a struggle between the forces of capitalism, defended by Western governments under the aegis of the US on the one hand, and communism, defended by the USSR and its Eastern European allies, on the other. Balance between the two groups was maintained by the threat of nuclear conflagration. The foreign policy of both the US and USSR was directed at maintaining their own spheres of power, while seeking some penetration of the other – at least from a Western perspective. In this construct, there was little space for either autonomous path for developing countries or of an alternative visioning of their realities. They were viewed, at least from the US's perspective, evident in the prevalence of the domino theory, as mere pawns in a game played out between two great powers. For the US's part, the Cuban missile crisis, which brought the possibility of nuclear confrontation to the region, justified the salience of this approach. This, supposedly, gave small states a degree of leverage far exceeding their size and political clout which was to redound to their benefit by way of increased aid and investments.

Developing countries' attempts to seek an alternative analytic path for addressing their development challenges gave rise to what is loosely referred to as the Bandung project led by governments of the South. This embraced the formation of the group of 77 as a distinct constituency within the UN system which sought to change the rules of the game by agitating for a New International Economic Order through UN agencies such as UNCTAD and UNESCO. Support for this project was also lent by the Non-Aligned Movement (NAM) which adhered to the possibility of alternative paths to the two dominant contending perceptual frames. This project succumbed in the 1980s to the restructuring of inter-state trade relations along neoliberal lines, first with the increased role of the International Financial Institutions (IFIs) in shaping developing countries' national economic strategies in the wake of the debt crisis, then consolidated in the formation, in 1994, of the World Trade Organization (WTO). The WTO oversees the phased liberalization of trade in goods and services, inter alia, within a system of binding rules. The ascendance of neo liberalism as the main paradigm for development, especially in the wake of the collapse of the Soviet system, served to discredit, for a time, alternative conceptualizations of development.

Communism's collapse across Europe and the ascendance of neoliberalism both as a tool for conceptualizing development and a means for achieving it, led to a shift in understanding small states and thus their economic and foreign policy concerns. In particular, the WTO's formation which was the formal vehicle for restructuring inter-state relations along neoliberal lines, led to an almost immediate restructuring of their established economic relations with major trading partners in Europe and North America. This was felt in the erosion of tariffs and the reformulation of trade and aid relations from non-reciprocity in favour of reciprocal trade negotiated under broad Regional Trading Agreements (RTAs). This move reflected a radical perceptual shift in the treatment of developing countries from an acceptance of specific national structural and historical factors conditioning their development to a rejection of particularities based on the notion of a level playing field of rules and regulations as the basis for achieving equity in inter-state relations. It also represented a rejection of deeper analyses into the causes of so-called underdevelopment and its particular manifestation in individual countries to a more superficial focus on rules and regulations justified by the simplicity of neoliberalism which located development within the narrow confines of trade. This was particularly problematic for small states as it failed to credit concerns that structure and the historical basis for their current integration in the global economic system might constrain development options.

The concern with small states' development challenges intensified from the 1990s when the embrace of neoliberalism as the principle guiding inter-state relationships foreshadowed the dramatic restructuring of their trading relationships and the very basis of the economic model they have pursued since independence. This restructuring of inter-state economic relations and the threat it posed to the economies of small states led to renewed interest in small state development problems both within academia and the state. Attempts were made to revive the small size debate with analytical innovations that included locating it within concerns for environmental sustainability which emerged in the 1980s and sought to ground claims for difference in scientific rigour. These were manifested in the development of the concept of vulnerability which led to indices that attempt to measure vulnerability. The Commonwealth (1985, 1997) played a significant role in recasting small states challenges in terms of vulnerability, supported by the World Bank (2000) and the United Nations.[4] Vulnerability thus functioned as a concept for challenging the dominant assumption of sameness along which the global trading structure was being restructured, thus emphasizing challenges of small size. Vulnerability as a concept was multi-dimensional, incorporating and expanding older insights on economic size and trade volatility, and adding new insights on environmental vulnerability, particularly for small island states, in keeping with broader concerns with environmental sustainability.

The debate has since expanded to include the concept of economic resilience as an attempt to soften the determinism inherent in the structural elements of the debate and to explain the perceived conundrum of successful small states (Briguglio's so-called Singapore paradox [200]). Briguglio (2004) sought to differentiate between what he saw as vulnerability deriving from immutable economic forces outside of a country's control and policy induced vulnerability arising from inappropriate policy, on the one hand, and resilience which could be inherent or nurtured, on the other. Policy played an important role in nurturing resilience and enhancing a country's ability 'to cope with or withstand its inherent vulnerability' (Briguglio 2004, 43). This led to attempts to identify a range of policy measures that would engender resilience, including macroeconomic policy, market reform, good governance, social cohesion and environmental management and the further generation of an index to measure economic resilience (Briguglio et al. 2006). The concept of resilience thus shifts the focus of debate from challenges to perceived positive attributes of small size (Baldacchino 2006), particularly the ability to recover from environmental hazards and economic shocks.

The discussion on resilience has broadened to include the concept of jurisdiction, (Baldacchino 2007; Baldacchino and Milne 2000, 2006), which examines the room for flexibility that state sovereignty allows these states for manoeuvre. Examples of the usage of jurisdiction include the sale of internet domains, country codes, orbital satellite slots, passports, votes in international bodies (Prasad 2004), and fishing rights; provision of military bases; shipping registries; and internet gambling, among others, (Prasad 2009). Prasad (2009) views these strategies positively, describing small island leaders as 'wise and intrepid...try(ing) to make the most of global opportunities while engaging the forces of globalization on its (sic) own terms' (60). The possibility that some of these strategies may serve to further erode the value of sovereignty which these states jealously guard, and thus their ability to raise the standard of living and dignity of their people, is not seriously considered. Furthermore, the focus on resilience, while important, runs the danger of shifting attention from immutable structural features, such as geography and inequities in inter-state relations, to the macroeconomic policies pursued by small states and the role these can play to 'mitigate the drawbacks of being small and economically fragile' (Winston Cox, Commonwealth Deputy Secretary General in Briguglio and Kasanga 2004, 15). This is most evident in the development of a resilience index by the Commonwealth Secretariat and the University of Malta (Commonwealth Secretariat c. 2009) as a 'guide for good practice' and 'emulation' by other states.[5]

Concepts such as resilience and jurisdiction, while important in seeking to identify room for small states to manoeuvre within the international economic system, run the danger of obfuscating the role of structure in constraining development options and ignoring specificities. Jurisdiction, in particular, represents an 'anansi' approach to foreign policy where the state uses cunning and agility in combating a bigger foe which it cannot hope to confront directly. It shifts the focus of the debate to the strategies and policy decisions of states, but leaves the broader more central problem of power and inherent inequality in the global economy now entrenched by rules, untouched.

Foreign Policy Practices in Grenada: Understanding the Foreign Policy of Small States

Pre-independence foreign policy

Jeanne Hey (2003, 193–94), in a summary chapter of her edited collection assessing the foreign policy of a range of small states, suggested that the following factors shaped small states diplomacy: 'systemic factors' or international constraints, level of development which privileges regime security as a foreign policy goal, and the role of leader which looms larger in 'less developed small states' (194). Braveboy-Wagner, in a more focused discussion on foreign policy of English-speaking Caribbean states, identified three specific goals which foreign policy was meant to achieve: 'territorial and political security, economic and social development, and global and regional prestige' (Hey 2003, 33).

The foreign policy approaches of post-independence Caribbean governments were clearly limited by international constraints that determined the options open to Caribbean small states, giving rise to a range of policies; although the occasion for exercising foreign policy arose only after the countries became independent. For countries of the West Indies Associated States,[6] which included Grenada, this occurred between 1974 and 1983. A common trend emerges in the conduct of state affairs that characterized their relationship with the colonial power before independence and shaped their post-independence foreign policy: the primacy of their economic challenges. One of the driving forces of independence in the Caribbean was restrictions imposed by the British colonial government on sourcing economic support even as Britain was reducing economic funding to the islands. Thus, Associated Statehood, which the small territories of the defunct West Indies Federation were forced to enter into with the British government, was considered second best to full independence as it placed constraints on their ability to conduct foreign policy which, with defence, remained within the purview of the colonial power (Spackman 1975). Thus, control over foreign policy was viewed as an essential prerequisite for achieving economic goals.

Colonialism ended leaving national governments with weak economies and severe development problems of limited social and physical infrastructure that required huge injections of finance to address. Countries were now able to source funding without constraint, although within the strictures of the Cold War. In Grenada challenges included low access to secondary and post-secondary education and rudimentary health care arising from low investment in human capital. The undiversified production structure of the economy, which was dominated by export agriculture, could not provide the resources necessary to address these problems or to alter the structural basis of the economy. In the 1970s, in the early post-independence period agriculture continued to dominate the economy, contributing just over 30 per cent to GDP, while tourism and manufacturing were insignificant, contributing just over 3 per cent and under 3 per cent, respectively (Ambursley 1983, 194). Arthur Lewis recognized this when he emphasized the importance of multilateral and government-to-government financing to underwrite costly infra structural projects that the private sector could not be relied upon to provide (Beckles and Shepherd, eds., 1996, 389).

In the post-independence period the primary concern of governments was securing funding for nation building. The main avenues for finance were the former colonial power and the European Community; the new regional hegemon, the United States; and the various international financial institutions (IFIs). This helped to shape the focus of foreign policy approaches which saw most countries privileging the Cold War perspective of security rather than the alternative approaches available at the time. Thus, for most Caribbean small states, especially given the US's pre-eminence in the region, foreign policy was viewed as a leverage to gain resources to address primarily economic concerns. This approach was useful as it allowed governments to subordinate domestic tensions, especially those arising from inequality and weak political institutions, to the Cold War preoccupation with ideological struggle and security. Thus governments deliberately used Cold War concerns to keep themselves in power and suppress opposition, while at the same time leveraging economic support from Western powers. This approach competed with structural perspectives on underdevelopment but won out in terms of foreign policy approaches adopted in the region. It is only Jamaica during the 1970s, Guyana up to the 1980s and Grenada, during the four years of the Revolution that consciously employed a broader analytical framework of underdevelopment as the basis for foreign policy. In the aftermath of the Grenada invasion OECS governments sought to shift the US's focus from viewing them in security terms towards a broader recognition of their economic challenges, without much success (Lewis 2002, 71–72).

Thus, in the initial independence period, the Eric Gairy government's foreign policy approach was to pursue a conscious alignment with US policy, which was dictated by the Cold War. In the region this meant supporting right-wing governments, even when these governments were repressive, and alienating governments or movements viewed as supportive of the communist bloc. This was manifested in Grenada's relationship with some of the most repressive regimes in the region, including the Pinochet regime in Chile, which helped to train and fund a newly created army.

On the economic front, the more permissive regulatory framework that existed allowed the government to utilize a range of fiscal incentives in order to facilitate the creation of nascent tourism and manufacturing sectors. Attempts at addressing highly skewed land distribution which led to the transfer of large private estates to government hands and to a lesser extent the peasantry (Ambursley and Cohen, eds. 1983), along with suspicions of electoral fraud, alienated important sections of the population, however. This, along with increasingly violent means of suppressing political dissent, led to the government's eventual overthrow. The economic and social conditions existing at the end of the period do not suggest that the supposed leverage Grenada, as a small Caribbean state, should have enjoyed contributed in any significant way to improving the conditions of life. Rather, it appeared to allow space for manoeuvre of a politically repressive state as long as it operated within the established parameters of the Cold War. Unemployment remained high, estimated at nearly 49 per cent at the time of the Revolution (1979); access to secondary education remained limited, with a mere 15 per cent of primary school students proceeding to the secondary level; and the quality of health care was poor (*Kairi* vol. 1, 15–17).

Foreign Policy during the Revolution

The first problem confronting the People's Revolutionary Government (PRG) was to address the low levels of economic and human development existing. Its economic strategy was aimed at diversifying the economy by regenerating agriculture and strengthening manufacturing and tourism. This required expanding infrastructure and enhancing human resources by broadening the reach and improving the quality of education and health care, but this was too costly for the country's economic base to support (Lewis 2010). The PRG viewed the state as playing a central role in providing the basis for this economic regeneration. Its prospects for supporting its economic and social platform from the usual sources of external financing – the US and Western governments and IFIs – however, were brought into question at the start of its hold on power. The US's response to the Revolution's broad appeal for assistance was delivered through Frank Ortiz, US ambassador at the time. The US indicated its preference for a multilateral approach involving international financial agencies rather than a more immediate bilateral approach for channelling funds to the new regime. Even then, political conditionalities were attached. Maurice Bishop summarizes his discussion with US Ambassador Frank Ortiz in this way:

> The Ambassador stressed the fact that his government will view with great displeasure the development of any relations between our country and Cuba. The ambassador pointed out that his country was the richest, freest, and most generous country in the world, but, as he put it, 'we have two sides' (Marcus and Taber 1983, 27).

The PRG responded by seeking to diversify its sources of assistance to include countries in the South and Eastern Europe, including the Soviet Union which, ultimately, represented a shift in foreign policy and placed it on a collision course with the US. In Cuba, with its tradition of offering fraternal assistance to other developing countries, the government found a willing source of support. Cuba's assistance was particularly important in the delivery of health care; providing scholarships to Grenadians to study in Cuba; developing agro-processing; constructing prefabricated houses; and in supporting the PRG's major infrastructural project, an international airport. The international airport was a major plank in the PRG's development agenda, considered essential to the expansion of the tourism sector and the diversification of export agriculture.[7] Through assistance in equipment, technology and labour, the Cuban government contributed to roughly half of the cost of the US$300m airport. A range of countries which were not traditional donors to the region, such as Libya, Syria, Iraq, Algeria, Venezuela as well as traditional donors such as the EC, contributed to its construction (Martin 1983). The PRG's platform for agricultural diversification included both diversification of products and markets. The latter led to arrangements to ship bananas to the German Democratic Republic (GDR) and nutmegs to the USSR (Searle 1983, 46), although the government collapsed before this could be cemented. From an economic perspective, the PRG's foreign policy thrust paid off in tangible initiatives, particularly the expensive infrastructure project of the airport. Dominica and St Vincent, long seeking support to construct international airports were to await the advent of ALBA, under which the governments of Cuba and Venezuela had promised support to construct an international airport in St Vincent and expand the Melville Hall Airport in Dominica. Grenada's success, nevertheless, was at the expense of increased hostility from the US administration which contributed to the Revolution's militarization and its eventual collapse.

The shift in foreign policy in support of the PRG's economic programme was reflected in cooperation agreements signed with a range of countries in Eastern Europe and 'fraternal' governments in the South, including Libya, although the government was careful not to sever ties with countries with which it had traditional diplomatic relationships. The exception here was the US which increasingly came to view the government as a threat to its national security. This openness to countries considered to be behind the curtain of the Cold War was mirrored by the unofficial embrace of Marxism/Leninism by the New Jewel Movement (NJM),[8] which had begun even before the revolution. Grenada's foreign policy shift was further reflected in open support for 'liberation movements,' many of which, such as the Farabundo Marti National Liberation Front (FMLN) of El Salvador, the US viewed with hostility. The strongest expression of this shift was the PRG's vote in the UN General Assembly in 1980 in support of the

USSR's intervention in Afghanistan, one of a minority of countries (18) that supported this action.

The PRG's courtship of governments within the Soviet bloc and among countries of the South not securely within the US's sphere of influence, drew a hostile response from the US, which was inclined to view the Grenada Revolution as a projection of Russian/Soviet influence and design, through its 'proxy,' Cuba, into a region that had been described variously as the US's 'soft underbelly' and its 'backyard.' This was compounded by the Nicaraguan Sandinista Revolution which, with Grenada, served as an inspiration for left-wing movements throughout the Caribbean and Latin America, many of which were in open conflict with their governments, thus cementing the US's view of the PRG as a threat to its national security interests. Gairy's overthrow, through the lenses of the Cold War, was viewed as Grenada succumbing to the Soviet Union's sphere of influence rather than as a response to internal political conditions.[9] The Grenadian government itself, between 1979 and 1983, increasingly located itself within a broader internationalist struggle against capitalist imperialism, represented by the US (Meeks 1988). It was the US's view of the Grenada Revolution as aiding the projection of Soviet influence in the region and the PRG's conscious identification with so called liberation struggles around the world and its embrace of countries considered hostile to the US that ultimately led to direct US intervention in the wake of the implosion of the process.

Post-invasion Foreign Policy

Foreign policy after the US invasion took a sharp shift back in line with US policy. Thus diplomatic relations forged during the revolution were either immediately broken, as with Cuba, or left to languish. The economic challenges remained largely unchanged, while the invasion itself, which had badly damaged infrastructure, introduced new challenges. The revolution had run upon the challenges of economic development common to small states. In the PRG's first year in power agriculture suffered from adverse weather that included a hurricane (August 1979) and floods (January 1980). It also suffered from external developments over which it had no control, primarily international recession and a fall in the value of the pound sterling that reduced revenue. In any event, four years proved too short to effect a radical transformation of the base of the economy, although tremendous inroads were made in expanding access to secondary education and health, and in reducing unemployment.

The invasion inflicted severe damage to infrastructure which now had to be rebuilt. Unemployment rose with the disbanding of the People's Revolutionary Army (PRA), which had become a significant employer, and the closure of many of the PRG's economic programmes. Unemployment for most of the decade of the 1990s was above the 14 per cent achieved by the PRG, with the exception of 1991 when it was recorded at 13.9 per cent (Central Statistical Office, Ministry of Finance Grenada 2008). The country continued to face decline in the earnings of its major productive sectors. The state's role was severely diminished with the immediate closure of some state-run enterprises, the return of land seized from Eric Gairy, which was the basis of a nascent cooperative movement, and the progressive divestment of government estates and state enterprises. Thus, the economic policies pursued after 1983 marked a decisive shift towards the embrace of neoliberal economic thinking which elevated the role of the market in development at the expense of the state. Challenges of economic diversification shifted from deliberate state action to largely unsuccessful attempts to lure private capital (Ferguson 1990), representing a return to a reliance on private FDI to drive economic development. In the years immediately following the invasion, the US government became the main source of financing. International financial institutions, primarily the IMF and WB oversaw the restructuring of the economy along neoliberal lines, and the EU resumed its role as a major donor. The IFIs, in particular, became the main channel for the progressive whittling down of the state through prescriptions directed at all governments after 1983 for sale of government assets and reform of the public sector in the direction of reducing its role as a major source of employment (Lewis 2010). While, arguably, the basis of this was justifiable on grounds of efficiency and productivity, nevertheless, it significantly eroded the state's ability to pursue alternative options for addressing its economic challenges and elevated the IFIs to the centre of policymaking.

Post-invasion governments found that Grenada's developmental challenges were no different from those that confronted the PRG. By the early 1990s, it was clear that the region, including Grenada, had lost any leverage it might have had during the Cold War. This was reflected in a significant reduction in US aid to the region and an apparent diversion of EC interest to the newly emerging states of Eastern Europe.[10] The economy remained fragile as agriculture weakened and manufacturing stagnated. Agriculture declined steadily after 1995, falling from 10.1 per cent of GDP to 8 per cent by 1999 (CDB 2006). Export agriculture, which constituted the bulk of earnings to the sector, suffered from the collapse of the banana industry and significant shortfalls in cocoa production. This trend continued into the 2000s, with nutmegs, which accounted for over half of agricultural earnings, declining by 20.8 per cent in 2003, with a corresponding 12 per cent decline in mace. The fall in agriculture's contribution to GDP may not necessarily be negative if it reflects a rise in the fortunes of other sectors. This was not the case, however, as manufacturing remained stagnant with some increase from 6.3 per cent in 1995 to 7.2 per cent in 1999, before falling back to 6.3 per cent in 2003. Tourism also declined over the period, moving from 9.7 per cent in 1995 to 9.3 per cent in 1999 and 8.9 per cent in 2003. The Pt. Salines International Airport's role in underpinning the diversification of the economy remained unrealized. Despite its greater capacity to accommodate large passenger carrying jets and to facilitate night landing, governments found that their lack of control over airlines and shipping had significantly curtailed ambitions for a significant growth in tourism and export agriculture. Further, their ability to secure favourable financing from the IFIs was diminished when Grenada, along with other middle income Caribbean countries was considered no longer eligible for concessionary financing. Grenada's woes were exacerbated in the wake of the damage done to the economy in 2004 by hurricane Ivan which reduced agriculture to 4.1 per cent of GDP, manufacturing to 5.5 per cent and tourism to 4.8 per cent (CDB 2006). Since then, governments' efforts have been directed towards rebuilding the basic structure of the economy. Whatever strides there may have been in enhancing the quality of human resources were set back by sustained high levels of out migration of skilled and highly trained people. The emigration rate of tertiary educated persons in 2000 was recorded at 66.7 per cent and 97.5 per cent of physicians (Ratha and Xu 2008).

The WTO's formation in 1994 also marked a significant transformation in the global environment in which the country had to operate. The WTO had far-reaching implications for the nonreciprocal market access agreements which Grenada, along with other CARICOM countries had enjoyed which were now deemed to be in violation of the WTO's non-discriminatory principle and were expected to give way to WTO compatible reciprocal trading agreements. Chief among these were the Caribbean Basin Initiative (CBI) with the US, which was expected to give way to the Free Trade Area of the Americas (FTAA) in 2005 with all countries in the hemisphere excepting Cuba; the trade protocols of the Cotonou Partnership Agreement (CPA) with the EC, which were replaced by an Economic Partnership Agreement (EPA) in 2008; and the Canada-Caribbean Agreement (CARIBCAN) with Canada, on which negotiations for an FTA began in 2008. These developments marked further constraints on CARICOM countries' exercise of economic policy, and catapulted trade to the forefront of their diplomatic agenda, as they struggled to influence the broader international agenda towards increased sensitivity to the development challenges of small states, and to craft agreements that took account of some of the asymmetries inherent in agreements among parties of widely differing size and resource endowments.

Keith Mitchell's NNP government undertook a number of initiatives geared at diversifying the economy and increasing revenue. These include the introduction of the offshore financial sector which swiftly succumbed to pressure exercised by the EU's Financial Action Task Force. More controversial was the sale of passports which had the negative consequence of the imposition of visa restrictions against Grenadians travelling to some destinations such as Canada. In the arena of foreign affairs, this meant a diversification of foreign relations that included a break in diplomatic relations with Taiwan in favour of China, the resumptions of close ties with Cuba, and closer cooperation with Venezuela, all of which represented a rupture in post-invasion foreign policy. This was symbolized by Fidel Castro's visit to Grenada in 1998. In 1997, two years after he had become Prime Minister, Keith Mitchell made an official visit to Cuba. This was a historic moment, as it represented the first such visit since diplomatic relations were frozen after the 1983 US invasion. By 2001, both countries had installed ambassadors. Cuba resumed its assistance to Grenada, very much in keeping with programmes provided during the revolution. This comprised health care delivery, including the training of intensive care nurses; free eye care in Cuba under Cuba's Operation Miracle programme with Venezuela; the construction of a biotechnology lab for food processing;[11] technical support in the construction of prefabricated housing for the poor; and construction of a new hospital on the site of the old General Hospital in St George's (Weathersbee).

China's relationship with Grenada brought immediate material gain reflected in its assistance to rebuild the national stadium destroyed in 2004 by hurricane Ivan, in time for the 2007 cricket world cup; the construction of low-cost houses; scholarships; and a US$6m grant to compensate for the withdrawal of Taiwanese support for projects after Grenada established diplomatic relations with China (Erikson 2004).[12] Grenada, as with most CARICOM countries, except for Trinidad and Tobago, and Barbados which declined to participate, benefits under Venezuela's PetroCaribe initiative which has, since 2005, provided direct supplies of oil, reducing the cost of middle men and soft loans for purchasing Venezuelan oil with long repayment periods. The value of this was realized when oil prices skyrocketed after 2008 and in the wake of the recession which reduced earnings from the main economic sectors. The savings from this arrangement were crucial to Mitchell's ability to finance social programmes to schoolchildren and the elderly, even before the recession (2008 interview).[13] Venezuela was also an important source of assistance after hurricane Ivan, providing low-cost housing, as it had done during the PRG's reign.[14]

In summary, Grenada's post-independence development problems remained largely unchanged and were not unique to Grenada, but were common to small states (and, in many instances to developing countries as a group). These included: the need for hugely expensive infrastructure, which could not be financed from domestic sources; difficulty in raising money from traditional sources of finance thus exacerbating the debt burden; the constant search for assistance to mitigate the effects of adverse weather on the economy; the need to diversify the economy to reduce economic vulnerability; the cost of financing social programmes necessary to mitigate the effects of high levels of unemployment and poverty; and challenges in retaining trained nationals to enhance economic, social and political life. Rather than abating, however, the global restructuring that occurred in the wake of the WTO which spelled progressive erosion in earnings from trade, exacerbated these challenges. In the context of diminished avenues for economic support and the prospect of punishing reciprocal free trade agreements with highly industrialized countries, Grenada once again turned to non-traditional avenues of financial support. Interestingly, the collapse of the Cold War, even as it consolidated the primacy of neoliberalism as the appropriate development model, also provided some space for alternative relationships. CARICOM countries grasped this when they embraced Cuba in the 1990s despite US opposition. Undoubtedly, the many foreign policy challenges, including wars in Iraq and Afghanistan and the so-called war on terror, which the US was confronting, allowed them important room for manoeuvre.

Regional Initiatives in Foreign Policy

The dramatic turn in Grenada's foreign policy under Mitchell cannot be analysed in isolation from a broader discussion of similar developments across the region which serve to underscore the commonality of the challenges facing a region of small states. Thus, while this chapter's primary focus is on the national policy thrusts of various Grenadian governments, this focus must be balanced by an acknowledgement of the role of regional action in sustaining national foreign policy goals. Regional action in defining and pursuing foreign policy goals of individual states has been one of the weakest areas of regional cooperation. Despite the formal recognition of foreign policy coordination as a goal of the Caribbean Community (CARICOM) (Revised Treaty of Chaguaramas Articles 6 and 16) attempts at formulating and coordinating foreign policy have been ad hoc. The OECS has been more active in pursuing joint initiatives in foreign policy both in the pre-independence and post-independence periods. Under the Associated Statehood arrangement, the formal meetings of Chief Ministers on matters of mutual interest provided the rudimentary basis for more structured cooperation in this area in the post-independence period (Lewis 2002). The goal of foreign policy coordination was formally incorporated in the OECS Charter (Article 3:1). Foreign policy initiatives included joint missions by various member states in capitals of interest, and the housing of different country embassies in the same building (Lewis 2002). Because these arrangements are based on the choice of individual countries and were not stipulated by the treaty, they have proved to be fluid, with countries entering and leaving such arrangements at will. This cooperation was not driven by a deliberate coherence of foreign policy goals, however, but primarily by cost concerns as the maintenance of individual country missions in various capitals proved costly.

The importance of joint diplomatic action was reinforced with the propulsion of trade to the forefront of the diplomatic agenda in the wake of the WTO's formation and consequent initiatives to restructure their traditional trading relationships. This underpinned the decision to establish an OECS mission in Geneva in 2005 to increase the countries' awareness of and input into the WTO negotiating process. It was both a response to the cost implications of maintaining national missions as well as reflecting a greater appreciation of common interests. The countries, in particular those of the Windward Islands[15] who were major banana producers, learnt the value of cooperation in their fight against the WTO decision on the legality of elements of the EU's regime governing the importation of bananas which threatened the sector's viability. At the wider regional level the Regional Negotiating Machinery's (RNM) formation was also driven by concerns that the renegotiation of trade relations with dominant trading partners, beginning with FTAA negotiations in 1998[16] and EPA negotiations in 2002,[17] held common threats to all CARICOM states. Further, the negotiations were expected to be too costly for individual states, even the larger ones. The role of the EC in insisting on negotiating with the region as a group which included the Dominican Republic cannot be ignored.

The RNM was important in translating the concerns of small states development expressed in the literature from the conceptual plane to the practical realm of trade negotiations, with mixed success. At the conceptual level some traction was achieved with the WTO's acceptance in the Doha Declaration (paragraph 34) of the need to examine trade-related issues affecting small economies and the formation of a work programme on small economies to examine these, although this was tempered by the proviso that it should not lead to a new sub-category of members. The RNM was also successful in the FTAA negotiating process in securing an acknowledgement in the Miami Ministerial Declaration (November 2003) that any agreement should take account of 'differences in the levels of development and size of economies of the hemisphere, through various provisions and mechanisms' (FTAA 2003, paragraph 6). In the more concrete arena of trade negotiations they have not achieved much success in translating this into concrete initiatives to reflect their concerns. Ongoing WTO negotiations are considering concrete proposals for reflecting small size concerns, but the broader negotiating process has been in trouble for a while. The major negotiating arena in which the countries have been engaged, the formulation of a new economic arrangement with the European Union, has yielded little by way of concrete concessions. The vast asymmetries that exist between the two groups of countries were acknowledged in differential time frames for liberalization and slightly lower liberalization commitments, the largest being in services where the EU's comparative advantage is vastly superior.[18] These have done no damage to the main principles of neoliberalism, namely the assumption of a level playing field among countries of varying natural and human resources and historical experiences; and the primacy of trade over production in development leading to a de facto equation of trade liberalization with development.

The general failure to get much traction at the international level for the challenges that neoliberalism and globalization pose for the development of small states, coupled with increasing difficulty in attracting development aid and FDI, are arguably the main factors in their decision to re-open old relationships, primarily with Cuba, and explore new initiatives with countries such as Venezuela and China. This trend towards a diversification of external relations is not unique to Grenada, but represents a broader resurgence of South/South Cooperation and begs the question as to what is driving this movement. It includes Cuba and Venezuela's ALBA initiative; Brazil's overtures for a CARICOM-MERCUSOR FTA; the formation of the Union of South American Nations (UNASUR) which is driven by Brazil and embraces all of South America including Guyana and Suriname; and the latest initiative of the Rio Group to form a regional LAC organization that excludes Canada and the US.

What is driving this process of S/S cooperation in which the Caribbean is engaged?

China

While one can argue that the region's interest in diversifying diplomatic and trade relationships is based on its need to find alternative sources of finance and trade, this does not explain the interest that this region of small states holds for the countries with which they are forming these new relationships. China's assistance to Grenada was one aspect of a broader Chinese approach to the LAC region. This was cemented in the February 2005 visit of Chinese Vice-President, Zeng Qinghong to Jamaica, where he met a number of officials, including the Prime Ministers of Jamaica, Dominica and Antigua and private sector representatives from nine countries in what was the first Ministerial Meeting of the China-Caribbean Economic and Trade Cooperation Forum (Embassy of the People's Republic of China in Ireland 2005; People's Daily Online 2005). He promised increased numbers of Chinese tourists, more trade, 'unconditional' aid and support in international fora, and pledged US$112m over six years to Dominica, whose economy had virtually collapsed with the decline of its banana industry (Erikson 2004). Mitchell's response to China's assistance is instructive in understanding what drives the foreign policy of small states: 'I cannot see that the Caribbean has any other choice but to develop a relationship with China' (Erikson 2004). This initiative to the Caribbean was preceded by discussions between MERCUSOR and China on trade and cooperation (INTAL, 2004).

It is possible, as some US commentators have done (Mosher 2006; Fraser 2006), to view China's overtures in geopolitical terms, as a projection of its designs, and as representing a victory in its struggle to gain recognition over Taiwan. It is also possible, however, to see China as operating within the rules of the game of the neoliberal trading framework, pushing to capture markets. China, now a member of the WTO, is fully in the race to capture markets which sees it competing with the US, not on ideological ground, but on trade based on goods produced along capitalist lines, while addressing the need for access to cheap sources for finances the region requires. Bryan (2009) characterizes China's interest in the region in what he terms 'resource diplomacy,' driven by its need for resources, particularly oil. Whatever China's motivations for deepening its relationship with the region, it provides a new avenue of financial support for most. The recognition of China's increasing global importance has been acknowledged in the shift from diplomatic ties with Taiwan, which most OECS countries had, to China.

ALBA

The Bolivarian Alliance for the Americas[19] (ALBA) initiated by Cuba and Venezuela in 2004 represents a different model of interstate relations than the trading schemes on offer to the region. ALBA was conceptualized as an alternative to the FTAA and the neoliberal premise that underpinned it, and was driven by Hugo Chávez's conceptualization of a unified LAC region inspired by Simón Bolivar's vision of a united region. ALBA has grown both in membership and scope. ALBA's membership includes Cuba and Venezuela, Nicaragua, Bolivia and Ecuador;[20] all with a more nationalist model of development; and three small states of CARICOM: Dominica, St Vincent and the Grenadines and Antigua and Barbuda.[21] Grenada is now an observer member.

ALBA embraces a number of areas of cooperation, some of which are extended to non-member states. The most important of these for CARICOM countries are the PetroCaribe agreement and health initiatives such as Operation Miracle. Under PetroCaribe Venezuela offers concessionary terms for the financing of oil imports from Venezuela. PetroCaribe beneficiaries can access concessionary loans to finance 40 per cent of the cost of oil when prices exceed $50 a barrel, which increases to 50 per cent when the prices reach US$100 a barrel. These loans are to be repaid over a 25 year period, including a two-year grace period, at one per cent interest (PSVSA [Petróleos de Venezuela, S.A.] 29 June 2005). The terms of the agreement were eased in July 2008 in response to rising oil prices. Signatories to the agreement are required to pay 40 per cent of the bill and the other 60 per cent within 25 years at one per cent interest when prices exceed US$100/barrel; and 30 per cent, within 90 days, with the remaining 70 per cent subject to 'special financing at the time of signing of final agreement' when prices reach US$150/barrel (*Stabroek News* 20 July 2008). Venezuela is also committed to building oil storage facilities and refineries in beneficiary states, including Dominica (*International Herald Tribune* 10 January 2008).

PetroCaribe is held out to be more than an arrangement for the concessionary supply of Venezuelan oil to recipients, but is viewed as a tool for the integration of regional economies and a mechanism for coordinating energy policies, including alternative sources of energy. It also incorporates a fund to finance social and economic programmes in participating states. The fund is financed from an initial capitalization by Venezuela of US$50m and 25 per cent of proceeds from revenues Venezuela receives from oil sold under PetroCaribe. The arrangement has been described as the 'largest single source of concessional financing to the Caribbean' (Girvan 2008, 7). An innovative feature is that it allows part of oil purchases to be financed by goods and services. Dominica is allowed to finance up to 40 per cent of its oil purchases with bananas (Girvan 2008, 4).

Central to ALBA are initiatives in health and education. Operation Milagros, probably the best known, provides access to eye surgery either in Cuba or by Cuban surgeons operating in beneficiary states. By 2007, some 9,799 OECS nationals had benefitted from eye surgeries and one in every 58 persons had been tested (OECS 31 May 2009). Cuba has also been instrumental in outfitting diagnostic centres in a number of OECS countries, an eye clinic in St Lucia and rebuilding the main hospital in Grenada (OECS 31 May 2009). There are plans for Cuba to build over 100 clinics in Haiti under the ALBA initiative (James Suggett 1 April 2010). Other initiatives include literacy programmes, the provision of scholarships and housing.

ALBA has made strides in introducing a whole range of initiatives among its member states that include a common currency, the sucre,[22] for the exchange of goods; a food security fund and the creation of a joint food company; the promotion of mixed enterprises; and the construction of oil refineries *(Dominican Today* 30 April 2007*).* Venezuela and Cuba have also committed to the construction of a long-desired international airport in St Vincent (*The Diplomatic Courier* February 2007). ALBA has also sought to define a political role for itself with the issuing of various statements including the ALBA Declaration on Copenhagen Climate Summit (28 December 2009), the Declaration of Cumana on the summit of the Americas and the ALBA Declaration on the Honduras' coup d'état (June 2009). The group also agreed to withdraw from the World Bank's International Centre for Settlement of Investment Disputes (Chris Carlson 30 April 2007). It is clear that ALBA is more than an alternative integration project but seeks to make a political impact.

ALBA has been met with some concerns. These include the viability of the economic arrangements which are driven by Hugo Chávez's vision and are therefore vulnerable to internal political shifts, especially given the fractious character of Venezuelan politics;[23] possible negative impact on derailing the implementation of the Caribbean Single Market and Economy (CSME); undermining CARICOM's cohesiveness (Bryan 2009); and concerns that the region's increasing dependence on Venezuela for oil and financing could compromise its stance on outstanding border issues involving Guyana, Dominica[24] and Venezuela (Bryan 2009). ALBA's political elements have also generated suspicions as to Chávez's broader political motivations. Bryan (2009) also employs the description of resource diplomacy to describe Venezuela's approach, arguing that Chávez was using Venezuela's oil to promote its vision of LAC integration and to undermine US influence in the region.

Brazil and UNASUR

Brazil's engagement with the region is more ambiguous. Brazil has been less than sympathetic to the economic concerns of Caribbean small states. In the FTAA negotiations it was not particularly receptive to their calls for special and differential treatment. Its challenge of the EU's sugar regime before the WTO triggered its reform leading to significantly reduced prices for Caribbean sugar which has led to the collapse or significant decline of the sector in most countries with the exception of Guyana. Brazil's approach to the region underwent a shift with the collapse of the FTAA negotiations and Ignacio Lula Da Silva's ascent to power. This is evident in Brazil's proposal for an FTA between MERCUSOR and CARICOM.[25]

Brazil has embarked on a broader project to create a broad regional alliance as an alternative to the US-conceived FTAA and sub-regional and bilateral FTAs, which has led to the creation of UNASUR in 2004. UNASUR envisages the gradual convergence of existing schemes: the Andean community and MERCUSOR and the inclusion of Chile and Guyana and Suriname, the latter being two members of CARICOM; and the incorporation of the Integration of the Regional Infrastructure of South America (IIRSA), which was accomplished in 2009. Key objectives of UNASUR are energy integration, addressing asymmetries and infrastructure integration. The IIRSA, which all 12 South American leaders signed on to in 2000, embraces the development of energy and communication and transport infrastructure. Central to IIRSA is a system of roads and bridges to connect various countries within the region. Of importance to CARICOM is the Guyana Shield Hub which aims to connect Guyana, Suriname and French Guiana, Brazil and Venezuela, a key element of which is the construction of a highway linking the Brazilian towns of Boa Vista and Bonfim to Lethem, Linden and Georgetown in Guyana. This has already led to the construction of the Takutu Bridge between Guyana and Brazil, linking the border towns of Bonfim in Brazil with Lethem in Guyana, financed by Brazil. The Bonfim to Boa Vista Brazil end of the highway project is already completed and Brazil is considering paving the Guyana end (Burt Wilkinson, IPS, 22 August 2009).

The broader refashioning of relations in the LAC region goes beyond the convergence of policy brought about by a resurgence of left-leaning governments coming to power at the same time in Venezuela, Brazil, Bolivia, Nicaragua *inter alia*, but represents a broader trend in the region to forge relations that are independent of US interests and more reflective of national concerns. The decision by members of the Rio Group to form a new organization among all countries in Latin America and the Caribbean, including Cuba, but excluding the US and Canada, suggests a broad detangling of a distinct regional agenda from the traditional dominance of US interests in the hemispheric Organization of American States (OAS). The Association of Caribbean States (ACS), the formation of which was driven by CARICOM, had reflected a similar sentiment but was derailed by the prospects of duty free access to the US market that the FTAA promised. The mooting of such an organization in a region still characterized by disparate political ideologies[26] appears to be driven by a desire for regional coherence and to increase the region's political profile by strengthening its voice vis-à-vis 'other world blocks.'[27] In Mexican President Felipe Calderón's words, it was expected to 'consolidate a global project in Latin American and Caribbean identity.'[28] The statement in support of Argentina's claim to the Falklands Islands, in the face of British exploration for oil that emerged from the Rio summit, marked a sharp distinction from the US's support of Britain in the issue and underscores an independent LAC interest (AFP Global Edition 24 February 2010).

One can argue that Caribbean small states' interest in participating in such an organization is directly linked to a sense of insecurity and limited ability to influence global developments. The region's engagement here can be seen as part of a longer history of supporting and even initiating organizations to increase their profile and bargaining strength of which the ACP group and the ACS are two examples. Further, the interest of individual countries in forging and deepening relations with Cuba and Venezuela – whose governments are viewed as outcast by the US – is arguably driven by the failure of traditional relations to provide the support needed to offset chronic budget deficits. In particular, the tide of liberalization which has transformed their trading relations with traditional partners, particular the EU, into FTAs, offering empty market access, while presenting the spectre of a wholesale collapse of domestic enterprises underscores this shift. It is also important to note that these various arrangements, even when underpinned by economic motivations, represent important alternative sources of support, in direct moneys and in kind, with no obvious strings attached.

Conclusion

This case study of Grenada suggests that small states' foreign policy is driven by a need to navigate global political and economic structures in an effort to address their limited ability to be economically competitive and to garner the financial resources needed to support their development aspirations. This presses them to form political and economic alliances to address these challenges. The alliances they have forged have shifted over time, reflecting broader global political dynamics and their attempts to ground their development strategies within particular political frameworks. Their weak political clout means that they are not always allowed the flexibility to do this, as the US's active hostility towards governments in the region who deviate from the dominant capitalist paradigm illustrates. The greater laxity seen since the 1980s can be attributed to the end of the Cold War which has served to shift the attention of the dominant capitalist countries – US and EU – almost exclusively to Eastern Europe and the Middle East. The collapse of the Cold War also served to remove the legitimacy of the geo-political framework of analysis, permitting instead a more meaningful discussion of the real challenges they face in seeking to exist as independent states.

The various tacks in foreign and economic policy taken by Caribbean small states, whatever the official rationale, cannot be disassociated from the limitations they face arising from small physical and population size which present economic and human resource challenges, but more importantly from their vulnerability to environmental changes. While they undoubtedly share much in common with other countries of the South in charting autonomous economic paths to address their specific realities, their vulnerability places them at the forefront of the fallout from the move towards global trade liberalization and environmental degradation associated with current models of development pursued. From this perspective, their challenges require a broader analysis of the dominant global economic framework, in particular its insensitivity to difference. Hence, the various approaches adopted to explain small states' foreign policy behaviour, particularly those relating to vulnerability and resilience, while important, have limited explanatory power unless grounded in a broader critique of the global economic system in which they participate. It is important to note, though, that some of their more creative strategies for raising funds, such as the sale of passports and diplomatic support, which fall within the 'jurisdiction' framework, hold negative implications for their already fragile hold on sovereignty and represent acts of desperation rather than strategies to be admired and emulated. Thus, while the internal policy choices of small states are important to navigate their inherent vulnerabilities, the strictures that international structures and power relationships impose are crucial to understanding their challenges.

Notes

1. It is important to note that this represents a shift in the relative importance of the main sectors of the economy in the wake of Hurricane Ivan which severely handicapped agriculture and tourism.
2. For a breakdown on the sources of Grenada's debt see CDB, 2007.
3. All references to $ are to United States (US) dollars.
4. The development of vulnerability indices and the role of these various organizations in contributing to these is detailed in Briguglio and Kisanga (2004), 15–26.
5. The need for such an index was supported at the AOSIS' Strategy for the further implementation of the Barbados Programme of Action, developed at the Inter-Regional Preparatory meeting of SIDS in Nassau, Bahamas, January 2004. See Briguglio and Kasanga, 2004.
6. This grouping comprised most of the members of the defunct West Indies Federation which remained left after Jamaica, Trinidad and Tobago, and Barbados proceeded to independence. They were considered too small to proceed to independence separately and thus entered into an arrangement with the UK that gave them some control over internal affairs while reserving foreign affairs and security to the UK government.

7. By providing access to wide bodied jets (rather than restricting capacity to small propeller planes which the existing airport could accommodate) as well as night landing facilities, it would boost the growth in the industry and thus its contribution to the economy. It would facilitate agricultural diversification by providing greater access to air transport for perishable agricultural products.
8. The New Jewel Movement was the party that seized power in 1979 and formed the new government.
9. Grenada was perceived within the framework of the Domino Theory employed by various US administrations since the Second World War as a foreign policy motif. Thus the Grenada Revolution conjured up images of collapsing dominos, beginning with Cuba, followed by Guyana, Jamaica, Grenada and Nicaragua, leading to ultimate Soviet control over a region which, because of its physical proximity to the US, would tip the military balance of forces in favour of the USSR, resulting in the collapse of the 'free world.'
10. Vincentian Prime Minister, James Mitchell, summed up the sense of abandonment that Caribbean small states felt in this period when he commented in a 1987 speech in which he called for a political union of the OECS countries as a way of addressing their economic and political marginalization: 'We have to behave like Fiji or Grenada to get attention....' (cited in Lewis 2002, 86).
11. A previous such lab established during the Revolution had been abandoned in the aftermath of the US invasion.
12. This shift to China angered Taiwan whose government had enjoyed a mutually beneficial relationship with various small Caribbean states where financial assistance, particularly for infrastructural projects was offered in return for diplomatic recognition. Mitchell's appeal to China for support in the wake of the economic destruction wrought by hurricane Ivan triggered Taiwan's severing of diplomatic relations and demands for the repayments of outstanding loans. This left the government facing high interest costs.
13. Author's interview with Prime Minister Keith Mitchell, 29 May 2008.
14. Ibid.
15. Grenada, Dominica, St Lucia and St Vincent.
16. Negotiations for a Free Trade Area of the Americas were launched in 1998 and were supposed to have been concluded in 2005. Negotiations collapsed in 2003, however, as a result of a deadlock primarily on agriculture and Singapore issues between the US and Brazil.
17. Although formal negotiations began in September 2002 with the ACP and the EC, specific negotiations for a Caribbean-Dominican Republic-European Commission EPA did not begin until 2004.
18. For critical reviews of the EPA by a range of Caribbean scholars see Norman Girvan's website: http://www.normangirvan.info/cariforum-ec-economic-partnership-agreement-epa/
19. The name was changed from the Bolivarian Alternative to the Bolivarian Alliance at the July 2009 summit held in Venezuela.
20. Honduras joined ALBA in 2008 under the government of Manuel Zelaya, but withdrew in January 2010 under Mauricio Funes who came to power

in elections in November 2009, held after the overthrow of Zelaya's government. See James Suggett, 15 January 2010, 'Honduras Withdraws from ALBA, El Salvador Won't Join Despite FMLN Support.' *Venezuelanalysis.com.* http://venezuelanalysis.com/news/5070.
21. Ecuador, St Vincent and the Grenadines and Antigua became members in 2009.
22. The sucre, or Unified System of Regional Compensation, was to operate initially as a virtual currency but was then expected to be converted into a hard currency. See Michael Fox. 17 April 2009. 'ALBA Summit Ratifies Regional Currency, Prepares for Trinidad.' Venezuelanalysis.com. http://venezuelanalysis.com/news/4373.
23. For a detailed treatment of Venezuela's foreign policy over successive regimes and its relationship to internal political dynamics, see Elsa Cardozo Da Silva and Richard S. Hillman. 2003. 'Venezuela: Petroleum, Democratization, and International Affairs,' In Frank O. Mora and Jeanne A.K. Hey, *Latin American and Caribbean Foreign Policy*. (Lanham. Boulder. New York. Toronto. Oxford: Rowman & Littlefield) 145–64.
24. Venezuela lays claim to Bird Island [Isla de Aves], an uninhabited island lying 90 miles off Dominica and 350 miles north of Venezuela. See Caribbean news net, 16 March 2006. OECS searching for Bird Island solution. http://www.caribbeannetnews. com/cgi-script/caArticles/articles/000008/000874.htm. Accessed 8 July 2010.
25. Lula da Silva, in his address to the Sixteenth Intersessional meeting of CARICOM Heads of Government, pledged that Brazil would 'proceed with flexibility and generosity' in an FTA between the two regions (CARICOM, 2005[a]). MERCUSOR representatives to a ministerial meeting with CARICOM to discuss the FTA promised to take account of differences between countries of both regions, and offered technical cooperation (CARICOM, 2005[b]).
26. Some of these divisions were in evidence at the very meeting that initiated the new organization, with reports of a heated exchange of words between Venezuela's Hugo Chávez and Colombia's president, Alvaro Uribe. See Olgar. Rodriguez, 2010.
27. Ricardo Patino, Ecuadorian Foreign Affairs Minister. Merco Press. 'Latinamerica agrees on new regional organization without US and Canada'. Merco Press. South Atlantic News Agency. 22 February 2010 //en.mercopress.com/2010/02/22/latinamerica-agrees-on-new-regional-organisation-without-us-and-canada
28. Mexican President, Felipe Calderón, 'Latin America creates bloc sans US; Spat mars mood.' Olgar R. Rodriguez, Associated Press, reported in Taiwan News Online. www.taiwannews.com/tw/etn/news_content.php?id=1187515&lang=eng_news&cate_...3/2/2010.

References

Ambursley, Fitzroy. 1983. Grenada: The New Jewel Revolution. In *Crisis in the Caribbean*, ed Fritzroy, Ambursley and Robin Cohen, Kingston, Port of Spain, London: Heinemann.

Associated Press. 2008. Venezuela to build oil refinery in Caribbean island of Dominica. *International Herald Tribune*, 10 January 2008. www.iht.com.

———. 2007. Chávez to discuss refinery with Dominica. Published by ABC money. co.uk, 16 February 2007. www.abcmoney.co.uk/.

———. 2007. Chávez pledges oil and financing for allies. *Dominican Today*, 30 April 2007. DominicanToday.com.mht.

Baldacchino, Godfrey. 2007. The Power of Jurisdiction in Promoting Social Policies in Smaller States. Thematic Paper, methodology workshop on Social Policies in Small States, United Nations Research Institute for Social Development (UNRISD) and Commonwealth Secretariat. October 2007, Geneva, Switzerland.

Baldacchino, G. and D. Milne. 2006. Exploring Sub-National Island Jurisdictions. *The Round Table: Commonwealth Journal of International Affairs*, vol. 95, no. 386, 487–502.

Baldacchino, Godfrey. 2006. Small States as Holons: The Transnational Survival Kit of Small Jurisdictions. In *Building Economic Resilience of Small States*, ed. Lino Briguglio, Gordon Cordina, Eliawony J. Kisanga, 212–24. Islands and Small States Institute of the University of Malta and the Commonwealth Secretariat.

Baldacchino, G. and D. Milne, eds. 2000. *Lessons from the Political Economy of Small States: the Resourcefulness of Jurisdiction*. New York: St Martin's Press, in association with the Institute of Island Studies, University of Prince Edward Island, Canada.

BBC Online Network. BBC news. 1998. Castro gets hero's reception in Grenada, 4 August 1998. www.bbc.co.uk.

Best, Lloyd. 1971. Size and Survival. In *Readings in the Political Economy of the Caribbean*, ed. Norman Girvan and Owen Jefferson. Kingston: New World Group.

———. 1968. A Model of Pure Plantation economy. *Social and Economic Studies*, vol. 17, no. 3. Kingston: University of the West Indies.

Braveboy-Wagner, Jacqueline Anne. 2003. The English-Speaking Caribbean States: A Triad of Foreign Policies. In *Small States in World Politics: Explaining Foreign Policy Behaviour*, ed. Jeanne A.K. Hey. Boulder. London: Lynne Rienner Publishers, 31–51.

Briguglio, Lino, Gordon Cordina, Eliawony J. Kisanga. 2006. *Building Economic Resilience of Small States*. Islands and Small States Institute of the University of Malta and the Commonwealth Secretariat.

Briguglio, Lino and Eliawony J. Kisanga (eds.). 2004. *Economic Vulnerability and Resilience of Small States*. Islands and Small States Institute of the University of Malta and the Commonwealth Secretariat.

Briguglio, Lino. 2004. Economic Vulnerability and Resilience: Concepts and Measurements. In *Economic Vulnerability and Resilience of Small States*, ed. Briguglio, Lino and Eliawony J. Kisanga. Islands and Small States Institute of the University of Malta and the Commonwealth Secretariat.

———. 2002. The economic Vulnerability of Small Island Developing States. In *Sustainable Development for Island Societies: Taiwan and the World*. Asia-Pacific Research Program w/SARCS Secretariat Publication, Taiwan.

———. 1997. *Alternative Economic Vulnerability Indices for Developing Countries*. Report prepared for the Expert Group on the Vulnerability Index. United Nations Department of Economic and Social Affairs.

———. 1995. Small Island Developing States and their Economic Vulnerabilities. *World Development*. Vol. 23 (9): 1615–32.

Byran, Anthony T. 2009. PetroCaribe and CARICOM: Venezuela's Resource Diplomacy and its Impact on Small State Regional Cooperation. In *The Diplomacies of Small States: Between Vulnerability and Resilience*, ed. Andrew F. Cooper and Timothy M. Shaw, 143–59. Houndmills, Basingstoke, Hampshire: Palgrave Macmillan International Political Economy Series.

CARICOM. February 2005[a]. Communiqué issued at the Conclusion of the Sixteenth Intersessional Meeting of the Conference of Heads of Government of the Caribbean Community, 16–17 February 2005, Paramaribo, Suriname. Press release 46/2005. www.caricom.org/jsp/Communications/Communiques/16inthgc_2005_communique.jsp.

———. February 2005[b]. Joint Communiqué Issued at the Conclusion of the CARICOM/MERCUSOR Ministerial Meeting 24–25 February 2005, Port of Spain, Trinidad and Tobago. www.sice.oas.org/TPD/CAR_MER/Negotiations/CARMERCOM_e.pdf.

Caribbean Development Bank. 2007. *Grenada Economic Review 2007*. www.caribank.org.

———. May 2005. *Annual Economic Review 2004*. www.caribank.org.

Caribbean Development Bank Economics Department. April 2006. *Social and Economic Indicators 2005. Borrowing Member Countries*. Vol. xvi. www.caribank.org.

Carlson, Chris. 30 April 2007. ALBA Summit Creates New Model for Latin American Integration. *Venezuelanalysis.com*. Accessed 23 January 2008.

Commonwealth Secretariat. c. 2009. Briefing Note Small States. http://www.thecommonwealth.org/files/216535/FileName/ComSec%20Briefing%20-%20Small%20States.pdf.. Accessed June 16, 2010.

Commonwealth Secretariat/World Bank Joint Task Force on Small States. 2000. *Small States: Meeting Challenges in the Global Economy*. Report of the Task Force, Washington, DC: World Bank. http://www.worldbank.org.

Commonwealth Secretariat. 1997. *A Future for Small States: Overcoming Vulnerability*. Report by a Commonwealth Advisory Group. London: Commonwealth Secretariat.

———. 1985. *Vulnerability: Small States in the Global Society*. Report of a Commonwealth Consultative Group. London: Commonwealth Secretariat.

Crowards, T. 2000. An Index of Inherent Economic Vulnerability for Developing Countries. *Staff Working Paper*, No. 6/00. Barbados. Caribbean Development Bank.

Demas, William. 1965. *The Economics of Development in Small Countries*. Montreal: McGill University Press.

Embassy of the People's Republic of China in Ireland. 3 February 2005. Zeng Qinghong Attends 'China-Caribbean Economic & Trade Cooperation Forum' and Delivers Speech. www.chinaembassy.ie/eng/NewsPress/t183690.htm. Accessed 7 June 2006.

Erikson, Daniel P. 2004. Castro and Latin America: A Second Wind? *World Policy Journal*. Spring. http://www.jstor.org/stable/40209900.

Erickson, Dan. 2005. China in the Caribbean: A Benign Dragon? *Focal Point Spotlight on the Americas.* April. Volume 4, Number 4. www.focal.ca.
Ferguson, James. c.1990. *Grenada: Revolution in Reverse.* Latin America Bureau: London.
Fox, Michael. 17 April 2009. ALBA Summit Ratifies Regional Currency, Prepares for Trinidad. Venezuelanalysis.com. Accessed 21 June 2010. http://venezuelanalysis.com/news/4373.
Fraser, Ron. 26 April 2006. China's Caribbean Strategy: China moves to sew up America's soft underbelly. The Trumpet.com. http://www.thetrumpet.com/print.php?id=2156. Accessed 7 June 2006.
FTAA Secretariat. Free Trade Area of the Americas Eight Ministerial Meeting, Miami, USA. 20 November 2003. *Ministerial Declaration.* http://www.ftaa-alca.org/Ministerials/Miami/Miami_e.asp.
Girvan, Norman. 2008. ALBA, PetroCaribe and CARICOM: Issues in a New Dynamic. http://www.normangirvan.info/girvan-alba-caricom-may0/
Guillermo Barros, Agence France-Presse. 24 February 2010. New Latin America bloc urges Falklands talks. http://www.globaltvbc.com/world/Latin+America+bloc+urges+Falklands+talks/2603252/story.html. Accessed 27 June 2010.
Hey, Jeanne A.K. 2003. Refining Our Understanding of Small State Foreign Policy. In *Small States in World Politics: Explaining Foreign Policy Behaviour,* ed. Jeanne A.K. Hey. Boulder. London: Lynne Rienner Publishers, 185–95.
Kairi Consultants Ltd. September/October 1999. *Poverty Assessment Report – Grenada. Volumes 1 and 2.* Prepared for the Caribbean Development Bank.
Lazare, Alick, Patrick Antoine, Wendell Samuel. 2001. RNM/OECS Country Studies to Inform Trade Negotiations: Grenada. www.crnm.org.
La Rose, Miranda. 2008. ALBA seen as avenue to economic aid for small Caricom states – Prof. Vaughan Lewis. *Stabroek,* 3 February 2008. *News*http://www.stabroeknews.com/2008/stories/02/03/alba-seen-as-avenue-to-economic-aid-for-small-caricom-states-prof-vaughan-lewis/
Levitt, Kari, Lloyd Best. 1984. Character of Caribbean Economy, in *Caribbean Economy Dependence and Backwardness,* ed. George Beckford, Mona, Jamaica: Institute for Social and Economic Research.
Lewis, Patsy. 2010. *Social Policy Challenges in Grenada.* No. 3 in Social Policies in Small States Series. UNRISD and Commonwealth Secretariat. Draft available at http://www.unrisd.org/unrisd/website/document.nsf/d2a23ad2d50cb2a280256eb300385855/fcafbb79786fa87ec12575f40030072c/$FILE/GrenadaWEBrev.pdf
———. 2005. Grenada: A Testing Ground for Lewis's Balanced Development Perspectives, *Social and Economic Studies,* vol. 54: 4, December, 204–37.
———. 2002. *Surviving Small Size: Regional Integration in Caribbean Ministates.* Barbados, Jamaica, Trinidad and Tobago: University of the West Indies Press.
Lewis, Arthur. 1955. *Theory of Economic Growth.* London: George Allen & Unwin.
———. 1938. The 1930s social revolution. In *Caribbean Freedom: Economy and Society from Emancipation to the Present,* ed. Hilary Beckles and Verene Shepherd, Princeton: Markus Wiener Publishers; London: James Currey Publishers; Kingston, Jamaica: Ian Randle Publishers.
Marcus, Bruce, Michael Taber. 1983. *Maurice Bishop Speaks: The Grenada Revolution 1979–83.* New York: Pathfinder Press.

Marriott, J.A.R. 1943. *Federalism and the Problem of the Small State*. London: George Allen & Unwin Ltd.

Martin, Tony (ed.). 1983. *In Nobody's Backyard: The Grenada Revolution in its own Words*. Vol. 1: The Revolution at Home. Dover, Massachusetts: The Majority Press.

Meeks, Brian. 1988. *Social Formation and People's Revolution*, PhD. Thesis, The University of the West Indies, Mona.

Mosher, Steven W. 2006. Red China on the March: The People's Republic moves onto Grenada. *National Review Online*, 14 February 2006. http:www.nationalreview.com. Accessed 7 June 2006.

Mora, Frank O. and Jeanne A.K. Hey, *Latin American and Caribbean Foreign Policy*. Lanham. Boulder. New York. Toronto. Oxford: Rowman & Littlefield

OECS. 31 May 2007. Cuba Commits to Further OECS Assistance. Accessed 13December 2009. http://www.oecs.org/news-a-events/9-secretariat/326-cuba-commits-to-further- oecs-assistance

———. 2004. *Grenada, Macro-Socio-Economic Assessment of the Damage Caused by Hurricane Ivan*. September 7, www.crnm.org.

People's Daily Online. 2005. China's vice-president terms China-Caribbean trade forum as milestone. 3 February 2005. http://english.people.com.cn/20050203/print20050203_172787.html. Accessed 7 June 2006.

PDVSA Petroleum de Venezuela, S.A., 2005, 'PetroCaribe Energy Cooperation Agreement'. http://www.pdvsa.com/index.php?tpl=interface.en/design/biblioteca/readdoc.tpl.html&newsid obj id=6213&newsid temas=111.

Prasad, Naren. 2009. Small but Smart: Small States in the Global System, in *The Diplomacies of Small States: Between Vulnerability and Resilience*, ed. Andrew F. Cooper and Timothy M. Shaw, 41–64. Houndmills, Basingstoke, Hampshire: Palgrave Macmillan International Political Economy Series.

———. 2004. Escaping Regulation, Escaping Convention: Development Strategies in Small Economies. *World Economics*. Vol. 5. No. 1. January–March, 41–65.

Spackman, Ann. 1975. *Constitutional Development of the West Indies 1922–1968: A Selection from the Major Documents*. Bridgetown, Barbados: Caribbean Universities Press.

Searle, Chris. c. 1983. *Grenada: The Struggle against Destabilization*. London: Writers and Readers Publishing Cooperative Society Ltd.

Stabroek News. 2008. Chávez eases PetroCaribe terms as oil prices rises. 20 July 2008. http://www.stabroeknews.com/2008/stories/07/20/chavez-eases-petrocaribe-terms-as-oil- price-rises/

Suggett, James. 2010. Venezuela, ALBA Countries Pledge $2.42 billion in Aid to Haiti. 1 April 2010. Venezuelanalysis.com. http://venezuelanalysis.com/news/5240. Accessed 21 June 2010.

The Diplomatic Courier. February 2007. Visit of H. E Hugo Chavez, President of the Bolivarian Republic of Venezuela to St Vincent and the Grenadines. News Letter volume 2. Office.foreignaffairs@mail.gov.vc.

Ratha, Dilip, Zhimei Zu. 2008. *Migration and Remittances Factbook. Grenada*. Migration and Remittances Team, Development Prospects Group, World Bank. www.worldbank.org/prospects/migrationandremittances.

Rodriguez, Olgar R., *Associated Press*. 2010. Latin America creates bloc sans US; spat mars mood. *Taiwan News*, 24 February 2010. www.taiwannews.com.tw/etn/index_en.php.

UNITAR. 1969. *The Status and Problems of Very Small States and Territories.*
Weathersbee, Tonyaa. n.d. Cuba and Grenada: An Enduring Friendship. http://www.ncat.edu/iajs/publications/Grenada/Ch8_Cuba_and_Grenada.pdf
Wilkinson, Burt. Guyana: Brazil Opens Gateway to Wider Caribbean. 22 August 2009. GALDU. Resource Centre for the Rights of Indigenous Peoples.

Contributors

John Aarons is the University Archivist, The University of the West Indies, and formerly Government Archivist, Jamaica Archives and Records Department, and Executive Director, National Library of Jamaica.

Derick Boyd is Reader in Economics at the University of East London, and former Executive Director of the Caribbean Centre for Money and Finance in Trinidad and Tobago.

Robert Buddan lectures in Caribbean politics and democracy in the Department of Government, University of the West Indies, Mona, and is a newspaper columnist.

Myrtha Désulmé is a Haitian-Jamaican who was born in Haiti and lives in Jamaica. She is President of the Haiti-Jamaica Society, an organization which advocates for Haiti, for Haitian refugees, and facilitates the integration of Haiti into the Caribbean Common Market (CARICOM).

Mark Figueroa of the Economics Department, University of the West Indies, Mona, has pursued research on Caribbean economic ideas, including thought prior to Economics becoming an academic discipline in the region, thus his study of W. Arthur Lewis, New World/Plantation School, and George Cumper.

Obika Gray is Professor in the Department of Political Science, The University of Wisconsin-Eau-Clair, Wisconsin, United States.

Anne Hickling-Hudson is Associate Professor in Cultural and Language Studies of the Education Faculty, Queensland University of Technology, Australia.

Robert A. Hill, Professor Emeritus of History, University of California, Los Angeles, is Editor in Chief of *The Marcus Garvey and Universal Negro Improvement Association Papers* in the James S. Coleman Center for African Studies.

Clinton Hutton lectures in political philosophy and culture in the Department of Government at the University of the West Indies, Mona. He is a noted painter and photographer.

Patsy Lewis is Senior Fellow at the Sir Arthur Lewis Institute of Social and Economic Studies (SALISES), researching on the development challenges of small states, regional integration movements, and international trade.

Rupert Lewis is retired Professor of Political Thought in the Departmet of Government at the University of the West Indies, Mona, and Associate Director of the Centre for Caribbean Thought.

Brian Meeks is Professor of Social and Political Change, and Director of the Centre for Caribbean Thought, and Director of the Sir Arthur Lewis Institute of Social and Economic Studies, University of the West Indies, Mona.

Louis Moyston lectures in Research Methods at the Vocational Training Development Institute/HEART NTA, and in the Philosophical Foundation of Education, The Mico University College, Kingston, Jamaica.

Margaret Stevens teaches history at Essex County College in Newark, New Jersey, where she is also the Director of the Urban Issues Institute.

Maziki Thame lectures in comparative politics and political thought in the Department of Government, University of the West Indies, Mona.

Rodney Worrell is a temporary lecturer in the Department of History and Philosophy at the University of the West Indies, Cave Hill, Barbados.

Index

Abeng Movement, 176, 178, 179, 180, 183
Abyssinian War, 108
Access to Information Act, 4, 5
ACP (African, Caribbean, Pacific), 281
Adams, Grantley, xxvii, 107, 108, 112
Adams, Inspector W.C., 94
Afghanistan, 213, 268, 273
Africa, 149, 150
African Blood Brotherhood, 126, 129, 130
African Diaspora, 108
African Methodist Episcopal Church, 105
Afro-Jamaicans, 171–98
Aiken, P.A., 45
Alba (Bolivarian Alliance for the Americas), 275, 277–79
Algeria, 267
Allan, Harold, xxxi, 79, 87
Allende, Salvador, 211
All-Jamaica Economic and Industrial Conference, 41
Als, Michael, 209
American Federation of Labor, 145, 146
American Negro Labor Congress, 132, 133, 145
Anderson, Oswald E., 41, 42, 43, 53, 54, 55
Anglican Bishop of Jamaica, 44
Anti-Imperialist League, 128
Antigua and Barbuda, 67, 69, 149, 166, 168, 276

Antigua Trades and Labour Union, xxvii
Argentina, 280
Ashenheims, 63
Association of Caribbean States (ACS), 280, 281
Augier, Roy, 21
Austin, Hudson, 205, 217

Bahamas, 70
Bailey, Amy, 53
Bailey, V.A., 53
Bain, Fitzroy, 221
Bain, Norris, 221
Bakan, Abigail, 52
Barbados, xiii, xxvi, 64, 67, 70, 102–15, 149, 272
Barclay, W.E., 94
Barclays Bank, 44
Batista, Fulgencio, 177
Batraville, Benoît, 162
BBC, 93, 254
Beckles, Hilary, 21, 105
Beckles, W.A., 105
Belize, 67, 69, 165
Bell, Wendell, 58, 61, 64, 66, 59
Belle, George, 105, 107
Bellview Estate, 94
Benjamin, P.A., 31
Bermuda, xxvii
Bernal, Richard, 61
Bernard, Aggie, xvii
Best, Lloyd, 167, 175
Birbeck College, 32

Bird, Vere, xxvii
Bishop, Maurice, xiv, 3, 199–226, 227, 254, 255, 266
Blackman, Courtney, 60
Black Nationalism, xiv, 118
Black Power, 115, 169, 176, 183, 206
Bogle, Paul, xix, 12, 93
    Paul Bogle League, 179, 180, 182
Bolivar, Simón, 277
Bolivia, 280
Bolshevism, 118, 122, 123, 125, 126, 129, 141
Bogues, Anthony, xii
Boston, 120
Bourne, Herbert, 107
Bowan, Jefferson, 105
Bowan, Keith, 105
Bowden, 94
Brathwaite, Kamau, 21
Brazil, 275, 279–80
Brereton, Bridget, 21
Briggs, Cyril, 130, 131, 132, 139
Britain, xxiv, 52, 60, 233, 248, 280
British Empire, xviii, 110, 119
British Government, 5, 63
British Guiana, xiii, xxvi, 106, 149, 154
British Guiana Labour Union, xxvii, 154
British Honduras, xiii
British-Jamaican Benevolent Association, 120, 122, 123
British Labour Party, xvii, xx, xxi, xxvi
British Medical Association (Jamaica branch), 45
British West Indies, 119
Brodber, Erna, 21
Brown, Ethelred, xvii, 120, 134, 135
Browne, David, 105
Bryan, Patrick, 21, 45, 57
Buchanan, Hugh, xv, xxii, xxv, 45, 140
Burke, Rudolph, 44
Burroughs, Williana, 132

Bustamante, Alexander, xi, xii, xv, xvi, xix, xx, xxxi, 43, 45, 76–90, 92, 110, 112, 113, 140
Bustamante Industrial Trade Union, xx, xxi, xxii, xxiv, xxix, xxxii, 6
Butler, Uriah, 99
Bybrook Sugar Estate, 113

Cacos, 161
Calderón, Felipe, 280
Cambridge GCE, 233, 238, 245
Cameron, Charlotte, 110
Campbell, Carl, 21
Campbell, Grace, 129, 130
Canada, 275, 280
Canada-Caribbean Agreement, 271
Cap Haïtien, 164
Caribbean Basin Initiative, 271
Caribbean Cement Company, 63
Caribbean Labour Congress, xiii, xiv, xxvi, xxvii, 1, 2, 5, 64, 65
Caribbean Single Market and Economy (CSME), 279
Caribbean Studies Association, 199, 200
Caricom, 271, 272, 273, 279, 280
    Caricom-Mercusor, 275
Carnegie, James, 57
Casimir, J.R., 137
Castro, Fidel, 177, 202, 205, 218, 220, 254, 271
Cawes, Major B.F., 96
Cedar Valley, 93
Cement Marketing Company, 74
Central Bank of Ireland, 74
Central Intelligence Agency, 211
Centre for Caribbean Thought, 3
Césaire, Aimé, 21
Chávez, Hugo, 254, 277, 278, 279
Chile, 211
China, 254, 271, 272, 275, 276
Churchill, Winston, xviii, xxxii,
Clarke, Bobby, 204
Clarke, Edith, 44, 53

INDEX

Coard, Bernard, 199–226, 235
Coard, Frederick, 200, 201
Coard, Phyllis, 204, 218
Coke, Burnett, 89
Cold War, vii, xi, xxiii, xxx, xxxi, xxxii, xxxiii, 194, 255, 259, 264, 265, 273, 281
Colonialism, 264
Colonial Office, xviii, 2, 5, 62
Colonial Standard, 13, 15
Committee of Industrial Organization, 140
Commonwealth Secretariat, 262
Communist International (Comintern), 128, 132, 133, 138, 144, 145, 146, 148, 151, 152, 156, 157
Communist Party (USA), 139, 145
Cooke, Howard, 41, 44, 52, 53, 54, 55
Cooke, Ivy, 54
Coombs, A.G.S., xvii, xxii, 43, 45, 97, 140
Copenhagen, 278
Cornwall, Leon, 205
Costa Rica, xxiv, 30
Cotonou Partnership Agreement, 271
Cox, S.A.G., 119
Creft, Jacqueline, 221
Cripps, Stafford, 2
Critchlow, Hubert, xxvii
Cronon, E.D., 35
Crusader, 126, 129, 137
Cuba, xxiv, xxxiii, 30, 149, 177, 208, 213, 220, 223, 236, 238, 246, 254, 266, 267, 268, 271, 275, 277, 278, 280, 281
Cudjoe, 9
Cutlass, xiii
Czechoslovakia, 92

Daley, Dennis, 175
Daley, Hubert, xvii
Da Silva, Ignacio Lula, 279
Dayan, Joan, 21
Deane Commission, 106, 107, 108

Decolonization, vii, xi, xxvii, 19, 29, 102, 103,104, 114, 115, 186
DeLeon, S.M., 33
DeLisser, H.G., 91
Demas, William, 258, 259
Democratic Socialism, 178
Dessalines, Jean-Jacques, 160, 170
Diplomatic Courier, 278
Domingo, Eulalie, 135, 136
Domingo, Wilfred, xvii, 13, 14, 118–43
Dominica, 67, 69, 149, 167, 168, 276
Dominican Republic, 274
Dominican Today, 278
Downes, Andrew, 64
Du Bois, W.E.B., 123, 124
Durham, Vivian, 31
Dutch Caribbean, 127
Dutch Guiana, 125
Duvalier, 177

Economic Partnership Agreement (EPA), 271, 274
Edwards, Adolphe, 39, 40
Edwards, Bryan, 17
Edwards, Roland, 108
Ehrenstein, R., 44, 91, 92
Emancipator, 126, 129, 131, 136, 137, 139
Emmet, Bishop, 44
England, xiii
Estimé, Dumarsais, 169
Ethiopia, xii, 108
Ethiopianism, 97
Europe, 257, 260, 266, 267
European Union (EU), 271, 275, 279, 281
Evans, Peter, 35

Facey, Cecil, 13, 31
Fairclough, O.T., xix, xxvi, 44, 46, 134
Falkland Islands, 280

Falmouth Post, 14
Fanon, Frantz, 103, 106, 115
Farabundo Martí National Liberation Front (El Salvador), 267
Farquharson, May, 44
Fascism, 135, 138
Federation of Citizens Associations, 42, 47
Fedon, Julien, 208
Fernando Po, 155
First World War, xi, 105, 124, 125,137
  post-First World War, 120, 122, 127, 128
Fisk University, 144
Flynn, Elizabeth Gurley, 125
Foley, Barbara, 131
Foster, William Z., 145
Francis, Delrosa, 94
Francis, Rothschild, 128
FTAA (Free Trade Area of the Americas), 274, 277, 279, 280, 281
Free West Indian, 206
Freire, Paulo, 236
French Guiana, 280
Frome, 95, 109

Gairy, Eric, xxii, 202, 209, 213, 222, 255, 269
Gallimore, Gideon, 81, 82
Gambia, 156
Garvey, Amy Jacques, 31, 36, 39
Garvey, Marcus, xxiv, 5, 24–39, 49, 53, 119, 120–21, 122, 123, 124, 126, 129, 137
Garveyism, xiv, 107, 110, 112, 125, 169
Gastonia, 146, 147
German Democratic Republic, 238, 267
Ginger Ridge, 43
Glasspole, Florizel A., xxix, 46, 83, 85

Gleaner, xxxi, xxxiii, 27, 42, 45, 46, 47, 48, 51, 53, 55, 56, 57, 91, 92, 93, 99
Gold Coast, 154, 156
Gomes, Albert, xxvii
Gomez, Antonio Soberanis, 165
Gordon, Derek, 179
Gordon, George William, xix, 12
Gore, James, 51, 62, 63
Gouldner, Alvin, 185
Grant, St William, xii, xvii, xxxii, 108
Gray, Obika, 110
Greenwich Town, 194
Grobble, Piet, 156
Great Depression, 71
Grenada, xxvi, 3, 67, 68, 69, 119, 149, 167, 168, 193, 199–289
  Butler House, 208, 217
  Centre for Popular Education, 241
  Electricity Company, 215
  Fort Rupert, 221, 222
  GDP, 247, 256, 270
  National In-Service Teacher Education Programme (NISTEP), 235, 239–40, 247
  New National Party, 255, 271
  Point Salines International Airport, 216, 270
  School of Nursing, 238
  Teachers' College, 240
  Technical and Vocational Institute, 239
  Revolution, xiii, 3, 199–226
Grenade, Wendy, 199
Gutzmore, Cecil, 105
Guyana, xiii, 67, 68, 165, 265, 275, 279, 280
Guys Hill, 43

Haiti, 18, 127, 149, 159–70, 278
Haitian Revolution, 10, 18

INDEX

Harlem, 118, 120, 121, 122, 123, 124, 126, 127, 128, 129, 130, 134, 140
Harlem Renaissance, 131
Harlem Tenants' Association, 133
Harper, Solomon, 133
Harris, Wilson, 21
Harrison, Hubert, 120, 121, 122, 132
Hart, Ansell, xii
Hart, Richard, vii, viii, xi–xxxiii, 1–11, 14, 15, 17–22, 24–40, 41, 42, 45, 47, 54, 55, 56, 57, 58, 59–63, 65, 66, 76, 87, 112, 113, 118, 128, 140, 141, 144, 159, 164, 165, 166, 169, 175
Hay-Webster, Sharon, 52
Hearne, John, xxii
Hearne, Leeta, 57
Heine, Jorge, 200, 201, 202, 203, 216
Henry, Arthur, vii, xxx, xxxi
Henry, Claudius, 175
Henry, Paget, 21
Higman, Barry, 21
Hill, Frank, vii, xxi, xxv, xxx, xxxi, 25, 27
Hill, Ken, vii, xxi, xxx, xxxi, 25, 26, 29, 28, 44, 45
Hill, Robert, 5, 24, 39
Hill, Wilfred, 52
Hitler, Adolf, xii, xiii
Honduras, 278
Hoover, Herbert, 163, 166
Hope, Donna, 57
Howard University, 43, 144
Howell, Leonard, xxiv, 91, 93, 94, 95, 96, 98, 99
Hughes, Langston, 139
Huiswoud, Otto, 125, 126, 130, 132, 137
Hungary, 218, 220
Hunter College, 203, 215
Hurricane Ivan, 272

Independent Trade Union Advisory Council (ITAC), 175
Imperial Trade Commissioner, 52
Indigéniste, 168
Institute of Commonwealth Studies, 2
Institute of Jamaica, 44
International Conference of Negro Workers, 149
International Convention of the Negro Peoples of the World, 49
International Herald Tribune, 277
International Monetary Fund (IMF), 216, 269
International Socialist League, 127
Iraq, 267, 273
Isaacs, Wills O., 43
Island Telephone Company, 82
Italy, xii

Jacobs, H.P., 44
Jagan, Cheddi, vii, xxvii, xxiii
Jamaica xiii, xxvi, 59, 60, 62, 63, 64, 67, 68, 69, 70, 76–90, 102–15, 119, 120, 124, 133–34, 137, 141, 165, 169, 171–98, 205, 206, 208, 216, 227, 265, 276
 Clarendon, 97
 Executive Council, 77, 78, 84
 House of Assembly, 15
 House of Representatives, 74, 77, 78, 87
 Legislative Council, 43, 44, 46, 47, 48, 77, 87, 88, 91
 Police Special Branch, xi
 St Elizabeth, 94
 St James, 94
 St Mary 97
 St Thomas, 90, 91, 95, 97, 98
Jamaica Agricultural Society, 44
Jamaica Archives and Records Department, 6
Jamaica Birth Control League, 45

297

Jamaica Broadcasting Corporation, 208
Jamaica Chamber of Commerce, 45
Jamaica Citrus Producers Association, 45
Jamaica Congress of Labour, 175
Jamaica Council of Human Rights, 175
Jamaica Democratic Party, xxii
Jamaica Fruit and Shipping Company, 113
Jamaica Imperial Association, 44–45
Jamaica Labour Party, xi, xx, xxii, xxvii, xxix, xxx, xxxi, xxxiii, 6, 78, 83, 84, 89, 90, 171, 178, 180, 185, 193, 194, 208
Jamaica Labour Weekly, xv, 2, 141
Jamaica Producers Association, 94
Jamaica Progressive League, xvii, 120, 133, 134, 141
Jamaica Standard, 97
Jamaica Times, 96
Jamaica Union of Teachers, 44, 53
Jamaica Welfare Ltd., 45
Jamaica Women's Liberal Club, 135
Jamaica Workers and Labourers Association, 33, 34
Jamaica Workers and Tradesmen Union (JWTU), xvii, 45, 113
Jamaica Youth Movement, 3
James, C.L.R., 21, 61, 71, 153
James, Liam, 204, 205, 217
Jim Crow, 120, 122, 130, 137, 144, 145, 146, 148
Johnson, Anthony, 57
Johnson, Charley, 113

Kerr-Coombs, Stennet, xv
Kerr-Jarrett, F.M., 44, 46, 47
Keynesian Demand Management, 65
Khler, Harvey, 146
King, Cleveland Antonio, xxv
Kingston, 118, 128

Kingston and St Andrew Corporation (KSAC), xv, xxx, 26–27, 42, 43, 44
Kirton, Claremont, 201
Knight, Franklin, 21

Latin America, 151
Lawrence, Chris, 175
Layne, Ewart, 204, 205, 208
League Against Imperialism, 149
League of Coloured People, 45
League of Nations, 155
Legislative Council, 43, 44, 46, 47, 48
Lenin, Vladimir, xxiii, xxv, xxxii, 122, 141, 211
Lescot, Élie, 169
Less Developed Countries, 67
Lewis, Gordon K., 24, 216
Lewis, Patsy, 200, 209
Lewis, W. Arthur, 57, 64, 72, 73, 258, 264
Liberia, 155
Liberty Hall, 120, 121
Liberty League, 121, 122, 123
Libya, 267
Lindo, Harold, 113
Lindsay, Louis, 104, 114
Linton, William, 83, 84
Livingstone, Ross, 43
Lloyd, Ivan, 79, 83
Locke, Alain, 131
London, xiii
London Star, 110
Louison, Einstein, 222
Louison, George, 205, 206, 218, 220, 221
Lovelace, Earl, 21
Lynch, James, 16
Lynch, Lionel, xxv

Malcolm X, 129
Manchester Guardian, 163
Manley, Michael, xiv, 99, 180, 227, 228

INDEX

Manley, Norman xi, xiii, xv, xvi, xviii, xix, xx–xxi, xvii, xxv, xxvi, xxx, xxxi, xxxiii, 2, 35, 43, 46, 77, 78, 79, 95, 110, 111, 113
Marcos, Ferdinand, 177
Marley, Bob, 175
Maroon wars, 9
Marriott, Alvin, 27, 28
Marryshow, T.A., xxvii, 119
Marshall Plan, 65
Marson, Una, 44
Marx, Karl, xxiii, 130
Marxism, xii
Marxism-Leninism, 171, 173, 179, 181, 183, 185, 206, 207, 212, 267
Maxwell, C.S., 45
McBean, Wellesley, xxv
McFarlane, W.G., 58
McGlashan, Adrian, 31, 35
McKay, Claude, 128, 130, 132, 133, 138
Meeks, Brian, 206–9
Mercusor, 276
Messenger, 126, 129, 137
Mico, 44
Mills, J.J., 44
Mitchell, Keith, 254, 255, 271, 272, 273
Montserrat, 67
Monroe, Ben, 175
Monroe Doctrine, 159
Moore, Carlos, 21
Moore, Richard, 125, 126, 130, 131, 132, 139
Morant Bay, 93
Morant Bay Rebellion, xviii
More Developed Countries, 67
Morning Journal, 14
Morris, Albreath, xxv
Morris-Knibb, Mary, 44
Moscow, 118
Moyne Commission, 55

Munroe, Trevor, 179, 180, 182, 193, 195, 206, 207, 208, 209

National Club, 119
National Heroes Park, 26, 28
National Library of Jamaica, 2, 4, 5
National Reform Association, 44
National Textile Workers Union, 146
National Workers Union (NWU), xxxii, 193
Native Industries Protection Committee, 45
Nazi, 139
Négritude, 169
Negro Champion, 148
Negro Worker, 122, 133, 137, 138, 152, 153
Negro Workers Educational League, xxiv, xxv, xxvi, xxxi
Negro World, 31, 123, 124, 125, 126
Nelson, Cecil, xxiv, xxv
Nethersole, Noel, xv, 43, 44
Nettleford, Rex, 21
New International Economic Order, 259
New Jewel Movement, 3, 119–226, 227, 228
New Negro Voice, xxiv
New World Group, 175, 183, 258, 259
New York, 120, 122, 137
New York Daily Tribune, 10
New York Times, 129
Nicaragua, 177, 211, 227, 280
Noel, Vince, 205, 222
Non-aligned Movement, 227, 260

OECS (Organization of Eastern Caribbean States), 66, 72, 265, 273, 276
Olivier, Lord, 99
O'Meally, James, xvii, 134, 135
Organization for Revolutionary Education and Liberation (OREL), 204, 205, 206, 209

299

Organization of American States
  (OAS) 236–37, 280
Ortiz, Frank, 266
Osborn, Robert, 15
Owen, Chandler, 122, 125

Padmore, George, 133, 144–58
Panama, xxiv, 30, 127
Parkes, Nathaniel, 44
Payne, Clement, 105, 106, 107
Penso, E.E., 32
People's Educational Association, 3
People's Education Organization, 30
People's Freedom Movement, xxxii, 3, 175, 183
People's National Party vii, xi, xiii, xiv, xx–xxii, xxiii, xxiv, xxvii, xxix, xxx–xxxiii, 2, 3, 4, 6, 8, 27, 28, 49, 77, 79, 80, 83, 84, 89, 90, 113, 135, 171, 178, 180, 182, 183, 185, 193, 194, 195, 196
People's Political Party, 36, 49
People's Revolutionary Army, 203, 219, 223, 269
People's Revolutionary Government, vii, xiv, 119–226, 227, 229, 230, 233, 235–40, 266, 267, 268, 269, 272
Péralte, Charlemagne, 161, 162
Petersfield, 93
Petrocaribe, 254, 272, 277, 278
Phillipines, 177
Phillips, A.W., 65
Pinochet, Augusto, 265
Pirow, Oswald, 155
Pittsburgh University, 199
Pixley, Frank, 83, 89
Plain Talk, 47
Poor Man's Improvement Land Settlement and Labour Association, xvii
Port-au-Prince, 162
Post, Ken, 42, 45, 108

Powers, Robert, 94
Public Opinion, xiii, xxxi, 35, 44, 46, 109, 134, 135, 136, 137, 138
Public Works Employees Union, xxxi
Puri, Shalini, 199

Radix, Kendrick, 205
Randolph, A. Philip, 122, 125
Rand School of Social Science, 125
Ranston, Jackie, 58
Rastafari, xiv, xxiv, 91, 94, 95, 97, 115, 175, 176, 179, 183, 189
Reagan, Ronald, 213
Richards, Arthur, 62
Richardson, Bonham, 106
Roberts, W. Adolphe, xvii, 134
Robinson, Randall, 200
Robotham, Don, 179, 195
Rodney, Walter, 21, 176, 183
Rojas, Don, 223
Roopnarine, Rupert, 199, 201, 209
Roosevelt, F.D., xii, 164
Rostow, W.W., 258
Rumble, Robert, xvii
Russell, John, 163
Russian Revolution, xi, 123

Sandinistas, 227, 268
Save the Children Fund, 45
Scholes, Theophilus E. Samuel, 11, 13
Schwarz, Bill, 107
Scottsboro committees, 127
Seaforth, 91, 92, 93, 94, 95, 99
Seaga, Edward, 194, 195, 196
Seale, Herbert, 112
Second World War, xii, xiii, xvi, 63, 66, 138
  pre-Second World War, 118
  post-Second World War, 157
Sekyi, Kobina, 156
Selassie, Haile, 28
Self-government, 118, 119, 134–36
Sen, Amartya, 189

INDEX

Serge Island Estate, 42, 91, 92, 93, 95
Seymour, George, 44
Shah of Iran, 177
Sharpe, Sam, 9, 19
Shepherd, Verene, 21
Sherlock, Philip, 44, 52
Silverman, H.P., 44
Singapore, 69, 70
Singham, Archie, xxii
Sir Arthur Lewis Institute of Social and Economic Studies, 1
Small, Hugh, 175, 183
Smith, Ferdinand, xxxii, xxxiii
Smith, J.A.G., xix, 43
Socialism Group, 179
Socialist Party (USA), 121, 126
Somoza, Anastasio, 177
South Africa, 127, 150, 156
Soviet Union, xxxii, 137, 138, 139, 141, 206, 213, 238, 246, 259, 266, 267, 268
Spanish Civil War, xii
Stanley, Colonel, 83
St Croix, 121
St George's, 201
St Kitts, xiii, xxvi, 67, 69
St Louis, 122
St Lucia, xiii, xxvi, 67, 69, 278
St Paul, Cletus, 218
St Pierre, Maurice, 58
St Thomas (Virgin Islands), 128
St Vincent, xiii, xxvi, 67, 69, 149
Stabroek News, 277
Stalin, Joseph, xii, xxxii, 207
Stalinists, xvii, 196, 206, 207
Stolbert, Claus F., 57, 58
Strachan, Selwyn, 203, 204, 205
Strachey, John, xii
Struggle, 197
Sugar and Agricultural Workers Union, xiii, xxxii
Sugar Manufacturers' Association, 45
Suriname, xxvii, 275, 279, 280

Survey Graphic, 130, 131, 133
Syria, 267

Tacky, 9
Taiwan, 254, 271, 272, 276
Tanzania, 238
Tate and Lyle, 108
The Blackman, 32
The Masses, 2
The New Jamaican, 32
The Worker, 2
Thomas, Audley, xxv
Thoywell-Henry, L.A., 27, 28
Times, 46
Trade Union Advisory Council, 43
Trades Union Council (TUC), xiii, xvi, xxx, xxxi, xxxii
Tramway Transport and General Workers Union, xxx
Trinidad and Tobago, xiii, xxvi, 10, 64, 67, 68, 70, 105, 127, 144, 149, 165, 205, 206, 233, 272
Trinityville, 93, 96
Trouillot, Michel-Rolph, 21
Tulsa, 129
Turner, Joyce Moore, 130

Unasur (Union of South American Nations), 279
Unemployed Workers' Council, 175
United Kingdom, 61, 67, 70
United Nations, 255, 259, 261, 267
General Assembly, 112
Institute for Training and Research, 255–56
UNCTAD, 259
UNESCO, 236, 259
United Nations Development Programme (UNDP), 257
UNICEF, 243
United States of America, 69, 70, 159-170, 187, 211, 215, 221, 233, 238, 248, 254, 255,

257, 259, 264, 266, 268, 273, 275, 281
National Archives, 209
Universal Adult Suffrage, 64
Universal Negro Improvement Association (UNIA), 27, 30, 32, 35–36, 45, 105, 119, 120, 123, 124, 126
University of London, 64
University and Allied Workers' Union, 181–82, 207–8
University of Toronto, 199
University of the West Indies, 29, 44, 60, 64, 181, 182, 209, 236, 238, 240
Faculty of Social Sciences, 64

Vastey, Pompée Valentin, 10, 11, 14
Venezuela, 254, 271, 272, 275, 277, 278, 279, 281
Ventour, John, 205, 220, 223
Vickars, Edward, 16
Victoria, Queen, 12
Vincent, Theodore, 37

Warner-Lewis, Maureen, ix, 21
Washington, Booker T., 124
Watson, Karl, 45
West India Royal Commission, 166
West Indies Associated States, 263
West Indies Federation, 263
Whiteman, Unison, 217, 218, 220, 221, 222, 223
Williams, Eric, 10, 11, 14, 15, 19, 21
Williams, Quintin, 51
Williams, Robert, 129
Wilson, Edward, 153
Women's Liberal Club, 45
Workers' (Communist) Party, 126, 129, 130, 132, 133
Workers' Liberation League, 183, 198, 207
Workers' Liberation Union, 175, 183
Workers' Party of Jamaica, 171–98, 206, 207, 208, 209
Workers Week Education Committee, 58
World Bank, 67, 68, 255, 261, 269, 278
World Federation of Trades Unions (WFTU), xxx
World Trade Organization (WTO), 256, 260, 270, 272, 274, 275, 276

Young Socialist League, 175, 183
Young Womens' Christian Association, 45

Zakheim, Dov, 213

Lightning Source UK Ltd.
Milton Keynes UK
UKOW040931231012

201016UK00001B/5/P